US Democracy Promotion in the Arab World

US Democracy Promotion in the Arab World

Beyond Interests vs. Ideals

Mieczysław P. Boduszyński

LYNNE
RIENNER
PUBLISHERS

BOULDER
LONDON

Published in the United States of America in 2019 by
Lynne Rienner Publishers, Inc.
1800 30th Street, Boulder, Colorado 80301
www.rienner.com

and in the United Kingdom by
Lynne Rienner Publishers, Inc.
Gray's Inn House, 127 Clerkenwell Road, London EC1 5DB

© 2019 by Lynne Rienner Publishers, Inc. All rights reserved

Library of Congress Cataloging-in-Publication Data
Names: Boduszyński, Mieczysław P., 1974- author.
Title: US democracy promotion in the Arab world : beyond interests vs.
  ideals / by Mieczysław P. Boduszyński.
Other titles: United States democracy promotion in the Arab world
Description: Boulder, Colorado : Lynne Rienner Publishers, Inc., 2019. |
  Includes bibliographical references and index.
Identifiers: LCCN 2019009322 (print) | LCCN 2019011752 (ebook) | ISBN
  9781626378315 (ebook) | ISBN 9781626378179 (hardcover : alk. paper)
Subjects: LCSH: Democratization—Government policy—United States. |
  Democratization—Arab countries. | United States—Foreign relations—Arab
  countries. | Arab countries—Foreign relations—United States.
Classification: LCC JZ1480 (ebook) | LCC JZ1480 .B62 2019 (print) | DDC
  327.1—dc23
LC record available at https://lccn.loc.gov/2019009322

British Cataloguing in Publication Data
A Cataloguing in Publication record for this book
is available from the British Library.

Printed and bound in the United States of America

∞ The paper used in this publication meets the requirements
of the American National Standard for Permanence of
Paper for Printed Library Materials Z39.48-1992.

5 4 3 2 1

For Ambassador J. Christopher Stevens

Contents

Preface	ix
Acknowledgments	xiii

1	US Democracy Promotion in the Arab World	1
2	On Democracy Promotion	35
3	Individuals	59
4	Institutions	111
5	Challengers	161
6	Trump and the Demise of US Democracy Promotion	181

Appendix: Foreign Policy Institutions and Their Stake in Democracy Promotion	205
References	215
Index	231
About the Book	241

Preface

Like any research project, this book is the product of an intellectual and professional journey. My first book analyzed regime change in the Balkans. It was published at the end of a decade in which Western democracy-promoting efforts in the region appeared to be succeeding. In placing themselves firmly on the path of European Union membership, states such as Croatia and Serbia had put aside nationalism and embraced democratic institutions. Free and fair elections brought to power parties that accepted the norms of liberal democracy. Civil society organizations flourished. Independent media and minority rights expanded. In that book, I expressed a healthy dose of skepticism about the ability of outsiders to overcome certain structural barriers to democratization in the Balkans. I nonetheless found that EU and US democracy promotion policies served as both a catalyst and motivator of liberal democratic reforms. By the time the book was published, I had joined the US foreign service and served in Albania, an experience that further convinced me that democracy promotion could work.

In the late 1990s and early 2000s, Western democratic leverage in the Balkans was at its peak, and Washington and Brussels worked in lockstep to exercise it. Western countries were ready to invest substantial financial and diplomatic resources in Balkan transitions, and comparatively high internal cohesion in both the United States and the European Union bolstered the capacity and will to promote democracy. In the case of the United States, the full range of institutional actors—the White House, State Department, military establishment, intelligence community, Congress, and others—lined up behind the project of democracy promotion in the region. The successful democratization of the Balkans was broadly understood to be in the national interest. The United States had not yet experienced the loss of confidence that resulted from failed nation-building experiments in Afghanistan and Iraq. In short, in both Europe and the United States, there was faith that democracy could succeed in the Balkans. Importantly, the international environment for democracy promotion was also favorable. Russia was not an active source of illiberal counterleverage, as it is today in the Balkans and other parts of the world, and the global economic recession that started at the end of the 2000s had not yet hit.

As the Arab Spring unfolded a number of years later, it was clear that these same circumstances would not be replicated. In the fall of 2010, I began my study of Arabic at the Foreign Service Institute in Virginia as part of my preparation for diplomatic postings to Egypt and Libya. Colleagues who knew the region assured me that the assignments would be quite boring. Libyan dictator Muammar Qaddafi had by then entered his fifth decade of rule, and Egyptian president Hosni Mubarak his fourth. Nobody predicted things would change. One day, I attended a presentation by a then-senior official of the State Department's Near Eastern Affairs (NEA) Bureau. Surveying US policy in the region and arriving at Egypt, the official intoned: "God help us if anything were to happen to Mubarak." It was a striking statement, not only because it was made just a few short months before the Egyptian strongman was deposed in February 2011, but also because of what it said about Washington's dependence on an aging, corrupt, and by that time largely illegitimate Arab autocrat.

Nevertheless, three months later, against the advice of many close advisers, and counter to the wishes of close US allies such as Israel and Saudi Arabia, President Barack Obama signaled that the United States no longer stood behind Mubarak and instead backed the calls for change of the young Egyptians who had amassed in Cairo's Tahrir Square. In spite of some mixed signals and the delay in Obama's response, it was a striking reversal in US policy given Mubarak's long and steadfast support of Washington's priorities in the region. Just weeks after calling for a democratic transition in Egypt, the Obama administration signaled its support for the rebels in Libya, and despite Obama's deep misgivings about another US military entanglement in the Middle East and North Africa, decided to join France and the UK in an air campaign designed to protect Libyan civilians from slaughter at the hands of Qaddafi's forces. In April, Obama criticized the Bahraini monarchy for its crackdown on peaceful protesters in terms that a US president had never used before. In a May 2011 speech to the State Department, Obama vowed to provide economic, diplomatic, and strategic aid to boost a swift transition to democracy in the Arab world. In August, he called for President Bashar al-Assad of Syria to step down. In November, the Obama administration backed a Saudi-brokered deal by which Ali Abdullah Saleh, who had ruled Yemen for thirty-three years, would give up power. That same fall, a special coordinating office for assistance to Middle East democratic transitions was established at the State Department. For these reasons, I went to my postings in the period after the Arab Spring with cautious optimism that US policy would finally turn to sincere democracy promotion in the Middle East and North Africa.

It was also immediately clear to me, however, that Obama's forward-leaning policy on Egypt did not reflect the preferences of his entire government. Indeed, some State Department colleagues with deep experience in the region expressed skepticism about the merits of democratic change in Egypt, not because they had reasoned arguments about the challenges to democratization in the Middle East, but because they had invested their entire careers in the status quo. When the uprising spread to the tiny Gulf monarchy of Bahrain, one senior US diplomat described the protesters there to me as a "mob." It was similarly telling on the eve of the Libyan uprising of February 2011 how many Washington "Libya hands" studiously avoided mentioning Qaddafi's horrific human rights abuses. Some were working with companies hoping to profit from Libya's extensive petrodollars. While there were exceptions, many of Washington's foreign policy elite simply did not see 2011 as a 1989 moment—that is, a moment when the old authoritarian Arab order would decisively crumble.

Washington's lack of faith in Arab democracy ultimately won out as the gains of the Arab Spring were turned back by authoritarian retrenchment and civil wars in the years that followed the uprisings. The resolve of the Obama administration to promote democracy dwindled and US policy reverted to well-established repertoires emphasizing stability, relationships with autocrats, and counterterrorism. The signs that the Obama administration would not follow through on the president's May 2011 promises were to be found everywhere, but two key decisions symbolized the retreat from democracy promotion: the administration's decision not to call the July 3, 2013, seizure of power by the Egyptian military from a democratically elected president a coup, and Obama's failure to take meaningful steps to follow through on his assertions that Syrian dictator Bashar al-Assad must step down and that the use of chemical weapons by the Assad regime would cross a "red line."

I had a front-row seat to Obama's retreat from post–Arab Spring democracy promotion in Libya after the attacks on the US diplomatic facility in Benghazi in September 2012, which resulted in the death of my boss, Ambassador J. Christopher Stevens. In Yemen, the Obama administration's initial support of a negotiated transition from the autocratic regime of Saleh ultimately turned to US logistical and political support for a Saudi-led military campaign that has helped to precipitate a humanitarian catastrophe. In Bahrain, early efforts to encourage reform disappeared by the end of Obama's presidency. Even in Tunisia, the lone democratic success story of the Arab Spring, the administration failed to provide a significant aid package to back the Tunisian transition, and Obama never visited the country. The Trump administration's seemingly unconditional embrace of Egyptian strongman Abdel Fatah al-Sisi and the autocratic Saudi and Emirati monarchies, which did everything in their power to counter the gains of the Arab Spring, signaled an end to US democracy promotion in the Arab world.

I write this book based on a normative commitment to democratization in the Arab world. I am convinced that decades of political repression have held back Arab societies from realizing their full potential. Decades of autocratic rule lie behind countless ills in Arab states, from corruption to sectarianism to extremism. I share the views of those who believe that it is not in the long-term interest of the United States to ignore political repression in the region and lend support to regimes that practice it. I do not mean to suggest that the United States can and should promote democracy in all places and at all times. Yet, the fact is that the United States is the external actor with the most power, leverage, and tools to encourage democracy in the region and beyond. Moreover, twice in the past two decades, Washington has signaled that backing democracy in the Arab world is not only the morally correct path, but also one compatible with US interests.

As a former diplomat, I also understand the dilemmas facing policymakers in a complex region such as the Middle East. The events of the Arab Spring and their aftermath were unexpected and overlapping crises, and while it is easy to evaluate how the United States responded with the benefit of hindsight, those who were charged with formulating and implementing policy responses—among them, many people I interviewed for this book—were confronted at that moment with no easy choices, much less morally clear ones. In short, I do not intend this book to be a form of armchair criticism launched from the Ivory Tower. In fact, I hope that one contribution of the book is to describe US foreign policy with the degree of nuance that does justice to the formidable challenges policymakers face.

Acknowledgments

I am deeply grateful to Lynne Rienner for taking on this project. I thank the many current and former US officials who sat down for interviews with me, sharing insights that were vital to my research. My final postings in the US foreign service—Egypt, Libya, and Iraq—were invaluable learning experiences that informed this book. In these assignments, I had the chance to work with some first-rate American diplomats, as well as military colleagues and local staff, among them: Larry Pope, Bill Roebuck, Deborah Jones, Ken Spear, Keith Philips, Mike Lebson, Joe Tordella, Hannah Draper, Josh Goldberg, David McFarland, Seraj Mshawet, Rana Duzan, Maysam Shebani, Ahmed Naili, Shana Kieran, Dan Hall, Walker Murray, Steve Walker, Faez al-Abdullah, Ali al-Kalbi, Imad Sabbak, Bill Cavness, and Jim Bullock. I am grateful as well to David Kirkpatrick of the *New York Times* and Fred Wehrey of the Carnegie Endowment for International Peace, both of whom allowed me to read their own book manuscripts. Their groundbreaking work on Egypt and Libya has made this book much stronger.

Many brilliant Pomona College students who took my foreign policy course helped to sharpen my thinking as I attempted to explain the "sausage-making" of US foreign policy. At Pomona, I benefited from the support of many colleagues, among them Pierre Englebert, who has been a steadfast source of encouragement. Ambassador Cameron Munter, who taught with me at Pomona during my first two years there, was a fantastic mentor as I reentered academia after a decade of working in diplomacy. Pomona College also helped to fund the research for this book through a startup fund and a Hirsch Research Initiation Grant, which allowed me to hire some excellent student research assistants: Jennifer Kim, Megan Schmiesing, Eileen Mahler, Kevin Wang, Gretta Richardson, Daniel Villars, Rachel Zimmerman, Adam Revello,

Zaza Chaplin, Jordan Carethers, Kamil Lungu, Ethan Kostishak, Preet Khowaja, Tariq Razi, Allie Pitchon, Nina Zhou, Scott Panek, Jacinta Chen, Lucy Onderwyzer-Gold, and Nils Skattum.

I did much of the writing while on a yearlong sabbatical from Pomona. I spent the bulk of that time at IAU College in Aix-en-Provence, France. I thank IAU's president, Carl Jubran, as well as the student research assistants who helped me during the writing phase: Leah Fayal, Lilah Wilder, Tiara Borneman, Alex Kirchner, Kevin Naseri, and Luis Arreola. I had three other affiliations during the sabbatical—Osaka School of International Public Policy; Varieties of Democracy Institute, University of Gothenburg; and Paris School of International Affairs, Sciences Po—and I am grateful, respectively, to Aki Matsuno, Staffan Lindberg, and Dania Del Ben for these opportunities. Philip Breeden and Michael Nelson read large parts of the early manuscript and offered invaluable feedback, Wendy Wei assisted with fact-checking, and James Ferencsik helped to update me on Trump administration policy. Amy Hawthorne generously organized a very useful roundtable at the Project on Middle East Democracy (POMED)—I am grateful to her and her colleagues Stephen McInerney and Andrew Miller. Andrew Lehman read the final manuscript with his ever-sharp eye. And I could not have accomplished this at all without the love and support of Sumin Sohn, my life partner.

I dedicate the book to the late Chris Stevens, who besides being an outstanding diplomat and inspiring boss, became a tennis partner and friend in the short time I was privileged to work for him at the US embassy in Tripoli. Ambassador Stevens sincerely wanted Libyans to realize the aspirations of the Arab Spring. He encouraged me to return to academia someday and take stock of what I had experienced as a diplomat. I was guided by his enduring optimism as I wrote this book.

1

US Democracy Promotion in the Arab World

On April 9, 2019, US president Donald J. Trump hosted Egyptian strongman president Abdel Fatah al-Sisi in Washington. Trump lavished praise on Sisi and the US-Egyptian relationship, saying nothing about the Egyptian leader's abysmal human rights record (Landler 2019). This was, in fact, the second time Trump had warmly welcomed Sisi; his first visit to the White House was almost exactly two years earlier, in April 2017, barely three months into Trump's presidency. The image of the Egyptian leader twice sitting alongside the US president in the Oval Office spoke volumes about the priorities of the Trump administration: Sisi's autocratic order, which most observers have described as more repressive than that of the deposed former president Hosni Mubarak, would be overlooked by the Trump administration in the pursuit of shared concerns, such as fighting terrorism (Nakamura 2017). The administration's transactional approach was confirmed during Secretary of State Mike Pompeo's visit to Egypt in January 2019, when human rights and democracy were barely mentioned. Perhaps nowhere else has Trump's distaste for human rights and democracy promotion come into sharper relief than in his support for Saudi Arabia, a country that worked tirelessly to roll back democratic gains in places such as Egypt and Bahrain. In the fall of 2018, as evidence mounted that de facto Saudi ruler and crown prince Mohammed bin Salman had ordered the execution and dismemberment of a dissident journalist, Jamal Khashoggi, Trump and his top advisers made clear that they would defy even their fellow Republicans in Congress to stand by the Saudi ruler.

However, Barack Obama, Trump's predecessor, also did not impose serious costs on the Sisi regime for its increasing repression of political freedoms or on the Saudi monarchy for its counterdemocratic meddling in

Egypt and other countries. While Obama never gave Egyptian president Sisi the highly prized platform of a White House visit, by the end of his presidency he had long retreated from the full-throated support he had offered to Egyptians and other Arabs who rose up in 2011 to demand change. In 2013, only two years after uprisings swept across the Arab world, the Obama administration remained largely silent as the Egyptian military, backed by Saudi Arabia and the United Arab Emirates (UAE), carried out a coup against democratically elected president Mohamed Morsi.[1] In his second term, Obama largely gave up on democracy promotion in the Arab world and diverted his attention to other foreign policy priorities.

In the years after the Arab Spring, euphoria turned to dysphoria as the aspirations of the youthful protesters were usurped by resurgent authoritarianism, civil wars, and terrorist groups. Tunisia was the only Arab Spring country in which the uprisings helped to usher in democracy. A sense of resignation took hold in Washington, accompanied by the belief that, compared to the chaos that has engulfed the region since 2011, autocracy no longer looked so bad. For the many US policymakers who harbored deep skepticism about the prospects for democracy in the Arab world, the aftermath of the Arab Spring was a self-fulfilling prophecy. To be sure, amidst the disorder of the post-2011 period, many Arabs, even those who had supported the uprisings, also began to express nostalgia for the certainty of authoritarianism.

But the fatalism that has engulfed Washington and other Western capitals, which sees Arab democratization as destined to fail and the United States as helpless in encouraging its success, may also be misguided. There is no question that the internal obstacles to democracy in the region were substantial: from a lack of institutions in Libya to deeply entrenched autocratic ones in Egypt, and from ethno-sectarian fragmentation in the Levant to the "resource curse" of the Gulf Arab states. Thus, I do not mean to suggest that democracy would have inevitably taken hold in the Arab Spring countries had the United States taken a consistently principled stance toward democratic reform. But I also see a problem with the argument, often repeated by government officials, that the United States did not have any leverage over post–Arab Spring developments. How can they be sure of this if they rarely, if ever, tested US leverage in the region in a meaningful way? For example, all too often, Washington threatened to cut off assistance in response to repression, but its bluff was called by Arab autocrats. And when the United States did suspend assistance, repression increased after it was reinstated. The fact is that the United States potentially had *some* leverage, but for reasons to be explained in this book, chose not to use it. While in retrospect the unsuccessful democratic transitions that followed the Arab Spring might be looked at with a sense of inevitability, at the time of the uprisings and in their immediate aftermath neither the United States nor local actors could definitively predict the final outcome. As Vali Nasr (2014, p. 163), a former official in Hillary Clinton's State Department, points out, nobody in Washington knew what path the Arab uprisings might take in 2011, "nor can we say now that the Arab Spring would have been such a disappointment had we engaged with the region quickly and forcefully."

Nasr's observation points to the lack of resolve in the US foreign policy community to advance the idea of Arab democracy, reflecting deep-seated beliefs among Washington policymakers about the poor prospects for democratization in the Arab and Muslim worlds, fears of political Islam and terrorism, and disappointment with the chaotic course of post–Arab Spring transitions. But the lack of resolve is also a function of bureaucratic interests and inertia. Indeed, the individuals and institutions responsible for formulating and implementing US democracy promotion efforts were sometimes the ones that undermined those efforts because they do not agree on what American interests in the Arab world are, including how best to achieve that vague and elusive concept known as "stability."

Overview of the Book

This book is about US democracy promotion in the Arab world since the uprisings of 2010–2011. In the decades leading up to the Arab Spring, the region remained in the deep freeze of authoritarianism. If Arab states were exceptional in their ability to resist democratization, US policy in the Middle East and North Africa (MENA) was also exceptional in its continuing focus on making pacts with Arab dictators in the name of stability rather than supporting the aspirations of ordinary people (Wittes 2008, p. 1). In Washington, DC, Arab democracy had few champions: Only a handful of interest groups advocated for US democracy promotion in the Arab world, none with the funding and influence of groups pushing for other foreign policy priorities. Congress rarely took up the issue of Arab democracy. Meanwhile, the US public was largely ignorant of the daily indignities suffered by ordinary Arab citizens at the hands of their regimes.

To some extent, this changed after 9/11, when American policymakers woke up to the idea that political repression, instability, and religious extremism might be linked, and as a result President George W. Bush launched an ambitious "Freedom Agenda" of worldwide democracy promotion in which he included the Arab world with great fanfare. But Bush's efforts were short-lived and derailed by the disastrous consequences of the Iraq War, overreach in the global war on terror, and an unwillingness to meaningfully challenge allied Arab autocratic regimes. Moreover, many institutions in the US foreign policy apparatus had continued a business-as-usual approach during the Freedom Agenda, talking to Arab authoritarian governments rather than ordinary people and relying on their intelligence services to understand developments (Panetta 2014, p. 303). By the end of Bush's presidency, few Arabs saw US intentions around democracy promotion as sincere (Telhami 2011).

The Arab Spring presented entirely new opportunities for US democracy promotion. Perhaps for the first time ever, democratization appeared as a possibility in a region that had resisted previous "waves" of democratic change sweeping the globe (Huntington 1993). Now, millions of ordinary Arabs from Morocco in the west to Oman in the east took to the streets to demand change. In Washington, the dilemma was no longer over whether and how much to prod an Arab strongman or monarch to open the political space here or there while never meaningfully challenging the durability of his rule, which was essentially the policy pursued under Bush. Now, such space had been opened in new and dramatic ways, and the agent of change was neither an Islamist nor a US Marine, but rather young Arabs calling for an end to dictatorship—and in some cases succeeding. US policymakers, in turn, faced stark policy choices: whether to stand or break with autocratic allies, and whether to encourage a process of democratic change with uncertain outcomes. If the United States had historically relied on authoritarian Arab regimes to expand Washington's influence, contain Iran, guarantee Israel's security, and protect access to oil resources, the Arab Spring decisively challenged the idea that autocracies could guarantee stability and uphold US interests. It was hard to argue that the US should uphold the status quo for the sake of stability when there was no stability. The challenge of the Arab Spring, then, was not only to the nondemocratic exceptionalism of the Arab world but also to the exceptionalism of US policy toward the region.

I tackle two tasks in this book. The first is to tell the story of US democracy promotion in the Arab world since 2011. A large part of the book focuses on the record of the Obama administration. Sufficient distance and the power of hindsight, as well as access to new sources on Obama's foreign policy, allow for the analysis of decisionmaking during these years. Obama's response to the Arab Spring simultaneously reflected both enthusiasm for and ambivalence about the prospects for democracy in the region. The policy was frequently reactive and inconsistent, with a mismatch between rhetoric and action. It featured courageous and dramatic policy moves such as the decision to drop support for Mubarak and to intervene in Libya. Yet it was also characterized by mixed messages and lack of strategy. After 2013, the general trajectory of the policy was clear: from an initial embrace of the protests and their aspirations, to a noble but restrained effort to push a democratic transition, and finally to a loss of resolve and a retreat from democracy promotion in the region, a retreat that has been furthered by the Trump administration's policies, which I cover in the last chapter.

The second task of the book is to explain this policy trajectory. US foreign policy dilemmas in the Arab world are often cast in terms of a tension between interests and ideals, with the former inevitably trumping the latter, thereby constraining democracy promotion. However, in this book I argue that it is not possible to understand outcomes in democracy promotion, or US foreign policy more generally, without appreciating the human, bureaucratic, and regional context from which it emerged.

Contributions to Scholarship

The larger question addressed in the book is where, why, and how the United States incorporates democracy promotion into its foreign policy, which in turn offers an opportunity to engage with several research traditions. In my effort to explain outcomes in US foreign policy, I aim to build upon the foreign-policy analysis tradition of Snyder (1962), Holsti (1976), Rosenau (1980), George (1980), Allison (1971), Janis (1972), and Saunders (2011). These scholars highlight the importance of learning about the narratives behind foreign policy decisions and encourage the use of midrange theories that push beyond the assumptions of international relations paradigms so as to capture the multiple influences on US foreign policy.

I also engage the literature on democracy promotion, which has grown in tandem with the end of the Cold War and the expansion of US democracy promotion to new parts of the world. There is now an impressive body of scholarship on why and how the United States and other states and multilateral organizations choose to promote democracy, and whether such policies work.[2] Some of this literature is descriptive, some is prescriptive, and less frequently it is theoretical. Yet, the Arab world is rarely mentioned in this body of work,[3] perhaps because there has been so little in the way of US democracy promotion in the region.[4] In this book, I aim to contribute to this body of research, especially those works that purport to explain the inclusion of democracy promotion in US foreign policy and variations in its application over time and space.[5]

My analysis of US democracy promotion in the Arab world engages another domain of scholarship, that on the international dimension of democratization. The "transitology" literature of the 1980s and 1990s largely omitted the influence of external powers.[6] By contrast, more recent research has found that it was "externally driven shifts in the cost of suppression, not changes in domestic conditions" that "contributed most centrally to the demise of authoritarianism in the 1980s and 1990s" (Levitsky and Way 2010). While much of the existing research focuses on whether and how external forces influence democratic change,[7] this book focuses on the factors that shape the will, policies, and capacity of democracy-promoting states such as the United States. In other words, rather than focusing on regime outcomes in Arab states as a dependent variable, this book is concerned with the determinants of the "prodemocracy" content of US foreign policy toward the MENA region. In my analysis of third-party spoilers of democratization (or "challengers"), I also engage the growing literature on autocracy promotion.[8]

While many academic and "trade" books, in addition to numerous articles in scholarly journals and the media, have analyzed the causes, events, and outcomes of the Arab Spring,[9] there remains a dearth of rigorous, scholarly analysis of US policy toward the region during and after this critical period in spite of the fact that the United States was the external actor with the greatest potential to influence developments.[10] Though this book is concerned mainly with the determinants of US democracy promotion policies rather than the internal dynamics of Arab states, I hope that my analysis will also contribute to our understanding of regime survival and change in MENA.

The Significance of the Arab Spring for US Democracy Promotion

The events of 2011 and the years that followed represented a *critical moment for US democracy promotion,* one in which a political opening in an autocratic regime creates not only prospects for domestic change in a democratic direction, but also an opportunity for external actors to apply heightened levels of democratic leverage. The period after the Arab Spring was a critical moment not because the United States or any other external actor was a catalyst for the uprisings—indeed, the fact that protests were entirely locally driven substantially boosted their legitimacy—but because they presented an opportunity for the United States to seize a locally induced political opening and respond in a way that advanced the calls for freedom.

Critical moments for US democracy promotion occur when there are protests against an authoritarian regime, but they may also be triggered by a multitude of events such as a coup in which the military overthrows a democratically elected leader, the refusal of an authoritarian leader to step down, the launch of negotiations to transfer power, when an election pits democratic against autocratic forces, or when another crisis occurs that could determine a democratic transition or reversion to authoritarianism. During and after the Arab Spring, furthermore, existing structures and institutions were potentially more malleable and susceptible to external democratizing pressures. At such moments, I argue, the United States has an opportunity to advance democratization. The United States has seized upon critical moments for democracy promotion before: in the Philippines in 1986, in South Korea in 1987, in Haiti in 1994, in Serbia in 2000, and in Côte d'Ivoire in 2011. In all of these cases, US presidents, albeit at times belatedly, stood on the side of democratic principles and deployed a range of tools to encourage a democratic outcome.

As a result of the events of the Arab Spring, opportunities for democracy promotion appeared in *autocratic allies,* nondemocratic regimes with whom the United States had long maintained close ties and provided security assistance, arguably giving Washington added leverage and an augmented motive to stand on the side of democracy. The United States had faced such critical moments in autocratic allies before. Two of the cases mentioned above, the Philippines and South Korea, are examples since they were both authoritarian regimes pivotal to the US Cold War strategy of containing Soviet influence. This fact complicated, but also enabled, democracy promotion as close ties, assistance, and security guarantees gave the United States substantial leverage. In both countries, then president Ronald Reagan and his advisers realized that it was no longer in the US interest to prop up ruling regimes because they were understood to be unstable.[11]

While the protagonists of Arab Spring were local actors, it is also a misreading of the extent of decades of US entanglement in the region to think that the US could avoid playing a role in what was happening, especially when it came to its autocratic allies. The survival of a number of regimes in the region, such as Egypt and the monarchies of Jordan and the Gulf Arab states, have depended to a large degree on US support. If US policies could help keep nondemocratic Arab regimes in power, then they should have the leverage to influence reform in a democratic direction. Nevertheless, there were those in the Obama administration who argued that the Arab uprisings were not about the United States and that therefore Washington should avoid any perception of meddling. Michael McFaul (2018, p. 214), a senior adviser to President Obama and a scholar of democratization and democracy promotion, writes that at the time of the Arab Spring he wondered privately "why these sovereignty champions had been so quiet during decades of American subsidization of Egyptian autocracy." Analysts such as Shadi Hamid (2015) have been similarly critical of the argument that the United States could not and should not influence post–Arab Spring events: "Where is the line between inaction and complicity? The notion of neutrality, for a country as powerful as the United States, is illusory. Doing nothing or 'doing no harm' means maintaining the status quo, which in the Middle East is never neutral, due to America's longstanding relationships with regional actors." Beyond this, would it have been morally feasible for the United States just to stand by and say or do nothing as millions of Arabs took to the streets to demand change?

The Arab Spring and its aftermath were also a critical moment for democracy promotion given the broad post-9/11 consensus that the internal dynamics of states—especially their practices vis-à-vis democracy and human rights—cannot not be divorced from the fight against violent extremism. The publication of an Arab Human Development Report in 2002[12] painted a dire picture of the state of freedom and economic opportunity in the region and was a wake-up call to many in the foreign policy establishment (Rice 2017). Even staunch realists such as then secretary of state Colin Powell could not ignore the connection between the sick state of Arab governments and societies on one hand and religious extremism on the other. As Condoleezza Rice, who succeeded Powell as secretary of state, put it, "the fundamental character of regimes now matters more than the international distribution of power."[13] It was no longer the lonely voices of activists, think tanks, and human rights nongovernmental organizations (NGOs) calling for Arab democracy in Washington policy circles.

In January 2011, just days before Zine el-Abidine Ben Ali relinquished power in Tunisia and the start of the Egyptian protests, then secretary of state Hillary Clinton gave a speech in Doha, Qatar, in which she highlighted the inability of Arab governments to meet their populations' aspirations using the poignant phrase, "the region's foundations are sinking in the sand."[14] While Clinton proposed only vague reforms, in retrospect the speech was a prescient one. Around the same time, key members of Obama's National Security Council were leading a policy review, or Presidential Study Directive, which concluded that the MENA region was ripe for reform and that the United States should adjust its policy accordingly (Sanger 2012). The intelligence community also produced studies that pointed to trouble for the authoritarian Arab regimes (Morrell 2016, p. 178). In other words, after 9/11 the issue of democratic reform in Arab societies and regimes moved to the center of US foreign policy debates. The Arab Spring should have only reinforced the imperative for a new approach.

The nature of the Arab Spring also defied many expectations about what kind of revolutions would take place in the Arab world. The uprisings challenged the assumption of some "neoconservative" thinkers that the United States needs to serve as the external catalyst of regime change. In fact, the Arab Spring's slogans and tactics diffused among the countries of the region (Lynch 2012) in a way that had little to do with the United States or other non-Arab powers. Contrary to the expectations of some in Washington, the protesters focused their ire on the failings of their own leaders and not foreign threats and enemies. And, contrary to conventional wisdom that the Muslim Brotherhood would inevitably lead any revolution, Islamists were not at the forefront of the Arab Spring protests.

The Limits of "National Interest" in Explaining US Democracy Promotion

The realist tradition in international relations maintains that policies such as democracy promotion will only emerge when security or vital economic interests are not at stake.[15] This view is supported by a long tradition in US foreign policy of relying upon autocratic allies in the service of counterbalancing foes. The United States benefited from alliances with the French monarchy during the American Revolution and the Soviet communist dictatorship during World War II to balance the British and Nazi threats, respectively. Throughout the Cold War, the United States maintained ties with right-wing dictatorships in Latin America, Africa, and other regions so as to balance the Soviet Union and contain the spread of communism. In the 1980s, the United States cultivated relations with Saddam Hussein's Iraq as a way to balance revolutionary Iran, looking the other way as Saddam used chemical weapons against his own citizens.

Realism might suggest that US interests are irreconcilable with the goal of promoting democracy in the Arab world. Yet, after 9/11 two successive US presidents and their surrogates argued that in fact there should be no tension between the two: Because political repression breeds both extremism and instability, promoting democracy and human rights should be easily reconciled with US interests. If interests were wholly incompatible with democracy promotion, then perhaps the United States would never promote democracy anywhere in the Arab world, and yet it has tried to do so at key junctures after 9/11. Conversely, if interests and values were fully harmonious, then the administrations of George W. Bush and Barack Obama would have easily reconciled the two, rather than ultimately backing away from democracy promotion in the Arab world. As Thomas Carothers (2004, p. 36) has written, in the end democracy promotion cannot be easily characterized as "a grand synthesis of idealism and realism."

Realism assumes the existence of an overarching "national interest." However, given the presence of multiple actors in the US foreign policy process, *whose* interests are at stake? For example, how can the Department of Defense's views on Egypt, where it has maintained a decades-long relationship with the Egyptian military, be reconciled with ideas about the importance of transition to civilian rule coming from parts of the White House, State Department, and US Agency for International Development (USAID)? What's more, can't interests change? Shouldn't the growing energy independence of the United States lead Washington to rethink its ties and military obligations in the Gulf? Such questions challenge the idea of a unified, objective, immutable, a priori identifiable US "national interest" in the Arab world that either constrains or supports democracy promotion. My aim is not to discount the influence of national interest entirely; rather, by using democracy promotion as an example, I seek to modify how we conceive of interest in explaining US policies toward the Middle East and North Africa.

There are many well-known instances of US foreign policy that cannot be easily explained by a priori existing, objectively identifiable interests. Consider US support for Israel, which has continued for decades despite complicating US relations with many Arab states. Mearsheimer and Walt (2007) have argued that pro-Israel policies run counter to the US interest, if for no other reason than that they inflame public opinion in the Middle East, adversely affecting US leverage over and relationships with Arab states. Or, consider another well-known case of US foreign policy: the longstanding economic embargo against Cuba that was in place prior to Obama's 2015 rapprochement with Havana. After the Cold War ended, it was hard to argue that a small island nation represented a strategic threat to the United States, and quite the contrary, there were economic incentives for the United States to engage with the Castro regime. And yet, the United States continued to pursue a policy of isolation that did little to change the character of the Cuban regime. It is hard to argue that these policies advanced the US interest in the realist understanding of the term. Instead, in both the Israel and Cuba cases, domestic interest groups—a well-organized and funded pro-Israel lobby and a conservative Cuban American voting bloc in Florida—contributed to shaping the foreign policy preferences of both elites and the public concerning US policies toward the two countries.

Counterterrorism and US Democracy Promotion in the Arab World

Countervailing interests such as counterterrorism do provide some explanation for the failure to follow through on post-9/11 promises of US democracy promotion in the Arab world. Democracy promotion policies push autocratic governments to "relinquish power across state institutions and to their citizenry," while cooperating on counterterrorism is easier when dealing with a strong, central leader (Hassan 2015, p. 480). Counterterrorism in particular is in tension with democracy promotion because it often reflects short-term considerations, while democracy is a longer-term goal that requires strategic patience. For instance, the use of armed drones relies heavily on cooperative regimes, ones that can respond quickly and discreetly while avoiding the "messiness" associated with democratic procedures.

Short-term thinking about counterterrorism also influenced the Bush administration's "extraordinary rendition" program in the 2000s, by which captured terrorism suspects were transferred to third countries for interrogation, and often torture. In Yemen, the Obama administration deferred to the Saudis and the Gulf Cooperation Council (GCC) to negotiate the resignation of strongman Ali Abdullah Saleh and the formation of an interim government to guarantee that the security apparatus needed for cooperation on drones and other counterterrorism programs remained in place (Nasr 2014, p. 181). In this manner, the short-term goal of locating and killing terrorists on foreign territory can "tie the hands" of the United States in promoting democracy (Nasr 2014, p. 181) while also raising questions about US complicity in human rights abuses and civilian deaths. Huber (2015, p. 702) refers to the tension between short-term and long-term interests as the "democracy dilemma": From the long-term perspective, it might be ethical or even strategic for the United States to pursue democracy promotion, but in the short term it can be a risky policy, especially when applied in allied autocracies that also serve as reliable partners on counterterrorism cooperation. Thus, even as the Arab Spring exposed the fragility of authoritarianism, it also gave rise to a great deal of uncertainty, which in turn posed a direct threat to counterterrorism and other short-term interests. Yet, the fact that years of counterterrorism cooperation failed to prevent the rapid expansion of the Islamic State and other terrorist groups raises questions about the effectiveness of the approach.

Assumptions About Stability

Many in Washington assume that alliances with autocratic states are stable. However, McFaul (2010, pp. 111–115) argues that the United States cannot depend on alliances with autocrats in the long run. First, autocratic regimes have no predictable or legitimate way to hand over power, meaning that transitions are precarious. Second, the struggle of autocracies to stay in power radicalizes opponents who might otherwise be moderated by the influence of elections. Third, since they do not answer to parliaments or voters, autocratic leaders can change their international allegiances unpredictably, which can be detrimental to US interests (witness Joseph Stalin after World War II).[16] Fourth, as I will discuss further below, autocratic allies extract "tremendous military and economic subsidies," which may sometimes be necessary (protecting South Korea against the North, for instance) but at other times is not the most effective way to pursue the national interest (McFaul 2010, p. 114). Fifth, the internal stability of many autocratic regimes, and by extension US alliances with them, is threatened by their inability to provide jobs and prosperity more generally (Wittes 2008, p. 57). Finally, supporting autocracy extracts a heavy price in terms of US credibility on the world stage.

At first glance, the Arab Spring might have convinced Washington policymakers that authoritarianism was inherently unstable, "producing the very problems [the United States] relied on it to contain" (Nasr 2014, p. 167). Instead, disillusionment about the outcome of the Arab Spring has led many in Washington and other Western capitals to revive the idea that only authoritarian Arab leaders can keep a lid on instability and terrorism.

However, it is worth taking a hard look at whether American alliances with Arab autocracies—countries such as Egypt, Jordan, Morocco, and the Gulf monarchies—actually deliver the stability their US proponents assume that they provide.

Even the resource-rich Gulf monarchies, which rely upon extensive oil and gas revenues to purchase the acquiescence of their populations, are not immune from popular revolt and other forms of instability. Saudi Crown Prince Mohammed bin Salman's push for social and economic reform and his moves against allegedly corrupt elites (including members of the Saudi royal family) reflect a recognition on his part that simply buying off citizens with subsidies cannot achieve stability in the long term (Cohen 2018), while his increasing reliance on brutal forms of repression points to the insecurity of the regime. Despite questions about long-term stability and Saudi Arabia's deplorable record on democracy and human rights, a strong bipartisan consensus in Washington has dictated that it is in the national interest to maintain strong ties to the Saudi monarchy and other Gulf autocracies. Many of the Washington policymakers who cheered the downfall of Ben Ali, Mubarak, and Muammar Qaddafi in 2011 said almost nothing about America's strong ties to equally repressive and corrupt Arab dictatorships in the Persian Gulf. In fact, until recently few in Washington policy circles have dared to seriously question exactly why a robust relationship with Riyadh or Abu Dhabi is essential.[17] As Chapter 6 will detail, the 2018 assassination of Saudi journalist Jamal Khashoggi produced unprecedented levels of bipartisan anger, and helped catalyze a resolution to end US involvement in the Saudi-led war in Yemen (Edmondson 2019), but it remains to be seen whether this will be translated into more far-reaching policy changes vis-à-vis the Saudi-US relationship.

Do Security Relationships Buy the United States Leverage?

There is also an assumption among some Washington foreign policy elites that long-standing relationships with autocratic Arab regimes gives the United States leverage over these states. However, evidence suggests that often the opposite is true. Security partnerships and the presence of US bases create the need to keep local partners "happy," which reduces diplomatic influence over a range of issues, democracy promotion included. Ruling monarchies in states such as Qatar, Kuwait, and Bahrain where the United States maintains military facilities know that the US military will not easily give up the valuable assets in their countries and therefore feel empowered to pursue internal repression and human rights abuses, all while "free riding" on US security guarantees. As one former senior official told me, "we think we are buying influence, when we are offering ourselves up as a hostage."[18] Some Department of Defense officials also argue that military ties afford the United States democratic leverage over Arab rulers. However, despite many years of US military engagement, assistance, and sales, the Middle East is no more democratic, not to mention stable, than it was since US involvement in the region intensified.

But it is not just that US support for autocratic Arab allies gives them the space to carry out domestic political repression. It also gives them carte blanche to implement a wide range of policies outside their borders that are harmful to US interests. Saudi and Qatari money has supported the spread of fundamentalist interpretations of Islam around the world, and both countries have directly and indirectly backed jihadist fighters in foreign conflicts from Bosnia and Herzegovina to Syria. Since 2015, Saudi Arabia (at times with US logistical support and tacit approval) has carried out a military intervention in Yemen that has resulted in catastrophic civilian suffering. The UAE and Qatar, as Chapter 5 will detail, have supported rival militias in post-Qaddafi Libya, contributing to state and social fragmentation. The policies of the Gulf states also destabilize their own relations, thereby hurting US interests in the region. In 2017, a GCC crisis based on personality and ideology broke out between Qatar and Saudi Arabia and led to the imposition of an economic embargo against Doha. The United States has not been able to put a stop to these detrimental policies despite acting as the security guarantor for the Gulf Arab monarchies.

US Security Partnerships in the Middle East and Their Consequences

US security relationships in the Arab world have entailed hundreds of billions of dollars in military aid and sales and include the presence of tens of thousands of US military personnel in the region. At this writing, there are approximately 52,612 US troops spread across the Middle East—with large military bases in Qatar (9,000 personnel), Bahrain (8,000 personnel), and Kuwait (15,600 personnel) and a smaller but significant presence in Iraq, Turkey, Egypt, Jordan, and Syria.[19] US service members at these facilities perform a range of missions, from patrolling commercial sea routes to training allied militaries to participating in counterterrorism operations.[20] Over time, however, the bases have become more than operational centers. Indeed, they are independent power structures, with their own interests. The American diplomat and historian George Kennan offered an early warning on military commands established abroad, writing in his memoirs that an overseas base is not just an "instrument of American policy" but "a new bureaucratic power structure situated far from our shores and endowed with its own specific perspective on all problems of world policy."[21]

However, US security partnerships with Arab states are rooted in much more than bases. Sales of arms and military equipment help "lock in" alliances and enable the "interoperability" of foreign and US militaries. US defense contractors earn tens of billions of dollars from military sales to Gulf countries; in the decade preceding the Arab Spring, over $72 billion in arms sales were approved for MENA countries ($10 billion of which went to Israel) (Thomas 2017).[22] These revenues are bolstered by the fact that Arab military partners prioritize expensive weapons such as fighters and tanks, even if they are not justified in terms of actual threats (Chollet 2016, p. 118). Consider the sales announced by the US government in the spring of 2018: $12 billion of F-15 fighter jets to Qatar and a staggering $110 billion worth of arms sales to Saudi Arabia—which, if it goes through, will be the single largest arms deal in American history (Filkins 2018). Security relationships also entail massive amounts of assistance to countries such as Jordan and Egypt. For example, between 1948 and 2016 the United States gave Egypt $77.4 billion in bilateral foreign aid, including $1.3 billion a year in military aid from 1987 to the present (Katzman 2017). As of 2019, US military assistance to Jordan totals approximately $400 million yearly, and total aid to the country over the past six decades has reached nearly $20 billion (Sharp 2018).

Security partnerships, as one top State Department official dealing with them admitted, "complicate" other foreign policy goals (Kaidanow 2017). Democracy promotion features prominently among these complications. The tension between maintaining security partnerships and promoting democracy comes to a head when we consider the role of the Department of Defense (DoD) in maintaining the partnerships. The literature on bureaucratic politics reviewed below hypothesizes that an institution is likely to "stand" where it "sits." Because the DoD "sits" on longstanding and multifaceted relationships with its counterparts in the Middle East, more often than not it "stands" on the side of stability, access, security, and force protection. Even when local, regional, and global dynamics might suggest that Washington should reassess the value of certain security partnerships, the reality is one of great inertia. From the perspective of the Pentagon, the costs of major shifts are simply perceived as being too high. While strategic considerations may have had primacy at the time security partnerships were first established, over time they have taken on a life of their own and become entrenched in multiple programs, sales, joint operations, and personal ties that link US and foreign military personnel.

Challenging the Rationale of US Military Partnerships in the Middle East

One argument commonly used to justify US military commitments in the Gulf is the imperative of securing oil resources. Every US president since Nixon has said that the country's dependence on foreign oil is a matter of national security (Rapier 2017). Toby Jones (2011a) argues that the American obsession with secure access to oil is rooted in the oil crises of the 1970s, when the Arab oil embargoes and the Iranian revolution constricted supply and helped push the US into recession. But as Jones (2011a) also points out, in today's world there is no shortage of oil thanks to new sources and extraction technologies. This is in part because the United States itself is energy independent thanks to fracking (or shale) technology. Obama's energy secretary, Ernest Moniz, called for a "new mentality" about America's energy position, with a "new political language to match" (Yergin 2013). Even before the fracking revolution, US energy dependence on the Middle East had declined as it bought more oil from countries such as Mexico, Canada, and Venezuela. However, access to domestic supplies does not insulate the United States entirely from oil price shocks: A shortage or high price in the Gulf can translate into higher prices everywhere else. At the same time, analysts point out that potential supply disruptions are actually less worrisome than scholars, politicians, and pundits presume (Gholz and Press 2010).

Close US allies such as Japan, South Korea, and European countries, however, do rely on Middle Eastern oil. Oil supply problems in these countries are likely to directly affect the US economy. Thus, the argument goes, the United States has an interest in continuing to secure transport routes from the Gulf to European and Asian markets. A failure to do so would allow the Chinese to quickly fill the void and perhaps one day deny the United States access (Snow 2016, p. 92). However, as with any policy, there are costs and benefits, and maybe the costs of keeping the Chinese at bay are simply too high. And perhaps, given a serious threat of US withdrawal from the region, Europeans or Asians could be convinced to take more responsibility over the security or transport routes. In sum, strategic concerns related to maintaining a stable oil supply make sense, but the shale revolution and growing energy independence of the United States should also call into question what have been regarded as rock-solid interests in the region and perhaps lead to a rethinking of US military obligations to Gulf states in particular. Moreover, as one analyst of Saudi Arabia has argued, it is in fact Riyadh's overdependence on oil revenues that gives the US leverage, since the Saudis will ultimately depend on American expertise and investment if they wish to diversify their economy (Wald 2018).

Counterterrorism is often another justification for ongoing military entanglements in the Arab world. US military facilities in both Qatar and Bahrain were used for operations in the recent war against the Islamic State. However, in an age when the main tools of counterterrorism are targeted strikes carried out by pilotless drones and covert operations conducted by small teams of special forces, it is more difficult to argue that a large troop presence is needed. The Obama administration preferred an approach to counterterrorism that favored covert operations and air strikes. The Trump administration has not indicated that it intends to change course. The drone- and special forces–focused approach certainly has a range of drawbacks—starting with ethical ones—but those drawbacks pale in comparison to the costs of large conventional deployments. Moreover, experts note that the presence of US troops and bases in the Middle East has long provided ideological ammunition and recruitment fodder for terrorist groups such as al-Qaeda (Ashford 2018b).

The need to check Iran is a further reason given for US security partnerships with Gulf countries. Gulf officials never miss an opportunity to remind their American counterparts of the existential threat posed by Iran.[23] To some extent, the fear of Iran is legitimate, but Gulf Arab leaders have also blatantly exaggerated the threat to sway US policymakers. It is true that Iran seeks regional influence, and does so in ways that undermine the stability and sovereignty of its Arab neighbors. Among other policies, Iran has supported Hezbollah in Lebanon, Syrian dictator Bashar al-Assad, and violent Shia militias in Syria and Iraq. However, Iran does not seek to destroy Saudi Arabia or overthrow the Arab regional order. It has its own internal problems, and its revolutionary legitimacy is an anachronism in which few Iranians still believe (Peterson 2018). Iran's nuclear weapons program is a real security concern, but the Joint Comprehensive Plan of Action (JCPOA), or "Iran nuclear deal," promised to neutralize this threat—at least until the Trump administration decided to pull out of the agreement in May 2018. According to both international inspectors and US intelligence agencies, Iran had been complying with the JCPOA's requirements at the moment Trump announced that the United States was quitting the accord (International Atomic Energy Agency 2018). Moreover, the Iranian challenge cannot be treated entirely through the lens of security—it is also a political problem that calls for diplomacy, as the experience of negotiating the JCPOA showed.

Then there is the argument that security relationships with Arab states "buy" peace for Israel, in terms of threats from both its neighbors and Iran. Israel, of course, fears Iran just as much as it fears Arab states, and Iran has certainly given the Israelis reason to be afraid. But the idea that US security partnerships with Arab countries are needed to ensure that they do not turn against Israel is unsubstantiated. Nasr (2014) notes that Gulf leaders publicly pledge their support for the Palestinian struggle, but in private meetings with US officials only want to talk about the Iranian threat. As of 2019, Gulf monarchies and Sisi's Egypt seem to have found common cause with Israel, and cooperate with Israeli officials quite well behind the scenes (Fraihat 2019).

US security partnerships with autocratic Arab regimes do not foster pro-American attitudes. Instead, cooperation with nondemocratic regimes fosters an anti-American outlook among a younger generation of Arabs. Moreover, they allow autocratic Arab regimes to build powerful domestic instruments of control and repression and advance corruption and cronyism. Consider Bahrain, one of the cases I examine in depth in this book and where the US Navy maintains a major facility. Washington's interests have been framed around ensuring a good relationship with the ruling monarchy, the al-Khalifa family. At the same time, al-Khalifa rule has been synonymous with corruption and nepotism, engendering widespread disaffection among the country's 70 percent Shia population. Thus, an alternate view of the US interest might be that the longer reforms are deferred, the harder it may be to ensure stability on the island and the safety of US basing and assets. Analysts have questioned the wisdom of propping up a minority Sunni monarchy that rules through repression rather than consent. Washington's "reluctance to condemn Bahrain," writes Jones (2011a), is the result of a deeply ingrained belief in Washington that the United States needs Bahrain to help it preserve regional stability and to protect friendly oil producers in the Persian Gulf. Jones (2011b) challenges these beliefs by offering a number of reasons why the "Fifth Fleet may well have become a political liability, irrelevant, or possibly even both." Jones argues that "the cost of maintaining a large military presence in the Gulf drains American resources and limits the United States' flexibility in dealing with regional crises" and "enables regional allies to act recklessly." Jones maintains that "Saudi Arabia would almost certainly not have sent its troops into neighboring Bahrain—a sovereign country—if the Saudi and Bahraini leaderships did not assume they were protected by their patrons in the U.S. military." Given the potentially explosive situation in Bahrain, Elliott Abrams (2015) asks "why it is smart to assume that the facilities the United States has in Bahrain will in fact be available—or safe to use—in the coming decades?" Noting growing Sunni extremism, Shia outrage, and deepening sectarian fragmentation in Bahrain and the wider region, Abrams wonders how the status quo can serve US interests. Abrams does not advocate doing away with the Fifth Fleet altogether, but he argues that its presence and the scope of US cooperation with the Bahraini military should be actively used by top US officials as a source of leverage over the Bahraini monarchy to encourage meaningful democratic reforms.

Challenging Security Partnerships from Libertarian and Realist Perspectives

Criticism of the costs of US security partnerships in the Arab world, however, does not come only from proponents of democracy promotion. This criticism can also be found in libertarian-leaning Washington think tanks such as the Cato Institute. For example, Cato's Emma Ashford (2018b, p. 128) writes that "it is unclear what goals this military presence is intended to achieve, other than to satisfy vague invocations of the need for 'engagement.'" Ashford observes that the current high force posture in the Middle East is a fairly recent phenomenon, which started only after the 1990–1991 Gulf War when increased numbers of troops in the region were justified by the need to contain both Iraq and Iran. President Bill Clinton's decision to keep sizable numbers of US troops in the region may also have had to do with domestic political benefits. If nothing else, it provided the "U.S. military a needed and not-too-costly new mission" in the aftermath of the Cold War (Ashford 2018b, p. 131). This policy of dual containment and the departure from "offshore balancing" in Ashford's view "was at best weakly justified" given that Iraq's armed forces had been crushed and Iran was still suffering from its war with Iraq. Moreover, in the preceding decades the United States had held the Soviet Union at bay and effectively managed both Iran and Iraq "through adroit balancing of aid and a swift military response to Iraqi aggression" without the large military presence (Ashford 2018b, p. 130).

From the realist perspective, Michael Wahid Hanna (2015) has challenged the idea that a continuing US security partnership with Egypt, which entails annual assistance on the order of $1.3 billion, falls within the US national interest. As noted earlier, despite its decades-long investment in Egypt, the United States has not achieved a professional military, a reduction in terrorism, or a stable democracy that respects human rights. Instead, successive Egyptian governments have propagated anti-Americanism in state-controlled media and attacked US-funded NGOs. Hanna notes that Egypt is no longer the Arab power that it used to be, and the benefits the United States supposedly derives from its relationship with Cairo are overrated. He describes the US-Egyptian relationship as "nakedly transactional," and one that "benefits the Egyptians more than the Americans." Like Ashford, Hanna is not an advocate of democracy promotion. But he nevertheless sees ongoing repression in Egypt as a long-term liability for the United States. He argues that the Obama administration's 2015 resumption of aid "implicated the United States in Egypt's repression of Islamists, secular activists, and journalists who have dared to challenge or even merely criticize Sisi." He concedes that at times the United States is forced to make deals with dictators but argues that "for such compromises to be worth it, the strategic benefits must outweigh the costs." Hanna concludes that the United States should distill its relationship with Egypt to core interests, such as overflight rights, some basic counterterrorism cooperation, and access to the Suez Canal. Egypt, Hanna maintains, is likely to cooperate in all of these areas because it is in its interest to do so.

Discussion

What the Washington foreign policy establishment defines as core US interests in the region are in part shaped by inertia and reinforced by longstanding security partnerships from which the United States finds it hard to extract itself. The "engagement" argument so frequently used by US military agencies to justify a continued presence in the Gulf conflates military presence with diplomatic influence (Ashford 2018b, p. 135). In reality, however, the two are actually in competition with each other when it comes not only to democratic leverage, but leverage over a whole host of other US priorities. Security partnerships with Gulf countries, in fact, have made it much harder for the United States to rein in Saudi Arabia, Qatar, and the UAE as counterdemocratic spoilers or "challengers" (described in Chapter 5). In reality, as Mara Karlin and Tamara Cofman Wittes (2019) write, these bases have "strategic implications" because of the "moral hazard" they create: "They encourage the region's leaders to act in ways they otherwise might not, safe in the knowledge that the United States is invested in the stability of their regimes."

Arguments about the perverse effects of the status quo come not only from democracy and human rights "types" but also from realists and libertarians who challenge whether the costs the United States pays for its alliances with Arab autocrats truly serve its interests. To understand how these "interests" are formulated and translated into policy, we must turn to the "agents" of national interest. In what follows, I highlight three additional determinants of democracy promotion policies—*individuals, institutions,* and *challengers*—each of which is elaborated in the subsequent sections.

Individuals and US Democracy Promotion

Consider the following scenario: Two senior foreign policy officials occupy the same position at different times. Each brings to the job a distinct set of psychological "baggage." The first believes that US interests in Arab states are best served by maintaining ongoing relationships with ruling regimes. This official also retains a deep aversion to political Islam. The second official is not immune to skepticism about democracy in the Arab world but is also willing to rethink US ties to Arab autocrats in light of pent-up economic and political frustrations among ordinary Arabs. This second official may also have doubts about political Islam but is willing to give Islamist parties a chance to prove that they are capable of adhering to democratic credentials. Each official presides over a critical moment for US democracy promotion in the same Arab country.

Though simplified a bit here, the scenario above describes two real US officials and the circumstances they faced: Secretary of State Hillary Clinton when the Egyptian uprising broke out in January 2011, and her successor, John Kerry, when a military coup threatened to bring down a democratically elected Islamist president in Egypt in June 2013. Each perceived the unfolding events through a unique filter. In 2011, Clinton perceived an opportunity for the United States to encourage the development of a pluralistic political order that was inclusive of Islamists, perhaps owing to her instinctive sense, as expressed in the 2011 Doha speech, that the status quo was unsustainable. She was less willing to accept the Arab autocratic narrative that free elections would inevitably lead to Islamist theocracy and the growth of terrorism, and in some ways was ahead of the risk-averse State Department she led in responding to the Arab Spring. Kerry, on the other hand, appeared to harbor a deep aversion to the Muslim Brotherhood and perhaps a belief that democracy was simply not possible in Egypt (Kirkpatrick 2018, p. 116). He also brought to the job relationships of many years with ruling Arab regimes, especially those in the Gulf. This and his singular focus on Israeli-Palestinian peace drew him away from democracy promotion in Egypt. No wonder then, that Kerry's "soft" positions on the 2013 Egyptian coup were out of sync with President Obama, who wanted the Egyptian military to pay some price for the coup and the brutal crackdown on Muslim Brotherhood supporters that followed. Differences in the worldview of individual policymakers, then, had direct consequences for US democracy promotion policies in Egypt.

The role of the individual—the experiences, personality, beliefs, and preferences that the president, his or her key advisers, and other foreign policy elites bring to the table—is understudied in international relations and foreign policy analysis. Although an actor-centric model is often helpful in explaining foreign policy outcomes, it is hard to research and theorize (Marsden 2005, p. 7). The beliefs that animate how individuals perceive foreign policy issues are based on a unique background and set of experiences. That is, they perceive the world subjectively, through a very personal set of psychological lenses. While institutions can powerfully shape individuals (Chapter 4), the opposite is also true: Individuals can shape both the character, priorities, and influence of the institutions they lead.

Any analysis focusing on the role of the individual in foreign policy making must start with the person of the president. The president is the head of state—and thus America's most recognizable symbol around the world—as well as the principal decisionmaker on foreign policy matters. The president also exerts influence on foreign policy by setting priorities, appointing senior officials, and acting as the chief executive of a vast foreign policy bureaucracy. The president acts, like all human beings, according to a personality, belief system, and leadership style. However, other individuals also influence foreign policy outcomes, especially those with direct access to the president. Among them are the president's top foreign policy advisers. Some of these advisers have access to the president by virtue of status and position: the chief of staff and the national security adviser, for example. Certain cabinet officials (secretary of state, secretary of defense) are involved in foreign policy decisions by law and custom. Other individuals the president regularly consults, depending on the issue, might include: the secretary of the treasury, the chair of the Joint Chiefs of Staff, the director of national intelligence, and the US permanent representative to the United Nations (UN). Yet, there are also those whose influence derives not from their title or position in the hierarchy but from their privileged relationship with the president. Such individuals could include members of the National Security Council or White House staff, members of Congress, politically appointed ambassadors, or even those outside of government (think-tank scholars, businesspeople, interest group representatives) who can reach the president directly.

The focus on the individual in the study of foreign policy decisionmaking is a perspective derived from psychology and cognitive science. *Homo psychologicus* is an umbrella term for a set of theories developed in the 1960s and 1970s about how individual decisionmakers process information (Houghton 2013, p. 18). Applied to foreign policy analysis, all of these theories begin with the observations that (1) individuals make key foreign policy decisions and (2) individuals make decisions with imperfect information and other cognitive limitations and thus rely on factors such as historical analogy, information shortcuts, scripts, and emotions. Individuals, then, are "boundedly rational" actors (Simon 1957, 1983) who frequently "cling to their existing beliefs and preconceptions, often rationalizing away the new information as insignificant or explaining it away so as to preserve their existing attitudes and mindsets" (Houghton 2013, p. 14) even when confronted with contradictory evidence and information.

One strand of theory drawing on the individual approach focuses on the "irresistible pull" of analogical reasoning (Houghton 2013, p. 68). Reasoning with the help of analogies is especially relevant in conditions of uncertainty and information overload around fast-moving events, when policymakers are most likely to resort to cognitive shortcuts such as analogies. Analogies, however, can mislead as well as illuminate because our minds "often downplay the differences between situations" (Houghton 2013, p. 69). Individuals, in other words, may assume parallels between a set of events and miss critical dissimilarities.

Robert Abelson (1981) highlights *cognitive scripts*—conceptual representations of stereotyped event sequences—as a way to understand the role of the individual in foreign policy making. He describes such scripts as "a particular kind of schema or mental box, which provides the typical default values for an event of some kind or an act which we are accustomed to performing."[24] In other words, individual decisionmakers fit new data into established mental categories based on experience, both "because it requires little effort and because it allows us to make sense of the outside world quickly and expeditiously."[25] This is particularly true in "conditions of high uncertainty and ambiguity, where the individual is being bombarded with too much information, or where he or she possesses too little of this." But just because something is "typically true" does not mean it will be true when a novel situation emerges, and these shortcuts can lead to oversimplification (Houghton 2013, p. 79).[26] In US foreign policy debates, the "Munich script" cautions about the dangers of appeasing a dictator, while the "Vietnam script" stresses the dangers of confrontation over accommodation. The former script can lead decisionmakers to overreact, while the latter can lead to overcautiousness.[27]

Institutions and US Democracy Promotion

Consider now this scenario: Protests challenging authoritarianism break out in an Arab country, and the regime responds with a violent crackdown, killing many unarmed, innocent protesters. This Arab state happens to be a close US ally and hosts a large US military installation. The fact that the state is a close ally does not stop the US government from being repulsed at the regime's brutal treatment of peaceful protesters, and both the White House and State Department issue statements condemning the violence and urging the offending Arab regime to enter into a dialogue with the opposition. A senior State Department official is dispatched to meet with regime leaders and communicates Washington's displeasure with the lethal violence inflicted upon unarmed protesters and implies unspecified damage to the bilateral relationship should the regime continue down the road of repression. Just a few days later, the head of US Central Command, the primary Department of Defense entity responsible for the Middle East, visits the country and meets with regime leaders as well. This official's talking points include a line taken from the State Department's script about refraining from violence and engaging with the opposition, but it is preceded by a number of other talking points emphasizing the importance of the military relationship, thanking the regime for its assistance on counterterrorism, praising the completion of recent joint exercises, and expressing concern about the safety and security of US personnel in the country given the recent unrest. Meanwhile, back in Washington, at interagency policy meetings on the country, Pentagon representatives remind participants of the vital strategic importance and irreplaceability of the base and the US relationship with the regime. Diplomats and lobbyists advocate for the regime, engaging with the Pentagon and congressional representatives. Meanwhile, the US ambassador meets with the regime and delivers a more conciliatory message.

This scenario is a composite of the dynamics that have often characterized US policy in Bahrain. While any constituent part of the US government would prefer a democratic Bahrain, the Pentagon has more immediate and narrow interests vis-à-vis the tiny Gulf state, resulting in multiple messages and policies on democracy promotion. As one retired US ambassador who worked closely with the military put it to me, the Department of Defense may think that it would be *good* to have democracy in an autocratic country where it operates, but it *must* have stability.[28]

In Bahrain, the Pentagon's interest lies first and foremost in protecting its strategically important base and preserving the security relationship. The US ambassador and the State Department's Near Eastern Affairs Bureau understand the destabilizing effect of Shia marginalization in Bahrain but are also interested in maintaining access and ties and not offending the royal family. Thus, a sub-bureaucratic entity, the State Department Bureau of Democracy, Rights, and Labor (DRL), is often the lone actor pushing for democratic promotion in Bahrain in a consistent and meaningful manner. As for the Bahraini royals, they readily recognize the internal US government divisions and see them as an opportunity to insert themselves into US interagency disputes, playing one institution off another.

Accounts of US foreign policy based on the institutional approach do not lend themselves to the elegant models associated with international relations theory. Bureaucratic politics are hard to discern since foreign policy debates generally happen behind closed doors and thus are often opaque to researchers, not to mention the general public. Yet, anyone who has worked within the Washington apparatus knows that foreign policy is often the outcome of a messy process of daily wrangling among various bureaucratic actors who look after particularistic, *institutional interests*. As James March and Herbert Simon (1958) have pointed out, the activities of a particular organization are concrete, while the generalized interest of the government is not. Thus, individuals come to see organizations as the way to operationalize the national interest. Bureaucrats come to identify strongly with their organizations and develop an awareness of the shortcomings of rival ones. For career officials, a strong identification with a particular institution and a personal interest in promotion often shapes the idea that their organization is vital to the national interest and leads them to defend it vigorously in interagency debates (Halperin and Clapp 2006). If a bureaucratic actor happens to be dominant on a specific issue, foreign policy outcomes may come to reflect that institutional actor's interests. Furthermore, as noted above for the case of US policy toward Bahrain, individual bureaucracies have subunits, each with their own functions, interests, and views.

Derived from organizational theory, the bureaucratic politics approach to US foreign policy decisionmaking was developed in the 1960s and 1970s by scholars such as Graham Allison (1971), but its insights remain strikingly relevant for understanding US foreign policy decisionmaking today. This literature's key assumptions are that (1) the United States is not always a unitary actor; (2) the instinct of any organization is self-preservation; (3) US foreign policy does not result from the intentions of any one individual; (4) US foreign policy is not based on a rational calculation based on interests, costs, and benefits; and (5) foreign policy bureaucracies may resist the preferences of presidents and other political leaders.

Seen from the bureaucratic perspective, foreign policy outcomes are less a reflection of deliberate choices than the result of bargaining between large agencies with very different ideas about how policies should be framed and pursued, and different tools with which to pursue them. Foreign policy decisions, thus, can end up as the least common denominator—one that everyone can agree on but fully pleases no one—or a collage of policies containing something for everyone (Houghton 2013, p. 9). In the face of bureaucratic wrangling, the president might end up as little more than a passive bystander or referee (Houghton 2013, p. 9).[29] The principal foreign policy bureaucratic actors, and their respective views on democracy promotion, are presented in an appendix at the end of the book.

The policy positions of institutional actors in the US foreign policy community also reflect unique organizational cultures. James Q. Wilson (1991, pp. 91–110) defines organizational culture as "a persistent, patterned way of thinking, which passes from one generation to the next." Edgar Schein (1984, p. 3) notes that organizational cultures inform basic underlying assumptions and encourage a "set of shared meanings" that influence the way in which individuals interpret and act upon their environment. Unique organizational cultures shape an institution's core goals, methods, and strategy, as well as the frames through which each institution sees foreign policy issues. At times, this results in the lack of shared definition among bureaucratic actors of what policy goals such as democracy promotion mean. The socialization of new employees into bureaucracies helps to perpetuate organizational cultures across generations and turn institutions into "mini societies" with processes, norms, and structures calibrated to uphold certain values (Allaire and Firsirotu 1984). However, as noted earlier, institutions are not unitary actors, and varying organizational cultures may exist at the subinstitutional level or in field offices versus Washington headquarters.

Institutions tend toward inertia; they move only when pushed hard and persistently (Halperin and Clapp 2006, p. 99). Bureaucrats prefer the status quo, and at any time only a small group among them is advocating serious changes in policy. Changes in administration and party have little effect on many foreign policy operations, and bureaucrats see elected officials as a temporary phenomenon that they can "wait out."[30] Moreover, the time and resources of any one person in the bureaucracy are limited, and he or she must pick battles over policy changes carefully (Halperin and Clapp 2006, p. 99). Arduous clearance processes, a focus on yearly performance evaluations, and a strict vertical hierarchy discourage the advocacy of meaningful change and tend to push bureaucrats toward "least common denominator" proposals. Democracy promotion is rarely part of such proposals as it tends to be disruptive to relations in a way that makes institutions nervous.

Bureaucratic actors have another advantage over the White House: the specialized knowledge and well-developed repertoires on which presidents rely to formulate and implement foreign policy. Because presidents have limited time and capacity to absorb all the complexities of a given issue, bureaucracies possess an information advantage that helps them frame an issue in a way that reflects their interests. At the implementation stage, there is a significant principal-agent problem that gives bureaucracies the room to shape, resist, distort, or even undermine a president's agenda. Thus, the bureaucratic politics model can help explain the gap between the intention of a policy as formulated by the president and the manner in which that policy is actually implemented.

Challengers to US Democracy Promotion

Consider this final scenario: After the Arab uprisings, wealthy but vulnerable Arab monarchies in the Gulf region are terrified of "people power" uprisings and their capacity to topple regimes. They are stunned that the US policy response to the uprisings has included, in some cases, withdrawal of support for allied autocrats.

They are even more concerned that ideological rivals such as the Muslim Brotherhood are ascendant in post–Arab Spring elections. In one case in particular, a member of the Brotherhood has been elected president in a reasonably free and fair election. The Gulf monarchies pull out all the stops to both discredit the Brotherhood president and influence US policy to turn against him. They start a media campaign demonizing the elected president, funnel millions of dollars to groups seeking to topple him, and after a military coup is successfully executed, pledge tens of billions of dollars to support the coup plotters, eclipsing whatever aid the United States threatens to cut. Meanwhile, lobbyists and diplomats acting on behalf of the Gulf countries mobilize to convince Washington executive and legislative branch officials that Muslim Brothers are closet terrorists whom the United States should actively oppose, while disparaging US officials who engage with Islamist political groups.

The scenario above describes Saudi and Emirati actions in 2013 around the Egyptian military coup, an event they backed in numerous ways while lobbying for US support. It reminds us that US policies in the aftermath of the Arab uprisings did not work in "splendid isolation" (Marsden 2005, p. 7). As Derek Chollet, a former senior Obama administration official said, the United States "was not the only player, and it was by far not the most active player in terms of resources."[31] During and after the Arab Spring, a number of external actors used their diplomatic, economic, and military muscle to interfere directly in the politics of Arab Spring states. The Arab Spring shook the wealthiest and most powerful Gulf monarchies to their core, not only because they despised ascendant actors such as the Muslim Brotherhood, but because they feared democracy itself. The tiny state of Qatar seemingly embraced the protesters in 2011, but it did so mostly in a gamble that its own ideological allies would prevail in transitions, and because the small kingdom's sheer wealth and small population made the possibility of rebellion within its borders unlikely (Walsh 2018). However, Qatar also played a democracy-undermining role at key post–Arab Spring junctures through its support for proxy militias and other actors with an undemocratic agenda.

The role of challenger is not a new one. The United States played it during the Cold War, propping up repressive right-wing governments as a way to contain Soviet expansion. States such as Russia, China, and France have all played it during the post–Cold War period, using economic, diplomatic, and other assistance to shore up autocratic governments in neighboring or former colonial states. Russia has backed authoritarian and corrupt governments in Armenia, Belarus, and Ukraine and blocked these states from closer association with the European Union. France has supported autocrats in former colonies such as Cameroon and Gabon. China has provided aid and investment with "no strings attached" to autocratic African states.

While individuals and institutions are variables endogenous to the US foreign-policy-making process, challengers are not exclusively exogenous to it. This is because the challengers of interest here—Saudi Arabia and United Arab Emirates in particular—are also close US allies with long-standing and deep networks of influence in Washington. As described earlier, the Washington consensus regards them as indispensable allies owing to hydrocarbon resources, security partnerships, and their role in balancing the Iranian threat. Consequently, challengers could be effective counterweights to US democracy promotion not only because they used their diplomatic, economic, and military muscle to interfere directly in the politics of Arab Spring states, but also because they harnessed their Washington linkages to influence or reinforce the beliefs of key US policymakers.

While the literature on democracy promotion and democratic diffusion is substantial, scholarship on exporting authoritarianism remains limited.

Scholars have highlighted the tools authoritarian powers use to support fellow autocrats, tools that mirror those used by democracy promoters. Authoritarian states, for example, can "bid" for loyalty by offering autocratic actors assistance that exceeds whatever democracy promoters threaten to take away as punishment for democratic transgressions. They can use diplomacy in multilateral organizations such as the UN Security Council to prop up allied autocrats. Or they can deploy their militaries to quell challenges to authoritarian rule. Investigating Russia's involvement in Belarus, Venezuela's engagement in Peru and Nicaragua, and Iran's connections to Lebanon, Rachel Vanderhill (2013) examines how states promote authoritarianism. She argues that authoritarian actors use both incentives (trade agreements, cheap supplies of energy, additional financial resources) and negative inducements (denial of energy supplies) to influence the calculations of local elites (Vanderhill 2013, p. 8).

While the tools authoritarian powers use to exert their influence are clear, there is less agreement about the motivations of autocracy-promoting states. For instance, one strand in the literature sees authoritarian powers as primarily interested in regional stability, and not necessarily reproducing their form of rule. Julia Bader, Jörn Grävingholt, and Antje Kästner (2010, pp. 88–91) find that powers such as Russia and China will prefer authoritarian rule abroad if a targeted country is already in some state of disarray. Moreover, "autocracy promotion" may be more about protecting or expanding regional spheres of influence than exporting a particular model of rule. Natalie Shapovalova and Kateryna Zarembo (2010), writing about Russia, claim that Moscow does not see the preservation of authoritarian rule as an end in itself, but rather as a way to maintain its privileged sphere of influence in the "near abroad." The 2018 Russian recognition of a reform-oriented leader in Armenia who came to power following mass protests lends some credibility to the idea that Russia is more interested in maintaining influence than fostering copycat autocratic regimes.

Similarly, Daniel Odinius and Philipp Kuntz (2015, p. 644) argue that states such as Saudi Arabia promote autocratic actors in the interest of self-preservation rather than for ideological reasons or access to resources. GCC countries, they write, "were mostly afraid of uprisings in states with monarchical rule and with similar domestic groups." This may also explain why the Saudis were more active autocracy promoters after the Arab Spring than the Qataris, since the former had greater fears of competing ideologies than the latter given Saudi Arabia's greater reliance on religious credentials for legitimacy. But if realpolitik considerations serve as the best explanation for the GCC's autocracy-promoting policies in Arab Spring countries, it is still necessary to explain why GCC countries chose not to support autocratic regimes in Syria, Yemen, and Libya in the name of stability. Here Odinius and Kuntz (2015) suggest yet another explanation, which are the "reputational gains" GCC monarchies might achieve domestically by standing up to atrocities committed by Qaddafi and Assad in particular. Opposing autocratic strongmen such as Qaddafi, Saleh, and Assad also offered the Gulf regimes "a way of diverting international attention from political oppression in the Gulf and gaining Western acquiescence over the GCC's own intervention in Bahrain" (Odinius and Kuntz 2015).

Then there is the question of whether efforts to promote autocracy actually work. Vanderhill (2013) aims to understand the impact of challengers on regime type, which she argues rests in part on the internal dynamics of target states. If certain political actors or segments of the population in target states have ties to an autocracy promoter in ethnic or ideological terms, it gives the autocracy promoter increased leverage. Shia in Lebanon (with ties to Iran) and ethnic Russians throughout the former Soviet space are a case in point. Vanderhill focuses on the balance of power among elites in a target state and the nature of linkages between the recipient state and autocracy promoter. She theorizes that if the target country is evenly divided between liberal and illiberal elites and there are economic, historical, or ideological linkages between the target state and autocracy promoter, then the promotion of autocracy is likely to be more effective (Vanderhill 2013, p. 8). Autocracy promotion, in other words, works in synergy with domestic factors.

The power of an autocracy promoter to challenge Western prodemocratic leverage also depends on the will and capacity of potential democracy-promoting states to stand up to the challengers. Gulf states can succeed as autocracy promoters in part because there is a transatlantic preference for stability and security in the Arab world over democracy and human rights. Moreover, Saudi Arabia is deemed strategically important for the West as an oil exporter and regional power (Hassan 2015).

Cases and Methods

The empirical material in the book focuses on three countries in which I argue that the United States had potential democratic leverage: two longstanding autocratic Arab allies of the United States—Egypt and Bahrain—and a state with which the United States had a much more complicated relationship prior to the Arab Spring—Libya. In 2011, all three countries experienced mass uprisings fueled by a desire for political reform and economic justice. In Egypt, the uprising toppled a strongman, Hosni Mubarak, and his hegemonic political party, if not the military system that guaranteed Mubarak's rule. In Bahrain, protests did not bring down the monarchy but shook it to its core and provoked a violent crackdown by both Bahraini authorities and intervening GCC troops. In Libya, protests turned into an armed rebellion that, with the help of external military intervention, succeeded in overthrowing the personalized dictatorship of Muammar Qaddafi. In all three cases, then, there was a significant political opening for democracy promotion.

In all three cases, moreover, there was evidence that the status quo was incompatible with long-term stability, suggesting a need to recalibrate how US interests were perceived. In Bahrain, a minority Sunni monarchy had failed to extend adequate political and economic rights to the country's Shia majority, and unrest was a regular occurrence. In Egypt, crony capitalism, corruption, massive inequalities, and continuing repression had led to widespread dissatisfaction. The existence of an anti-American and anti-Israeli state media had already led to questions in some parts of the US government as to what benefits the United States was deriving from its support of the authoritarian status quo.[32] In Libya, there was also extensive corruption and a dearth of economic opportunities for a bulging youth population. This was accompanied by high levels of repression that left almost no room for freedom of expression or civil society.

Promoting democracy in Bahrain and Egypt promised special benefits. Close US relations with both countries, manifested in military-to-military ties and extensive security assistance programs, suggested a high degree of US leverage. By promoting democracy, the United States could counter accusations that it is not interested in democracy where friendly regimes are concerned. Moreover, both countries had a history of political and economic reforms that could serve as a foundation for democracy promotion. Egypt in the latter years of Mubarak had become a "liberalizing autocracy,"[33] while in Bahrain there was a well-organized opposition, and the country had taken steps toward constitutional monarchy. In both Egypt and Bahrain, there were civil society groups and media outlets critical of the government. Both countries had parliaments and judiciaries that exhibited streaks of independence. By comparison, such a foundation for democratization did not exist in US allies such as Saudi Arabia, the United Arab Emirates, or Qatar, and existed to a more limited extent in allies such as Morocco and Jordan.

Libya, by contrast, was not an autocratic ally of the United States prior to 2011, and as such is a case that allows one to test the role of individuals and institutions in a context not characterized by decades of close military-to-military relations. Here, the story of potential US democratic leverage is more nuanced. During the 2011 Arab Spring, the lack of sufficient strategic and bureaucratic interest in maintaining the status quo in Libya meant that institutions such as the Department of Defense, while opposing the intervention, did not constitute as much of an obstacle to robust forms of democracy promotion as they did in Egypt and Bahrain. While US leverage over the Qaddafi regime was limited at the time of the 2011 uprising owing to a lack of close ties such as those that connected the United States to

Egypt and Bahrain, it was heightened during the post-Qaddafi transition owing to US support of the rebel government.

The choice of cases allows me to test the central premise of the book: that the notion of a clear and unified national interest that can explain why the United States tends not to pursue democracy promotion in the Arab world is elusive. The constellation of US interests in Libya, Egypt, and Bahrain did not necessarily predict the initially bold democracy promotion moves the Obama administration made in all three cases in 2011. In Egypt, despite extremely close US relations with Hosni Mubarak for nearly three decades, Obama ultimately made the decision to call for him to step down. In Bahrain, despite a close relationship with the ruling family, the presence of a major naval base, and pressure from ally Saudi Arabia, Obama criticized the monarchy for its violent crackdown and instituted a "pause" on weapons sales. In Libya, despite a *lack* of sufficient strategic interests, Obama made the risky decision to join a military intervention that helped topple the Qaddafi regime.

All three cases—Egypt, Bahrain, and Libya—allow one to observe the role of challengers, or third-party spoilers of democratization. Emboldened by Obama's perceived withdrawal from the Middle East and alarmed by his readiness to reconsider long-standing alliances and engage Iran, Gulf Arab states launched their own campaigns of counterleverage in the region, simultaneously limiting the influence of US democratic pressure and convincing Washington policymakers that their efforts would make little difference in the face of overwhelming Gulf money and influence. In Libya, Egypt, and Bahrain, we witness three different ways Gulf Arab countries such as Saudi Arabia, Qatar, and the United Arab Emirates have countered US democracy promotion: financial guarantees to authoritarian forces, the cultivation of proxy militias, and direct military intervention.

For each case, I focus on a number of critical events in post–Arab Spring transitions and analyze how the United States responded to them—violent crackdowns, constitutional and legislative crises, elections, and other important developments. For example, in Egypt, I look at the 2011–2012 protests against the military council that governed the country after the ouster of Mubarak, the 2011–2012 parliamentary elections, the 2012 presidential elections, the 2013 coup, and the growing atmosphere of repression after 2015. In Bahrain, such critical moments included the violent crackdown on Pearl Roundabout in March 2011, the release of the Bahrain Independent Commission of Inquiry (BICI) report in November 2011, and the events surrounding the run-up to the November 2014 election. In Libya, critical events include the 2012 decision by interim governing authorities to deputize militias as providers of security, the 2012 elections to an interim parliament, the 2013 Political Isolation Law, and the fragmentation of the country into competing power centers in the summer of 2014.

Alongside the comparative case study approach, I utilize methods such as process tracing of foreign policy decisionmaking and counterfactual reasoning. My data comes from multiple sources. I garnered firsthand knowledge of the events and policies covered in the book as a US diplomat posted in Egypt and Libya immediately after the Arab Spring. Thus, my understanding of both US policies and conditions in those two countries stems in part from those experiences. After leaving government, I made fieldwork visits to a number of Arab Spring countries and talked to former and current government officials, analysts, and, when it was possible and safe for my interview subjects, to democracy activists, with the goal of understanding how local actors perceive US democratic leverage. In 2017 and 2018, I conducted over fifty interviews with key decisionmakers in the Obama administration. Given that they were now out of government, many of these former officials could be more open about the deliberations within the administration, but many still requested to be interviewed on background or off the record.

In choosing US officials to interview, I was careful to elicit perspectives from across the interagency: State Department, Department of Defense, National Security Council, and other institutions. I also interviewed senior diplomats who were in the region during the period analyzed. When inquiring about the debates that went into key policy decisions, I made sure to ask different officials the same question so as to corroborate facts and better understand different institutional and individual perspectives. Outside of government, I spoke to experts at Washington, DC–based think tanks and other analysts with knowledge of the countries I cover and of the US foreign-policy-making process. Finally, I relied on multiple primary sources: memoirs, statements, speeches, assistance data, human rights reports, published interviews, and other government documents that detail US policies toward the Arab world after 2011.

Organization of the Book

Chapter 2 outlines what democracy promotion is (and isn't), presents its tools, and discusses how one can identify a high versus low degree of democracy promotion. It also contains a brief history of US democracy promotion in the Arab world, focusing on the limited efforts of the George W. Bush administration to promote democracy in the region. In the ensuing three empirical chapters I show how individuals, institutions, and challengers shaped Obama's approach to democracy promotion during and after the Arab Spring. Chapter 3 focuses on individuals; Chapter 4 is about institutions; and Chapter 5 covers challengers, the third-party spoilers of US democracy promotion. Chapter 6 summarizes US policy under Obama and analyzes US democracy promotion in the Arab world and beyond during the first two years of the Trump presidency. An appendix provides an overview of US foreign policy institutions and how they relate to democracy promotion.

Notes

All interviews cited were conducted by the author unless otherwise noted.

1. The change in approach was reflected in Obama's public oratory: compare, for example, his May 2011 speech on the Arab Spring (Obama 2011b) with his September 2013 speech before the UN General Assembly (Obama 2013).

2. Notable books on US democracy promotion include Smith (2012); Carothers (2004); Cox, Ikenberry, and Inoguchi (2000); and McFaul (2010).

3. For example, Smith's (2012) seminal work on the history of US democracy promotion very rarely mentions the Arab world.

4. An example is Nau's (2013) essay on Reagan's democracy promotion policies. Some authors highlight the democracy promotion efforts of certain US presidential administrations while barely mentioning that those same presidents were content with propping up the authoritarian status quo in the Arab world.

5. Examples include Marsden (2005) and Huber (2015).

6. For example, Linz and Stepan (1996).

7. For example, Whitehead (2001); Levitsky and Way (2010); and Gleditsch and Ward (2006).

8. For example, Vanderhill (2013).

9. Scholarly books on the Arab Spring are too numerous to list here, but examples include Lynch (2014); Diamond and Plattner (2014); and Lynch (2016). Trade book examples include Worth (2016) and Kirkpatrick (2018).

10. There seems to be more scholarly work on EU democracy promotion before and after the Arab Spring, including Van Hüllen (2015) and Balfour (2012). There are some more recent works on the United States and the Arab Spring. Abrams (2017) covers the US response to the Arab Spring from a democracy promotion advocacy vantage point, while Wahlrab and McNeal (2018) edited a volume that employs critical theory to illuminate Washington's policy responses to the Arab uprisings.

11. Interview with Elliott Abrams, Washington, DC, February 2018.

12. See United Nations Development Programme (2002).

13. Rice, quoted in Traub (2008, p. 3).

14. Clinton, quoted in Landler (2011).

15. The realist approach also assumes perfect information and a rational and orderly approach on the part of policymakers who consider all available options and calculate their relative costs and benefits (Houghton 2013, p. 7). There are those realists who see the United States as a liberal power and thus its interests as moral. But, as Kaplan (2013) notes, these interests are only "secondarily moral." This is because adjusting the balance of power in one's favor has been throughout history an amoral enterprise pursued by both liberal and illiberal powers (Kaplan 2013). Moreover, even if the United States pursues balancing in the service of a noble goal, such as preventing war among states, it is not necessarily promoting democracy.

16. Egypt's peace agreement with Israel, for example, rested "on a narrow pedestal of just a few leaders—like Mubarak" (Morrell 2016, p. 181), but was and

remains deeply unpopular among the Egyptian public. This is hardly the recipe for a stable alliance.

17. In the wake of the killing of Saudi dissident journalist Jamal Khashoggi in October 2018, influential voices in Congress began to question the relationship in more poignant terms.

18. Phone interview with former US official, November 2017.

19. In December 2018, President Trump announced a pullout of US troops from Syria.

20. Phone interview with former US official, May 2018.

21. Quoted in Halperin and Clapp (2006, p. 280).

22. The UAE, for example, was the first Gulf country to purchase the Terminal High Altitude Area Defense (THAAD) system from the United States, in 2012 (Defense Security Cooperation Agency 2012).

23. Phone interview with US official, May 2018.

24. Quoted in Houghton (2013, p. 75).

25. Ibid.

26. Realists argue that the individual level of analysis is irrelevant when seen from the perspective of global power politics. Rational-choice theorists and those who employ formal modeling do not dispute the central relevance of human beings in foreign policy decisionmaking, but they see them simply as utility-maximizing rational actors rather than complex individuals animated by their past experiences, beliefs, emotions, and analogical reasoning.

27. Role theory, first articulated by K.J. Holsti (1970), also incorporates the influence of individual agency into foreign policy analysis. Holsti argued that decisionmakers' conceptions of their state's role in international politics influence that state's foreign policy behavior. Role theory was subsequently further developed and connected with psychological approaches to foreign policy analysis.

28. Interview with Ambassador Cameron Munter, Aix-en-Provence, March 2018.

29. The bureaucratic politics approach was further elaborated in another seminal contribution, Morton Halperin's (1974) exhaustive *Bureaucratic Politics and Foreign Policy,* an updated edition of which appeared as Halperin and Clapp (2006).

30. When asked about the impact of the transition from Lyndon Johnson to Richard Nixon, outgoing secretary of state Dean Rusk suggested the importance of continuity and consistency in government behavior: "A transition is not so earth-shaking. Of the thousand or so cables that go out of here every day, I see only five or six and the President only one or two. Those who send out the other 994 cables will still be here. It is a little bit like changing engineers on a train going steadily down the track. The new engineer has some switches he can make choices about—but 4,500 intergovernmental agreements don't change." Rusk, quoted in Halperin and Clapp (2006, p. 308).

31. Interview with Derek Chollet, Washington, DC, November 2018.

32. Interview with former US official, Washington, DC, February 2018.

33. On liberalizing autocracies, see Brumberg (2002).

2
On Democracy Promotion

Since the early twentieth century, US foreign policy has been distinguished by its commitment to the construction of a liberal world order—sovereign nation-states bound together by international law, multilateral institutions, and free trade—an arrangement that was broadly understood to coincide with American national interests. As Tony Smith (2012, p. xxi) elegantly demonstrates, during the presidency of Woodrow Wilson (1913–1921) a powerful idea became deeply embedded in US foreign policy thinking: "If democracy were to spread, America's place in the world would be more secure." Democracy promotion was born of this view of America's role in the world. Since that time, Smith (2012, p. xviii) writes, "no theme has figured more prominently in the annals of US foreign policy than the repeated presidential calls to promote the creation of democratic government abroad." These calls were further rooted in the idea of the United States as a "shining city on a hill" and an accompanying missionary zeal to export the American model.

While the belief in the compatibility between the expansion of democracy and US national interest has been a constant since the early twentieth century, the actual implementation of foreign policies designed to encourage and uphold democratic governance has been highly inconsistent over time and space. Presidential rhetoric notwithstanding, over the years the way in which the US national interest has been framed could not in fact be easily reconciled with democracy promotion. Yet, the empirical record also shows that US democracy promotion policies have gone beyond rhetoric in numerous instances. Each presidential administration has genuinely promoted democracy in some countries while upholding the authoritarian status quo in others, and US policy toward individual countries has often reflected a complex mix of sometimes contradictory approaches. However, as the brief historical survey presented later in this chapter demonstrates, even as US democracy promotion efforts expanded to new parts of the globe and became institutionalized in democracy assistance mechanisms, in the Arab world the United States remained staunchly supportive of autocracy until the mid-2000s.

The United States is not the only power with the capacity to promote democracy. Other states and international organizations, from the Netherlands and Japan to the European Union (EU) and the Organization for Security and Cooperation in Europe (OSCE), have democracy promotion missions and mechanisms. However, despite a marked decline in its power in the twenty-first century, the United States remains the "most important protagonist" of democracy promotion (Huber 2015, p. 393). "Given the reach of its military power, the size of its economy, and its diplomatic-legal position in the UN Security Council," write David Forsythe and Patrice McMahon (2017, p. 35) in their otherwise skeptical look at America's commitment to promoting democracy and human rights, "the United States remains the indispensable nation—whether it likes it or not. In terms of being well positioned to have an impact if it wishes to try, there is no other country like the United States."

What Is Democracy Promotion?

Democracy promotion refers to the full range of tools, instruments, and mechanisms available to Washington policymakers to influence the political development of another country toward democratization, either by way of a transition from autocracy or the consolidation of a new or unstable democracy (Bush 2015, p. 205). However, the meaning of democracy promotion can also vary according to the promoter's conception of democracy (Hobson and Kurki 2012). This book argues for a political and electoral definition of democracy. Given that I focus on a set of cases where a peaceful rotation of power determined by a free election had never occurred, and since this is what the Arab Spring protesters demanded in 2011, it makes sense to emphasize the basic ingredients of democracy. Thus, I tend toward the minimalist definition, which sees democracy as "the institutional arrangement for arriving at political decisions in which individuals acquire the power to decide by means of a competitive struggle" (Schumpeter 1942, p. 269). In other words, democracy consists of elections in which all citizens have the right to vote, are held for offices that actually have the power to govern, the playing field is even, and results cannot be reversed by those who lost or opposed the outcome (McFaul 2010, p. 40).

Democracy Promotion vs. Human Rights Promotion

Human rights and democracy promotion are closely related, but not always the same. At times, US policies place greater weight on human rights promotion over democracy promotion. For instance, the United States might push for the release of specific political prisoners, better treatment of LGBTQ (lesbian, gay, bisexual, transgender, and questioning) persons, and expanded rights for women, all without challenging the authoritarian structure of a regime. Some human rights advocates are reluctant to package human rights and democracy promotion together (Carothers 2004, pp. 9–22). They emphasize that human rights are embedded in international legal norms, which the United States has the right and duty to promote, while democracy is not. These advocates further argue that state-sponsored torture or murder needs to be addressed immediately, while democracy-building is a longer process. Moreover, some human rights advocates have been critical of elections, or the equating of elections with democracy. The promotion of democracy through elections can produce unintended negative consequences for human rights. For example, the United States might support elections that bring to power groups that espouse ethnocentrism and repress minorities. Democracy promotion advocates, by contrast, see elections as a necessary step to foster political participation, legitimacy, and accountability.

Could an authoritarian regime do a better job of respecting human rights than a democratic but weak state where militias and other groups regularly abuse ordinary citizens? Singapore limits free speech and is dominated by a single party but offers more security to its citizens than democratic Nigeria.[1] Would then the United States not do better to support strong central authority in a country such as Nigeria rather than free and fair elections? However, as James Traub (2008, p. 225) notes, it is difficult to conceive what it means, practically, for the United States to support human rights without encouraging democracy in a broader sense: "Does it mean that we will help train judges and prosecutors and policemen and jail wardens, but not political parties? That we will not exert diplomatic pressure to ensure that the elections are transparent—or that they occur at all? Will we protest when prisoners are abused but not when newspapers are shut down?" For these reasons, I see human rights promotion as a vital part of democracy promotion, particularly in the Arab context.

The United States, in fact, does fund numerous assistance programs focusing on economic development, market liberalization, and the rule of law, many of which aim to reform and strengthen the capacity of institutions. The logic underlying these programs is that economic reform and strong institutions are a prerequisite to both democratization and the respect for human rights, and therefore that the United States should put its resources into helping countries build strong economic foundations and institutional capacity before supporting elections or civil society. However, in the Arab world, economic liberalization has not spurred political reforms in the past. Quite the contrary, it has strengthened the hold of ruling cliques over politics and the economy. The crony capitalism and corruption that were a hallmark of the "liberalizing" Mubarak and Ben Ali regimes in Egypt and Tunisia, respectively, and became a source of popular rage are a case in point. The lack of political reform, in fact, may be precisely what undermines efforts to undertake economic reform (Wittes 2008). Tamara Wittes (2008, pp. 65–66) notes that efforts at economic reform in autocratic Arab regimes are "deeply constrained by the problem of vested interests" and "economic reform alone will not necessarily improve the prospects for rule of law or other democratic reforms down the road."

To be sure, the argument that only democratic reform can ensure the rule of law, security, and human rights protections has been challenged by the chaotic aftermath of the Arab Spring. Citizens of states with functioning governments and institutions (i.e., Morocco, United Arab Emirates, Jordan), no matter how autocratic, are arguably better protected from arbitrary violence than those where the state is absent or predatory (Libya, Yemen, Syria) or weak even and deeply corrupt while being ostensibly democratic (Iraq). At the same time, Arab authoritarian regimes are adept at playing up the threat of instability, terrorism, and the specter of Islamist rule to justify continued undemocratic rule and repressive state measures. Post-2011 developments have allowed the surviving autocrats of the region to more forcefully make the argument that stability can only be guaranteed by their strong, central authority.

The Tools of Democracy Promotion

Table 2.1 presents a typology of tools for democracy promotion. The first item in the toolbox is US soft power (Nye 2004), which relies on the attraction of the US democratic model and its diffusion around the world. Here, State Department public diplomacy programs that aim to increase knowledge and understanding of the United States can play a role, but diffusion of the US democratic example can also happen without US government intervention. The United States can also deploy officials to make public statements encouraging democratic change or calling out regimes that engage in repression, or it can publish and amplify democracy and human rights monitoring reports (the next tool in the typology). There are those who argue that public "naming and shaming" is ineffective and prefer quiet advocacy, but others maintain that only public criticism can compel a change in authoritarian regime behavior. The use of multilateral diplomacy, in forums such as the UN Security Council, or the Organization of American States, can also advance democracy promotion, though policy outcomes in such forums often get mediated and diluted by the competing goals of other states.

Moving on in the typology, US democracy assistance programs are present in more than 100 countries today and might entail support for democratic elections to assure they are free and fair; training for judicial, police, and other institutions to strengthen the rule of law; backing of civil society groups; and strengthening of independent media organizations. Funding for US democracy assistance increased significantly in the 1990s and 2000s and is implemented by the "democracy establishment" (Bush 2015, p. 267), the hundreds of for-profit and not-for-profit organizations who design and execute programs in the areas identified above. Next in the typology are tools that aim to create material incentives for democratization. These can include positive inducements such as aid or membership in international organizations as a way to compel democratic reforms, or alternatively diplomatic isolation, withdrawal of assistance, and sanctions to punish regimes for democratic infractions. Finally, while highly controversial, and arguably ineffective (Rice 2017), the toppling of authoritarian regimes (the final tool) through the use of military force can also be seen as a form of democracy promotion.

Table 2.1 Tools of Democracy Promotion

Tool	Examples
Soft power	Diffusion of example of United States as a democratic and open society
	Promotion done organically and through public diplomacy programs
	Aid without conditionality
Rhetoric	Positive reinforcement or public criticism of transgressions against democracy
	Naming and shaming
	Monitoring reports on democracy and human rights
Diplomacy	Pressure through bilateral diplomacy and through multilateral action in forums such as the UN Security Council, Organization of American States, Community of Democracies
Assistance	Support for elections
	Training for political parties
	Support for civil society
	Governance and rule of law capacity-building
	Training of judges, prosecutors, and police
Conditionality	Withholding of assistance to punish undemocratic behavior
	Positive inducements such as aid to reward democratic reforms
Force	Intervention (unilateral, UN approved, or invited)
	Setting up of protectorates
	Military occupation

The Degree of Democracy Promotion

While there are multiple tools of democracy promotion, how they are applied, and in what combination, determines the *degree* of democracy promotion. Sarah Bush (2015, p. 205) observes that in some cases, "all the tools of democracy promotion work together," while in others they "can become decoupled, or separated, from the other tools of democracy promotion as well as states' broader foreign policies." For example, democracy assistance programs are the most popular form of democracy promotion. However, they are weakened in the absence of what Carothers (2004) calls "high policy"—diplomatic pressure and conditionality in the typology presented above. US democracy assistance programs were present to varying degrees in the Arab world even before 2011. They often function on "autopilot," benefiting from multiyear congressional allocations. They continued to operate in the Arab Spring countries even after Obama turned his attention away from democracy promotion in the region. Many of them continue under the Trump administration, though there have been moves to cut certain programs that cannot be justified by "countering violent extremism" goals.

Bush's (2015) study of US assistance to civil society organizations highlights the limitations of democracy assistance in fostering reform. Rather than looking at the motivations or strategies of the US government and other funders of democracy assistance, Bush examines the "survival instincts" of the nongovernmental organizations (NGOs) that implement the assistance programs. She hypothesizes that these NGOs want to foster democratization, but they also want to survive and thrive—by obtaining donor government funding, for which they need to show "measurable" results,[2] all while maintaining access in authoritarian regimes. As a consequence, they tend to design and implement programs that do not directly challenge authoritarianism. Using both large-N analysis and a detailed study of democracy assistance in Tunisia and Jordan, she finds that not only do such programs fail to confront dictators, but also over time programs that do challenge autocracy have been replaced with "tame" ones that conform most closely to their host environments (Bush 2015, p. 170). In some cases, Bush argues, democracy assistance programs may actually boost the legitimacy of authoritarian governments.

Bush (2015, p. 302) describes a longstanding support program for women parliamentarians in Jordan that may have enhanced women's participation in politics, but it mainly empowered female supporters of the autocratic regime. Moreover, experts suggest that these improvements "have done more to enhance the regime's international reputation than they have to advance democracy" (Bush 2015, p. 326). The Jordanian parliament, after all, is a tool that the monarchy uses to distribute patronage: It is thus an instrument of autocratic survival rather than an engine of democratization (Lust-Okar 2009). Other authoritarian regimes will readily restrict funding if an NGO challenges existing power structures while still claiming democratic credentials for having allowed the NGO to operate in the first place. As one activist told Wittes (2008, p. 68), civil society assistance programs are designed to help local NGOs "be more efficient, to organize. But there is something before this—to have the *right* to organize." Bush's book has detractors in the Washington-based democracy assistance community. Some point out that she relies on a sample of programs drawn from National Endowment of Democracy (NED)–funded projects, which are by design not "confrontational" in part to protect their local partners. They also observe that confronting regimes was never in the mainstream of democracy assistance programs, which, as one expert on democracy assistance told me, are designed not to foment a breakdown but to "prepare people for when that breakdown arrives."[3] Such criticisms notwithstanding, Bush's study points to the fact that democracy assistance, no matter how well-intentioned, cannot be effective in isolation from other tools of democracy promotion.

A high degree of democracy promotion requires the deployment of significant resources, diplomatic weight, and the attention of high officials. While effective democracy promotion cannot consist merely of words, when the power of the United States stands behind words emanating from a senior official in Washington, those words can carry weight and change behavior. Amy Hawthorne, a leading expert on democracy promotion in the Arab world, has noted that "strong presidential rhetoric combined with strong presidential action behind the scenes can move the needle."[4] When the president, for example, directly pressures a foreign counterpart on democratic reform, or the secretary of state cancels a foreign visit in protest at repressive acts, it signals a high degree of democracy promotion. Such measures bring more leverage to the table than a low-level human rights officer from the US embassy delivering a demarche on reform, details of nondemocratic practices in a report that is not widely read, or talking points about democracy at the bottom of a briefing memo given to an official.

At the same time, diplomatic pressure is unlikely to be taken seriously by the target regime if continued financial or security assistance is never in doubt. Thus, a high degree of democracy promotion entails matching conditionality policies—rewards and threats—to diplomatic pressure and public statements. The rewards and threats, furthermore, need to be credible in order to be effective. In Jordan, a close US ally, democracy declined between 1993 and 2011 (the country moved from "partly free" to "unfree" on the Freedom House scale), despite substantial US investment in Jordanian civil society throughout the 2000s (Forsythe and McMahon 2017, p. 54). When the Arab Spring broke out, Obama's first impulse was to give more cash to the Jordanian monarchy, assuring it of continuing US support

(Forsythe and McMahon 2017, p. 54) without requiring any pledges of reform in exchange. Existing forms of assistance are often described as buying the US leverage over autocratic allies, but they need to be explicitly linked to democratic reform in order to have an impact. While elections do not a democracy make, elections matter and democracy promotion strategies need to incorporate them. Military assistance, a pillar of US foreign policy for many decades, is a prime example: Besides doing little for democracy promotion in autocratic allies, it has also failed to achieve narrower goals such as reform of foreign militaries (Karlin 2017).

Finally, a high degree of democracy promotion entails a coordinated and unified message from across the US government with senior officials from various agencies issuing and repeating it. Calls for democratic reform need to be at the top of the agenda and talking points of all US officials engaging their foreign counterparts. Autocratic regimes can quickly read and exploit divisions among US officials and agencies, seeing them as carte blanche to avoid reforms. The degree of democracy promotion is lowered when the secretary of defense emphasizes the centrality of a military partnership while the secretary of state talks about the need for political openness. The messaging on reform, furthermore, needs to be consistent over time.

With all of this in mind, the following criteria will be used to evaluate the degree of US democracy promotion policies in the Arab world:

- *Very high:* Statements by top officials supporting democracy are combined with high-level, consistent diplomatic pressure and the use of credible conditionality. US messaging is unified. Autocracy-challenging democracy assistance programs focused on parties, unions, and civil society and other sectors support the efforts.
- *High:* Statements supporting democracy are combined with some pressure, but not always at the highest levels. Democracy assistance programs are paired with some conditionality. Messaging is not always unified and consistent.
- *Medium:* Democracy assistance programs continue, but many of them are "tame." High-level engagement and pressure on the part of US officials is episodic. Conditionality policies are weak. Messages delivered on democracy are divided.
- *Low:* Democracy promotion rhetoric may or may not exist, but it is not backed by any real pressure, conditionality, or high-level attention. Democracy assistance programs are also present but limited to "tame" civil society, rule of law, or governance projects.

In Table 2.2, these categories are presented in the context of the range of tools available for democracy promotion described in Table 2.1.

In Table 2.3, I apply this measurement framework to US democracy promotion policies in the three Arab Spring countries most closely examined in the book from 2011–2019. Here, these policies are characterized in broad strokes over a longer time period, while more specific policies are described in subsequent chapters.

How We Got Here: US Policy in the Arab World Before and After 9/11

In sharp contrast to Woodrow Wilson's liberalism, influential twentieth-century foreign policy realists such as George Kennan, Reinhold Neibuhr, and Hans Morgenthau saw relations between states as a struggle for power, "modified only by the different conditions under which this struggle takes place in the domestic and in the international spheres."[5] The internal character of regimes was of little consequence. Realism counseled modesty, restraint, and the shameless pursuit of national interest in US foreign policy. Shaped by interests such as access to oil, support for Israel, and, after

Table 2.2 Degree and Tools of Democracy Promotion

Degree	Soft Power	Rhetoric	Diplomacy	Assistance	Conditionality	Force
Very high	Yes	Yes, frequent and consistent	Yes	Yes	Yes, credible	Possible[a]
High	Yes	Yes, but not consistent	Some, not always at highest level, some mixed messages	Yes, including a focus on elections and parties	Some use of conditionality, not always credible	No
Medium	Yes	Some, not at high level	Episodic and not at high level, mixed messages	Some assistance, mostly focused on "tame" nongovernmental organizations	Minimal use of conditionality	No
Low	Yes	Very rare	No, besides publication of human rights reports	Limited to "tame" nongovernmental organizations	No	No

Note: a. Since outright coercion rarely works as a tool of democracy promotion, it is included here only as a tool that might potentially work in harmony with other tools—for example, a military presence can help support a democratically elected government during a fragile transition.

Table 2.3 Degree of US Democracy Promotion, 2011–2019

Time Period	Libya	Egypt	Bahrain
2011–2012	*High:* Obama calls for Qaddafi to step down; joins international intervention; recognizes opposition; assists in early transition, though in a limited way.	*Medium-High:* Obama calls for Mubarak to step down, supports elections, engages in dialogue with Muslim Brotherhood, and institutes new democracy assistance programs, but also continues to work with military rulers and overlooks Morsi's abuses. Mixed messages on US policy.	*Medium:* 2011 is a period of high-level attention and engagement. Obama issues condemnations of violent crackdown; United States "pauses" military aid and supports establishment of investigative and truth-telling commission.
2012–2016	*Low-Medium:* Engagement was limited from 2012–2013, with some assistance programs and a focus on counterterrorism. After 2014, support for political settlement among fighting factions.	*Low-Medium:* United States does not call the coup as such, cuts assistance from 2013 to 2015, but in general remains silent on growing repression. Different US officials deliver varying messages to Egyptians.	*Low:* Things are back to status quo, with weapons embargo mostly lifted, weak push for reform, sporadic engagement on democracy. Bifurcated messages come from Department of Defense and State Department.
2017–2019	*Low:* Trump signals he is not interested in Libya; there is no ambassador or special envoy after 2017; focus is on counterterrorism; turns to Department of Defense and its Africa regional command (AFRICOM); influence policy.	*Low:* Trump signals early and strong support for Sisi; there is limited pressure over political prisoners; aid is briefly withheld, mainly over North Korea issue.	*Low:* Trump administration forges close ties with Bahrain's Saudi patrons; no public and very limited private pressure is placed on reform.

1979, the desire to contain Iran, a realist framework came to exercise a seemingly unshakable hold on US policy in the Arab world for nearly six decades following the end of World War II.

The cultivation of friendly Arab regimes also reflected the cynical "the enemy of my enemy is my friend" logic of Cold War–era US foreign policy. This logic led Washington not only to support numerous nondemocratic governments committing major human rights abuses as a counterweight to Soviet influence, but also, in several key cases, to topple democratically elected governments that were seen as prone to fall under Moscow's tutelage. Cold War realist thinking had such a powerful, bipartisan hold on Washington and public opinion that it went virtually unchallenged for nearly three decades. It became embedded in a powerful foreign policy institution, the US defense establishment, as well as the military-industrial complex that sprung up around containing the Soviet Union. This complex included an extensive network of US military bases around the globe and a corresponding web of defense contractors, which employed massive amounts of American workers and generated billions of dollars in revenue for their owners.

Although Congress to some extent checked the more extreme realist impulses of the Nixon administration in the 1970s (Snyder 2018), the first major challenge to the Cold War realist consensus arrived with the administration of President Jimmy Carter (1977–1981). Carter declared human rights promotion to be the "soul" of US foreign policy. Carter, deeply shaped by his religious faith, criticized Americans for the "inordinate fear of communism" that led his predecessors to look the other way or even lend support to human rights abuses carried out by allied regimes. While Carter's focus on individual rights fell short of a more expansive ideal of democracy promotion, his administration helped to institutionalize its practice in the US foreign policy apparatus. However, despite his pledge to put human rights at the center of US policy, Carter largely ignored human rights abuses in the Arab world. For example, Carter's promotion of Egyptian-Israeli peace in the end did little to encourage democratic reform in Egypt (Brownlee 2012).[6]

Ronald Reagan (1981–1989) similarly did little to change the status quo of US policy toward the Arab world, even as democracy promotion became a more conspicuous part of his foreign policy in his second term. Among those members of the Reagan administration committed to promoting democracy, there were no individuals pushing for attention to Arab autocracy, and institutions such as the State Department and Department of Defense decidedly preferred the status quo in the region. Perhaps a triggering event in the Arab world would have forced Reagan's hand, as did popular uprisings in the Philippines and South Korea in the latter half of the 1980s. Conversely, there were mass strikes and protests throughout the 1980s in Egypt, but by that point the United States was deeply entangled in a defense relationship with Cairo, giving its ruling autocratic regime hundreds of millions of dollars in military aid every year. This and the fear that genuine democracy would challenge Egypt's peace treaty with Israel made US democracy promotion in Egypt undesirable, even for a president who had used lofty rhetoric about freedom when speaking about the Soviet Union and other regions of the world.

The tradition of accepting the authoritarian status quo in the Arab world continued under President George H. W. Bush (1989–1993). Rather than issues of human rights and democracy, Bush and his advisers were focused on the Arab-Israeli peace process and the 1990–1991 Gulf War. Saddam Hussein's defeat in Kuwait helped catalyze Shia and Kurdish revolts against the Iraqi dictator's repressive rule, but despite the presence of US troops on Iraqi soil, the Bush administration refused to take any actions to support the uprisings. In the Gulf Arab states, the Bush administration maintained the status quo, expanding military cooperation with Bahrain. The fear of Islamic fundamentalism held back US democracy promotion in countries such as Yemen and Jordan, despite liberalizing trends underway in both countries. In Algeria, the Bush administration did not raise any objections when the regime annulled an election that was seen to favor Islamists.

President Bill Clinton (1993–2001) ran on a platform of criticizing George H. W. Bush for not doing enough on democracy promotion. Yet, once Clinton was in office, the Middle East remained a "no-go area for American democracy promotion" (Bouchet 2015, p. 135). The Clinton administration's focus was on the dual containment of Iraq and Iran, promotion of Arab-Israeli peace, and nonproliferation (Bouchet 2015, p. 118). Policy toward Egypt, Jordan, and the Arab Gulf states remained supportive of autocratic regimes. When Egyptian president Hosni Mubarak stole yet another election in 1996, the Clinton administration's silence was deafening (Brownlee 2012). The same perceived interests and deeply seated fears of Islamist political forces that had shaped US foreign policy in the MENA region for decades persisted despite the growing consensus that the end of the Cold War represented a triumph of democracy, the market, and unchallenged US leadership.[7]

George W. Bush and US Democracy Promotion in the Arab World After 9/11

Hearing George W. Bush's (2001–2009) rhetoric during the 2000 presidential campaign, it would have taken a leap of imagination to envisage him as a future democracy promoter. Candidate Bush railed against "nation-building," by which he meant, among other things, democracy promotion. In 2000, his foreign affairs adviser and future national security adviser and secretary of state, Condoleezza Rice, wrote a widely read article in *Foreign Affairs* arguing for a realist US foreign policy, one that avoids overstretch and is narrowly focused on America's national interest (Rice 2000). Top foreign policy jobs in the Bush administration went to individuals known for their Cold War realism, such as Dick Cheney, Colin Powell, and Donald Rumsfeld. Accordingly, the preoccupations of the early months of the Bush administration included trade, national missile defense, and the charting of new relationships with Russia, India, and Mexico (Traub 2008, p. 102).

However, a nation-builder and democracy promoter is exactly what Bush became, and he was motivated by the tragedy that came to redefine US foreign policy: the terrorist attacks of September 11, 2001. Both policymakers and ordinary Americans came to realize that while the perpetrators of the attacks were few in number, hatred of the United States ran broad and deep in the Islamic world. While some critics on the left argued that the problem lay inside US foreign policy, the more popular view became that the problem lay inside the character of Arab societies and regimes. This view was reinforced by an influential publication released in 2002, the Arab Human Development Report, whose findings could not be ignored even by staunch realists such as Colin Powell. Moreover, as Traub (2008, p. 108) observes, "the fact that it was produced by leading Arab academics made it impossible to impeach on grounds of Western bias or neocolonialism." The report argued that the Arab world suffered from a "freedom deficit," a "women's empowerment deficit," and a "human capabilities/knowledge deficit." It insisted that "education, political freedom, and economic development were all bound together" and that "freedom is the guarantor and the goal of both human development and human rights" (United Nations Development Programme 2002). This idea—the linking of political repression and religious extremism—captivated the president and key members of his team and helped shape one of the most ambitious US democracy promotion agendas ever, one that for the first time challenged deeply entrenched policy orthodoxies toward the Arab world.[8]

Bush's first National Security Strategy, which appeared in September 2002, expressed that the "non-negotiable demands of human dignity" could be met in "many ways," depending on local traditions of governance (White House 2002). Over time, this more limited view of the possibilities for accountable government in the Arab world began to evolve into a more expansive one. Bush's vision of democracy promotion was influenced in part by ideas in a book written by the Israeli politician and former Soviet dissident Natan Sharansky, who argued that it was a terrible mistake to coddle authoritarian regimes in the pursuit of stability, since such stability was ephemeral (Traub 2008). Sharansky further argued that the United States could put pressure on autocratic Arab regimes to democratize just as Reagan had put such pressure on the Soviet Union, leading to Mikhail Gorbachev's reforms and, eventually, regime collapse (Traub 2008). The evolution in thinking culminated in Bush's second inaugural, in which he declared that it is "the policy of the U.S. to seek and support the growth of democratic movements and institutions in every nation and culture, with the ultimate goal of ending tyranny in our world" (Bush 2005).

The rather revolutionary idea that Arabs, too, deserve democratic governance was put into practice by the Bush administration in ways that it never had been before, at least for a time and in certain places. Moreover, as Yom (2008, p. 133) observes, "more than a handful of democratic activists in the region saw a historic opportunity to assemble unprecedented American support for their campaigns for liberal reforms." One of the places where democratic activists seized this opportunity was Egypt, where Hosni Mubarak, then in power for twenty-five years, had already been under some pressure to reform, encouraged by modest aid conditionality emanating from the State Department. Traub (2008, p. 133) writes that strangely, "the Bush administration could be simultaneously despised for its policies and welcomed for its democratic advocacy." Indeed, a number of leading Egyptian dissidents encouraged Bush's prodemocracy approach and were disappointed when he pulled back from it by the end of his presidency. Perhaps this reflected the fact that Arabs were "accustomed to America's centrality in their world, schizophrenic in their simultaneous resentments and expectations of American influence" (Burns 2019, p. 296).

Bush repeatedly pushed Mubarak in private to open the political system. In response, Mubarak allowed opposition political parties to register, permitted demonstrations, and welcomed election monitors. He also agreed to allow a real opposition candidate to challenge him in the 2005 presidential election. However, when that candidate, Ayman Noor, appeared to pose a serious challenge to the regime, Mubarak locked him up. In response, Secretary of State Rice canceled a planned trip to Cairo. Traub (2008, p. 131) writes: "The regime was stunned; Washington had never before extracted any price for acts of domestic repression." It is notable that the move was opposed by many in the foreign affairs agencies, including State Department and military officials with close ties to the Mubarak government.[9]

When Rice finally did travel to Egypt, she gave a strikingly candid speech at the American University of Cairo in which she declared: "For sixty years, my country, the United States, pursued stability at the expense of democracy in this region here in the Middle East—and we achieved neither. Now we are taking a different course. We are supporting the democratic aspirations of all people" (Rice 2005). She added that "success in our relations will require the decent treatment of their own people" and called for free and fair elections. This was unprecedented language for a senior US official to utter in Egypt: "no high-ranking American official had ever admonished the regime so publicly" (Traub 2008, p. 132). Bush's new approach to the Arab world also entailed the establishment of new democracy assistance mechanisms. Under the influence of Elizabeth Cheney, a daughter of the vice president and a senior State Department official, the State Department launched the Middle East Partnership Initiative (MEPI), a democracy assistance mechanism designed to bypass the Arab state (the traditional recipient of assistance) and instead target civil society. While novel in its approach, MEPI's outlays were modest, a total of about $100 million throughout the Middle East and North Africa during Bush's term.

The 2005 presidential election in Egypt was followed by a parliamentary election in which Muslim Brotherhood candidates were allowed to run as independents. The Mubarak regime responded with harassment and violence directed against Brotherhood voters, tainting the election. In the second round, the violence was ramped up further and there was open stuffing of ballot boxes. Despite the overwhelming obstacles, Brotherhood-affiliated candidates won over half the seats. The State Department initially issued a statement indicating that the elections went just fine. Outrage among Egyptian and international activists later pressured the State Department to revise this message and criticize the conduct of the election (Traub 2008, p. 133). However, then US ambassador Francis Ricciardone declined to publicly or privately criticize Mubarak (Abrams 2017).[10] Signals from the US government that it would accept a highly flawed election left Egyptian democracy activists feeling deeply betrayed (Traub 2008, p. 169).

Later, the State Department only offered weak criticism after the regime conducted a referendum on a package of constitutional amendments designed to give the Egyptian executive more power and curtail civil liberties, ostensibly as a way to fight terrorism. Preserving channels of access and influence mattered most to the State Department, and particularly to US diplomats on the ground in Cairo. The Mubarak regime understood this, and as Traub (2008, p. 133) observes, called Rice's "bluff." There were other institutional actors skeptical of Bush's democracy agenda in Egypt, among them the DoD, which had a deep and longstanding relationship with its Egyptian counterpart, and the intelligence community, which had established cooperation with its Egyptian counterpart on counterterrorism. Mubarak instinctively understood these internal US government divisions and skillfully tried to exploit them to his advantage. In a 2008 meeting with the Egyptian president, former Central Intelligence Agency (CIA) director Michael Hayden (2016, p. 319) recounts Mubarak's criticism of the Freedom Agenda, his "paternalistic" assertions about the unreadiness of Egyptians for democracy, and his denigrating comments about Secretary of State Condoleezza Rice, whom he referred to as "that woman."

The belief that the Muslim Brotherhood was a dangerous actor was deeply entrenched in Washington. The dominant perception was that the Brotherhood was tied to terrorism and would never accept the existence of an Israeli state, thereby making it an enemy of the United States. Of course, the Brotherhood in the past had not helped itself by taking anti-Israeli, anti-Semitic, and other positions that helped turn US policymakers against the group (Hamid 2015). Brotherhood-affiliated parliamentarians succeeded in alienating key democracy promotion–minded individuals in the Bush administration, such as Elliott Abrams, Michael Gerson, and Liz Cheney with their virulent anti-Israeli rhetoric. Yet, when meeting with their American counterparts, Egyptian officials also played up the idea that the Brotherhood was incapable of change, arguing that just as the Nazi Party is forbidden to operate in Germany, so should the Brotherhood be banned in Egypt (Traub 2008, p. 176). Many in the Bush administration readily accepted this narrative. Never mind that the Egyptian Muslim Brotherhood was by then a diverse organization with both progressive and conservative factions, and one that had denounced violence. Or that its counterparts in countries such as Jordan, Kuwait, Yemen, and Morocco were successfully participating in parliamentary politics. Or that the United States maintained close ties with the Saudis, whose state is built upon a fundamentalist interpretation of Islam. Or that the United States worked closely with Shia religious political parties in Iraq. Or that "secular" Arab parties, the ostensible alternative to the Islamists, were hardly a better democratic alternative, and had a weak base of support (Boduszyński, Fabbe, and Lamont 2015). "What put the Muslim Brotherhood beyond the pale," writes Traub (2008, pp. 177–178), "was that Hosni Mubarak had declared them his sworn enemy."

The Muslim Brothers performed well because they reached the grassroots, and because they were seen as an uncorrupted organization—one committed to helping ordinary people, in contrast to the crony capitalism espoused by Mubarak's misnamed National Democratic Party and the urban elitism of the secular parties. Many of the Brotherhood-affiliated parliamentarians elected in 2005 were technocrats and professionals such as engineers, doctors, and lawyers. They worked diligently once in office, leading two political scientists to conclude that they were attempting to make the Egyptian parliament a real representative institution (Shehata and Stacher 2006). However, as others in the administration noted, it is not that the Muslim Brotherhood was an extremist alternative to Mubarak's repression, but rather that real extremists and poorly organized secular democratic parties with no connections to the grassroots were the alternative to the Brotherhood.[11] It was not an ideal scenario from the perspective of Western liberalism, but it was a reality that the Bush administration could have chosen to shape by meaningfully engaging with the Muslim Brothers.

The Brotherhood's strong showing in the 2005 Egyptian election proved to Washington-based skeptics of Arab democracy that free and fair elections were unlikely to produce a democratic outcome in the region, as they had in postcommunist Eastern Europe. A year later, the victory of

Hamas in the Palestinian elections was in many ways the final nail in the coffin for Bush's bold plans for democracy promotion in the Arab world. The American refusal to deal with Hamas,[12] Hezbollah, and the Egyptian Muslim Brotherhood in spite of their electoral successes led to even further skepticism among Arab publics that the United States was seriously committed to democracy promotion. As J. Scott Carpenter, who worked on the frontlines of the Freedom Agenda in the Bush administration said, "I felt that the chill was on. Rice and Bush were still committed to the idea. But for those who were implementing the policy, it became much more difficult."[13]

Broader strategic interests also played a role in the rollback of the Freedom Agenda in Egypt. Increasing Iranian influence in Iraq led many to fear the consequences of a newly emboldened regime in Tehran. The Bush administration was egged on by its Saudi allies, who were alarmed by the Shia resurgence in Iraq and had the most to lose from a resurgent Iran. The outbreak of war between Israel and Hezbollah in Lebanon in 2006 further instilled fear in Washington. These developments, argues Traub (2008, p. 134), led the administration to lean more on its "moderate" Sunni allies, Egypt included, with *moderate* defined in terms of regional policy rather than commitment to democratization. Again, Egypt and Arab regimes instinctively understood the geopolitical dimension and thus correctly calculated that when push came to shove, the United States would not shove. And it didn't: in 2006, Secretary Rice opposed the efforts of Congressman David Obey from Wisconsin to condition part of the military aid package to Cairo on political reform (Brownlee 2012, p. 111). In January 2007, when Rice returned to Cairo, she said nothing about democratization and instead emphasized the US "strategic relationship" with Egypt (Slackman 2007). In other words, there was no longer robust institutional or individual backing for a high degree of US democracy promotion in Egypt.

The Credibility Gap

Bush and his top advisers failed to see the credibility problems that arose from simultaneously calling for democratic reforms in autocratic states while defending "enhanced interrogation techniques" and other abuses of the war on terror. Mikaela McDermott and Brian Katulis (2004) found that reformers in Syria, Bahrain, and Jordan were wary of even using the terms *human rights* and *democracy* in their campaigns because they had become "synonymous" with "military occupation, civilian casualties, and abuse of prisoners."[14] Karen Hughes, Bush's top public diplomat, openly admitted that two of her greatest challenges in explaining US policy in the Middle East were detainee abuse and Iraq.[15] One top aide to Condoleezza Rice told Traub (2008, p. 141) that the widespread perception that the Bush administration did not really care about the rule of law or the values it claimed to espouse did the United States "deep and lasting damage."

The Iraq invasion and what was perceived as a botched US occupation also caused irreparable damage to the Freedom Agenda. It was just three weeks before the first US bombs fell on Iraq in March 2003—after months of emphasizing the existential threat posed by Saddam's alleged weapons of mass destruction—when Bush stated that a new, democratic Iraq would serve as a "dramatic and inspiring example of freedom for other nations in the region" (Bush 2003). The sudden insertion of democracy promotion into an invasion that had been previously sold in security terms was received with much skepticism around the world, in no small part by experts who understood that many obstacles stood in the way of Iraqi democratization. But it was the idea that the United States would deliver democracy to Iraqis at the barrel of a gun that alienated many Arabs and international public opinion more generally and took the attention away from Bush's otherwise welcome assertion that it was "presumptuous and insulting" to suggest that Arabs and Muslims were not ready for democracy. At the very moment when US officials were attempting to argue that the United States had turned a new page in terms of its decades of support for Middle East dictators, headlines continued to be dominated by abuses at Abu Ghraib, detentions at Guantanamo Bay, and the rendition of detainees (Traub 2008, p. 5).

Putting aside the failures of postinvasion stabilization and the abuses of Abu Ghraib, was the act of invading Iraq and toppling Saddam Hussein, one of the most brutal dictators of the twentieth century, an act of democracy promotion? Most foreign policy and regional experts, as well as a wide swathe of the US political elite, came to see the Iraq invasion as an unmitigated policy disaster, and one that forever discredited Bush's Freedom Agenda, with the costs of toppling Saddam far outweighing any benefits derived by Iraqis and Americans. Moreover, contrary to Bush's predictions that Iraq would serve as a beacon of democratic hope for the Arab world, many Arabs saw the chaos of postwar Iraq as a demonstration of precisely the opposite. Even when the Bush administration delivered the "right message" about democracy, writes former senior diplomat William Burns (2019, p. 298), "the Bush administration was the wrong messenger."

Perhaps the most damning short-term indictment of Bush's policies, democracy promotion and otherwise, were the views Arabs and Muslims expressed toward the United States in opinion polls taken at the end of his term as president. Favorable attitudes had fallen to dismal lows, even in the states understood to be "mainstream" or "moderate," meaning close US allies such as Jordan, Morocco, and Egypt. In these countries, only 20 percent or less of respondents held favorable views of the United States (Pew Research Center 2007). This was especially striking given that (1) the majority of these same citizens despised their corrupt political leaders and expressed strong support for democracy in other surveys, and (2) Bush had declared democratization of the Arab world as one of his main foreign policy goals. It showed that credibility does matter, and the Bush administration had little of it when it came to Iraq, its about-face on policies in Egypt and Palestine, or its continuing close relations with the Gulf Arab monarchies.

Democracy Promotion and Counterterrorism

Traub (2008) writes that by late 2007 "the Freedom Agenda had disappeared into the war on terror." Attempts to link democracy and counterterrorism undermined genuine efforts at democracy promotion in at least three ways. First, and most important, the global war on terrorism (GWOT) conditioned US policymakers to seek counterterror partnerships around the world to facilitate intelligence sharing, joint operations, terrorist detentions, and other objectives. This included relationships with a number of states with authoritarian or semiauthoritarian governments that the Bush administration cultivated as security partners: Algeria, Bahrain, Egypt, China, Jordan, Kazakhstan, Kuwait, Malaysia, Pakistan, Qatar, Uzbekistan, Yemen, and Syria (Carothers 2004, p. 79). Even as the administration spoke of the need to spread democracy and implemented democracy assistance programs, it issued public words of praise for autocratic GWOT partners during high-level visits, enhanced security cooperation agreements, and enlarged aid packages (Carothers 2004, p. 79). A "partner in the GWOT" rarely was at the receiving end of pressure or criticism for undemocratic behavior.

Second, contradictions between democracy promotion and the "hard" foreign policy tools of the GWOT not only harmed the credibility of US democracy promotion efforts under Bush, but also led autocrats around the world to believe that when push came to shove, democracy was not *really* what the Bush administration wanted.[16] This, in turn, allowed wily strongmen such as Yemen's Ali Abdullah Saleh to skillfully exploit Washington's deep-seated fear of radical Islamic groups in their favor. When US officials, from the president down, attempted to push autocrats such as Saleh and Egypt's Mubarak on human rights and democracy, their response was immediate and quite predictable: Opening up the political space could only empower the radical Islamists. Whether this was true or not, and whether all Islamists were violent jihadists, did not matter, because the point was to frighten the Americans from applying any real democratic pressure, thereby preserving the regime and its privileges.

Third, the focus on the hard tools of the GWOT greatly empowered the agencies that specialized in the use of such tools, notably the intelligence community and the Department of Defense, which benefited from a massive influx of funds, even greater global reach, and added clout in the interagency policy process. In an atmosphere of zero tolerance for another terrorist attack on the "homeland," and a stated mission to eliminate terrorism and terrorist groups wherever they exist, the institutions that served as the GWOT's "tip of the spear" could easily subvert the democracy-promoting agendas of competing institutions and individuals. The hard tools of terror—armed drones, kill and capture operations, and so on—were politically popular (at least initially), while democracy promotion became much less so over time (Smeltz 2012).

The Bush administration responded to a public mandate to take a hardline approach to terrorism, but in the process, it unleashed a host of institutional and legal forces that helped to make the GWOT a "forever war." Put differently, the Bush administration had policy choices in pursuing terrorism. If we accept the premise that the war on terror must be fought simultaneously on multiple fronts, from the physical battlefield to the battlefield of ideas, then where that balance is struck is a policy decision. The extrajudicial detention system at Guantanamo Bay, the use of extraordinary renditions, and outsourced, torture-driven interrogations were choices, not necessities, and we have little evidence that these policies either foiled a major terrorist attack or reduced the appeal of extremism. David Kilcullen (2016, p. 211), a noted counterinsurgency expert who advised top US generals and diplomats, writes of the "addiction" of US policymakers to unilateral air strikes, which can undo Washington's ability to defeat terrorists in the long term by inadvertently killing civilians. The balance the Bush administration struck in terms of its counterterrorism policy choices in the end led to an undermining of its own democracy promotion goals.

Has the anger directed against Bush's more harmful policies blinded his critics against some sincere and perhaps even effective democracy promotion efforts? There is an argument to be made that the Bush administration's policies did open some doors, at least a crack—a crack that remained open and served as the foundation for the Arab uprisings of 2011 (Abrams 2017). Bruce Gilley (2013) argues that the Freedom Agenda weakened authoritarian regimes and strengthened their opponents, helping to create conditions for democratic openings. The Iraq War also may have further galvanized ordinary Arabs against their own corrupt and authoritarian governments. As Amy Hawthorne (2005) writes, "Widespread anger over the [Iraq] war and over Arab governments' inability to prevent it exposed Arab governments to fresh charges of incompetence from their citizenry and to new expressions of discontent with the status quo." Bush's democracy promotion policies in Egypt helped spur new media outlets, new civil society actors, and perhaps even a newly empowered public. We may never know for sure whether Bush's limited efforts, or the rhetoric around them, yielded results that in any way enabled the 2011 uprisings. What is clear is that the Freedom Agenda never seriously challenged the authoritarian structures dominating Arab polities.

In sum, the approach of George W. Bush laid the ideological, legal, and institutional foundation for a schizophrenic policy torn between an instinct to spread freedom as a means of decreasing the appeal of Islamic extremism on one hand, and on the other, an unrelenting global pursuit of terrorists using the hard tools of drone strikes and covert operations, which also entailed cultivating relationships with nondemocratic regimes and their instruments of repression. Ironically, by trying to link the two, he blurred the line between them, which only served to lower the credibility of the United States as a democracy promoter. Obama inherited, and never fully resolved, this tension.

Enter Obama

President Barack Obama thus inherited democracy promotion policies whose credibility was badly damaged by its association with the war on terror, invasion of Iraq, and a bellicose, heavy-handed foreign policy more generally (Traub 2008, p. 4). America's standing as a global symbol of democracy and human rights had declined greatly under the Bush presidency. In one of his first acts as president, Obama sought to repair America's damaged "brand" by issuing executive orders to shutter the Guantanamo detention facilities (a goal that soon proved very hard to realize), end the CIA's program of secret "black site" detention facilities, and prohibit torture. The incoming Obama administration also sought to capitalize on the young president's compelling personal story and what the election of an African American president said about the strength of US democracy (Carothers 2012, p. 11–12).

Bush's policies and their effect on America's reputation notwithstanding, Obama entered the White House in a difficult global climate for democracy promotion. Democracy seemed to be in retreat around the world (Freedom House 2009), and as a result many had lost faith in what was assumed to be its natural counterpart, the free market. But as Chapter 3 elaborates, Obama as an individual also lacked faith in the ability of the United States to transfer democratic norms to foreign societies. Thus, as Carothers (2012) observed just two years into Obama's presidency,

> recalibration on democracy promotion was not just a reaction against the negative legacy of the Bush approach. It also embodied some deeper core instincts of the new chief executive and his top foreign policy advisors.... President Obama clearly resonated with the inspirational power of democracy and its centrality to the American place in the world. Yet that outlook was mixed with strong pragmatic instincts—a wariness of overstatement, a disinclination to lead with ideology, and the desire to solve problems through building consensus rather than fostering confrontation. And Obama appeared to be especially disinclined to put the United States in the position of imposing itself politically on other societies, telling others what to do, or assuming that the United States has all the answers.

As a result of the Bush legacy and the new president's own cautious instincts about the limits of American power, in the first phrase of his presidency, Obama and his incoming team took pains to distance themselves from what they saw as Bush's messianic rhetoric about spreading democracy. Tellingly, President Obama did not mention democracy promotion in his first inaugural speech. Incoming secretary of state Hillary Clinton similarly said little on the subject in her confirmation hearings (Carothers 2012), instead focusing on "development, diplomacy, and defense," while leaving out a fourth *D,* democracy.

Obama's early caution about full-throated democracy promotion was reflected in the lack of a forceful call for democracy in the president's much-heralded June 2009 "reset with the Muslim world" speech at Cairo University (Obama 2009b). In the speech, Obama equivocated, saying that the desire for freedom is universal but that every country must decide the proper form of government for itself. And he emphasized that it is certainly not the place of the United States to impose its ideas about the best kind of government on others. Some Egyptian democracy advocates had hoped that Obama would resume the real pressure his predecessor had put on the Mubarak regime.[17] Instead, just a year later, the Obama administration remained silent as the Mubarak regime stole yet another election. Moreover, the Obama administration came under criticism from democracy activists for cutting USAID's funding for Egyptian civil society, limiting it instead only to "official" NGOs recognized by the Mubarak government. Carothers (2012) points out that in fact Obama was just continuing the approach of all of his predecessors since 1979 of propping up the Egyptian strongman and directing the vast majority of Egypt's aid package toward the Egyptian military, but in the eyes of some, these policies sent the wrong signal—that the United States was stepping back from any efforts to democratize Egypt. The Obama administration's more skeptical approach to democracy promotion was also very much in evidence in US policy toward Iraq, where the Bush administration had spoken of Saddam Hussein's fall as the catalyst for a democratic revolution that would then spread across the Middle East. The Obama administration, by contrast, expressed skepticism about the prospects for democracy in Iraq.

Obama readily adopted the Bush administration's ideas and tools related to the "kinetic" side of counterterrorism in terms of the perceived imperative of degrading and defeating terrorist groups around the world. He increased drone strikes in countries such as Somalia, Yemen, and Pakistan multifold. Finally, Obama's early emphasis on engagement with nondemocratic states such as Iran and Russia further lessened the administration's willingness to engage in robust forms of democracy promotion. This was the background against which the Obama administration would respond to the events of the Arab Spring.

Notes

1. On illiberal democracy, see Zakaria (2007).
2. Carothers (1999) concludes that the emphasis on quantitative results harmed democracy promotion by encouraging myopia and wasting time and resources.
3. Interview with democracy assistance expert, Washington, DC, October 2018.
4. Hawthorne, quoted in Hubbard (2019).
5. Morgenthau (1948), quoted in Traub (2008, p. 45).
6. In addition to turning a blind eye to repression in the Arab world, Carter said little about human rights abuses in Iran, toasting the autocratic shah in Tehran in 1977 as a great leader who could guarantee stability (Smith 2012, p. 258).
7. A small exception was the slightly tougher line that the Clinton administration took on Algeria, mostly in reaction to the deepening civil war there in the 1990s (Carothers 2004, p. 28).
8. Of course, this idea runs into very serious empirical challenges. For example, as Traub (2008, p. 7) points out, the democratic Philippines produces many more terrorists than authoritarian China.
9. Interview with former US official, Washington, DC, July 2015.
10. Another former ambassador openly admitted to me that he refused to carry out Secretary of State Rice's instructions to meet with the political opposition in another Arab country because he knew the Bush administration's time was almost up. Interview with former US official, Washington, DC, February 2018.
11. Interview with State Department official, December 2014.
12. Hamas presented political (its refusal to recognize Israel's right to exist) and legal (its designation as a foreign terrorist organization) problems for the United States.
13. Quoted in Traub (2008, p. 136).
14. US foreign service officers engaged in public diplomacy, as I was at the time, saw the effects of the credibility gap. As we tried to highlight US good deeds around the world and religious tolerance inside the United States, we invariably faced questions about Guantanamo, Abu Ghraib, extraordinary renditions, and so on.
15. Interviewed by Traub (2008, p. 145).
16. Interview with US official, Washington, DC, February 2018.
17. Interviews with Egyptian democracy activists, Cairo, December 2014.

3

Individuals

Given the high stakes involved and the resulting level of presidential involvement, the role of Barack Obama as an individual is central to understanding the nature of the administration's policy responses to the Arab Spring. So is the role of some of Obama's top advisers who helped shape what was at least initially a forward-leaning response to the uprisings. The Arab Spring and its aftermath was a time of great uncertainty, when Arab leaders, institutions, and modus operandi familiar to US foreign policy bureaucracies were suddenly swept aside or marginalized, replaced by unrecognizable and unpredictable actors, groups, and developments. Decisionmaking in a crisis situation, Irving Janis and Leon Mann (1979) find, "tends to highlight the importance of personality and ideology."

Bureaucracy is an unresponsive, slow-moving ship at the best of times. But in 2011, as events spun out of control in a region where the status quo had prevailed for so many decades, institutions such as the State Department and the Department of Defense were unprepared to respond quickly, especially given their decades of relationships with Arab autocrats; their shared frames, which associated stability with ruling Arab regimes; and their cumbersome internal hierarchy and processes, which tend to discourage bold policy proposals. Of equal importance, these institutions did not possess the fresh ideas with which to harness the Arab Spring. The intelligence community had not predicted that protests could spread so quickly and challenge so many Arab autocrats. This further provided individual democracy promoters in the foreign policy apparatus with an unprecedented opening to advocate for their ideas. But, as this chapter will show, not all individuals in Obama's government were behind the project of democracy promotion, leading to mixed messages at key junctures.

Barack Obama as an Individual

President Obama came to the job with limited experience in foreign policy making but nevertheless had well-developed views on foreign policy owing to the international experience he garnered growing up, his time as a US senator, and his own intellectual curiosity. Yet, Obama readily deferred to the expertise of others in policy areas in which he was not knowledgeable, engaging in prolonged decisionmaking processes in which he listened to debates among his advisers. At the same time, he also participated actively in most key foreign policy deliberations and decisions. According to James Mann (2012, p. xviii), by virtually all accounts, the dominant influence on the Obama administration's foreign policy was the president himself: "He was the main strategist. It was Obama's own ideas, sometimes changing over time, that have determined America's role in the world during the presidency." Another high-level official who advised the president told me, "Obama was his own man and had his own ideas on the Arab Spring and most other foreign policy issues."[1]

Obama was a consensus builder, often asking for unanimity among his advisers before making a final decision on an important issue. Though Obama did not shirk from difficult decisions, he was afraid of making mistakes, accounting for his cautious, risk-averse approach. His legal background meant that rigor, logic, and rationality, rather than emotions or reactions, shaped his response to international events. Thus, while Obama's rhetoric on issues such as justice, human rights, and democracy may have been at times soaring and emotional, the president's decisions often reflected a cool, rational temperament. Obama believed that decisions made out of a sense of moral outrage did not lead to good policy. Ben Rhodes, Obama's closest foreign policy adviser, noted that "one of the president's core things" is not to make choices "that don't work just so that we feel pure. And there is an element of realism to that, but there is also an element of pragmatism."[2]

Obama spent his childhood in Hawaii and in Indonesia, which may have contributed to his signature "pivot to Asia" foreign policy initiative. He spoke passionately and optimistically about Asia as the dynamic, forward-looking continent of the future, in sharp contrast to his pessimism on the Middle East. Interviewees who worked in the White House told me that Obama tended to see the Middle East as a troubled region where change would not come for perhaps more than a generation, and such sentiments only increased over time.[3] William Burns, a legendary State Department diplomat and senior official under Obama, writes in his memoirs (2019, p. 333) that Obama's explicit strategy was to "gradually break the [Middle East's] decades-long psychological, military, diplomatic, and political hold on American foreign policy." Obama came to believe that only a handful of threats in the Middle East conceivably warranted US military action: the threat posed by al-Qaeda; threats to the continued existence of Israel; and, not unrelated to Israel's security, the threat posed by a nuclear-armed Iran (Lynch 2017). In general, Obama saw the Arab world as one in which to avoid US entanglements. Jeffrey Goldberg (2016) writes: "The rise of the Islamic State deepened Obama's conviction that the Middle East could not be fixed—not on his watch, and not for a generation to come."

One of the beliefs that may have shaped Obama's lack of faith in the capacity for change in the Arab world was the tribalism he encountered while visiting his father's native Kenya. In his first book, *Dreams from My Father,* Obama (2004) describes how tribal conflict in postcolonial Kenya helped shape his father's life. "It is literally in my DNA to be suspicious of tribalism," Obama told Goldberg (2016). In post–Arab Spring civil wars such as Yemen, Syria, and Libya, Obama saw intractable, age-old and primordial hatreds based on clan, village, sect, and creed that neither the United States nor any other outsider could solve (Goldberg 2016). Indeed, as Ben Rhodes (2018, p. 298) writes in his memoir, "Obama was more sanguine about the forces at play in the world . . . as an African-American, he had an ingrained skepticism about powerful structural forces." And yet, in *Dreams from My Father,* Obama (2004, p. 300) also emphasizes the fine line between cynical fatalism and racism.

Obama saw terrorism as a threat that merited constant attention and a military response, though not necessarily a conventional one. At times, Obama tried to publicly downplay the threat of terrorism, for which he was criticized as being out of touch. But he felt that politically, especially as a Democratic president, he had to show "toughness" on terrorism, and his policies reflected this. Even before the appearance of the Islamic State in Iraq and Syria (ISIS), Obama had increased the number of drone strikes in Yemen and Pakistan and, in May 2011, decided to carry out a daring raid on Osama bin Laden's Pakistan hideout. Early in 2014, Obama's intelligence briefers told him ISIS was but a marginal threat. But by the late spring of that year, after ISIS conquered the Iraqi city of Mosul, Obama "came to believe that U.S. intelligence had failed to appreciate the severity of the threat and the inadequacies of the Iraqi army" (Goldberg 2016).

Obama has been described as a relativist, unattached to a core set of values and suspicious of rigid ideologies. In *The Audacity of Hope,* Obama (2006, p. 40) wrote, "it's precisely the pursuit of ideological purity, the rigid orthodoxy, and the sheer predictability of our current debate that keeps us from finding new ways to meet the challenges we face as a country. It's what keeps us locked in 'either/or' thinking." His willingness to understand perspectives other than the US view of the world may have led him to relativize issues and take the middle ground. His tendency to see other countries on their own terms may have come partly from his upbringing in multicultural Hawaii and Indonesia, his personal contacts with Kenya, or his travels as a student. Or, as Mann (2012) suggests, it may have been generational: Yes, Obama came from a unique multicultural background, but he was educated in elite private schools and universities, much like his presidential predecessors. The difference was that he was the first president too young to have been drafted for service in Vietnam, and his career as a politician took shape with the United States already in decline as a great power.

Perhaps more than any other aspect of Obama's beliefs, personality, and leadership style, the extent to which Obama was driven by realism could help enlighten us on his approach to democracy promotion in the Arab world. There were already strong signs of a tilt toward realism by the time he ran for president. Unlike one of his top advisers, Samantha Power, who had worked in his Senate office, Obama generally did not believe a president should place US soldiers at risk in order to prevent humanitarian disasters unless those disasters posed a direct security threat to the United States, especially in the Middle East (Goldberg 2016). He expressed admiration for prominent realists such as George H. W. Bush, Colin Powell, and Brent Scowcroft while criticizing his predecessor's penchant for proselytizing about democracy. Like most realists, he saw the United States as secure, with nuclear terrorism and climate change as the "only existential threats it faces for the foreseeable future" (Walt 2016). Obama once said, "The truth is that my foreign policy is actually a return to the traditional bipartisan realistic policy of George W. Bush's father, of John F. Kennedy, of, in some ways, Ronald Reagan" (Lizza 2011).

Instead of abstract moral values or brute military strength, Obama tended to emphasize relationship-building and shared interests. He repeatedly spoke of burden-sharing with other states (Hachigian and Shorr 2013). Obama opened his presidency with bold overtures to Russia and Iran, both autocracies and foes of the United States. To engage China on economic issues, he deemphasized human rights. He opened his 2009 Nobel Peace Prize acceptance speech by reminding the audience that he was the commander in chief of a military engaged in two wars and argued that states at times will inevitably "find the use of force not only necessary but morally justified" (Obama 2009a). He thus defended the need for military power and reminded the Nobel audience that the United States "helped underwrite global security for more than six decades with the blood of our citizens and the strength of our arms" (Obama 2009a).

Observing his realist impulses, critics accused Obama of abandoning the "democracy promotion tradition" of American foreign policy and turning instead to "ideological pragmatism."[4] From the left, Obama was criticized for his administration's extensive use of the armed drones and covert operations to pursue terrorists (Friedersdorf 2016). Obama, in turn, was unapologetic about his tough counterterrorism policies. Goldberg (2016) writes: "This is one of the larger ironies of the Obama presidency: He has relentlessly questioned the efficacy of force, but he has also become the most successful terrorist-hunter in the history of the presidency, one who will hand to his successor a set of tools an accomplished assassin would envy."

However, Obama's aversion to the use of *conventional* military force led Michael Clarke and Anthony Ricketts (2017) to see him as operating within the Jeffersonian tradition of US foreign policy. Described by Walter Russell Mead (2002) as the least prominent of four currents of US foreign policy thinking, Jeffersonianism holds that the United States should focus on putting its own "house" in order and adheres to the realist belief that only direct threats to the United States can justify the risks and costs of military interventions overseas. A more concise rendering of this idea was Obama's private admonition not to "do stupid shit" in foreign policy (Rhodes 2018). Robert Tucker and David Hendrickson (1990, p. 139) see the Jeffersonian tradition as rooted in the belief that "the objectives of foreign policy were but a means to the end of protecting and promoting the goals of domestic society, that is, the individual's freedom and society's well-being." In contrast to George W. Bush's National Security Strategy (NSS) documents of 2002 and 2006, which focused mostly on US involvement in the world, Obama devoted a significant section of his NSS to "strengthening America at home." One of Obama's former advisers told me that the president believed that foreign policy was "eating up too much of the nation's bandwidth."[5] Obama's early focus on domestic recovery from the devastating 2008 recession, and his push for the Affordable Care Act, very much reflected Jeffersonian thinking.

Obama's identification with popular protests during the Arab Spring and elsewhere recalls another part of Obama's background, as a community organizer in Chicago's South Side. Even as he often observed the world through a realist lens, he also believed in the power of civil society and bottom-up change, which might explain his early sympathy for the Arab uprisings, and his desire to engage and support civil society as a core part of promoting democracy. At the same time, Obama's writings on this period in his life also reflect an emphasis on getting things done and a pragmatism in finding the means to do so. Obama's experience with Kenya may have also taught him that "liberation without mature institutions is its own form of oppression" (Rhodes 2018, p. 48). "Yes, Obama believes in the liberation of peoples," Rhodes writes, "but he is at his core an institutionalist, someone who believes progress is more sustainable if it is husbanded by laws, institutions, and—if need be—force" (2018, p. 48).

Another core Obama belief and one directly relevant to his positions on democracy promotion was his view that American power faced real limits, especially in the Middle East. While he may have seen the United States as "indispensable," he also understood it must be "careful in its ambitions" (Chollet 2016, p. x). In this he frequently drew on the analogy of the Iraq invasion (Hamid 2016), which he saw as an example of misguided overreach that only inflamed anti-American passion among Arabs. Rhodes (2018, p. 48) noted that Obama "harbored a deeper concern about overreach—how our policies affect people in places like Indonesia; the casual manner in which, from Vietnam to Iraq, we failed to consider the consequences of our actions; the dangers of unchecked executive power." Goldberg (2016) writes that he "came to see Obama as a president who has grown steadily more fatalistic about the constraints on America's ability to direct global events." Obama thus criticized the Washington establishment for pushing a certain foreign policy playbook on him, saying it "makes a fetish of 'credibility'— particularly the sort of credibility purchased with force."[6] He saw this kind of thinking as precipitating a quagmire in Vietnam. Obama also railed against "free riders," such as those states pushing him to intervene in Syria without being willing to share any of the cost.

When asked to describe the "Obama doctrine" at the end of his first term in the White House, Obama responded, "[Mine is] an American leadership that recognizes the rise of countries like China, India and Brazil. It's a US leadership that recognizes our limits in terms of resources and capacity."[7] The experience of Libya after 2011, according to Goldberg (2016), only further strengthened Obama's belief that the Arab world was a region to be avoided. This adhered closely to his deep belief in the historical lessons of great power overextension: "Almost every great world power has succumbed" to overextension, Obama told Goldberg (2016). "I suppose you could call me a realist in believing we can't, at any given moment, relieve all the world's misery. . . . We have to choose where we can make a real impact."

The picture of Obama that emerges from the above is a complex one in terms of its implications for democracy promotion. Obama was mindful of the possibility for unintended consequences in the exercise of American power, even when that power was used for noble purposes. He was humble about America's ability to change the world. But he also seems to have understood that autocracies are never going to be stable or durable, even in the Arab world. This accounts for the Presidential Study Directive (known as PSD 11) he commissioned in 2010, in which policymakers imagined a postauthoritarian Arab world. Yet, the directive also reflected his caution, given that the document prescribed a rather timid, hands-off approach for how the United States should encourage democratization in the Arab world (Sanger 2012, p. 281). The PSD group, writes McFaul (2018, p. 205), had focused on "gradual, evolutionary change," not unlike Bush's Freedom Agenda. No doubt Obama was again heavily influenced by the analogy of Iraq, which analysts such as Shadi Hamid have criticized as "warping" his view of the Syrian conflict and Arab Spring more generally (Hamid 2016).

Moreover, Obama's frequent return to what he perceived as core US interests in the Middle East, among them counterterrorism and the denuclearization of Iran, took him away from democracy promotion, especially in the latter part of his presidency. And his penchant for compromise and taking the middle ground on many complex issues meant that he was unwilling to take a strong stand on democracy promotion in Arab Spring countries. Some of his principal heuristic devices—the focus on tribalism, the lack of faith in US leverage over issues such as democracy—suggested that Obama had little faith in either Arab democracy or the US ability to influence it. His adherence to a relativist worldview, and accompanying belief that the United States could not impose its values on others, also lowered his propensity to be a democracy promoter in the Arab world.

How then do we square this with Obama's optimistic rhetoric in May 2011, when he came as close as he ever would to embracing the rhetoric of George W. Bush's Freedom Agenda? Perhaps the answer is that Obama was never able to reconcile these contradictory impulses himself. Obama's May 2011 speech equated protesters in Tunisia and Egypt's Tahrir Square with Rosa Parks and the "patriots of Boston." In announcing his decision to intervene in Libya, Obama said that "some nations may be able to turn a blind eye to atrocities in other countries. The United States of America is different" (Obama 2011a), expressing the kind of idealism that contradicted his realist impulses on so many foreign policy issues.

Individuals and the US Response to the Arab Spring in Egypt

When it comes to individual influence over US policy toward Egypt, two moments stand out. The first occurred during the 2011 Egyptian uprising, when a constellation of close Obama advisers, many (but not all) of whom later argued for the Libya intervention, drew on analogies and scripts that saw the Tahrir Square uprising as a historical opportunity for the United States to stand on the right side of history and successfully overcame substantial institutional and individual resistance to abandoning Mubarak. However, the often-contradictory messages emanating from the White House and other agencies and officials in early 2011 showed that other influential individuals in the Obama administration read US interests in Egypt from an entirely different script. And Obama's own ambivalence about how strongly to respond to the Egyptian revolution also shaped some of the zigs and zags in the US policy response.

The second took place in the run-up and aftermath of the 2013 military coup. There were again mixed messages—both private and public—emanating from a cast of high-level US individuals, each with very distinct views about what was "best" for US interests in Egypt. The key questions in this period were how to respond to increasing pressures against democratically elected president Mohamed Morsi of the Muslim Brotherhood, and then how to respond to the coup led by his own defense minister, Abdel Fatah al-Sisi. Some individuals, drawing on a well-honed Washington habit of cozying up to Egyptian military leaders while buying into their fear of political Islam, first delivered inconsistent messages about how the United States would respond to a possible coup and then gave ambiguous signals about Washington's resolve to punish the new ruling clique for its abuses. Yet, others (including the president himself) remained at least nominally committed to a democratic transition in Egypt. Obama and his surrogates passed their own messages to Egypt's leaders, but the Egyptians were quick to catch on to the inconsistencies. This contributed to an incoherent policy in which anything approaching robust US democracy promotion was greatly diminished. After 2013 Obama had lost faith in the Arab Spring and become focused on other diplomatic priorities. He was less personally engaged in the policy deliberations, yielding policy implementation and formulation to others. Here, the fact that in 2013 John Kerry took over from Hillary Clinton as secretary of state turned out to matter a great deal.

The Significance of Letting Mubarak Go

How path-breaking was President Obama's February 2011 phone call to Mubarak, in which he informed the embattled strongman that he no longer had the backing of Washington? A cynical view might see it as a delayed move, taken only once it was clear that Mubarak had lost all support, and only once the United States could be assured that a friendly successor, intelligence chief Omar Suleiman, would take over. But such cynicism does not consider the formidable constellation of forces that were in favor of continued US support for Mubarak: elements within institutions such as State, Defense, and the CIA; prominent individuals in Obama's inner circle; and Israel and Saudi Arabia, two key US allies. Seen from this perspective, it was a courageous and game-changing decision.

It was also a bold move if we consider that it came from a president who at any cost did not want to *own* these events. That is, at least some of Obama's cautiousness, and his belated response, can be attributed to his desire to back the protests, but at the same time not use US power in any way that could be seen as meddling in a domestic process. Obama did not want to be seen as preventing the wave of change, or encouraging it with a visible US stamp of approval that might someday be used against the prodemocracy protesters. Driven in part by the analogies of Iraq and Afghanistan, he believed that the United States could not shape the trajectory of Egyptian developments even if it wanted to.[8] And yet, his caution about the projection of US power had the unintended consequence of making his administration look indecisive in response to a historic popular uprising against a despot who happened to be a close US ally.

Indeed, many Egyptian activists I met in Cairo after the 2011 uprising expressed disappointment with Obama's response. From the perspective of Tahrir Square, Obama's support came too late in the game. When Secretary of State Clinton visited Cairo in March 2011, she was snubbed by some of the youth activists "based on her negative position from the beginning of the revolution and the position of the US administration in the Middle East" (Sanger 2012, p. 310). William Burns, who was then Under Secretary of State for Political Affairs, describes the young Egyptian protesters he met as equally skeptical of the Egyptian military and the United States (Burns 2019, p. 304). While this was an early expression of the nationalist undercurrents that came to define post-Mubarak Egypt, it was also a reflection of the lack of trust engendered by decades of American support for Mubarak and other Arab autocrats. Based on this mistrust, Egyptian activists saw ulterior motives in the delayed US response to their revolution. One activist told David Sanger (2012, p. 302): "Obama changed his decisions . . . once he knew the revolution would win, he sided with the revolution. I don't trust a man like that." Sanger's (2012, p. 302) comment on such attitudes is telling: "It was a strange reaction—for years Egyptians have complained about Americans meddling in their politics; this time they complained about not enough meddling."

Individuals vs. Institutions, and the Initial US Response to the Egyptian Uprising

In early 2011, Obama was simultaneously caught between his own conflicting instincts about the Egyptian uprising and between institutions and individuals advocating caution and those pushing for him to seize the historical opportunity and stand with the people. He was further caught between the Egyptian protesters who had been inspired by his message of hope and the Mubarak regime (as well as its Gulf and Israeli backers) who expressed anger and disbelief that the United States seemed to be prepared to abandon its support for its longtime Egyptian ally (Rhodes 2018, p. 101).

On one side were bureaucratic actors such as the State Department, CIA, and the Pentagon. All three had pursued a status quo–focused policy approach for decades in Egypt (Brownlee 2012). The CIA's relationship with Mubarak's *mokhabarat* (intelligence services) had become robust in the post-9/11 years, leading the agency to argue that any disruptions in that relationship could harm US counterterrorism efforts. The Department of Defense (DoD) had for decades benefited from close relations with the Egyptian military in the form of joint training, military sales, exchanges, and of course the generous assistance program totaling $1.3 billion per year. DoD argued that all of this bought it tremendous access and influence in Egypt that would be hard to replace should Mubarak be toppled in a revolution. In the DoD's view, the US-Egyptian relationship was built on stability, and stability depended on Mubarak's continued rule.

The US military establishment had come to see Egypt as uniquely vital: the guarantor of the peace with Israel, the gatekeeper of the Suez Canal and strategic flight routes, the crossroads of three continents, and the "regional bellwether" (Kirkpatrick 2018, p. 19). The State Department's Near Eastern Affairs Bureau had similarly built deep and long relationships with the Egyptian Foreign Ministry and urged caution at interagency meetings, preferring the status quo. At one point, Rhodes (2018, p. 102) recounts, the heads of foreign affairs agencies proposed inviting leaders of key Arab countries to Washington to reassure them of US support. Rhodes (2018, p. 12) recorded his own bold response to this proposal during an interagency meeting: "Maybe if we're going to have all the corrupt autocrats over, we could just think about actually inviting some of these young people, too . . . for balance."

In fact, it was the State Department, supported by the CIA and DoD, that came up with a plan to encourage Mubarak to hand power to his seventy-four-year-old intelligence chief, Omar Suleiman.[9] Suleiman had been Egypt's main liaison to both Washington and Jerusalem, and US lawmakers, diplomats, generals, and spies all knew him well. Former CIA deputy director Michael Morrell (2016, p. 181) praises Suleiman in his book as "very wise" and notes that the CIA would often seek his views on "complex issues." Former National Security Agency and CIA director Michael Hayden (2016, p. 318) refers to Suleiman's "wise counsel" and his support on counterterrorism. Inside Egypt, however, Suleiman was known for leading a brutal apparatus of internal repression that tortured political prisoners. Senior US foreign policy leaders were accustomed to making one phone call to get things done with Cairo. Who would they call if Mubarak were gone? Suleiman could be just that person.

Early Mixed Messages

Reflecting the tussle in Washington over how to deal with the events in Egypt, the initial US response to the Egyptian uprising was "hesitant and confused" (Sanger 2012, p. 291). This reaction reflected the influence of institutions who were not prepared to deal with the new reality, but it also was driven by individuals whose first instinct was to preserve the Mubarak regime. Secretary of State Clinton's early statements in response to the protests came, as Sanger (2012, p. 288) writes, "from the traditional American script." On January 25, 2011, Clinton told reporters: "Our assessment is that the Egyptian government is stable and is looking for ways to respond to the legitimate needs and interests of the Egyptian people."[10] Two days later, Vice President Joe Biden argued that "he would not refer to [Mubarak] as a dictator" (a statement about which he later expressed regret) (Nichols 2011). Robert Gates, secretary of defense, urged Obama to stand by a stalwart US ally. Individuals such as Gates, Biden, and Clinton may have been channeling the interests of the institutions they led, but their public statements reflected decades of socialization in the US foreign policy apparatus, which could not imagine life without Mubarak.

Clinton made the argument that the right path was to pressure Mubarak for change using as many threats as necessary, but not to remove US support (Sanger 2012, p. 293). She and other senior members of Obama's cabinet had dealt with Mubarak for many years, and some had personal relationships with the Mubarak family.[11] A former official told me: "[The secretary of state] and others, whether consciously or unconsciously, had simply bought into the idea Mubarak had lectured them about for years: that the Egyptians could not handle democracy, that the only alternative to his rule was the radical Brotherhood."[12] Other advisers reminded the president that dropping support for Mubarak would send the wrong signal to allies—that the United States was ready to abandon its friends when the winds shifted (Sanger 2012, p. 293). National security adviser Tom Donilon privately cautioned Obama about the risks of a Mubarak departure.[13] Such individuals saw Mubarak's continuation in power as aligned with US interests, this despite the fact that the majority of Egyptian people—and at some point, even the Egyptian military itself—had given up on him.

By contrast, many of the younger individuals in the White House who had worked on Obama's campaign were not committed to the entrenched ways of framing US interests in Egypt. They were convinced of the unsustainable corruption of the Mubarak regime and ahead of the intelligence community in predicting the spread of protests beyond Tunisia (Rhodes 2018, p. 99). To challenge the Pentagon's equation of stability with autocratic rule, the younger advisers would say that "Mubarak no longer represented stability . . . his dictatorship was a source of instability" (Rhodes 2018, p. 100). In this group was Samantha Power, who was to play a major role in the decision to intervene in Libya, along with aides such as Ben Rhodes, Tony Blinken, Denis McDonough, Susan Rice, and Michael McFaul, all of whom saw this as a pivotal moment for the United States to stand with the Egyptian people rather than with an aging, corrupt, and, by 2011, largely illegitimate dictator. They pressed Obama to take a principled and bold stand in support of change, especially as the regime began to use violence against the Tahrir Square protesters. Rice, then the US ambassador to the UN, asked Obama if he wanted to be remembered as the president who sided with Mubarak, or with the people of Egypt (Dyer and Saleh 2016). Clinton later described these advisers as being "swept up in the drama and idealism of the moment."[14] Somewhat surprisingly, John Brennan, a career CIA official who was then Obama's counterterrorism adviser, also lined up with the younger aides on the side of letting Mubarak go (Dyer and Saleh 2016).

Obama himself, who did not have personal ties to Mubarak or his family, was pressing his advisers to come up with more aggressive responses, sensitive to the fact that the United States was already seen by the protesters as being behind the curve based on its delayed response to the Tunisian uprising (Sanger 2012, p. 293). According to Kirkpatrick (2018, p. 35), Obama's feeling early on was that Mubarak's fate was sealed:

> Obama, perhaps remembering the tumult he lived through as a child in Indonesia, told his advisers that day that Mubarak was doomed. "He took one look at what was happening in the streets and he thought, 'We ought to get on the right side of this,'" Ben Rhodes, the deputy national security adviser and a long-time aide to Obama, later told me. "He knew that the old order was rotten and the status quo was unsustainable," Rhodes said. "Obama thought this was an opportunity that had to be tested. He wanted the future of Egypt to be the people in the square—not Mubarak."

Obama's instincts were one thing, but his cautious approach and pressure from the older advisers led to a series of ambiguous actions and statements. In a January 28, 2011, phone call with Mubarak, Obama was careful not to imply to the Egyptian president that he had lost US support (Sanger 2012, p. 291). His ensuing public message about the call was vague: "When President Mubarak addressed the Egyptian people tonight, he pledged a better democracy and greater economic opportunity. I just spoke to him after his speech. And I told him he has a responsibility to give meaning to those words, to take concrete steps and actions that deliver on that promise" (Obama 2011c). Obama's apparent caution frustrated both the Tahrir Square protesters and those within his administration pressing for a more forceful approach. In fact, Rhodes wanted to place the words "pursue a path of political change" in Obama's statement, but Clinton, Gates, and other principals vetoed it as being too forward. Every word about the grievances of the protesters and human rights was also taken out (Rhodes 2018, p. 101). Obama's acceptance of the principals' veto reflected his inner conflicts about wanting to encourage change without taking sides and without inserting the United States too far into Egyptian politics, an approach he felt could backfire. On January 31, at the suggestion of then-senior State Department official William Burns, Obama sent Frank Wisner, a veteran American diplomat and former US ambassador to Egypt to reason with Mubarak (Burns 2019, p. 301). He instructed Wisner to tell the Egyptian leader two things: refrain from using force to crush the protests, and cede power to someone outside the Mubarak family, but only after the September elections.[15] This was the cautious Obama hedging his bets, caught between forward-leaning advisers pushing him to be on the "right side of history" on one hand, and on the other hand a foreign policy bureaucracy and its career officials reminding him of the multiple threats to US interests that might arise should chaos prevail in Egypt.

Obama Calls for Transition, "Now"

On February 1, Mubarak delivered a defiant speech, using a time-tested threat. "The events of the past few days impose on us . . . the choice between chaos and stability," he said. Obama happened to be chairing a National Security Council (NSC) meeting in the White House Situation Room, and everyone stopped to watch Mubarak's speech. Afterward, the debate over how to respond continued. Obama asked everyone at the table to offer their views on whether he should ask the Egyptian leader to leave office now (Burns 2019, p. 292). Gates again came out firmly against pushing Mubarak out, voicing his concerns about an uncertain transition (Dyer and Saleh 2016). Clinton now took a more nuanced approach, arguing that the United States should apply private pressure but avoid a strong public push lest it anger its Gulf allies (Dyer and Saleh 2016), who were already intensively lobbying on behalf of Mubarak. After calling Mubarak again, Obama went against the advice of the pro–status quo group in his administration and made his most forceful statement to date, saying: "Now, it is not the role of any other country to determine Egypt's leaders. Only the Egyptian people can do that. What is clear—and what I indicated tonight to President Mubarak—is my belief that an orderly transition must be meaningful, it must be peaceful, and it must begin now" (Obama 2011d). There was in fact a tussle over the words "it must begin now," with senior leaders at the Pentagon and State Department lobbying the White House to take them out (Rhodes 2018, p. 105). While at first glance the statement was bold, indicating that the United States was prepared to let go of a linchpin of US policy in the region for three decades, it was also vague on the point of exactly what an "orderly" or "meaningful" transition would entail. As a result, the next day, Obama's spokesperson, Robert Gibbs, struggled before the press to explain what Obama meant. In the end, Gibbs clarified that Obama was *not* in fact asking for Mubarak's departure. Mubarak and Egypt's generals undoubtedly picked up these mixed signals.

On February 2, the Mubarak regime deployed thugs riding camels and horses to raid Tahrir Square and beat protesters. The shocking, almost medieval, scenes were captured live on Al Jazeera and other media outlets. It is unclear who ordered the crackdown, though a number of ruling National

Democratic Party (NDP) officials were later tried and acquitted of charges relating to the incident. It was clear, however, that the attack on Tahrir Square was not spontaneous. The military stood by and watched, eventually firing warning shots to disperse the thugs, but did not intervene forcefully to stop them. Despite these disturbing scenes of violence in Cairo, the view among the prostability faction in Obama's circle of advisers was that the "Battle of the Camel," as February 2 came to be known, was not a government-ordered crackdown but instead clashes between rival groups (Kirkpatrick 2018, p. 50). This view shocked the younger coterie of NSC staff, who continued to push for a more forceful policy. Obama's view was also hardening in response to the ongoing violence. Yet, the individuals wedded to scripts in which only Mubarak could guarantee stability seemed unable or unwilling to change their views. Adding to the chorus of mixed messages, during a video appearance at the Munich Security Conference on February 6, Wisner, Obama's special envoy to Cairo, publicly backed Mubarak by saying that the Egyptian president's continued leadership until the fall elections was "critical." Obama was furious, and Burns apologized to the president for sending Wisner in the first place (Burns 2019, p. 302). At the same conference, Clinton expressed support for a transition led by Suleiman, as if "the old spy were perfectly well suited to lead a transition to democracy" (Kirkpatrick 2018, p. 50).[16] Rhodes (2018, p. 106) writes that he was "increasingly frustrated" that the "bold step" Obama had taken "to embrace a social movement that was demanding change" was being undermined by ambivalent individuals in his own administration.

Different Individuals, Different Scripts

Thus, while Obama may have seen little hope for Mubarak's rehabilitation, a substantial number of individuals in his administration thought otherwise (Rhodes 2018). Well into the protests, Clinton and Gates continued to oppose withdrawing US support for his rule (Sanger 2012, p. 295). Other advisers suggested meager steps, such as further statements and phone calls urging restraint. This was despite the violence of the regime against peaceful protesters, and despite the fact that the burning of Mubarak's immense NDP headquarters should have sent a signal about the depth with which Egyptians had come to loathe their autocratic leader. It was only after Mubarak's defiant speech of February 10 that Obama decided to call Mubarak and tell him the game was up. The call turned into a heated conversation between the two men, with Mubarak lecturing Obama on his naivete about the realities of Egypt. Obama, in turn, advised Mubarak to seize the historic moment before it was too late (Sanger 2012, p. 295).

How could two groups of advisers perceive the stakes for US interests in Egypt so differently? The *homo psychologicus* approach to foreign policy analysis, particularly its focus on analogical reasoning, can help us understand the divergence. McFaul (2018, pp. 205–206), who took part in the White House debates on how to respond to the Arab uprisings, writes the following:

> In my experience, historical analogy is the analytic method of choice for senior foreign policy makers trying to get a handle on world events unfolding in real time. When trying to understand a new problem, they rarely use or even read analyses informed by social science methods . . . and logically, these analogies are made to historical cases with which the individuals are most familiar. I watched this play out dozens of times over my five years in government, and it was particularly striking during our struggles to understand the Arab Spring, and especially events in Egypt in the winter of 2011.

The status quo group saw an uncertain Iranian revolution–like scenario where chaos could be exploited by radicals, especially parts of the Muslim Brotherhood,[17] leading to unforeseen consequences for US interests: perhaps war with Israel, or denial of access to the Suez Canal. In this analogy, Obama was cast as Jimmy Carter, and its champions noted Carter's weakness, excessive focus on human rights, and neglect of America's security interests (McFaul 2018, p. 206). Don't repeat Carter's mistakes, senior officials such as Clinton initially argued (McFaul 2018, p. 206). As Kirkpatrick (2018, p. 35) writes, "they worried about other autocratic Arab allies across the region, like the hereditary monarchs of Jordan, Morocco, and the Persian Gulf. What if citizens marched on those royal palaces, too?" The United States should not "throw them to the wolves," as Gates (2014, p. 506) put it in his memoir.

The group of advisers pressing Obama to abandon the sinking ship that they saw in the Mubarak regime, by contrast, was operating from a different set of analogies and scripts, perhaps based on US policy during the height of the Cold War: The United States stands by a repressive and corrupt dictator at all costs, thereby delegitimizing itself in the eyes of the local population and lessening its leverage and thus hurting its interests in the long term. McFaul, who was part of this group, writes (2018, p. 208) about what he told Obama at the time:

> On Egypt, I told him I recognized the appeal of the Iranian analogy, but suggested that there were dozens of cases of autocratic breakdowns that might illuminate alternative trajectories for the state. The Egyptians were not doomed to follow the Iranian script. Even the outcome of the Iranian Revolution was more contingent than most assumed. . . . I focused in particular on three other analogies: Chile, the Philippines, and South Korea in the 1980s.

These analogies, in turn, cast Obama as Reagan rather than Carter.

The group of advisers in favor of maintaining the status quo emphasized the leverage that close military-to-military ties gave the United States, pointing to the fact that US military personnel at all levels of the hierarchy were being mobilized to engage their Egyptian counterparts and implore them not to use force against the protesters. The pro-change group, by contrast, argued that years of "leverage" and over a billion dollars in annual aid had done little to prevent Egypt's economic decline or deplorable record on human rights. While the status quo group emphasized loyalty to a leader who had stood by the United States for decades, the pro-changers pointed to the costs of the alliance with the Mubarak regime. The difference was based on different backgrounds and beliefs, but it was also generational: Some of Obama's younger advisers could imagine themselves with the protesters in Tahrir Square (Sanger 2012). If the older, status quo group read from an "Iran in 1979" script, the younger group followed an "Eastern Europe in 1989" one, emphasizing the historic wave of change sweeping the Arab world. In this manner, the individual level of analysis can help us understand why two different groups of foreign policy elites from the same administration diverged on the question of how to respond to the Egyptian uprising.

That Obama ultimately chose to drop US support for Mubarak certainly reflected the influence and arguments of the younger, pro-change advisers. It also helped that the Mubarak regime stirred outrage by using violence to attempt to disperse the protests. This eventually led Clinton, originally part of the status quo group, to reach the same conclusion as Obama: Mubarak must go (Dyer and Saleh 2016). But the manner in which Obama reached his decision was also very much in line with his worldview and style, as analyzed earlier. This worldview was perfectly encapsulated in an aside to McFaul about the Egyptian uprising: "What I want is for those kids in the square to win and the Google guy to be elected president. What I think is we're going to be in for a long, protracted transition."[18] In these words, we see the multiple, and at times contradictory, dimensions of Obama: the community organizer who campaigned on a message of change versus Obama the sober pragmatist, with—depending on one's perspective—a realist or pessimistic view of the chances for democracy in Egypt.

US Democracy Promotion in the Months After Mubarak

Mubarak bowed to popular and US pressure and stepped down on February 11, ceding power to the military. If the uprising of 2011 represented a critical moment for US democracy promotion, the fall of Mubarak represented another kind (the chance to push a democratic transition forward). The initial US response to early post-Mubarak Egypt was just as full of contradictory messages and policies as the reaction to the uprising. On one hand, the United States seemed to throw its weight behind a democratic transition. "The White House and State Department now gushed with enthusiasm for the Egyptian revolution," Kirkpatrick (2018, p. 60) writes. Clinton made a triumphant visit to Tahrir Square in March 2011. And the Obama administration announced that it was shifting $65 million in economic aid toward democracy assistance in Egypt (Essam El-Din 2011).[19]

On the other hand, the pledges of democracy assistance were not matched by higher-level engagement on pressing the Egyptian generals to end military rule. Even as the Obama administration was announcing its support for the post-Mubarak transition, it was more quietly embracing the interim military government that emerged out of the revolution, the so-called Supreme Council of the Armed Forces (SCAF), as "the best guarantee that the 'revolution' would not go against American interests" (Kirkpatrick 2018, p. 60). Already, the individuals and institutions that had been skeptical of the revolution were reverting to familiar policies to ensure that the United States had a credible interlocutor in Cairo who could protect core US interests: the peace treaty with Israel, access to the Suez Canal, and counterterrorism cooperation. The Pentagon began to see the military chief of staff, General Sami Anan, as its point man in Egypt and the country's next ruler (Kirkpatrick 2018, p. 60). Ben Rhodes told Kirkpatrick (2018, p. 60) that the de facto policy was "to hug SCAF as closely as possible." In fact, the US approach was conflicted, as William Burns (2019, p. 304) describes: on one hand, US officials warned the SCAF of moving too quickly, while on the other they cautioned against the perpetuation of military rule. "We should have pressed harder for a more deliberate transition timetable," reflects Burns (2019, p. 312).

Insofar as the success of Egyptian democracy would depend on visible improvements in the lives of tens of millions of ordinary Egyptians, one road for a high degree of US democracy promotion after Mubarak's ouster might have been positive inducements, including a massive aid package to help Egypt deal with its economic woes. The democracy assistance package announced by the Obama administration did not rise to that level. As one former White House official told Sanger (2012, p. 313), the Marshall Plan was approximately $150 billion in today's dollars, while the "Middle East Fund" Obama ultimately proposed to support reforms in the Arab Spring countries was $1 billion—for the entire region. The Europeans did not do much better. Sanger (2012, p. 313) notes that the "easy" answer to why the United States did not pledge more is the atmosphere of budget austerity that prevailed in Washington in the years following the Great Recession of 2008. It is true that Congress was in no mood to offer billions of dollars to support uncertain transitions in Egypt or other Arab countries. Many Republicans were ambivalent about Obama's withdrawal of support for Mubarak, describing it as throwing a longtime US ally "under the bus." As a result, many of Obama's proposals for economic aid got little traction in Congress (Rogin 2012b). Instead, assistance coordinators in the State

Department, such as then deputy assistant secretary Tamara Wittes, were forced to cobble together and reprogram funds that were already committed. "It was money we found in the couch cushions," Wittes told me, "there was no new money."[20]

It also seems that the Obama administration did not try too hard to pull together a more generous assistance package for reasons that went beyond budget limitations and Congressional support. Obama's ambivalence about the prospects for change in the Arab world and focus on other foreign policy priorities meant that he did not want to expend significant amounts of political capital by asking Congress to pony up a Marshall Plan for the Arab Spring. Beyond that, there was a sense, based on decades of US foreign policy practice in the Arab world, that the United States could not pledge an aid package until an acceptable leader or government was in place, one that could guarantee US interests. Thus, as some senior officials conceded to Sanger (2012, p. 313), fiscal belt-tightening was as much an excuse as an explanation of the failure to follow up with a significant assistance package to bolster the Egyptian and other Arab Spring transitions. Sanger (2012, p. 313) writes: "In short, America would talk about democracy promotion. But it would no longer be democracy's venture capitalist."

Obama's landmark speech about the Arab Spring, delivered at the State Department on May 19, 2011, reflected his own conflicted thinking and the contradictions in Washington opinions about how and how much to seize on the historic moment in Egypt and its neighbors. It is notable, in retrospect, that Obama waited until months after the major protests of the Arab Spring to deliver such a speech. This was classic Obama—cautious about reacting to events prematurely and carelessly. For these same reasons, Obama chose not to visit Cairo after the Arab Spring.[21] The speech struck a very forward tone on democracy promotion, but at the same time reflected the reluctance to expend major US political or financial resources on the Arab Spring. Of equal importance, after the speech the administration did not lay out a strategy for how US diplomats in Arab states should begin to do their jobs differently, and where to put their focus. In other words, foreign policy institutions were left without clear instructions on how to operationalize Obama's call for a "new chapter." Michael Crowley (2016) writes: "The bureaucracy was partly unsure about how to implement Obama's vision and partly unwilling to do so. . . . The State Department's Bureau of Near East Affairs showed little appetite for following through. The same held for a Pentagon mindful of assets like its giant air base in Qatar and the Fifth Fleet's base in Bahrain."

McFaul (2018, p. 218), Obama's senior adviser at the time, notes that in the May 2011 speech about democracy promotion in response to the Arab Spring, the only four concrete policies Obama announced were economic in nature: an International Monetary Fund (IMF) and World Bank stabilization plan for Tunisia and Egypt, $1 billion in debt relief and $1 billion in credit for Egypt, the creation of enterprise funds in Tunisia and Egypt, and a trade partnership. Saad Eddin Ibrahim, the Egyptian democracy activist, wrote to McFaul after the speech thanking him for the economic aid but lamenting the lack of concrete support for democracy fighters in Egypt and the region (McFaul 2018, p. 218). "We were presented with an opportunity to do something big," McFaul concludes, "but we did not deliver." He adds: "What at the time seemed to me like one of the greatest achievements of Obama's foreign policy now feels in retrospect like a squandered opportunity" (McFaul 2018, p. 218).[22]

Meanwhile, in Egypt, throughout 2011, protesters were keeping up the pressure on the SCAF, making demands and threatening protests if they were not met. The SCAF, in turn, would usually offer a concession in response to a planned Friday protest: shaking up the cabinet; jailing Mubarak and putting him and his interior minister on trial for murder and his sons on trial for corruption; scheduling elections; repealing the emergency law; and meeting other demands (McGreal 2011). The Obama administration's internal divisions—between a group of advisers hoping for a real democratic transition in Egypt and those individuals and institutions seeing continued military rule in Egypt as the best way to achieve stability and guarantee US interests—helped shape a democracy promotion policy that was ambiguous and inconsistent.

The Transition Gets Complicated

In the summer of 2011, the Obama administration issued a series of statements pressing the military to set a roadmap for transition. But in September 2011, when the Israeli embassy in Cairo was attacked by soccer hooligans, leaving staff trapped in a safe room in the building, Washington leaned on the SCAF even more closely as fears about Israeli security took hold among Pentagon officials in particular. Panicked Israeli officials called their American counterparts and warned of the growing "Islamization" of Egypt (Kirkpatrick 2018, p. 62), which struck a chord with those US policymakers who had always feared what a transition to civilian rule might mean for Washington's close ally. By this point Leon Panetta, until then the CIA director, had replaced Gates as secretary of defense. Panetta was of the generation and worldview that saw military rule in Egypt as firmly in the US interest. During the NSC deliberations over how to respond to the 2011 uprising, Panetta had been firmly in the status quo camp. Now, he called SCAF head Mohammed Hussein Tantawi to implore him to protect the Israelis, which, according to Panetta (2014, p. 364), was the start of a close working relationship.

Throughout the fall of 2011, the SCAF pursued a two-track approach of embracing the revolution and hailing its "martyrs" while ramping up repressive measures and violence against protesters demanding a definitive end to military rule. In October 2011, armored personnel carriers rolled over Coptic Christians demonstrating near the Maspero media complex, killing dozens. In November 2011, soldiers were caught on video brutally kicking a partially disrobed woman. Reports about the military's use of "virginity tests" as a way to shame female protesters were making headlines (Zayed 2011). These and other ongoing abuses were greeted with mixed signals from Washington. Despite having pledged support for a democratic transition, it was clear that key individuals in the Obama administration were reluctant to criticize or push the Egyptian military too hard (Kirkpatrick 2018, p. 92). The generals in the SCAF, one Egyptian political analyst told me, understood the ambivalence within the US government well and felt that they could pursue a violent path without serious censure from Washington.[23]

A turning point came in November 2011 when a small protest of families demanding compensation for their relatives who had been killed during the revolution earlier that year soon escalated into a much bigger demonstration calling for the SCAF to step down and yield to a civilian government. The ensuing confrontation with the military and hired thugs lasted for days. When the smoke cleared, hundreds of protesters were dead. The response from Washington might have been as ambivalent as before if it were not for determined individuals in the Obama White House, including Ben Rhodes and deputy national security adviser Denis McDonough. They seized upon the fact that much of Washington (including their boss, national security adviser Tom Donilon) was away for the Thanksgiving holiday to draft and release a statement that for the first time called for the "full transfer of power to a civilian government" to take place "as soon as possible" (White House 2011). Donilon apparently was furious about the statement, seeing it as too critical of the Egyptian military (Kirkpatrick 2018, p. 101).

Enter Ambassador Patterson

By August 2011, another key individual was shaping the US response to the Arab Spring in Egypt: newly appointed ambassador Anne Patterson, who soon became an influential voice in policy debates (Lake and Rogin 2013). An experienced career diplomat, Patterson was hardly a dyed-in-the-wool champion of democracy promotion. Nevertheless, she arrived in Cairo to replace Ambassador Margaret Scobey armed with a set of experiences and beliefs that led her to adopt a pro-democracy approach at a number of key junctures after 2011. First, she believed that too many Washington policy elites were used to dealing with a narrow band of Egyptian actors in Cairo, while neglecting to listen to the conservative smaller cities and countryside (Lake and Rogin 2013). Second, as a former ambassador to Colombia and Pakistan, Patterson had extensive experience dealing with transitions from military rule and worked to bolster weak civilian rulers threatened by military coups and insurgencies. In Pakistan, importantly, Patterson had worked with Islamists committed to democratic governance. These formed some of the analogies Patterson carried with her to Cairo.

Prior to Patterson's arrival, the US embassy in Cairo followed a policy established by then secretary of state Condoleezza Rice six years before: eschew all contact with the Muslim Brotherhood other than rare meetings with lawmakers who were affiliated with the movement but entered the parliament as "independents" (Brooke 2015).[24] This policy, in part, was designed not to anger Mubarak.[25] As a result, the State Department had limited contacts within the movement on the eve of the Arab Spring. A presidential directive issued after the uprisings authorized contact with a broader set of political actors. But national security adviser Tom Donilon refused to clear a cable to the US embassy in Cairo that instructed US diplomats in Egypt to make contacts with the Islamists, changing course only when he heard that the British had opened a dialogue with the Brotherhood (Kirkpatrick 2018, p. 117).

However, in a classic display of bureaucratic reticence, the embassy did not even react to the cable immediately, fearing that contact with the Brotherhood could become a liability once the Obama administration was out of office. In June 2011, outgoing US ambassador Scobey initially refused to approve the visit of a State Department adviser to establish contact with Brotherhood leaders, eventually relenting after she was assured that embassy staff would be able to sit in on the meetings (Kirkpatrick 2018, p. 117). Administration officials understood the difference between the Brotherhood and violent extremist groups, but they knew that many members of Congress and the wider American public did not, and were thus wary of a political backlash.

In November 2011, despite the ongoing violence in the streets, the SCAF had decided to go ahead with promised parliamentary elections, which occurred in stages at the end of 2011 and beginning of 2012. The United States hailed the elections, and several American NGOs participated as observers. One of Patterson's most important actions was to launch a program of US engagement with ascendant Islamist political groups, which immediately aroused resentment among those in Egypt, the wider region, and Washington who were deeply suspicious of the Muslim Brotherhood in particular. But from the point of view of Patterson and those in the White House, it was critical for the United States to engage with emerging political actors who had made a commitment to the democratic process and were likely to prevail in elections. According to Patterson, it was natural for her as a career diplomat to engage with the Islamists to ensure that the United States would have good lines of communication to the group, especially if they gained power.[26] Though Patterson was not necessarily a democracy promoter, she believed US interests in Egypt should align with popular will rather than familiar authoritarian faces. Moreover, the feeling in the White House among those who had pushed for Mubarak's departure was that the United States would end up looking like it was out of touch if it continued its old policy of eschewing contact with the Brotherhood. Moreover, the new approach was in line with Obama's approach of not interfering with the local will, which in this case seemed to be leaning toward political Islam. Finally, the strategy of outreach was also envisioned as a way to legitimize and moderate the Islamists.[27]

Thus, Patterson had changed the approach radically. In one of the more memorable moments of my foreign service career, I remember vividly an embassy-wide meeting at which the ambassador announced the policy of engagement with the Brotherhood and their Islamist counterparts, the Salafists. She told the assembled staff—American and Egyptian—that everyone should reach out to a Salafi or Muslim Brother, "take them to lunch," as Patterson said. I also remember the wary reactions of many of the embassy's Egyptian employees, some of whom were Coptic Christians and instinctively fearful of the Islamists.

Despite misgivings all around, the policy held. Besides reaching out to the Islamists, the US government allocated funds to democracy assistance organizations such as the International Republican Institute (IRI) and National Democratic Institute (NDI) to train the Muslim Brotherhood–affiliated Freedom and Justice Party and the Salafist al-Nour Party in organizational and messaging strategies, help that both groups gladly accepted. In the 2011–2012 parliamentary elections, the two parties together won over 60 percent of the vote, a stunning outcome just a year after Mubarak's ouster. The legislature that formed (and was later dissolved by the Egyptian high court on a technicality) was popularly known as the "Parliament of Beards" owing to the enormous presence of pious men in its ranks. To be sure, it was a largely powerless body, with the country still under de facto military rule and with no progress toward a new constitution. But unlike the Bush administration seven years earlier, the US government had taken the bold position of both recognizing the election outcome and engaging with the Islamist parties as legitimate democratic players. This policy change is not to be underestimated, and it was largely thanks to the individual roles played by officials such as Patterson, as well as Obama and his younger advisers, that enabled this transformation.

That being said, there are to this day deeply conflicting views in the United States and Egypt of Patterson's embrace of the Islamists. One view is of a brave policy that encouraged political inclusion, pluralism, and the "democratization" of political Islam in Egypt. An alternate perspective holds that it was just based on a realpolitik acknowledgment that the Brotherhood was now the strongest political force in Egypt and that the United States would need to work with it in order to protect its interests. A third view, held by many of Patterson's Egyptian critics, is that she was naively enamored by the Brotherhood's slick exterior while failing to see its inherent fundamentalism. These debates notwithstanding, it is also arguable that the policy of reaching out to the Islamists was in line with a high degree of democracy promotion. The Mubarak regime had long marginalized the Brotherhood, imprisoning and torturing its members. Knowing that the group had deep roots in smaller cities, towns, and villages; that it generated broad popular support through its social welfare programs; and that it was seen as uncorrupted even by those who were suspicious of its religious goals (Kingsley 2013; Al Jazeera 2017) all meant that it would have been folly for the United States to *not* pursue a program of engagement with the movement. The policy of continuing to support the democratically unaccountable and heavy-handed SCAF was clearly not a viable one for the long term, yet there were those in Washington who pushed for it nonetheless.

The 2011–2012 NGO Crisis

In late 2011 and early 2012, Patterson and the Obama administration were confronted with an unexpected crisis when the Ministry of International Cooperation, controlled by Fayza Abou Naga, a Mubarak hold-over with strong nationalist sentiments, ordered raids against US-funded NGOs and issued arrest warrants against a number of US citizens working for these organizations. Burns (2019, p. 306) explains the move as an effort on the part of the SCAF to burnish its nationalist and revolutionary credentials at a time of falling support. The Egyptian government accused the NGOs of operating without proper registration. Egyptian officials further announced that they had ordered the surprise raids because the CIA had been using NDI and IRI to weaken Egypt for the benefit of Israel (Awad and El Madany 2011). One official claimed that Freedom House, a congressionally funded group hit by the raids, was "founded by the Jewish lobby" (Kirkpatrick 2012). Some of the Americans working for the NGOs were forced to seek refuge in the US embassy. The issue consumed the US government for several months in 2012, while many critical policy questions about the structure and timetable of Egypt's transition were set aside. The United States threatened to withdraw its entire annual assistance package if the Egyptians did not back down and hinted it might also block a multibillion-dollar aid package from the World Bank and the IMF. In the end, however, the United States not only kept the aid intact but paid what amounted to ransom to get the Americans out of Egypt (Fadel and Wan 2012). The Egyptian government actions hardly befitted those of a US ally; yet, the generals suffered no repercussions. Indeed, as Kirkpatrick (2018, p. 143) writes, the Egyptians had called the United States' bluff. The issue of the NGOs continued to irritate US-Egyptian relations for years afterward.

The 2012 Presidential Election and the Morsi Presidency

One of the most critical moments for Egypt's post-Mubarak transition, and for US democracy promotion, came after the second round of the Egyptian presidential election in mid-June 2012. That month alone, the SCAF had dissolved the fledgling parliament, reinstated the so-called emergency laws, and decreed a constitutional amendment that stripped the presidency of many powers (Hamid 2015). Thus, when results showed that the Muslim Brotherhood candidate, Morsi, had prevailed over his opponent—Ahmed Shafik, a holdover from the former regime—by 800,000 votes, there was fear in Washington that the SCAF would falsify the election. Saudi Arabia and the United Arab Emirates, fearing both Islamists and free elections, were pushing the SCAF to do just that. Many in the US military and intelligence establishments dreaded the prospect of an Islamist president too, but they understood in the end that throwing US weight behind a stolen election simply could not be justified. "You could tell a lot of the people in the room were sympathetic to the Shafik play," Rhodes told Kirkpatrick (2018, p. 148) about the NSC discussions at the time. "But even those people just could not sustain knowing that the other guy won a free election and we were acting against it."

Thus, the Obama administration embarked on a campaign to implore the SCAF to recognize the outcome of the election. Clinton declared that it was "imperative" for the generals to "turn over power to the legitimate winner" (LaFranchi 2012). The administration again deployed assistance conditionality, threatening to cancel the $1.3 billion annual military assistance package if the military council attempted to falsify the results. Senior US diplomats also engaged the Emiratis and Saudis, who were encouraging the Egyptian military to hand the election to Shafik. All of this reflected a high degree of democracy promotion. Still, it did not guarantee that the Egyptian ruling generals would recognize the results if Morsi won. After some delay, on June 24, 2012, the electoral commission (barely) recognized Morsi as winner,[28] a watershed in Egyptian and Arab politics: An Islamist had won the first fair presidential election in Egyptian history. Marc Lynch (2016, p. 147) writes: "The administration clearly recognized that no political system which excluded a group the size of the Muslim Brotherhood could ever be democratic. Obama was prepared to pay the short-term costs of an unsympathetic Egyptian president in order to achieve a long-term consolidation of Egyptian democracy." However, in the eyes of many Egyptians and American critics of US policy, it appeared as if the United States was simply returning to its policy of supporting the powers-that-be and ignoring abuses and democratic transgressions to guarantee its interests in Egypt.

Upon taking office, Morsi immediately turned his attention to the drafting of a new constitution. Frustrated by the intransigence of his opponents in the judiciary, which he saw as stacked with Mubarak loyalists, in November 2012 Morsi attempted to appropriate judicial powers for himself. Many Egyptians saw this as a blatant attempt to undermine the separation of powers. But by this point there were those in Washington who wanted to ensure that Morsi would remain in sync with US objectives on issues such as Israel and terrorism. Morsi had been particularly helpful in using his line to Hamas to lower Gaza-Israel tensions in the fall of 2012. This may have also shaped the reluctance of Obama advisers such as Donilon to criticize Morsi too strongly. When Prem Kumar, senior director for the Middle East and North Africa at the NSC, attempted to draft a strong condemnation of Morsi's decree, he was thwarted by Donilon (Kirkpatrick 2018, p. 182). The final statement was vague: "The current constitutional vacuum in Egypt can only be resolved by the adoption of a constitution that includes checks and balances." Hamid (2015) argues that Obama had boxed his administration in with his weak response to the SCAF's abuses: "The unwillingness to pressure the SCAF would make it all the more difficult for the U.S. to hold [Morsi] to democratic standards. SCAF wasn't elected. How, then, could Washington justify withholding U.S. assistance to Morsi's administration—the country's first democratically elected government?"

The lack of a US response to Morsi's misdeeds helped to convince many in Egypt and the Gulf that Obama was now fully "in bed" with the Muslim Brotherhood. Indeed, the tepid response had not reflected a high degree of democracy promotion. And yet, it is important to remember that widespread conspiracy theories, fueled by a hostile state media and "fake news" on social media, would have likely led many Egyptians to see a hidden US hand no matter what route the White House or Patterson had pursued.[29] It was also clear the Egyptian "deep state"—the military (or at least large parts of it), Interior Ministry, and other security services—were trying to sabotage Morsi's presidency from day one (Childress 2013). Examples of this abound, from the failure of the police to protect the presidential palace against violent demonstrators, to inexplicable cuts in electricity and oil supplies. Morsi's supporters, in response, turned to vigilantism to protect the president, leading to further violence and galvanizing the anti-Brotherhood opposition (Abe and Gebauer 2012).

The 2013 Coup, Individuals, and Mixed Messages on Democracy Promotion

The turning point for US democracy promotion in Egypt was 2013.[30] By the spring of that year, the anti-Morsi opposition was a well-organized movement engaged in relentless protests against the Egyptian president. The White House policy—firmly backed by Ambassador Anne Patterson—was that Morsi was imperfect as a politician, but that he had been democratically elected, had ascended to the presidency through a nonviolent transition of power, and was more likely to guarantee stability than the military.

Patterson worked hard to convince both the military and Muslim Brotherhood to remain committed to the democratic process. However, institutions such as the Pentagon remained wary of Morsi. Kirkpatrick (2018, p. 209) writes that ongoing contacts between Egyptian and US military officers had become "bitch sessions" about the Morsi government. Key individuals reinforced this anti-Brotherhood worldview. For example, General James Mattis of US Central Command in Tampa, Florida, believed that the Brotherhood and al-Qaeda were "swimming in the same sea" (Kirkpatrick 2018, p. 115). He visited Cairo in February 2013 to meet with Sisi, who was now Morsi's defense minister, and affirmed Washington's commitment to the Egyptian military alliance. In the spring of 2013 at an Aspen, Colorado, security forum, Mattis harshly criticized Morsi and falsely claimed that the 2012 constitution that Morsi backed had been "rejected immediately by over sixty percent of the people" (Kirkpatrick 2018, p. 209).

There was another individual in the Pentagon with even more uncompromising views: General Michael Flynn, then the director of the US Defense Intelligence Agency, was outspoken about his conviction that the Brotherhood could not be differentiated from al-Qaeda. He spoke of Islam as a political ideology that "hides behind the notion of it being a religion."[31] In an interview with Kirkpatrick (2018, p. 209), he warned that "Muslim Brothers had infiltrated Washington." Both President Obama and Ambassador Patterson were dangerously close to the Islamists, he also told Kirkpatrick (2018, p. 209). Flynn enjoyed a close relationship with Sisi and other top Egyptian military figures. When Flynn visited Cairo in the spring of 2013, the Egyptian generals welcomed him as an old friend (Kirkpatrick 2018, p. 209).

Regardless of exactly what messages Flynn and Mattis delivered to their Egyptian interlocutors about US policy intentions, the divisions within the US government were becoming obvious to the Egyptians and others in the region. Obama and his pro–democracy promotion advisers were rooting for Morsi, while top Pentagon leaders had adopted the view of their Egyptian counterparts that saw Morsi as a danger. US government officials were not even informing each other of their engagements with the Egyptians: One senior DoD official, Deputy Assistant Secretary Matt Spence, was not aware that Flynn had visited the country and met with Sisi (Kirkpatrick 2018, p. 211).

Mixed Messages from Individuals: Kerry, Hagel, and the Run-Up to the 2013 Coup

Owing to the influence of individuals, US messaging and policy toward Egypt became further muddled in the run-up to the July 1, 2013, coup and its aftermath. Secretary of State John Kerry, who replaced Hillary Clinton in January 2013, had previously expressed anti-Brotherhood views. In Ambassador Scobey's 2008 confirmation hearing before the Senate Committee on Foreign Relations, then led by Kerry, the future secretary of state asked only about "the current state of threat" posed by the Muslim Brothers. "I've heard this from President Mubarak," Kerry said, advancing the idea that democratic elections in Egypt would inevitably precipitate a Brotherhood takeover.[32] Kerry was also proud of his extensive relationships with Arab leaders (Kirkpatrick 2018, p. 211). In Washington and overseas, Kerry frequently socialized with the diplomats and princes of the Persian Gulf monarchies, including UAE ambassador Yousef al-Otaiba and Crown Prince Mohammed bin Zayed. As one interviewee noted, Kerry had long been "wrapped around the finger of the Gulf monarchies."[33] Former Obama adviser Ben Rhodes was more nuanced in his analysis, telling me that Kerry always had a foreign policy objective that "superseded everything else and on which he believed he needed to bring the Gulf Arabs along."[34] Another official who knew Kerry well spoke about his particular style and how that influenced his dealings with the Egyptians:

> His diplomatic style is face to face, it is all about him. Anyone who worked with him will tell you this, if it had not worked before it was because *he* didn't try it. He was never willing to give up on anything until he personally had done it himself and seen it fail. What that meant with the Egyptians, for example, is that they would sell him the same bullshit they had sold the three previous people and he would buy it. He very much wanted to not be the one to criticize them, he would let the spokesman criticize, he would let the president criticize! But *he* didn't want to do it because he wanted to keep his relationship because he believed that he could get things done that no one else could.[35]

The evidence suggests that, upon becoming secretary of state, Kerry had not abandoned his old beliefs. In March 2013, he paid a visit to Egypt during which he pressed Morsi to undertake painful economic reforms needed for IMF assistance. Kerry walked away from the meeting frustrated by Morsi's intransigence. "He is the dumbest cluck I ever met," Kerry told his chief of staff. "This isn't going to work. These guys are wacko" (Kirkpatrick 2018, p. 212). During that same visit, Kerry met separately with the defense minister, General Sisi. When told by Sisi that the general would not allow Morsi to take his country "down the drain," Kerry barely pressed for an explanation (Kirkpatrick 2018, p. 212). He knew then that "Morsi was cooked," as Kerry later told Kirkpatrick (2018, p. 212). One former official who worked on Egypt told me that it was often hard to know what Kerry was telling Egyptian interlocutors, since his aides avoided reporting on their meetings through regular channels.[36] However, upon coming back to Washington he did little to hide his preference for the Egyptian military, which he called a "bulwark against extremism" in testimony before Congress (Kirkpatrick 2018, p. 213).

Just weeks after Kerry's visit, the National Salvation Front (NSF), a group organized to oppose Morsi, seemed to turn toward the military as the only way to oust the democratically elected Egyptian president. The alliance of democracy activists with the military left the Muslim Brotherhood without allies (Lynch 2016, p. 151). By April 2013, liberal parliamentarian and member of the NSF Amr Hamzawy said, "the plan was spelled out quite clearly—popular mobilization, followed by tanks, followed by early presidential elections. I sensed that the National Salvation Front was dead set on its decision to call on the army to intervene."[37] The leader of the NSF, Mohamed ElBaradei—a former UN official and Nobel Peace Prize recipient—who had until then opposed military intervention against Morsi also seemed to be on board, as were wealthy business figures with ties to the old regime and the Gulf (Lynch 2016, p. 151). A new group, Tamarrod (or "Rebellion"), appeared and organized a petition demanding that Morsi step aside by June 30, 2013, the one-year anniversary of his inauguration.

Chuck Hagel, who had recently replaced Leon Panetta as defense secretary, was sent to Cairo in April 2013 to deliver tough talking points to Sisi. The White House wanted to warn the Egyptian military that there would be consequences for a coup. Hagel, however, delivered a message that was much softer, apparently infuriating the White House (Kirkpatrick 2018). Hagel later told Kirkpatrick (2018, p. 227) that he responded to Sisi's ominous suggestions that a coup may be imminent with the following: "I don't live in Cairo, you do, so I will never tell you how to run your government or run your country. You've got to figure that out. I would never put myself in your shoes . . . you do have to protect your security, protect your country." Some former officials, however, insist that Hagel had not intended to soften the White House stance.[38]

Taking stock of the mixed messages, Kirkpatrick (2018, p. 228) concludes: "Obama was trying to help Morsi, Patterson was warning the Muslim Brothers, Kerry had given up on Morsi, and Hagel was reassuring Sisi." Each thought they were doing the right thing, and each thought they were acting in US interests. As Rhodes (2018, p. 50) realized early in his tenure as one of Obama's closest foreign policy advisers, though his boss was "uniquely revered by people around the world," his "views did not necessarily reflect the views of the U.S. government." In the end, Sisi may have interpreted the mixed messages as a green light to go ahead with the coup. As one former official told me,

> you know, counterfactuals are difficult, but if there were a unified US position and they were hearing from everyone, "don't do this, there will be consequences," it could have affected their calculations. That wouldn't

have changed the fact that certain Gulf countries were encouraging them to take this action and promised to bankroll them, but the Egyptian military does value its relationship with the United States and if they thought and heard from all relevant US actors that it would have a negative impact on their standing, they may have been a bit more hesitant.[39]

After the June 30, 2013, mass protests against Morsi, Obama and Ambassador Patterson made last ditch efforts to encourage Morsi to make power-sharing concessions so as to save his presidency. On June 18, Patterson gave a speech reiterating the US position that change should not come from the street, but from the ballot box. As Chapter 5 will detail, in response she was savaged by anti-Morsi forces in Egypt and the Gulf, who portrayed the ambassador as a lackey of the Brotherhood (Ibrahim 2013).

Disregarding Patterson's admonition, the coup-plotters went forward with their plans on July 3, forcibly removing and then detaining Morsi. The pro-coup coalition behind Sisi was broad: the military, intelligence services, judicial sector, the Coptic Church, the Al-Azhar Islamic establishment, and the Gulf monarchies, among others (Kirkpatrick 2018, p. 262). Despite Patterson's efforts to avert the coup, the inconsistent messages emanating from US officials certainly did not give the impression that the United States was firmly opposed. Just days before, Obama and Patterson had told Morsi and his inner circle that the United States could not control the Egyptian military, but Morsi's people could not believe that Washington lacked the leverage to stop the coup (Kirkpatrick 2018, p. 262). Maybe the United States indeed lacked such leverage; however, had Washington tried to avert the military takeover with the kind of real "sticks" that constitute a high degree of democracy promotion?

The US Responds: To Call a Coup a Coup?

On July 4, 2013, a day after the coup, Obama called a meeting of the NSC. Surprisingly, Obama opened the meeting by noting that it would be impossible to call the events a *coup,* apparently believing that US legal restrictions would require the Egyptian military to reinstate Morsi in order to continue sending aid to Egypt (Kirkpatrick 2018, p. 241). But some advisers immediately reassured him that this was not the case: The "coup law" just required a reinstatement of democracy, not the ousted ruler. Philip Gordon, NSC senior director; Martin Dempsey, chair of the Joint Chiefs of Staff; and Ben Rhodes, deputy national security adviser, all made the case that the United States should in fact call the action what it was, a *coup.* They were backed by Republican senators Lindsey Graham and John McCain, who wrote in the *Washington Post* that the United States "may pay a short-term price by standing up for our democratic values, but it is in our long-term national interest to do so" (Graham and McCain 2013).

Secretary of State Kerry, by contrast, argued forcefully at the July 4 meeting that Morsi's ouster was *not a coup*. Sisi, in Kerry's view, was acting at the behest of the Egyptian public, a view that mimicked Sisi's own public justification for the unconstitutional move. Kerry insisted that Sisi and the generals had a transition plan, including elections, in place. "If we called it a coup and walked away," Kerry later told Kirkpatrick (2018, p. 243), "we would lose any leverage and other countries would have happily filled the void." Hagel, the intelligence community, and in the end, Dempsey, all stood with Kerry on the side of not designating the takeover a coup: They argued that the alliance with Egypt was too important to jeopardize and continued aid gave Washington leverage over Sisi.[40] Michael Morrell, then the deputy CIA director, has subsequently admitted in his memoirs (2016, p. 196) that he cheered the coup in a phone call with a "senior Arab ambassador to the United States" (likely the Emirati or Saudi ambassador), saying, "This is a good thing. Morsi was leading the country to ruin, to instability, and to extremism. Now Egypt has a chance again." "Not every country is ready for democracy," Morrell (2016, p. 196) concludes. Hagel argued that Sisi would simply turn to Moscow or other sources if the United States dropped its assistance. Kerry likely also had other priorities in mind for which he would need allies such as the Israelis and Gulf Arabs, both of whom supported the coup: the Iran nuclear deal, Israeli-Palestinian peace, and Syria.[41] He did not want to "get into a fight with [the Egyptian military] over something as historically clear as how Egypt works," Kerry said to Kirkpatrick (2018, p. 243). Indeed, Kerry's rationale appeared to be less about competing interests and more about a lack of belief in the prospects for Egyptian democracy:

> In Egypt, what was the alternative? It wasn't Jeffersonian democracy. Was it Morsi? Or the Salafists? Or was it Sisi and company, and the establishment that has been there awhile. Are they democratic? No. Are they something to brag about at home? No. But over whatever number of years we have put about eighty billion dollars into Egypt. Most of the time, this is the kind of government they had—almost all of the time. And the reality is, no matter how much I wish it was different, it ain't going to be different tomorrow.[42]

The dominant view expressed by career officials representing foreign policy institutions was that the United States had little leverage. A State Department official who worked on Egypt policy told me that the best the United States could do post-coup was to "acknowledge reality" and "limit damage," including working to "prevent extreme violence."[43] In the end, the White House cancelled the shipment of certain weapons systems and asserted that no judgment on whether this was a coup was required by law. Again, Obama had split the difference, but in the process "managed to antagonize just about everyone—besieged Islamists, repressed revolutionaries, our regional friends and partners, and of course the Egyptian military and Congress" (Burns 2019, p. 308).

Individuals and US Democracy Promotion Beyond the 2013 Coup

The story of the US response to the 2013 Egyptian coup is very much about the lack of individual will to promote democracy. As expressed by Kerry above and reflected in the views of multiple individuals, US interests continued to be framed around the stability of an ongoing US relationship with the autocratic Egyptian military. Kerry's cynicism, however, was not an option after the post-coup crackdown resulted in the August 14, 2013, massacre of over a thousand pro-Morsi protesters at Raba'a Square in Cairo. The violence forced Obama's hand.[44] As one official put it, "the coup was not the real turning point. The turning point was Raba'a."[45] The administration first canceled US military exercises with Egypt and later that fall announced a partial military aid freeze, with Congress refusing to disburse any aid pending "credible progress" toward free elections and a "democratically elected civilian government." While human rights advocates argued that Obama had only put a "symbolic dent" in aid to Egypt (Crowley 2016), the irony is that the reaction from Egyptian officials was furious. "You turned your back on the Egyptians, and they won't forget that," Sisi told the *Washington Post* (Weymouth 2013). Despite the partial suspension, the Obama administration continued its full range of engagements with the Egyptian government: Relations were not downgraded; the US ambassador was not recalled.

The internal struggle over how much to censure Cairo for the coup and the wave of repression that followed continued for months, through endless interagency meetings. Throughout this time, Secretary of State Kerry was a consistent advocate for reinstating aid and full engagement with the new Egyptian regime. Just a few weeks after the coup, he declared that Egypt's generals were "restoring democracy" (Gordon and Fahim 2013). He had an ally in Secretary of Defense Hagel, who had been in constant communication with Sisi for weeks. Both Kerry and Hagel argued that they could moderate Sisi through engagement rather than the deployment of further sticks, and that democracy and human rights could wait until Egypt was stabilized.[46] Both believed that with the ouster of Morsi the United States had "dodged a bullet."[47] Both had been intensely lobbied by Gulf Arab allies, as Chapter 5 will describe. At a certain point, Crowley (2016) writes, the Egyptians "even told Pentagon officials that they no longer wanted to speak with the White House, where officials like Rhodes and Power supported punishing their thuggish behavior." During a June 2014 visit to Cairo, Kerry said that Sisi "gave me a very strong sense of his commitment" to human rights issues, adding, "I am confident that we will be able to ultimately get the full amount of aid" (Kerry 2014). To the Egyptians, it was a clear sign that divisions in the Obama administration would prevent any meaningful punishment from being carried out (Crowley 2016).

Despite Kerry's argument about how US engagement would moderate Sisi's behavior, over the next three years, the Egyptian president ramped up the repression to new heights. Tens of thousands of alleged opponents of the regime were thrown in jail. The police repeatedly used live bullets against unarmed protesters, killing some. In 2017, the State Department Human Rights report estimated the number of political prisoners in Egypt—only part of them Brotherhood members—at more than 30,000 (US Department of State 2017). Yet, Kerry and many members of Congress continued to view Sisi as a secular, stabilizing force, despite an increase in terrorist attacks in Egypt and in spite of Sisi's cynical use of religion—for example, cultivating the support of the Al-Azhar religious establishment—to rally further public support. Members of Congress visited Cairo and expressed their support for Sisi, and argued that the suspension of aid was having little effect (Halime 2013).

Meanwhile, over time the Obama administration lowered its standard of what a restoration of democracy would mean. At the beginning it had pushed for a full restoration of democracy, then for a loosening of restrictions on nonprofit groups, and finally only for the release of a few political prisoners (Wittes 2015). Sisi did not budge in response. Instead, members of his regime trotted out the same talking points that Mubarak once used: "We may not be perfect, but what better choice do you have?"[48] They deployed the Muslim Brotherhood bogeyman, equating the group with the Islamic State of Iraq and the Levant (ISIL). They argued that the withheld aid was threatening their counterterrorism capabilities (Chollet 2016, p. 121). Threatened with further suspensions of assistance, Sisi indicated that he was ready to go to Russia. As one senior official said to me, "it was a bluff, but not a cheap bluff."[49] And the Egyptians attempted to trade their support for the December 2015 Libyan Political Agreement, detailed in Chapter 4, for US silence on human rights issues. As one former official told me, Sisi's people staked their bets on the idea that Egypt was too important, and that in the end the United States would back the regime.[50] For those who never came to grips with a post-Mubarak Egypt, these arguments resonated.

By 2015, most of the heads of foreign policy institutions, as well as the new US ambassador to Egypt Robert Beecroft, were pushing to reinstate US assistance. Beecroft in particular argued that Sisi could not control the "deep state" and its apparatus of repression anyway (Crowley 2016), an argument I have heard from a number of pro-Sisi Egyptians in recent years. Obama was not convinced, at least until March 2015, when he finally "caved" to the individuals and bureaucracies calling for a return to the status quo (Crowley 2016). Shortly thereafter, Obama called Sisi to inform him of his decision to allow delivery of withheld weapons, but halt the privileged cash-flow financing program, which allows beneficiaries such as Egypt and Israel to buy sophisticated weapons systems on credit (Chollet 2016, p. 122). According to one former official who worked on Egyptian affairs, Obama was personally inclined to go much further in "remaking the relationship" with Egypt, but "he was reined in to some degree by the concerns of his cabinet" about any further punishments that might hurt US access to the Egyptians.[51]

The Egyptian coup and its violent and repressive aftermath, and the failure of the United States, European Union, and other Western states and organizations to forcefully condemn it, was a major turning point in post–Arab Spring politics for Egypt and the entire Arab world. The "Sisi model"—rule by a military strongman combined with an uncompromising campaign against Islamists—was readily adopted by General Khalifa Haftar in neighboring Libya. It strengthened the hand of authoritarian apologists and promoters in the Gulf monarchies. Pointing to Washington's failure to meaningfully condemn Sisi's takeover and subsequent crackdown, jihadist groups such as al-Qaeda could now credibly argue that US claims to support democracy were empty words. Among Sisi's justifications for the coup was the need to preserve the state and fight terrorism, but acts of terror only increased in the ensuing years.[52] The hope of 2011 had faded. As Kirkpatrick (2018, p. 286) writes, "What Tahrir ignited, Raba'a extinguished."

Discussion

The preceding account has highlighted the central role of individuals in the formulation and execution of US democracy promotion policies toward Egypt from 2011 to 2013. We saw the critical role played by President Obama himself, whose desire to support the protesters while avoiding any entanglements in the region shaped mixed US messages in the early months of the uprising. We witnessed the part played by the younger individuals among White House advisers who saw a new relationship with the Egyptian people as compatible with US interests and pushed for strong statements and actions supporting democratization well beyond the 2011 uprising. The part played by individuals was further evident in the person of Ambassador Anne Patterson, whose forward-leaning approach on outreach to the Islamist camp stood in sharp contrast to both the State Department bureaucracy and her immediate predecessor and successor. While other US ambassadors to Egypt had watered down democracy promotion messages to stay in the good favor of their hosts, Patterson was in sync with Obama's desire to promote a democratic transition in Egypt, even if she acted from the instincts of a career diplomat.

The role of one key individual—Secretary of State John Kerry—in shaping US responses to the events around the summer 2013 coup also comes into sharp relief if we construct a counterfactual in which we assume that Hillary Clinton had remained in the position of secretary of state beyond January 2013. Clinton was a pragmatist, no doubt, and she harbored deep skepticism about the chances for a successful democratic transition in Egypt.[53] She may have been motivated by her presidential ambitions and considerations of legacy.[54] In the end, however, Clinton also subscribed to the view that the United States should at least give the Egyptian transition a chance and saw no future for continued military rule. And, importantly, she was not subject to the same anti-Islamist prejudices as Kerry. If anything, Clinton had proven that she was able to update her views in the face of new information. It is highly unlikely that Clinton would have carried the same ambiguous messages to the Egyptian leadership in the run-up to the coup, or argued that Sisi genuinely wanted to lead a democratic transition. Conversely, imagine if Kerry had been at the helm of the State Department in January 2012, when the Islamists prevailed in Egypt's parliamentary elections. Given his demonstrated aversion to the Brotherhood, would he have recognized the Islamist victory as readily as Clinton did, and on top of that encourage US diplomats to engage with them? We can never be certain, but knowing Kerry's beliefs about the Islamists, it is highly likely that the contours of US democracy promotion would have been quite different.[55] Normally, a secretary of state is the one who lobbies for human rights, democracy, and a long-term view of stability. After the 2013 coup, John Kerry's position lined up squarely with the DoD's focus on access and perceived stability.

In the response to the 2013 coup, we also witnessed what can happen when important individual advocates of democracy promotion are absent from the policymaking debates. Samantha Power, often the most vocal supporter of a human rights and democracy-focused policy, was preparing for her confirmation as ambassador to the UN at the time and could not join the policy debates. Michael McFaul had become ambassador to Russia. Susan Rice, in her new role as national security adviser, was more constrained than she had been as ambassador to the UN, now having to represent the views of the cabinet more broadly. This left Ben Rhodes and, once she was confirmed, Samantha Power as among the few high-level advocates of vigorous democracy promotion in the Arab world in the second half of the Obama presidency. Power, by all accounts, remained a consistent and principled supporter of democracy promotion through the end of Obama's second term.[56]

Thus, different individuals argued for a unique understanding of what was better for the United States in Egypt, and at the end of the day, not enough of them saw democracy as the best outcome. Egypt's authoritarian forces, for their part, readily perceived that American officials failed to speak with a single voice backed by a threat of real punishment and almost certainly felt empowered by the lack of a coherent US policy. While certain individuals in the Obama administration were able to momentarily overcome tremendous institutional interests in maintaining a status quo, military-focused relationship with Egypt, the balance of forces was not in their favor. In the next chapter, I return to Egypt and illustrate how institutions reasserted themselves and pulled the Obama administration away from democracy promotion in its final years.

Individuals and Intervention in Libya

The US decision to intervene militarily in Libya in 2011 is a compelling case study of how individuals with a certain set of beliefs and influence on the president can overcome both bureaucratic and presidential reticence in pursuit of democracy and human rights–related goals. But it is also a case study of how a president's worldview consciously put self-imposed constraints on what was otherwise a bold policy move. One of the central characters in the Libya story is Samantha Power, who at the time of the Libya uprising had the rather innocuous bureaucratic title of "special assistant to the president and senior director for multilateral affairs and human rights." This meant that she was part of the National Security Council staff, a senior one no doubt; even so, there were many other "special assistants" and "senior directors" in the Eisenhower Executive Office Building. However, the title belied Power's close relationship with, and direct access to, Obama (Osnos 2014). Before he became president, Obama had read Power's Pulitzer Prize–winning book about the repeated US failure to respond to genocide in the twentieth century and invited her for a conversation in Washington, DC, where he was serving as a senator from Illinois. During that conversation, Obama asked Power to work for him in his Senate office. Power obliged, leaving her post as director of a human rights center at Harvard's Kennedy School (Pazzanese 2018). Power subsequently worked as an adviser to Obama's 2008 presidential campaign and then followed him to the White House (Osnos 2014).

Power came to her position with a well-formulated set of beliefs and policy preferences. She was a humanitarian interventionist, believing that the United States and the broader international community had not only the power, but also the responsibility, to act to prevent atrocities in the world. In addition to her prize-winning book on the subject, she had also worked as a journalist in the former Yugoslavia, where she witnessed the West's failure to intervene and stop the slaughter of civilians in Bosnia and Herzegovina. In 2004, she criticized the international community over its inaction in Darfur. "Tens of thousands of Africans are herded onto death marches," she wrote, "and Western leaders are again sitting in offices. How sad it is that it doesn't even seem strange" (Power 2004). In February 2011, in her role as a senior foreign policy adviser, Power began receiving regular reports about the protests in the Eastern Libyan city of Benghazi, long neglected in Qaddafi's Libya and the locus of strong anti-Qaddafi feelings. "It started to stand out as a place where people were taking tremendous risks," Power told Wehrey (2018, p. 37). "It was an inspiring tale; people coming to the square and reading poetry. It stood out because there was this place and a set of images." Contrary to the forecasts of analysts in the US government, the Arab Spring had arrived in Libya, and protests soon spread to other cities, including Tripoli. Shortly afterward, reports of Qaddafi's crackdown started to trickle out. Power's portfolio in the White House and special access to the president gave her a central role in coordinating the administration's response to the crisis in Libya. Not long before the outbreak of the Arab Spring, Power had co-chaired the Presidential Study Directive mentioned earlier, which concluded "that the region was ripe for political reform and that the old American pattern of backing authoritarian regimes needed to change" (Wehrey 2018, p. 38). That review was ending just as the Arab Spring was beginning. Suddenly, Power's background, beliefs, and work on the policy review became directly relevant.

The Libyan Uprising and US Policy Dilemmas

While responding to the Egyptian uprising presented Obama with one kind of policy dilemma—how to deal with an allied autocratic regime and strongman under immense popular pressure to resign—the Libyan situation added more dimensions to the US decision calculus. In Libya, the calls for regime change and democracy came in the context of a regime with which the United States had only recently reconciled and with which it had a difficult relationship, albeit a sometimes fruitful one in the area of counterterrorism. Although Libya was a major oil producer, the United States imported only small amounts of its reserves. Had it been only protests that demanded Washington's response, the dilemma may have been easier, since the lack of sufficient countervailing interests might have conditioned an unequivocal call for democratization by Obama.

However, the Arab Spring in Libya also confronted the White House with a different kind of crisis: the threat of a civilian massacre. The grim prospect only intensified when Qaddafi gave a speech threatening to hunt down his people like "rats." We now know that some atrocities by Qaddafi's forces reported at the time by media outlets such as Al Jazeera were exaggerated or even fabricated (Hashem 2012). And some scholars have questioned the veracity of Qaddafi's threats and pointed out that he offered amnesty to those who abandoned the rebellion (Kuperman 2015). Nonetheless, Qaddafi had demonstrated his brutality and capacity to kill political opponents at will, most notoriously in the Abu Slim prison massacre of 1996 (Matar 2016).

Lacking solid intelligence assets in Libya, White House advisers were dependent on reports coming from the media and anti-Qaddafi Libyan exiles. Power, for example, met with Libyan Americans who were in contact with their relatives in Libya and provided further information about the regime's human rights abuses (Wehrey 2018, p. 38).

Individuals and the Road to Intervention

Initially, the administration reached for what liberal interventionists such as Power referred to as the "diplomatic toolbox" of atrocity prevention. The UN became the focus of US initiatives in this regard, in part because of Obama's preference for multilateralism, and also because it was easy to generate international support given the antipathy toward Qaddafi among many world leaders, including Arabs. Perhaps not wanting to go down with a sinking ship, Qaddafi's own diplomats were turning against him and declaring their support for the opposition. All of this made it easier to pursue a UN consensus on tough diplomatic actions. Here the role of Obama's ambassador to the UN, Susan Rice, became critical. Rice, like Power, had worked closely with Obama during the 2008 campaign and earned his trust. She also shared Power's views on humanitarian intervention, having written and spoken forcefully about the need for international action to prevent further killing in places such as Darfur. Rice also referred to another "script" that was very close to her own experience: that of the 1994 Rwanda genocide and US inaction at the time (Rhodes 2018, p. 112). In 1994, as the killing in Rwanda unfolded, Rice was a member of President Bill Clinton's National Security Council covering Africa. At the time, she had argued that using the language of genocide would adversely affect the Democrats in the upcoming midterm elections (Kamola 2018). However, Rice had subsequently expressed particular regret about not pushing for a US response. Now, she told Obama that "We have a moral responsibility to act" (Rhodes 2018, p. 113). Rice and Power became the two most forceful advocates within the administration for a robust US response to the unfolding situation in Libya. Meanwhile, from outside the government, human rights organizations, opinion writers, and various pundits were demanding that the United States rise to the occasion.

On February 26, 2011, UN Security Council Resolution 1970 was approved unanimously by all permanent and nonpermanent members of the UN Security Council. It included a referral of the unfolding Libyan situation to the International Criminal Court (ICC).[57] The resolution also imposed sanctions on Qaddafi family members. Despite its significance, Resolution 1970 by itself was not an act of democracy promotion. It did not call for elections or regime change, instead focusing on curtailing the violence. Nevertheless, it was a powerful signal of support for the aspirations of the anti-Qaddafi opposition. Soon afterward, Obama called for Qaddafi to relinquish power, saying that "when a leader's only means of staying in power is to use mass violence against his own people, he has lost the legitimacy to rule and needs to do what is right for his country by leaving now."[58] But the threat of a massacre by Qaddafi's forces also called for policy responses that went beyond the standard tools of democracy promotion, given the widespread perception that Qaddafi would not accept a negotiated exit, as was made apparent by his son and heir-apparent Seif al-Islam's chilling public speech on February 20.[59]

As Qaddafi's columns continued their march to the east, the French and British began to advocate for military action. On March 3, 2011, Obama underscored US support for regime change in Libya, saying that Qaddafi needed to "step down from power and leave" and announcing that the United States was considering a no-fly zone (Landler 2011). Still, despite pressure from the French and British, the administration remained wary of provoking a war with Qaddafi without being able to neutralize his tools of repression. I was in Washington, DC, at the time and in contact with US embassy staff, by then "exiled" to Washington. Given Obama's steadfast opposition to US military entanglements in the Middle East, nobody I talked to in the US government thought that Obama would take further action.

An intense debate in Washington over how to respond in Libya soon spilled into the public arena. Defense Secretary Robert Gates gave six public speeches against intervention in Libya, telling Congress that US involvement would harm an already-overstretched American military trying to wind down ongoing wars in Iraq and Afghanistan. Gates, in fact, emerged as the most vocal opponent of military action, arguing that a no-fly zone was insufficient and, in the end, would require ground troops to protect civilians. As Derek Chollet (2016, p. 99) observes, the defense secretary "appealed to the president's cautious instincts." But there were a number of other individuals in Obama's inner circle who opposed a military option: Mike Mullen, chair of the Joint Chiefs of Staff; Denis McDonough, deputy national security adviser; Vice President Joe Biden; William Daley, chief of staff; and John Brennan, counterterrorism adviser. Secretary of State Hillary Clinton, who at times operated from realist instincts and had sided with the military on every major decision in the early part of the Obama administration (Rhodes 2018, p. 64), was also in the anti-intervention camp at this point. Concerns were raised about whether the rebels included extremists in their ranks. Other skeptics of intervention worried about whether a post-Qaddafi Libya might look like Iraq after Saddam.

Importantly, Gates and other opponents of intervention in the Obama administration made the argument that US interests in Libya did not rise to the level of justifying military action (Gates 2014). They contended, as then secretary of state James Baker had argued in 1991 when confronted with growing violence in the former Yugoslavia, that the United States had "no dog in this fight." Yet, part of the argument of intervention opponents also boiled down to *political* risk. Advisers to the president such as national security adviser Tom Donilon were concerned about how Obama could convince American public opinion of the need for another US military entanglement in a Muslim country. After all, polling in early March 2011 suggested that only one-third of Americans supported military action against Qaddafi (Pew Research Center 2011). However, intervention advocates Power and Rice found support among other individuals in the bureaucracy who saw unfolding events in Libya through the Tunisian and Egyptian scripts: Gayle Smith, NSC senior director; Ben Rhodes, national security adviser for strategic communication; Ivo Daalder, US ambassador to the North Atlantic Treaty Organization (NATO); and Jeremy Weinstein, NSC director for human rights (Blomdahl 2016).

The balance of power among opponents and advocates of a military intervention shifted on March 1 when Clinton, having until then opposed any military action, now stated that a no-fly zone was not off the table. When the Arab League requested UN action on March 12, Clinton split from Gates and began to actively support intervention. She embarked on a flurry of consultations with European counterparts and representatives of the Libyan opposition, who said all the right things about the democratic direction in which they would take a post-Qaddafi Libya, which likely also influenced her change of heart. Clinton was also under substantial pressure from the French and British (Sullivan 2016). However, the story of Clinton's "flip" to the pro-intervention camp may have had other roots as well, from a desire to have the State Department play a bigger role, as well as her own future presidential ambitions.

Obama was now seriously considering US military participation, but demanded an Arab stamp of approval and participation. He got both: On March 12, the Arab League approved intervention under a UN mandate, and Clinton received pledges of military contribution from several Arab countries including Jordan, Qatar, and the United Arab Emirates (Warrick 2011). But the Obama administration was still divided internally. The pro-intervention camp was now arguing that a Qaddafi victory would embolden other Arab leaders to choose the route of repression and that an extended civil war could cause instability in neighboring countries (Wehrey 2018, p. 41). Pro-interventionists also argued that the French and British could not carry out the operation without US technology and intelligence (Wehrey 2018, p. 41), but the anti-intervention camp continued to maintain that US interests could not justify US military involvement.

Obama, Intervention, and Democracy Promotion in Libya

With a divided NSC principals' committee, it would be up to Obama to make the final call on US participation in an international intervention. He made the decision after an intense set of NSC meetings on March 15, which the president himself chaired. Members of the intelligence community told the participants that Qaddafi's troops had pushed to the edges of Ajdabiya, which supplied water and fuel to Benghazi (Wehrey 2018, p. 42). US ambassador to Libya Gene Cretz, who had been forced to leave Libya just weeks before the revolution, warned of Qaddafi's history of violence against Libyans (Wehrey 2018, p. 21). Clinton was away on official travel, but by that point, her pro-intervention views were well known. Gates had resigned himself to a possible no-fly zone but was still wary of deeper involvement. However, Obama's instinct was that a no-fly zone alone would do little to stop the killings, a conviction confirmed by the chair of the Joint Chiefs of Staff, Mike Mullen. Frustrated, the president asked NSC principals to come up with more options as he dined with the joint chiefs of staff (Chollet 2016, p. 97). The NSC reconvened later that evening, and this time the president received a range of approaches (Rhodes 2018, p. 114): (1) use no US force at all, simply leaving it to others; (2) set up a no-fly zone; (3) strike Libyan ground targets to block Qaddafi's forces from entering Benghazi. Gates and others again voiced their reservations about an intervention. Nevertheless, Obama chose the third option, later telling Gates that it was a "51-49" decision (Becker and Shane 2016).

Obama then directed Ambassador Susan Rice at the UN to take a French and British proposed draft resolution and strengthen it further. Rice and her team worked furiously to do just that (Wehrey 2018, p. 43). On March 17, 2011, UN Security Council Resolution 1973, which authorized UN member states to use any means necessary to protect civilians, passed in the UN Security Council. Remarkably, China and Russia, usually opposed to any kind of intervention, abstained rather than block its passage. Just two days later, French fighter jets were bombing Qaddafi's forces outside of Benghazi. When Obama publicly announced his decision, however, he dialed back some of the more forceful language, removing phrases such as "never again" and references to the Holocaust. Even at a moment like this, Rhodes (2018, p. 116) writes, "Obama didn't want to overpromise."

Obama's bold decision to intervene militarily in Libya went against many of his instincts, but he helped justify it by reasoning that the United States would provide its military capabilities to facilitate the air strikes but then hand over responsibility to the Europeans. Because it was supported by the UN and Arab League and included the participation of a broad coalition of states, including Arab ones, it satisfied Obama's desire for multilateralism and burden-sharing, which Hachigian and Shorr (2013) called the "Responsibility Doctrine." Moreover, since Obama had avoided sending ground troops and implied that the United States would not be responsible for what happened afterward, it also could be squared with his desire not to become embroiled in Libya (Chollet 2016, p. 105). As Samantha Power told Fred Wehrey (2018, p. 43), Obama's thinking came "from a desire to help these people, but not a desire to do what we did in Afghanistan and Iraq, to *own* this to the point that it sucks the air out of our foreign policy and our domestic agenda." Here we see the staying power of the analogies, especially the perceived failure of nation-building in Iraq and Afghanistan, that repeatedly drove Obama's thinking on foreign policy.

A limited mandate of humanitarian protection in itself is not democracy promotion. But by then Obama had already stated that Qaddafi must step down, and inside his administration there was a growing sense that the Libyan dictator was finished. Combined with the euphoria of the Arab Spring, which by then had spread to even more countries, US support for regime change in Tripoli felt inevitable. How did that translate into the intervention in Libya, whose command was taken over by NATO in April 2011? There was in fact a great deal of ambiguity about whether NATO's mandate was simply to protect civilians or actively aide the rebels in their fight against Qaddafi. Russia and China, for their part, were already arguing that NATO was pursuing regime change and criticized it sharply. Obama publicly pushed back, but already in March 2011 reports suggested that he had signed an order to provide covert assistance to the anti-Qaddafi rebels (Hosenball 2011).

At its April 2011 Ministerial Summit, NATO changed its definition of "threat to civilians" to apply exclusively to Qaddafi's armed forces, a clear implication that NATO had chosen sides (Wehrey 2018, p. 45). Yet, NATO officials also continued to insist that they were not an "air force" for the rebels. It is true that NATO as a coalition was careful not to declare support for regime change per se (Wehrey 2018, p. 45). But the reality is that individual intervening states, United States included, were clearly pursuing overt and covert policies that supported the rebels (Beaumont 2013). This, as McFaul (2018, p. 226) writes, "created the permissive conditions for regime change." The fact that intelligence assessments indicated Qaddafi was unwilling to surrender power (Clapper 2018, p. 164) further hardened views in the direction of regime change.

Signs that the United States saw the intervention as part of a larger push for a democratic transition in Libya went beyond just this. Starting in late March 2011, the Obama administration also took a number of steps suggesting that it was on the road to recognizing the Libyan opposition, which had coalesced around a "National Transitional Council" (NTC) in Benghazi. On April 5, 2011, the administration sent J. Christopher Stevens as the special envoy to the NTC (Pincus 2015). On May 13, 2011, national security adviser Donilon met with NTC chair Mahmoud Jibril and said the United States recognized the body as "a legitimate and credible interlocutor of the Libyan people," though he stopped short of recognizing it as the legitimate government (BBC 2011). On May 24, the NTC opened a diplomatic office in Washington, DC (Epstein 2011). On June 9, Secretary Clinton repeated Donilon's words about the NTC being a legitimate interlocutor, though she did not go as far as the French, who were already dealing with the NTC as the government of Libya (Reuters 2011). Then, on July 15, at an international conference on Libya in Turkey, Clinton declared that the United States had finally decided to formally recognize the NTC as the country's "legitimate authority," which in turn permitted the United States to divert $30 billion of Libyan sovereign funds that had been frozen in US banks to the Benghazi government (Lee 2011). In early July 2011, the Obama administration made one last attempt to offer Qaddafi a way out (Chollet 2016, p. 106), which the dictator did not accept. On July 19, the United States sent Qaddafi a message saying that negotiations for his removal were over and that he must yield power immediately, and it began urging other countries to recognize the NTC as well.[60] Thus, in a head-spinning period of only a few months, the United States had actively worked to overthrow a dictator using a range of diplomatic and military tools. While the military intervention's role in toppling Qaddafi might at first glance recall the 2003 Iraq invasion, the means by which regime change was accomplished in Libya were in fact quite different: Libyans themselves had asked for an intervention; the Arab League and UN Security Council had approved it; intense diplomatic pressure on Qaddafi preceded the intervention; and no ground forces were used. Qaddafi's final demise was at the hands of Libyan rebels. If the use of military force can ever play a legitimate role in democracy promotion, then the Libya intervention may be the model.

After Qaddafi's fall, however, if the desire to see a democratic transition in Libya still existed in Washington, it was no longer backed by the will or resources to meaningfully promote democracy. In its messaging to Congress and the wider public, the Obama administration had emphasized the highly "limited" nature of the Libya operation. After Qaddafi's fall, whatever attention there was to democracy would be soon overtaken by a turn to counterterrorism as the central preoccupation of US policy in Libya.

Discussion: The Role of Individuals and the US Intervention in Libya

Though the intervention opened the door to a democratic transition in Libya, its proponents argued they were acting to protect civilians in the short term and not necessarily driven by a desire to promote democracy in the longer term. Advocates of intervention thus framed their policy preferences in a way that would most likely solicit support from a reluctant president. In fact, given Obama's dim view of US attempts to bring democratic governance to Iraq by force, democracy promotion arguments would probably not have swayed the president on military action in Libya. By contrast, the idea of limited participation in an international coalition to save lives is something that *could* motivate the US president. The fact that the UN, Arab League, and Libyans themselves all asked for an intervention helped a great deal in this regard. From Obama's point of view, the Libya intervention, unlike Iraq, was not about the United States unilaterally imposing its values at the barrel of a gun. The form of intervention, furthermore, played to Obama's penchant for taking the middle ground: The United States would act, but in a self-limiting way.

We saw individuals shape the US response to the Libyan uprising in a number of ways. As Blomdahl (2016, p. 155) argues, it is unlikely that top Obama advisers such as Power and Rice would have changed their beliefs on the proper US response to the unfolding drama in Libya if they had worked for different bureaucratic actors. US ambassador to the UN Susan Rice was part of a larger State Department bureaucracy whose Near Eastern Affairs Bureau did not rally behind intervention. The rebuilding of contacts with Libya had been a long, painful process, and at least some State Department diplomats did not want to destroy all that had been accomplished since the rapprochement of the early 2000s. Instead of acting based on institutional interest or culture, Rice viewed Libya "as an opportunity to enact a new form of humanitarian intervention, one contemplated for nearly a decade" (Blomdahl 2016, pp. 151–152). As for Power, had she been driven only by the bureaucratic interests of the institution she represented, she might not have come out against her own boss, national security adviser Tom Donilon. Moreover, as an NSC staffer, she might have been more concerned about the substantial political risk to Obama of the Libya intervention.

Thus, there is a strong argument to be made that the policy preferences of both Power and Rice reflected their *individual* beliefs, which featured a career-long advocacy of humanitarian intervention, driven by the analogies and scripts derived from the Balkans and Rwanda. Political appointees unconstrained by the caution of the State and Defense Departments who viewed the Arab Spring as a sign of a new era, Rice and Power were in a position to frame US interests in Libya in a fresh way. Though the decision to intervene in Libya may have been a compromise in Obama's mind, it was not necessarily a "least common denominator" policy that emerged from interagency wrangling, as the bureaucratic politics model might predict. Instead, it reflected the influence of certain individuals—those with a preexisting ideological commitment to intervention.

Power and Rice, along with Ben Rhodes, were well-placed to influence Obama not only because of the power of their ideas but also because of their direct line to the president. Secretary of Defense Gates, for instance, while highly valued by Obama, did not enjoy this same kind of access. Obama often relied heavily upon a small informal network of close aides, of which this triumvirate was a key part, to formulate ideas and deal with the foreign policy bureaucracy. They were the kind of advisers who could linger in the Oval Office after a meeting was over and use that crucial added time with the president to make their case. The relationships Obama enjoyed with these advisers were characterized by high levels of trust. Obama elevated both Power and Rice to cabinet-level status when each took on the job of permanent representative to the UN, meaning that they could attend all NSC principals' committee meetings. He wanted to make Rice secretary of state in his second term, but the political furor that followed the 2012 Benghazi attacks made her confirmation unlikely, and she became his national security adviser instead. Rhodes had some of the best access to Obama of any foreign policy adviser.

At the same time, "the idea that the president was a passive player being shoved around by advisers" is also inaccurate, as former Obama official Derek Chollet (2016, p. 103) notes. It is true that the policy process around Libya depended much on Obama and his beliefs, personality, and leadership style, which sought multiple views on an issue and relied on careful, deliberate decisionmaking. His deep personal involvement on Libya and other Arab Spring countries at the time of the uprisings also reflected the unprecedented nature of the developments and shaped what might have otherwise been a decisionmaking process dominated by institutional actors and interests. Yet, even if we take into account the fact that ultimately the decision to intervene was Obama's alone, if we imagine a counterfactual scenario in which individuals such as Power did not exist—that is, if key advisers with privileged access to the president who held strong humanitarian intervention beliefs were not at the policymaking table as the Libyan uprising began—then it is hard to imagine that President Obama, given his reluctance to further entangle the United States in the Middle East, would have acted. That Obama's decision to intervene in Libya was, in his mind, such a close call perhaps further accentuates the ability of these individuals to sway him in one direction, as does the fact that at least two other advisers who outranked Power, Rice, and Rhodes and also enjoyed direct access to Obama—Vice President Biden and national security adviser Donilon—had opposed the intervention. Another way of looking at this is that the views of Power, Rice, and Rhodes prevailed in part because they connected to Obama's *own belief* that the United States could, in limited circumstances, use its military power to protect civilians without "owning" a conflict.

Other accounts highlight the decisive role of Secretary of State Hillary Clinton (Becker and Shane 2016). As Blomdahl (2016, p. 152) notes, Clinton's "decision to side with the intervention advocates strengthened their bargaining influence and placed additional political pressure on the president to use military force." In part this was for political reasons. Clinton had run against Obama for the nomination in 2008 and still had a large and loyal following among Democrats. This, in turn, translated into bargaining power at the policy table (Blomdahl 2016, p. 152). Clinton also provided Obama with the political cover to pursue a military option.

However, some opponents of intervention may have been working not only from personal belief, but also based on institutional interests. The Pentagon often worried about military overextension and getting involved in a conflict without clear long-term objectives, which may account for Gates's anti-intervention stance. The DoD at the time was facing spending cuts as a result of the recession, thereby constraining military operations (Blomdahl 2016, p. 152). Donilon, as mentioned earlier, wanted to protect the president from any political fallout that would inevitably follow an intervention that had gone wrong—something that national security advisers tend to do based on their institutional interests.[61]

Individuals and the Initial Push for Democracy Promotion in Bahrain

The next chapter makes the case that institutionally framed perceptions of US interests in Bahrain constrained the possibilities for democracy promotion there from the moment the 2011 uprising broke out. I argue that the presence of a major US military installation in Bahrain (US Naval Forces Central Command [NAVCENT], or the Fifth Fleet) gives the Department of Defense the motive and bargaining power with which to oppose a high degree of democracy promotion, such as incorporating conditionality into the security relationship. This helps explain why the US response to the Bahraini uprising emphasized dialogue and modest reforms rather than full democratization. And yet, the Obama administration's public statements and high-level diplomatic engagement in 2011 on issues related to greater inclusion, respect for human rights, and democratic reforms went further than any other presidential administration had attempted in the past. This needs to be explained in light of the institutional obstacles to democracy promotion, and the individual level of analysis can help.

While it would be tempting to attribute the flurry of US democracy promotion activity in Bahrain in 2011 and 2012 entirely to President Obama, that would overstate Bahrain's significance in Washington. While the country is important to the US Navy, that does not mean that Bahrain frequently, if ever, reaches the president's desk. One interviewee observed that there probably had been as many interagency meetings on Bahrain in the year after the uprising as there had been in the entire decade that preceded it.[62] Bahrain is tiny, with a population of under 700,000 citizens and another 800,000 foreign residents. Yes, the fact that there was an outbreak of protests following similar uprisings throughout the region put Bahrain on the radar screen, but the kind of high-level attention that it received in Washington in much of 2011—multiple visits by assistant secretary of state for Near Eastern affairs Jeffrey Feltman and other senior officials, in addition to mentions in presidential speeches and statements—required that a constellation of individuals in the foreign policy apparatus made a determined effort to ensure that the Bahraini struggle for democracy was not overshadowed by attention to larger countries such as Egypt. Advisers such as Power, Rice, and Rhodes may have favored a Bahrain policy that was consistent with Obama's calls for change in other Arab Spring countries, but they also had to pick their battles, and Bahrain was unlikely to be one of them, at least on a consistent basis.

Part of the task of ensuring that Bahraini voices calling for change were heard in the policy deliberations fell to determined junior and mid-level officers in the bureaucracy. These officers, in turn, were able to get the attention of Michael Posner, who was then assistant secretary of state for democracy, rights, and labor (DRL).[63] The ability of DRL assistant secretaries to successfully advance democracy and human rights issues in the interagency process depends on their relationship with other key actors in the bureaucracy. Posner was a skillful operator who understood that in order to make headway on democracy and human rights issues in a country such as Bahrain, he would have to solicit high-level support and build strong ties to the Pentagon.

Posner was able to do all of this, even before the Bahraini uprising. He got the attention of Secretary Clinton on Bahrain, making it, along with Myanmar and China, one of the handful of countries that were consistently on the human rights radar screen. After the uprising broke out, Posner built excellent working relations with then commander of the US Central Command (CENTCOM) James Mattis, and the two traveled together on several occasions to Manama to jointly push the Bahraini monarchy to institute reforms.[64] One of the areas they focused on was making the security sector, especially the police forces, more inclusive of Shia personnel. The integration of the police in Northern Ireland was used as an example. These combined State Department–DoD efforts became a critical ingredient of the Obama administration's democracy promotion measures in Bahrain following the Arab Spring. Posner and Mattis were also important advocates of setting up the Bahrain Independent Commission of Inquiry, a truth commission established by the monarchy in 2011 to investigate and report on abuses committed during the uprising.

Mattis's role as an individual was key to these democracy promotion measures. As a top military officer, he had the cover to advocate for an approach focused on human rights and democracy in a way that State officials did not. His involvement was critical to convincing individuals such as Secretary Clinton (who to some degree had accepted the argument that

Iran was behind the protests) that a US push for reform on the island was a worthy endeavor.[65] And, critically, from his perch at CENTCOM, Mattis was able to push the Fifth Fleet Command in Bahrain to fall in line with the push for a Bahraini dialogue on political reform in spite of its reluctance to put pressure on the monarchy. "The Fifth Fleet was not on board until Mattis was on board," as one former official told me.[66] Moreover, the presence of a senior US military official helped convince the Bahrainis that the Obama administration meant business. Mattis often turned to Posner for talking points prior to engagements with Bahraini military officials.

This rather improbable working relationship between a combatant commander and a senior State official responsible for human rights was based first and foremost on personality, and showed that individual will can overcome institutional divisions. It also showed that a single individual's role on democracy promotion can differ among policy areas: As we saw earlier, Mattis's fear of the Muslim Brotherhood made him a less-than-forceful democracy promotion messenger on Egypt policy in the spring of 2013. However, the downside of democracy promotion based on individual engagement is that in the US foreign policy bureaucracy, people rotate among positions. Mattis moved on from CENTCOM in March 2013 and was replaced by General Lloyd Austin. This change and the rising position of the hardliners in the Bahraini regime led to the end of the joint State Department–DRL reform push. Austin was much less likely to raise issues of democratic reform and human rights in his engagements with Bahraini officials. Furthermore, he was reluctant to join State Department human rights officials on joint engagements as his predecessor, Mattis, had done.[67]

However, the fact that DRL became a leader on Bahrain initiatives, as noted above, was also thanks to the efforts of the junior and midlevel officers in the bureau. Some of these officers were civil servants who had long worked on Bahrain and established lines of contact to the Bahraini opposition even prior to the uprising, and when the protests broke out, they were able to gather real-time information to place in the all-important briefing memos that would end up on Posner's desk.[68] "We had to convince Posner that a country like Bahrain was worth the US effort," one of the DRL officers who worked on Bahrain at the time told me.[69] The officer also noted that framing the human rights and democracy issues around stability and security was key to being effective, and the DRL officers made sure that the briefing documents and press statements they drafted did just that. In other words, the officer said, they had to "translate" the "hippy zippy human rights language" of various human rights NGOs lobbying the Obama administration to do more on Bahrain into talking points that linked democracy and human rights concerns with security.[70] Posner was then able to pass all of this up to the secretary and other top-level officials.

The junior and mid-level DRL officers also established good working relations with the State Department's Near Eastern Affairs (NEA) Gulf Desk, the nerve center of policy toward the region and one usually predisposed to status quo relations with the monarchies. "The desk is the gatekeeper," the officer who worked on Bahrain told me. "If you can't get in with the desk, if the mission did not align with the desk and the embassy's policy, you were dismissed as irrelevant."[71] At the time, the desk was full of "hard-core realists," an interviewee told me.[72] The DRL officers also had to establish a line to diplomats at the US embassy in Manama, a task that was difficult at first given their reluctance to anger the Bahraini government. Some of this work involved overcoming gender stereotypes, as those who work on the security aspects of US relationships with the Gulf tend to be men, while those who work on human rights issues are more frequently women.[73] At first, DRL was the lone voice on human rights and democracy issues in Bahrain, but over time it succeeded in getting NEA at least partially on board. As the crisis in Bahrain heated up, DRL officers covering Bahrain skipped the usual chain of command and took to emailing Posner directly with the latest developments and suggestions on a US response.[74] They also found a willing ally in Samantha Power at the NSC, and helped bring human rights–focused NGOs into the policy discussions.

Other individuals were also key to getting traction on democracy promotion in Bahrain. Even realist-leaning senior officials such as then undersecretary for political affairs Bill Burns, perhaps believing that the United States had more leverage than it did, supported the pressure on the monarchy to do more to carry out promised reforms. Tamara Wittes, a political appointee who was a deputy assistant secretary of state at the time, was also very vocal on the need to promote democracy in Bahrain. In 2014, Tom Malinowski replaced Posner at the helm of DRL, but only after a ten-month gap, which some former officials told me was harmful to the bureau's efforts. Like Samantha Power, Malinowski had an impressive background in human rights advocacy. Prior to assuming the DRL role, he had worked for Human Rights Watch in Washington, DC, putting him at the center of policy battles over human rights and US foreign policy. Malinowski's experience in Bahrain afforded him a seat at most interagency debates, and he used it to continue to press the US government and the Bahraini regime on reform in the country. At the time, part of the US security assistance package to Bahrain was still on hold owing to the monarchy's violent actions against protesters, and Malinowski argued for keeping it and tying it to progress on particular issues, especially the release of political prisoners. Malinowski also developed excellent working relations with Ambassador Anne Patterson, who by 2014 had become the assistant secretary of state for Near Eastern affairs. Patterson had not really "dived into Bahrain" when Malinowski arrived in the State Department in January 2014, but he helped convince her to do so in advance of the critical 2014 elections.⁷⁵ The partnership with Patterson, Malinowski told me, was key not only to winning bureaucratic battles within the US government, but also in applying high-level pressure on the Bahrainis since it precluded them from playing State-NEA and State-DRL off of each other. He was able to convince Patterson of the need to continue US democracy promotion in Bahrain, and she became a willing partner, traveling to Manama together with Malinowski.

Institutional factors, as Chapter 4 describes, posed a significant obstacle to the democracy promotion efforts of Malinowski and his deputy, Dafna Rand, who served in DRL from 2015 to 2017. The Pentagon consistently opposed the instrumentalization of security assistance and in general did not always reinforce the messaging of the Malinowski-Patterson duo. But Malinowski was not an ideologue. He knew how to work within the institutional constraints with which he was confronted so as to achieve larger goals. For example, in 2015 he deferred to the Pentagon and the Bahraini monarchy in devising a plan by which the regime would release some political prisoners in exchange for lifting the hold on assistance.⁷⁶

In 2016, as the Bahraini regime was ramping up the level of repression, Malinowski and others argued that it was not in the US interest to let the behavior go unpunished as it would only drive further instability on the island. As it had many times before, the interagency sat down to look at Bahrain's "wish list" of military equipment to see what could be cut. The list included a shipment of F-16 warplanes. Malinowski maintained that the planes should be among the items withheld, since fighter jets are prized possessions. Withholding them, he argued, would show the Bahrainis that the United States meant business. However, the Pentagon was opposed, and much like on Egypt, Secretary of State Kerry stood not with DRL but with his military colleagues. In a classic Obama act of splitting the difference, the president decided to leave the F-16s on the list, but delay their delivery until the Bahraini government showed progress on human rights.

Notes

1. Phone interview with former US official, April 2018.
2. Quoted in Crowley (2016).
3. Interview with former US official, Washington, DC, February 2018.
4. Muravchik (2009); Nau (2010, pp. 27–47); Drezner (2011); Walt (2014).
5. Phone interview with former US official, June 2018.
6. Obama, quoted in Goldberg (2016).
7. Obama, quoted in Zakaria (2012).
8. Interview with US official, Washington, DC, February 2018.
9. The CIA was particularly enthusiastic about Suleiman. Author interview with US official, Washington, DC, February 2018.
10. Clinton, quoted in Reuters (2011).

11. For example, since her time as first lady, Clinton maintained relations with Suzanne Mubarak, and one well-placed interviewee told me that the Egyptian first lady had sent a gift to Chelsea Clinton for the occasion of her wedding a year before. By contrast, Obama once noted that it was easier for him to withdraw US support for Mubarak because he did not have a personal relationship with the Egyptian leader. He said it would have been much harder to do that with King Abdullah of Jordan, whom he considered a friend (Rhodes 2018, p. 107).

12. Phone interview with former US official, November 2017.

13. Interview with former US official, Washington, DC, October 2018.

14. Quoted in McFaul (2018, p. 207).

15. Interview with former US official, Washington, DC, February 2018.

16. Ironically, not understanding that Obama had already given up on Mubarak, Clinton worried at the time that she had gone too far in her statement (Kirkpatrick 2018, p. 50).

17. Sanger (2012) points out that intelligence reports had been circulating in the Washington policy community suggesting that there was a group of more radical Brotherhood supporters in the Egyptian military waiting for the chance to seize power.

18. Quoted in Sanger (2012, p. 295). The "Google guy" was Wael Ghonim, who had set up a Facebook page that became a rallying point for the uprising.

19. The Obama administration also announced the launching of a Middle East Response Fund, the creation of a new US-Egyptian Enterprise Fund, relief of up to $1 billion of Egypt's debt, provision of Overseas Private Investment Corporation loan guarantees of up to $1 billion, and support of job creation through small and medium-sized enterprise development. The administration also mobilized Middle East Partnership Initiative (MEPI) funds for democracy assistance.

20. Interview with Tamara Wittes, Washington, DC, February 2018.

21. Interview with former US official, Washington, DC, February 2018.

22. I saw firsthand during my time in Egypt in the months after Mubarak's overthrow how unprepared the State Department was to put Obama's words into action. Lacking direction from Washington, many in the US Embassy continued to operate in a "business as usual" mode. The Public Affairs office remained shockingly unimaginative in its approach.

23. Interview with Egyptian political analyst, Cairo, December 2014.

24. Even then, when such contact occurred, the United States felt the need to publicly justify it and say it was not deviating from policy (Tau 2012).

25. Interview with US official, Washington, DC, February 2018.

26. Phone interview with Anne Patterson, May 2018. The strategy apparently paid off, since, as one official who worked in Cairo told me, "we had good inroads into the presidential palace under Morsi." Interview with US official, Washington, DC, February 2018.

27. Interview with former US official, Washington, DC, November 2018.

28. According to Ambassador Patterson, the election commission would have falsified the election were it not for the intervention of one member who refused to go along with the ploy. Phone interview with Anne Patterson, May 2018.

29. Phone interview with former US official, June 2018.

30. Interview with analysts, Washington, DC, February 2018.

31. Flynn, quoted in Benaim, Awad, and Katulis (2017, p. 22).

32. Kerry, quoted in Kirkpatrick (2018, p. 116).

33. Interview with former US official, Washington, DC, October 2018.

34. Interview with Ben Rhodes, Claremont, CA, April 2019.

35. Interview with former US official, Washington, DC, February 2018.
36. Ibid.
37. Hamzawy, quoted in Kirkpatrick (2018).
38. Interview with former US official, Washington, DC, November 2018.
39. Ibid.
40. Interview with former US official, New York, February 2018.
41. Ibid.
42. Kerry, quoted in Kirkpatrick (2018, p. 243).
43. Interview with former US official, Washington, DC, October 2018.
44. Undersecretary of State William Burns was dispatched to Cairo in an attempt to broker an agreement, but as one former official told me, the Emiratis were "basically there as soon as he left the room telling the Egyptians, 'don't worry about it. We've got your back. We'll make sure the U.S. comes along.'" Interview with former US official, Washington, DC, October 2018.
45. Interview with former US official, New York, February 2018.
46. Interview with former US official, Washington, DC, February 2018.
47. Interview with former US official, New York, February 2018.
48. Interview with US official, Washington, DC, February 2018.
49. Interview with former US official, Washington, DC, November 2018.
50. Ibid.
51. Interview with former US official, Washington, DC, October 2018.
52. Michael Morrell (2016, p. 180), the former CIA deputy director, argues that contrary to initial assessments about how the demise of authoritarianism would undermine the narrative of extremists, the Arab Spring in fact emboldened terrorist groups. This is a common view in the intelligence community and makes sense when seen from the perspective of failed states such as Yemen and Libya. But it makes less sense for Egypt, where terrorist attacks increased commensurate with Sisi's repression.
53. Interview with former US official, Washington, DC, October 2018.
54. Leaked emails show advisers encouraging Clinton's stance on recognizing the Islamist victory in the 2011–2012 parliamentary election, saying it would be good for her legacy. Other leaked emails show confidants encouraging Clinton to seize on her historic role in pushing for regime change in Libya.
55. Many former US officials I spoke with noted that the policy would have looked different if Clinton was still secretary in 2013 and afterward.
56. Interview with former US official, Washington, DC, October 2018.
57. Libyan ambassador Abdulrahman Mohamed Shalgham, who had defected from the regime, personally pressed for the ICC referral to be included.
58. Obama, quoted in Mason (2011).
59. In a rambling late-night speech, Seif suggested that the protests were overblown and manipulated by outside actors, and he promised to "fight to the last bullet." Nor were others in Qaddafi's inner circle willing to abandon him. Morrell (2016, p. 194) describes how Libyan intelligence chief Abdullah al-Senussi told him that Qaddafi was more important than his own family after the former CIA deputy director urged him to abandon the embattled dictator.
60. Interview with former US official, Washington, DC, February 2018.
61. But as one interviewee who worked in the White House told me, Donilon often wanted to protect the president in spite of the president. Interview with former US official, Washington, DC, October 2018.
62. Interview with former US official, Washington, DC, February 2018.
63. Phone interview with former US official, March 2018.

64. Interview with Michael Posner, New York, January 2018.
65. Phone interview with former US official, June 2018.
66. Ibid.
67. Ibid.
68. Phone interview with former US official, March 2018.
69. Ibid.
70. Ibid.
71. Ibid.
72. Ibid.
73. Ibid.
74. Ibid.
75. Phone interview with Tom Malinowski, June 2018.
76. Ibid. Malinowski told me that the Obama administration was careful not to call the plan a "deal" so as to help the more moderate forces in the monarchy save face. Ironically, the Bahraini hardliners did not even know that the prisoner release had been part of an agreement when they rearrested some of the same opposition figures months later.

4

Institutions

This chapter considers how the bureaucratic politics approach can help explain US democracy promotion policies in the years after the Arab Spring. It begins with Libya. During the period immediately following the intervention and Qaddafi's killing, the United States pursued a restrained path of democracy promotion in Libya, one whose reach was constrained by Obama's desire not to "own" the country and by Congress's refusal to bankroll the Libyan transition. However, the Obama administration's post-2012 retreat from democracy promotion in Libya was also shaped by institutions, especially the DoD and the intelligence community. The bargaining power of these actors was enhanced by the security frame through which Libya came to be viewed after the September 2012 attacks on the US diplomatic facility in Benghazi, and they actively pushed for a counterterrorism-focused agenda in interagency debates. The dominance of counterterrorism, in turn, crowded out other US policy priorities in Libya, democracy promotion included, by sidelining the individuals and institutions pushing for a broader approach. The appearance of an Islamic State affiliate in Libya in 2014 only reinforced these trends.

The chapter goes on to demonstrate how Bahrain's importance to US foreign policy has been constructed and reinforced through institutional interest. It argues that Washington policymakers' conception of US interests in Bahrain is often inseparable from the institutional interests of the Department of Defense (DoD), which often does not consider what repression in Bahrain means for long-term stability. The military's role in the formulation of US policy toward Bahrain has been so central that other institutional actors such as the State Department's Bureau of Near Eastern Affairs, successive ambassadors to Manama, and large parts of Congress largely adopted a DoD-centric perspective on Bahrain. After 2011, they only reluctantly signed on to Obama's short-lived push for reform, but over the long term advocated a return to the status quo. In fact, it is often a de facto alliance among these various institutional actors that serves as an impediment to more robust approaches to democracy promotion in Bahrain. Finally, the chapter briefly analyzes the role of the DoD and other bureaucratic actors in constraining US democracy promotion in Egypt after the 2013 coup.

Institutions and the Retreat from Democracy Promotion in Libya

Chapter 3 demonstrated that Obama's "51-49" decision to join an international intervention in 2011 in Libya was influenced by individuals who saw the 2011 Libyan uprising and Qaddafi's violent crackdown as an opportunity for the United States to use its military power to protect civilians from atrocities.[1] Institutions, by contrast, were mostly opposed to the intervention in Libya. DoD, led by Defense Secretary Robert Gates, opposed military intervention, arguing that US interests in Libya were not sufficient to justify it. The intelligence community was ambivalent about the intervention too, since it benefited from some valuable counterterrorism cooperation with Qaddafi's intelligence services in the years leading up to the Arab Spring (Morrell 2016, p. 188).[2] After 9/11, the CIA and Britain's Secret Intelligence Service (also known as MI6) had transferred al-Qaeda suspects to the Qaddafi regime (Wehrey 2018, p. 19). US and British intelligence officers visited Libyan jails to conduct interrogations or let the Libyans use torture to obtain the information (Pitter 2012). Though the United States had shown interest in a terrorist rehabilitation program championed by the Qaddafi regime in its final years, US intelligence agencies were not focused on understanding popular grievances and potential opposition in Libya. Other institutions with stakes in the Libya relationship, from State Department to the Commerce Department, were engaged in building ties to a capricious regime, in part motivated by Libya's petrodollars and the potential for lucrative contracts for US businesses. In sum, democracy promotion and human rights were not part of the US policy mix during a period in which arguably Qaddafi was most susceptible to external democratic leverage. Former CIA deputy director Michael Morrell (2016, p. 188) writes: "While we had no illusions about the harsh, authoritarian nature of the regime led [by Qaddafi], in the aftermath of 9/11 we were more than prepared to work with his regime if it would help in our efforts to prevent attacks and defeat al Qa'ida and similar organizations."

At the same time, the level of US institutional investment in the relationship with the Qaddafi regime never matched the entanglements of the Pentagon with Egypt or Bahrain. As a result, the costs of withdrawing from the existing relationship were much lower. Events in the final two years of the Qaddafi regime confirmed just how tenuous US-Libya relations were. A US diplomat was expelled for meeting with members of the Amazigh minority. US businesses operating in Libya found the operating environment to be untenable due to the unpredictable nature of the regime. The publication of tens of thousands of US diplomatic cables by Wikileaks in late 2010, some containing unflattering accounts of Qaddafi's inner circle, led to the expelling of then ambassador Gene Cretz from the country and a general deterioration in bilateral relations.

The foreign policy institutions involved in Libya policy, as noted earlier, were blind to the pent-up resentment against the regime. Wehrey (2018, p. 22) cites US embassy insiders who recall that as protests raged in Tunisia and then Egypt in 2010 and 2011, "the CIA representative, concerned with preserving his agency's counterterrorism relationship with the regime, was the most forceful in arguing against the likelihood of serious unrest." I was present at high-level briefings on Libya in February 2011, just days before the revolution broke out, at which top officials with deep knowledge of Libya emphatically predicted that Libyan youth were far too lazy and apolitical to launch a protest movement.

After the fall of the Qaddafi regime, institutions such as the DoD and CIA, in spite of their misgivings about the 2011 intervention, could not use the same kind of arguments they might use to oppose democracy promotion in autocratic allies, where they enjoyed productive access and relationships. But the potential for a high degree of democracy promotion was tempered by a president who wanted to avoid deep US entanglement in Libya. After the fall of Tripoli and the death of Qaddafi at the hands of rebels in October 2011, the Obama administration took a self-limiting approach to US democracy promotion in Libya. Wehrey (2018, p. 67) reports that as a result, Obama's reticence consigned an existing policy planning process for post-Qaddafi Libya at the NSC to irrelevance. The number of interagency meetings devoted to Libya dropped dramatically, and high-level attention devoted to Libya's transition dwindled (Wehrey 2018, p. 68). Wehrey (2018, p. 67) adds that "a mindset of 'we did our part' and 'no ownership' seemed to take hold across the NSC, enforced by Obama's chief of staff." Obama's reticence was based in part on the hope that the Europeans would play a bigger part. But Europe, rather than taking the leading role that Obama had counted on, pushed for the UN to play a central part in post-Qaddafi reconstruction. In the end, however, the UN also decided to limit its role in the new Libya, rejecting the deployment of peacekeeping troops or military observers (Wehrey 2018, p. 68).

A Light Footprint

The Obama administration's self-limiting approach to democracy promotion and other forms of engagement in post-Qaddafi Libya focused largely on democracy assistance programs. US-funded NGOs played an active role in supporting the organization and execution of the 2012 elections to the General National Congress (GNC), Libya's new democratic parliament. These elections, in which "secular" parties came out ahead of Islamists, were hailed as a success (United Nations 2012). The State Department and US Agency for International Development (USAID), through its Office of Transitional Initiatives (OTI), were at the forefront of these efforts (Boduszyński 2015, p. 742). OTI disbursed money to support local governance through civil society engagement, while State Department Middle East Partnership Initiative (MEPI) funds went to support women's and youth activist groups. Many of these groups were composed largely of urbane expatriate Libyans who had returned to the country after Qaddafi's fall, with the best of intentions but shallow roots. This and the fact that their work was often confined to the capital, Tripoli, meant that they had limited impact and legitimacy. Still, the presence of democracy assistance mechanisms such as OTI and the State Department's Conflict Stabilization Office (CSO) meant that democracy promotion was at least part of the US policy mix. While the DoD via its Africa regional command (AFRICOM) ran a small counterterrorism-force training program, the overall role of the US military was minuscule compared to the role the Pentagon played in Afghanistan and Iraq. Instead, diplomacy and diplomatic tools were front and center. Most important, while Washington policymakers certainly viewed Libya through a security lens—in no small part owing to the countless weapons on the loose in the country at the time—they also viewed it through a democratic transition frame. As Ben Fishman, who was responsible for Libya on the NSC at the time, told me, it was after all Libyans who repeatedly told US officials that democracy was their goal.[3]

Despite Obama's insistence on a minimalist role for the United States in Libya, there was a sense in 2011 and 2012 that the fact that Libya was starting from scratch might actually enable a democratic transition, as the kinds of "deep state" institutions that were similar to the ones holding back change in countries such as Egypt and Syria were already weak during Qaddafi's rule and had collapsed along with the former regime (Vandewalle 2012). Opinion polls reflected a deep reservoir of goodwill among Libyans toward the United States given its support of the revolution. Indeed, in polls taken after 2011, the majority of Libyans expressed some of the warmest feelings toward the United States ever recorded for an Arab public (Benstead and Boduszyński 2017).

In Washington, the advocates of the intervention wanted to capitalize on the US role in removing Qaddafi.[4] Hillary Clinton and Susan Rice were welcomed as liberators when they visited Libya in the wake of Qaddafi's death. Other high-profile US figures, such as Senator John McCain, also visited Libya during the successful 2012 election to show US support for the post-Qaddafi democratic transition. It was a hopeful time for Libyans, and for those in Washington who supported Libyan democratization. But the "light footprint" approach of the Obama administration had consequences that would not become fully clear until later. In the spring of 2012, the National Transitional Council (NTC), Libya's interim government, made a series of decisions that essentially legitimized the revolutionary militias rather than encouraging them to disband in favor of forming state-controlled security structures. Some Washington-based analysts, such as Fred Wehrey, saw the looming danger of the militias and attempted to alert policymakers.[5] The reconstituted US embassy in Tripoli, however, acting on what it perceived as the White House's "light footprint" policy, turned down a number of agencies that wanted to install security assistance programs in the country. Letting Libyans "own" the process effectively meant that nothing would happen (Chollet 2016, p. 110).

The NTC's decision to legitimize the militias was not made in a vacuum. In previous attempts to create centralized security forces, Libya's interim rulers faced resistance from militia commanders who refused to consider reviving any security structures or personnel connected to the former system. The rank and file of Libya's security forces had often been dissuaded from returning to work by the revolutionary fervor of the militias. Many, fearing for their lives, fled to Tunisia or Egypt (International Crisis Group 2013). But Libyans I interviewed also say that the NTC, interested in broadening its support base, acquiesced to the militias too quickly, thereby fostering an outsourcing of security that had begun during the uprising. The NTC legitimized these trends by allocating funds to localities to form their own military councils. Then minister of defense Osama al-Juwaili offered cash handouts of between $1,800 and $3,000 to get militia members to register themselves only, not their weapons (International Crisis Group 2013). This, in turn, incentivized a growing number of young men to sign up for militias. Emboldened by social prestige and funding, militias turned to both political agendas and criminal activity. As oil production came back on line in 2012, billions of dollars flowed to the militias (Wehrey 2018, p. 86) despite a lack of command and control structures over them. This directly challenged the limited efforts to create official security units operating under the Ministry of Interior, often by cobbling together what was left from the Qaddafi regime.

Thus, one of the great failures of Libya's transitional authorities was their inability to institute effective mechanisms to disarm the militias and create security forces under state control. Some Obama administration officials who worked on Libya argue that there is little the United States could have done to make a difference on this front, given the militias' power and the complete collapse of Qaddafi's already-weak security sector. However, as in other critical moments of the post–Arab Spring period, they make this assertion without having tested its veracity. There were arguably diplomatic and conditionality tools that Washington might have deployed to compel the NTC to do more on militia demobilization, or to put together an international peacekeeping force to protect critical infrastructure from colonization by the militias. Instead, as the NTC yielded the Libyan security sector to the militias, the Obama administration mostly just watched the undermining of the central state from the sidelines, unwilling to insert itself too deeply into the Libyan transition at fear of getting entangled in the way that Washington had in Iraq over the past eight years. Now, experts such as Wehrey say that this was a missed opportunity to help guide the Libyan transition on a more stable path.[6]

Libya Unravels; the United States Retreats

The attacks on the US diplomatic and CIA outposts in Benghazi on September 11, 2012, quickly shifted the shared frames through which officials viewed developments in Libya away from democratic transition and toward security and counterterrorism, which in turn put an end to the already limited focus on issues of democracy and human rights in Libya. The killing of Ambassador Stevens was an enormous loss to already limited US engagement in post-Qaddafi Libya. As Samantha Power told Fred Wehrey (2018, p. 145), it is not just that the United States lost its "eyes and ears," but that it also lost its "best advocate"—someone who, no matter how bad things got, would always suggest things the United States could do to make it better. Stevens was not a forceful advocate of democracy promotion per se, but he believed deeply that Libyans deserved better than what they had under Qaddafi. He was also optimistic about the possibilities for a new Libya and, although highly constrained in the tools he could deploy to assist the country in its transition by the Obama administration's light footprint policy, was keen on building relations with a broad array of Libyans. He understood that decades of estrangement had greatly reduced the possibilities for contact and cooperation between Libyans and Americans. The great irony and tragedy after the Benghazi attacks and Stevens's death were that US policy in Libya turned in exactly the opposite direction of what Stevens had advocated (Boduszyński 2013). While Stevens was the guy who "pushed the envelope" on US engagement in Libya, the attitude in the White House after his death became "the hell with it" (Wehrey 2018, p. 147).

The post-Benghazi shift toward a preoccupation with security and away from democracy promotion was also largely the story of the sidelining of certain institutions—notably the State Department, USAID, and their democracy promotion programs—at the expense of others such as the DoD and CIA. In the year following the death of Ambassador Stevens, the US embassy in Tripoli was massively "securitized" in countless ways: Over fifty Marines deployed from Spain to help guard the embassy compound; a team of Federal Bureau of Investigation (FBI) agents arrived to investigate the attacks; and DoD and CIA, now seeing Libya as the newest front in the war on terror, began examining ways to expand their counterterrorism operations in the country. The defense attaché's office made plans to increase its presence, and the embassy began to take on a highly militarized atmosphere. A robust, counterterrorism- and operations-focused intelligence presence overshadowed a greatly reduced State Department one. Frequent intelligence briefings on various jihadist groups meant that both the embassy's work in Tripoli and Libya-focused policymakers in Washington were increasingly occupied by counterterrorism concerns.

In addition, the focus of US foreign policy turned to bringing the perpetrators of the Benghazi attack to justice. In operational terms, this meant that the daily activities of US diplomats in Libya, who had been until then devoting at least part of their time to engagement on issues related to the fragile post-Qaddafi transition, were now sidelined by the security agencies. Bodyguard resources available at the embassy were prioritized for the FBI team. The activities of the few US diplomats who remained after the attacks (of whom I was one) were severely curtailed, while officials of other agencies had free rein. This often meant that Libyans were meeting US intelligence and military officials much more frequently than they were meeting diplomats, and predictably, these officials were not engaged on issues of political reform. When State officers did meet their Libyan counterparts, they were instructed to deliver Washington-furnished talking points focused on apprehending the perpetrators of the Benghazi attacks and broader terrorism concerns, but rarely concerns related to the post-Qaddafi transition.

In Washington, State officials, wary of weakening the feeble Libyan government any further, pushed back on DoD and CIA plans to expand counterterrorism in interagency debates, arguing that the Libyan government needed some breathing room. They succeeded for a while, but soon enough the logic of counterterrorism had taken over. Those attempting to draw attention to human rights and other drivers of extremism in Libya were marginalized. In other words, the bargaining power of the DoD and CIA had increased greatly commensurate with the heightened salience of counterterrorism in Libya. NEA Libya Desk and DRL officials found that they had to frame issues in terms of security just to get heard. DoD and CIA officials giving briefings on security in Libya dominated interagency meetings.[7] Meanwhile, ever-expanding investigations searching for the purported "truth" about Benghazi—some would say witch hunts—by

Republican members of Congress made Libya increasingly "radioactive" in the Washington policy community (Wehrey 2018, p. 146).

Standing up to a counterterrorism-focused agenda in the charged post-Benghazi climate was particularly difficult. One midlevel official who participated in interagency discussions on Libya observed the immense power the intelligence agencies wielded at these meetings. "I saw that this was the way the cookie crumbles on Libya policy," the official told me. "Obama had a great relationship with the [CIA]," this same official told me, "and CIA folks were constantly pushing him to take a tough line on Libya."[8] In my own attempts to raise political or human rights issues at the embassy level and in discussions with colleagues in Washington, I at times felt as if I was almost being accused of being unpatriotic by refusing to focus only on "catching the bad guys." With the congressional witch hunt in full force, nobody wanted to take responsibility for Libya. The Obama administration did not want to admit defeat in Libya, but it also did not want to take any risks. As diplomats in Tripoli, we often felt like pawns of the Washington paralysis, playing second or third fiddle to other agencies with terrorism-focused agendas. A former senior Libyan official later told me that the militias were emboldened by the US silence. "I tried to tell the Americans that they should pay attention to more in Libya than just terrorism," he told me, "but they were focused on one thing only."[9]

The US retreat from democracy promotion, and indeed from any kind of broader engagement, "was happening precisely when the Libya revolution started turning on itself" (Wehrey 2018, p. 145). The weak central government elected in 2012 encountered tremendous pressure from militias and was further paralyzed by internal divisions. Nascent Libyan civil society, particularly in the east, was under increasing threat from armed groups. Regional, tribal, ideological, and other kinds of divisions were deepening. The militias were becoming bolder and more entrenched, demanding privileges and access to resources and power based on their heroic role in liberating the country from Qaddafi. But it was also clear that thousands of the men profiting from militia activity had never fought in the revolution.

The Political Isolation Law

It was in this environment that a controversial piece of legislation, the so-called "Political Isolation Law" (PIL), was introduced in Libya's young parliament. It proposed to disqualify anyone who had held any of a wide range of positions in Qaddafi's state apparatus between September 1, 1969, and October 23, 2011, from participation in the new government. The proposed law, in fact, went further than the widely criticized Iraqi de-Baathification laws of the 2000s (Boduszyński and Wierda 2017). State Department officials in Tripoli and Washington were aware of the potential dangers of the law, and from the embassy's perch in Tripoli we tried our best to alert Washington of its potential dangers. However, the dominance of a security discourse made it difficult to get the attention of senior officials. Libyan legislators ultimately passed the PIL under threat from armed militias in May 2013. On May 28, 2013, Mohamed Magarief, president of the GNC and de facto head of state, was forced from his position in spite of his status as a leading dissident from Qaddafi's regime because he had briefly served it as a senior diplomat. Other prominent leaders of Libya's 2011 uprising, among them Mahmoud Jibril and Mustafa Abdel-Jalil, both of whom held senior positions in Qaddafi's regime but defected early in the revolution, were also forced out of the new government (Boduszyński and Wierda 2017). Many observers now see the PIL as the end of the experiment with representative democracy in Libya, and the beginning of the unraveling.[10]

During this period, the United States courted Prime Minister Ali Zeidan as its principal interlocutor on counterterrorism and other pressing issues. As with Morsi in Egypt, desperate for a local partner it could trust, the United States may have invested too much in Zeidan as the person to fill the power vacuum created by the external intervention and Qaddafi's overthrow. The intense focus on supporting the embattled prime minister as a counterterrorism partner and as the best hope for building a central authority in Libya led the Obama administration to lower the pressure on Zeidan's government around key human rights and democracy concerns. From the perspective of some institutional actors in the Obama administration, something resembling a central state needed to precede any discussion of democracy or human rights. US foreign policy bureaucracies tend to prefer a stable, trusted interlocutor. However, in ignoring some of the Zeidan government's policies, such as its systematic marginalization of towns and regions seen to be pro-Qaddafi, US policy was also not supporting the creation of an inclusive government. Former deputy secretary of state William Burns (2019, p. 321) summarizes the lack of post-Qaddafi US engagement in Libya as such: "Without a strong post-intervention American hand, our neat 'long game' coalition stumbled—the incapacity and irresolution of most of the Europeans painfully exposed" and "most of the Arabs reverting to self-interested form."

Limited US Reengagement: The General Protection Force Plan

After a year of relative disengagement beyond counterterrorism, by March 2013 Obama and his team were searching for a low-risk way that the United States could help stabilize Libya (Wehrey 2018, p. 156). Susan Rice, who was now the national security adviser, was willing to be much more forward-leaning on Libya than her cautious predecessor, Donilon.[11] Given the reluctance of Congress to fund anything having to do with Libya, the policy initiative would have to be low-cost as well.¹² In a March 2013 visit to Washington, then Libyan prime minister Ali Zeidan pitched White House officials on a proposal for the West to train a "General Protection Force" (GPF) to protect the Libyan government and some of its institutions. The White House responded positively, but stipulated that the Libyans would have to pay for any such initiative. The training of the GPF was designed to be a joint project of the Americans, British, Turks, Italians, French, and others. The Libyans would pay the exorbitant amount of $600 million for the American part of the training (Wehrey 2018, p. 157). However, there was immediate skepticism about the plans among DoD officials, who were concerned about how recruitment, logistics, and retention would function in Libya's chaotic atmosphere. Moreover, Libya lacked the institutions needed to support a new army, while militias controlled the bases and most arms depots (Wehrey 2018, p. 154). AFRICOM officials pointed out that the plan would take five to eight years, "yet the life span of Zeidan's government could be counted in months, if that" (Wehrey 2018, p. 155).

In another sign of the Obama administration's limited reengagement in Libya, by the summer of 2013 it had sent a new US ambassador, Deborah Jones, to Tripoli. Jones had amassed years of experience in the Arab world, including an ambassadorship in Kuwait and work as a senior diplomat in the UAE. She also brought an intense leadership style to the embassy and used the force of her personality when meeting with Libyan interlocutors. Jones was committed to both the GPF and to a broader agenda of diplomatic engagement in Libya. AFRICOM was tasked with planning for the GPF training, which was to be conducted in Bulgaria. However, using a common tactic of bureaucratic obstructionism, the AFRICOM commander "slow-rolled" the initial process, convinced that it was unworkable in the context of Libya's divided society and weak institutions (Wehrey 2018, p. 154). Defense officials at the embassy in Tripoli also opposed it, and Jones clashed with them bitterly.¹³ Part of the problem was that the Obama administration and Congress wanted Libya to foot the bill, while the Libyan government simply did not have the coherence to pay for the training despite having pledged to do so. Some of DoD's objections were borne out by training that was carried out in the UK. A group of Libyan recruits sent to the UK abandoned their base, got drunk, assaulted women in a nearby town, and as a result were sent home (Wehrey 2018, p. 158).

The US failure to enact the GPF plan also reflected a lack of will among Washington policymakers. Support for the GPF may have been a kind of indirect democracy promotion, but it was also about protecting Washington's sole interlocutor on counterterrorism in Libya, which one former official described to me as the "fourth, fifth, and sixth priority" in 2013 (after the first three, which were keeping US diplomats in Libya safe).¹⁴ Yet, it did reflect an approach to Libya that went beyond a narrow counterterrorism focus. It was also intended to provide a threshold of security to fragile government institutions as a way to give the transition a chance to succeed. However, DoD's resistance, the Congressional refusal to fund the program, and Obama's reluctance to "own" the Libya problem weakened Washington's resolve to follow through. A smaller AFRICOM effort to train a counterterrorism force went ahead in Tripoli. However, the recruits were almost exclusively from the western part of Libya, especially Zintan, thus sending a message of US favoritism to certain cities and tribes. In August 2013, their training camp was raided and pilfered by rival militias.

The Rise of Khalifa Haftar

Even as the Obama administration made a rather weak attempt to salvage the Libyan transition in 2013, the focus on counterterrorism and the corresponding importance of security institutions in policy formulation remained. In subsequent years, counterterrorism operations became a staple of US policy in Libya. On October 5, 2013, US Army Delta Force operators working with the CIA and FBI snatched a terrorism suspect, Nazih Abdul-Hamed Nabil al-Ruqai (also known by the alias Abu Anas al-Libi), from the streets of Tripoli, symbolically opening a new front in the war on terror. Al-Ruqai was wanted for his involvement in the 1998 bombings of US embassies in Tanzania and Kenya. Though the operation did not generate widespread protests against the United States, experts agree that it did weaken the Zeidan government. At the time, Zeidan was trying to co-opt the more pragmatic Islamist commanders, but their position became undermined after the al-Ruqai raid. As Wehrey told me, "the fact that Zeidan was seen as complicit in this breach of sovereignty strengthened the radicals' argument for disassociation with his government" and "contributed . . . to the marginalization of the pragmatist, pro-state Islamist commanders from the scene in Benghazi by the end of 2013 and the strengthening of the radicals."[15] This, according to Wehrey, contributed to Benghazi's dissent into violence in late 2013. Analyst David Kilcullen (2016, p. 64) ascribes direct responsibility to the raid for the fall of Zeidan's government in the spring of 2014:

> The single terrorist captured in the October 2013 Tripoli raid, Abu Anas al-Libi, was wanted for an attack fifteen years earlier, was already seriously ill with liver cancer, and died in January 2015, ten days before his trial could begin. It's hard to see how that outcome justifies the government collapse, the fragmentation of Libya and the deaths of ordinary Libyans that resulted, in part, from the raid.

Meanwhile, many ordinary Libyans had grown tired of the revolutionary militias. Activists, judges, and others were being assassinated by the dozens in Benghazi. It was a ripe time to seize on public dissatisfaction with extremists in the east of Libya and deploy policies that went beyond hunting terrorists. But there was little will to do more at top levels of the Obama administration, and on top of that US diplomacy was completely absent in eastern Libya. Ambassador Jones came up with a plan to use her UAE connections to arm embattled Libyan special forces fighting extremist militias in Benghazi, but it was turned down owing to a continuing UN arms embargo (Wehrey 2018, p. 169).

As the disorder in Libya deepened in 2014, General Khalifa Haftar, a former Qaddafi ally turned opponent who had been sidelined by rebel groups in 2011, reappeared on the scene. He announced the formation of a new armed group, the Libyan National Army (LNA), and spoke, much like Sisi in neighboring Egypt, of his duty to cleanse the nation of terrorists. Many Libyans were fearful of the Islamist militias and were attracted to Haftar's rallying cry (Anderson 2015). Haftar's militias drew on a hodgepodge of tribal and regional elements opposed to dominance of militias from the city of Misrata (Toaldo and Fitzgerald 2016). The murder of Benghazi-based civil society activists such as Salwa Bugaighis, apparently by Islamist extremists, galvanized Haftar's support base further (Daragahi 2014). Like Sisi, Haftar revered the military and appealed to segments of the population who were weary of chaos and insecurity, despite having supported the 2011 revolution. But, also like Sisi, Haftar had little patience for human rights or democracy, and he did not distinguish among various shades of Islamists. To him, they were all terrorists. Indeed, Haftar saw the kind of strongman rule and repression that Sisi had installed in Egypt as perfect for Libya.

The rise of Haftar presented the United States with a new policy quandary in Libya. The debate over how to respond divided Washington along institutional lines (Wehrey 2018, p. 180). The CIA and DoD, fixated on the growing terrorist threat in Libya, were sympathetic to the fact that Haftar's forces were pursuing "bad actors."[16] The State Department, however, had a broader agenda in Libya—political reconciliation of opposing factions as a way to build the Libyan state—and, as such, argued against showing too much favoritism for Haftar. Such policy debates were put to the test in the summer of 2014 when Misratan militias launched a surprise attack on their Zintani foes at Tripoli International Airport. The Misratans and their "Islamist" allies had suffered losses to the more "secular" groups affiliated with the National Forces Alliance in June 25, 2014, elections to a new national parliament, the House of Representatives (HoR), and declared that the contest was flawed. The Zintanis, in turn, were associated with the "secular" camp. The fighting laid waste to the airport and ultimately led to the division of Libya into two parts. The newly elected House of Representatives fled to the eastern Libyan city of Tobruk; set up a government in another eastern city, Bayda; and allied with Haftar's LNA, which was now leading an anti-Islamist campaign called "Dignity" (Karama) (Wehrey 2017).

Meanwhile, the remaining members of the General National Congress set up their own government in Tripoli and allied with an array of militias under the "Libya Dawn" (Fajr) umbrella, many of them Islamist in orientation—but not all (Glenn 2017). If anything united the Dawn militias, it was their "revolutionary" character, meaning that "they sought the complete remaking of Libya's political order and security institutions" (Wehrey 2018, p. 191). Foreign powers stepped in to back their favored proxies: the Qataris (working through Turkey and Sudan) supported Dawn, while the Emiratis (working with the Egyptians) stood behind Haftar and Dignity. In 2014, the UAE carried out air strikes against Dawn positions in Tripoli, violating the no-fly zone in effect since 2011. Obama personally admonished Gulf leaders for their meddling in Libya at a Gulf-US summit in May 2015, while the US special envoy for Libya, Jonathan Winer, tried to get all the parties supporting Libyan proxies on the same page, but (as Chapter 5 will discuss) the administration was never fully able to put an end to external backing of favored proxy militias.

In December 2014, the Tripoli-based Libyan Supreme Court ruled that the constitutional amendment giving rise to the Tobruk-based HoR was procedurally invalid, that the June 2014 election should never have happened, and consequently that the HoR was not legitimate (Pack 2015). The US response was weak and suggested that the ruling was made under pressure from the Misratan militias that now ran the city. Jason Pack (2015) argues that at this moment the United States and other Western powers might have used as a pretext to withdraw their recognition of the Tobruk-based parliament in order to force the warring parties to reach a settlement. But, as Pack (2015) observes, at that point Tobruk's attractive claims to be fighting Islamist militias made it hard for the West to be truly neutral. In fact, some in the Obama administration did want to freeze Libya's overseas assets and establish an international trusteeship as a way to cajole the warring sides to make compromises, but the plan was opposed by the White House and some European governments.[17]

Critics pointed to the Obama administration's retreat from the Middle East as one reason for the Gulf countries' increasingly aggressive stance (Wittes 2016). While the administration was only moderately engaged in Libya in 2014, at the very least it was trying to promote inclusion and dialogue among Libya's various factions, peaceful Islamists included. The State Department again began to exercise influence over Libya policy and maintained a focus on encouraging an inclusive process of political reconciliation despite the Pentagon and CIA's push to throw US weight behind Haftar and the LNA. State's efforts to promote dialogue among the various Libyan factions—a natural task for a bureaucratic actor interested in using the tools of diplomacy—was not necessarily intended as democracy promotion. Indeed, Jonathan Winer's orders were more basic: prevent Libya from becoming a chaotic failure.[18] But as a counterweight to bureaucratic actors interested mainly in counterterrorism, State's role was extremely important. Having missed important opportunities to support the transition before Libya unraveled, this was perhaps the best the White House and State Department could do in terms of democracy promotion. However, following the summer 2014 fighting in Tripoli, US diplomats in Tripoli had evacuated to Tunisia and Malta, leaving the US embassy unable to engage with Libyans directly.

By late 2014 Benghazi had devolved into all-out conflict between the Dawn and Dignity coalitions and their affiliated militias, which destroyed large parts of the city that just three years before had been the cradle of the revolution against Qaddafi. By labeling all of Benghazi's diverse revolutionary militias as Islamic radicals, Haftar had paradoxically forced them into a united front (Wehrey 2018, p. 198). But the battle lines soon became extremely complicated, cutting across tribes, regions, towns, and even families. The warring sides began to co-opt various factions in southern Libya, where tribal conflicts between Arab and Tebu were already raging. Dawn backed the Tuareg, and Dignity, the Tebu. Libya had become an immensely complex battlefield with multiple and shifting loyalties.

The Rise of the Islamic State

The Islamic State first appeared in Libya in the spring of 2014 and drew its recruits from young Libyans, some of whom had gone to fight the Assad regime in Syria and some who had previously joined other extremist groups (Wehrey 2018, p. 229). It started to consolidate authority in the eastern city of Derna, long a bastion of jihadist fighters supplying fighters to wars in Afghanistan in the 1980s and Iraq in the 2000s. Later, the Islamic State skillfully exploited tribal divisions and resentment against mistreatment by Misratan forces in the coastal city of Sirt, a former Qaddafi stronghold, and turned the city into the "caliphate's" provincial capital in Libya. Foreign fighters streamed into Derna, Sirt, and other Libyan cities and gradually co-opted other Islamist militias. By the end of 2015, the Islamic State had as many as 3,000 fighters across Libya and controlled a 155-mile stretch of territory on the country's central coast (Baroudos 2016). A decision by Benghazi-based Islamist militias to form a tactical alliance with the Islamic State against Haftar offered a tremendous propaganda boost for the self-styled strongman. As Wehrey (2018, p. 234) notes, Haftar now had "an easy pitch to the world, not just to his longtime patrons such as Egypt and the UAE, but to the United States and Europe." At least parts of the US Africa Command leadership bought the pitch at the time. Retired Army Brigadier General Don Bolduc, who headed AFRICOM's special operations forces between 2015 and 2017, has since said the United States made a mistake by not working more closely with Haftar in the fight to defeat the Islamic State's Libyan branch. "We kind of botched it at every single level, both on the [Defense Department] and the Department of State side, the U.S. policy side, on how we should have been dealing with this guy," Bolduc said. Haftar was "a very reliable guy, a guy that we could trust, a guy that we knew wasn't going to sell us out, a guy that we knew was wanting to take it to ISIS and al-Qaida and hand them their ass."[19]

Libya's collapse into two competing governments combined with the lawlessness that gave rise to the Islamic State further pushed Washington (and Europe) toward a counterterrorism-driven approach. The United States continued to observe and encourage the UN-led peace process between Dawn and Dignity, but the White House was now consumed by how to defeat the Islamic State. Once again, the institutions with the most valuable counterterrorism tools—the DoD and CIA—had the strongest bargaining power and initially argued, as they had a year earlier, that the United States should throw its weight behind Haftar since he was already fighting various jihadist groups.[20] Once they realized that Haftar refused to work with the Misratans, however, the push to support his operations was weakened. Instead, the United States turned to cooperation with the Misratans and other anti–Islamic State militias and unleashed air strikes targeting Islamic State leaders and bases (Ryan and Raghavan 2016).

Even as it vigorously pursued a counterterrorism-focused agenda in Libya, for most of 2015 the Obama administration, working through the State Department and its special envoy, continued to support the UN-sponsored political dialogue, which aimed at reaching a final settlement and establishing a unified central government (Winer 2016). The DoD, and especially AFRICOM, however, also saw the agreement as a way to establish a legitimate interlocutor with which to work on counterterrorism operations. President Obama hinted at this short-term line of thinking in his 2015 UN General Assembly speech, saying that the "Government of National Accord will serve as the legitimate entity in Libya to ensure the protection of civilians and to confront the growing threat of terrorist groups before they become more entrenched" (Obama 2015). Notably, he did not mention democracy and democratization, instead using words such as *prosperity, stability,* and *unity.* During the final push for the agreement in December 2015, in an off-the-record briefing with the press, a senior State Department official said that the settlement "allows the government to ask for help . . . we expect that they will do so, and that outsiders will then help with training and equipping in appropriate ways."[21] Secretary Kerry, however, did announce targeted sanctions against Libyan figures who "obstruct and undermine Libya's democratic transition" (Kerry 2015). Special Envoy Winer and the State Department wanted to put more pressure on Haftar to join a unity government, but the DoD and intelligence community argued for "keeping the lines open" to the LNA commander.²² Later, some officials argued for targeted sanctions against Haftar, but they also lost out to the DoD and CIA.

In December 2015, a deal—the so-called Libyan Political Agreement (LPA)—was struck among the feuding factions in Skhirat, Morocco, on a governing formula. Soon afterward, a shaky Government of National Accord (GNA) arrived in Tripoli by boat. The GNA was immediately criticized for its unwieldy institutional arrangement and its exclusion of certain groups and tribes (International Crisis Group 2016, p. 14). Moreover, the deal did not solve the problem of the Libyan Central Bank, one of post-Qaddafi Libya's only functioning institutions, which continued to pay all the warring sides, including elements who refused to sign on to the LPA. Meanwhile, Haftar and his militia and tribal supporters refused to pledge allegiance to the GNA because of its designation of the newly created Presidency Council as the supreme commander of the Libyan armed forces (International Crisis Group 2016, pp. 14–15). This prompted the Tobruk-based House of Representatives to refuse to endorse the LPA (International Crisis Group 2016, p. 21). Nor did the LPA meaningfully deal with the militia problem. As Lacher and al-Idrissi (2018, p. 3) have noted, the UN and Western powers "encouraged the GNA's Presidency Council to move to Tripoli under the protection of the militias, then tacitly supported the expansion of these militias."

Thus, the UN-backed GNA was a paralyzed entity from its genesis. Dependent on militias, it was unable to exert its authority beyond a few ministries in Tripoli. Yet, for Washington and its European allies, it was indispensable to have a partner with whom to coordinate the overarching policy goal of defeating the Islamic State, and that goal, rather than a truly sustainable and inclusive agreement, may have overwhelmed Western motivations.²³ With Haftar still refusing to cooperate with his bitter enemies, the Misratans alone took the leading role on the ground in clearing Sirt of Islamic State fighters, while the United States and Britain supported the ground effort with special forces, intelligence, and air strikes. Despite superior resources, it took the United States and its Misratan partners on the ground months to route the Islamic State fighters. Only in December 2016 were the Misratan militias able to declare victory, after losing more than 700 men. Three thousand others were injured (Wehrey 2018, p. 261).

Before the end of its second term, the Obama administration carried out several other air strikes to eliminate remaining pockets of Islamic State fighters. The US counterterrorism mission in Libya had succeeded to a degree. But Libya remained divided as ever. Haftar, supported by French special operators, the Emiratis, Russians, and Egyptians, all in violation of the LPA, continued his uncompromising campaign against Islamist militias in Benghazi, committing countless human rights abuses and killing untold numbers of civilians (Kirchgaessner and Michaelson 2017). Nevertheless, the Obama administration had come to the realization that Haftar had to be part of any future political settlement. At a meeting in Abu Dhabi in 2016, US diplomats "presented Hiftar with an offer they thought he couldn't refuse" (Wehrey 2018, p. 265). In a deal endorsed by the UAE, they proposed that Haftar be made commander in chief of the Libyan military in a new unity government that would also include greater representation from factions loyal to him. Haftar refused: He wanted to govern Libya himself and evidently thought he had the support and political capital to do so. But Haftar had shown his true colors too often and in too many ways, revealing that he was an autocrat determined to take power by force and rule through coercion. Already, he ruled the eastern part of Libya through intimidation, an intelligence apparatus staffed by Qaddafi-regime figures, and control of the media (Wehrey 2017). He dismissed elected city councils in Benghazi and other eastern cities, replacing them with military governors (Hanly 2016). Haftar justified all of these undemocratic moves by invoking his antiterrorist and anti-Islamist credentials (Wehrey 2017). And yet among his militia ranks were hardline Salafi fighters who were enforcing ultraconservative morality laws in neighborhoods they controlled, not to mention being involved in smuggling, extortion, and trafficking of migrants (Wehrey 2017).

US democracy promotion, then, had been largely overwhelmed by the logic of counterterrorism and the institutions charged with executing it. But even where the Obama administration tried to encourage the foundations of a future democratic order by pushing the Libyans toward compromise and inclusion, its efforts and leverage were thwarted by outside actors with their own agendas.

Institutions and Constrained Democracy Promotion in Bahrain

The Bahraini uprising that started on February 14, 2011, and was brutally put down a month later presented the United States with dilemmas that epitomize the tension between interests and ideals in US foreign policy. However, the case of Bahrain also provides an opportunity to critically analyze US policy choices in ways that go beyond this binary and examine how interests are perceived, formulated, and transmitted by key institutions. The DoD plays a central role in shaping Washington's policy toward Manama given its institutional interests in maintaining close ties to the Bahraini monarchy owing to the presence of a major installation, the Fifth Fleet, on Bahraini soil. Over the years this has made Bahrain mostly "untouchable" territory for robust US democracy promotion, despite multiple openings and widespread resentment among ordinary Bahrainis toward the ruling family.

Though the United States buys virtually no oil from Bahrain, it derives considerable benefits from its security relationship with the monarchy. In 2002, President George W. Bush designated Bahrain a major non-NATO ally by presidential decree. The designation "qualifies Bahrain to purchase certain US arms, receive excess defense articles (EDA), and engage in defense research cooperation with the United States for which it would not otherwise be eligible" (Katzman 2017, p. 20). For sixty-five years Bahrain has been the host for a US naval presence, a nerve center for the American presence in the Gulf, and has been seen as a crucial tool with which to contain Iran, ensure the free flow of commerce, and protect Gulf oil reserves. In 1991, the United States and Bahrain formalized their security relationship through the signing of a defense cooperation agreement (DCA), which granted US forces access to Bahraini facilities and ensured the right to pre-position material for future crises (Katzman 2010). Bahrain also hosts US Air Force planes and personnel at Shaikh Isa Air Base, and Bahraini Defense Forces (BDF) work closely with the United States on counterpiracy and counterterrorism roles (US Department of State 2018). Moreover, DoD-related defense contractors have benefited from considerable military sales to Bahrain. In the decade immediately preceding the 2011 uprising, about 85 percent of Bahrain's defense equipment was of US origin and valued in the billions of dollars (Katzman 2010).

In addition, the monarchy has directly supported a number of critical US military missions. During the 1990s, Bahrain reinforced US maritime interdiction efforts against Iraq and housed over 1,300 US military personnel supporting Operation Southern Watch. Since 2001, Bahrain has allowed US forces to fly combat missions from Shaikh Isa Air Base for Operations Enduring Freedom and Iraqi Freedom (Katzman 2010, p. 6). In 2008, the US Defense Department estimated that about 45 percent of Bahrain's forces were fully capable of integrating into a US-led coalition (Katzman 2010). Bahrain sent its own ground and air assets to the wars in Afghanistan and Iraq, and its forces have also participated in regional security initiatives promoted by the United States, such as the 2006 Proliferation Security Initiative (PSI) (Nikitin 2012, p. 12).

The Bahrainis also derive significant benefits from the military relationship with Washington. The United States has long been the kingdom's security guarantor, both as a provider of arms and a protector against regional aggressors. US funding for conventional and counterterrorism security assistance efforts from 2005 to 2010 averaged $22.78 million per year (Katzman 2010). Bahrain's dependence on the United States for its security stems both from its small size and the threats it has faced from the Islamic Republic of Iran. From the 1980s to the mid 1990s, Iran supported a Shia revolutionary movement in Bahrain, and figures associated with the

Iranian regime have claimed that Bahrain rightly belongs to Iran and that the al-Khalifa monarchy should be toppled (Alhasan 2011).

Manama has also relied on the US security partnership to balance its patron, Saudi Arabia. US military sales and training substitute for what the Saudis would otherwise provide. Moreover, in 2003 Bahrain signed a free trade agreement (FTA) with the United States, provoking a torrent of criticism in Riyadh, which claimed that the move undermined Saudi efforts to form a unified trade bloc within the Gulf Cooperation Council (Sturm and Siegfried 2005, p. 23). The fact that the United States has consistently provided support and protection to the al-Khalifa family against Iran and helped it balance Saudi Arabia should, in theory, give Washington some leverage over democracy and human rights issues in Bahrain, but such leverage has rarely been tested. This is in large part because the DoD has consistently opposed applying meaningful pressure on the al-Khalifa regime, fearful that it could backfire and threaten its facilities in Bahrain and its cooperation with the BDF.

On one hand, given Iran's history of meddling in Bahrain, it is not surprising that the al-Khalifa monarchy would be suspicious of Iran. On the other hand, the ruling family, which is Sunni, has frequently played up the Iranian threat to discredit Shia opposition movements and to justify repressive measures against the majority Shia population (most of whom are not loyal to the Iranian religious hierarchy). Bahrain's rulers, for example, make frequent accusations that the Iranian Revolutionary Guards or Lebanese Hezbollah provide material support to Shia terrorist groups, though often such claims are unsubstantiated (Knights and Levitt 2018). Since the uprisings of 2011, the Bahrainis and their GCC allies have increasingly deployed such messaging. While a number of policymakers I interviewed readily admit to the exaggerated claims of Iranian meddling, they also concede that these claims resonate with certain members of Congress and parts of the foreign policy bureaucracy that see containing Iran and protecting its Bahraini partners from the Islamic Republic as one of its most important goals in the region.[24]

It is ironic, therefore, that at least before 2011, much of the opposition to the Fifth Fleet came from hardline Sunni parliamentarians protesting US policies in Israel, Iraq, or Afghanistan rather than the marginalized Shia opposition (Wehrey 2013a, p. 10). Experts and US officials who have served in Bahrain point out that none of the Shia opposition groups were anti-base before 2011, and in fact some oppositionists believed that moving the base would only worsen the lot of the Shia as it would likely empower the hardliners.[25] They saw NAVCENT as a counterweight to both Saudi and Iranian influence. Moreover, many Shia depend on NAVCENT for employment opportunities.

Roots of Unrest

Yet, within this framework of mutual benefit in the US-Bahrain security relationship, the possibility for unrest and violence in Bahrain was rarely a topic discussed between Washington and Manama prior to 2011. US ambassadors and Fifth Fleet commanders posted to the island often expected a quiet, uneventful, family-friendly, warm-weather assignment spent playing golf and attending royal banquets. Ambassador Tom Krajeski, who served in Bahrain from 2011 until 2014, told me that he had actually at first turned Bahrain down, saying it was just "too boring." "I said, we have a great relationship," Krajeski told me, "nothing ever happens in Bahrain."[26] No senior US officials I interviewed who came to Bahrain prior to the 2011 uprising told me that they had extensively discussed the potential internal drivers of instability on the island in their Washington consultations. And yet, on so many dimensions, Bahrain was probably the Gulf monarchy most prone to instability. The rule of the Sunni al-Khalifa dynasty was long characterized by a lack of transparency, corruption, and nepotism, and as a result engendered widespread distrust among the country's 70 percent Shia population. Bahraini Shia were excluded from the security forces and other government jobs and economically marginalized (Hinnebusch 2014, p. 215). However, it would be a mistake to see Bahraini opposition politics exclusively through the prism of sectarianism. Indeed, Bahrain also has a history of leftist, class-based, and cross-sectarian opposition movements. One of the founders of the main opposition movements, al-Haq, is a Sunni leftist, despite the group's domination by Shia (Katzman 2018, p. 3). In part, this is due to class divisions, economic inequality, and corresponding anger at the royal family, which is the kingdom's largest property owner (Hinnebusch 2014, p. 215).

Hinnebusch (2014, p. 215) writes that Bahrain is the "weak spot of the GCC," a Gulf state that is "less tribal, with a bigger middle class and a 90 percent literacy rate, and with less rent with which to anesthetize opposition." Indeed, the push for political reform in Bahrain has deep roots, and periods of change and opening have often been followed by suppression of opposition activity. There is a tradition of protest in Bahrain dating back to the 1920s (Ulrichsen 2013). Opposition campaigns for more rights occurred at regular intervals in 1921–1923, 1934–1935, 1938, 1947–1948, 1953–1956, 1965, and 1975 (Ulrichsen 2013, p. 2). In the 1950s, Bahrainis created a nonsectarian social movement that openly challenged the ruler, Shaikh Salman bin Hamad Al-Khalifa, and his longstanding British adviser, Sir Charles Belgrave (Ulrichsen 2013, p. 2). In the 1990s, there were sustained protests against the government demanding political and economic reform, but the ruling al-Khalifa family stood firm, determined to maintain the status quo and avoid diluting or distributing its power (Ulrichsen 2013, p. 2).

Leadership change brought new political openings. The longstanding ruler, Salman Al-Khalifa, died unexpectedly in March 1999 and was succeeded by his son, Hamad bin Isa. Following Hamad's accession to the throne, the regime embarked on a program of reforms, including the announcement of a National Charter that would lead to parliamentary elections and ostensibly make Bahrain a constitutional monarchy. However, from the perspective of much of the opposition, such reforms hardly characterized a genuine step toward democratization. The elected Bahraini parliament lacked real power: It could not exert oversight over ministries or enact legislation, for instance. In addition, a new constitution was announced in 2002, creating an appointed upper house of parliament that basically blunted the power of the elected lower house (Wittes 2008, p. 72). Genuine power, instead, continued to reside with the monarchy, leading parts of the opposition, including the mainstream Shia opposition "society," al-Wifaq, to boycott the 2002 elections and participation in what they saw as a toothless parliament.[27] At the height of Bush's Freedom Agenda, the State Department took notice of these dynamics, and the United States used its democracy assistance tools to encourage the Shia political societies, activists, and NGOs to channel their demands through the existing parliament, however imperfect a democratic institution that was (Huber 2008). At the same time, consistent with its approach in other countries, the Bush administration focused on incremental change. Although some Shia activists participated in a regime-sponsored "dialogue," many felt that political participation got them nowhere, and regime-driven reforms were merely window dressing: The decision to participate achieved little in terms of delivering significant reforms or improvements in living conditions for the Shia, such as government jobs.

The Bahraini regime responded to the surge of activism in the late 2000s by creating a state-led "human rights council," but one stacked with loyalists. In addition, the government instituted new rules requiring all civil society activity to take place under a state umbrella, and prohibiting foreign funding (Wittes 2008, p. 72). A number of Bahraini NGOs had received support from the Middle East Partnership Initiative. In the early years of the Obama administration, State Department Bureau of Democracy, Rights, and Labor (DRL) efforts to push back on these restrictions led to a bureaucratic battle between the deputy assistant secretary responsible for MEPI funding and the US ambassador to Bahrain, Adam Ereli.[28] Ereli felt, as ambassadors in the field often do, that Washington policymakers were tone deaf to the realities of Bahrain: Namely, the activities of certain NGOs funded by Washington were angering the regime and thus making his job of engaging with the Bahrainis harder.[29]

Although al-Wifaq and most of the opposition societies decided to end their boycott and participate in the 2006 and 2010 elections, "the former were marred by allegations of systematic fraud and gerrymandering while the latter followed a heavy-handed clampdown on opposition members and human rights activists" (Ulrichsen 2013, p. 2). During the 2010 election, there were allegations of torture and other forms of repression. The Obama administration's response was timid at best. Secretary of State Clinton's public statement on the October 2010 contest spoke volumes: "I am impressed by the commitment that the government has to the democratic path that Bahrain is walking on" (Tran 2011).

By 2011, Bahraini Shia youth had grown tired of both the regime's failed promises of political and economic inclusion and the impotency of their supposed political representatives in the opposition to effect change. The outbreak of protests in Tunisia and Egypt was bound to resonate on the streets of Bahrain. The 2011 uprising in Bahrain represented the culmination of frustration that was brewing since the 2006 elections, in which the institutionalized opposition failed to deliver any meaningful reforms. This convinced a younger generation of activists that participation in the regime's "dialogue" and quasi-democratic structures such as the parliament were ultimately an exercise in futility. Yet, many US officials working on Bahrain seemed unaware of the depth of resentment, and the potential for instability.

The Uprising Breaks Out; Washington Responds

Imitating their counterparts in Tunisia and Egypt, groups of loosely organized Bahraini youths established Facebook pages calling on their followers to mobilize against the regime on February 14, 2011. At this early stage, the calls to protest were mostly nonsectarian in their messaging and goals. The demonstrations gained momentum after the killing of two protesters by Bahraini police and shifted from villages outside the capital to Manama's Pearl Roundabout. Sunni and Shia Bahrainis protested together in unprecedented numbers, chanting slogans such as "No Shiites, no Sunnis, only Bahrainis" (Slackman and Audi 2011). Others focused their anger on the prime minister of over four decades, Shaikh Khalifa bin Salman Al-Khalifa, considered an uncompromising hardliner. By contrast, the crown prince, Salman bin Hamad bin Isa Al-Khalifa, was seen as a reformer (Henderson 2014).

The protest organizers demanded political reform but refrained from directly criticizing the monarchy or calling for its overthrow. However, certain elements of the opposition ultimately did adopt the Arab Spring–wide slogan, "the people want the downfall of the regime" (*assh'ab yuridh isqat al-nidham*) (International Crisis Group 2011, pp. 1–2). Such voices played into the hands of regime hard-liners, who could argue that there was little point in negotiating with the opposition. Over time, more and more voices among the protesters shifted from "reform" to "toppling" the regime (Bassiouni et al. 2011, pp. 69–70). The monarchy reacted by sponsoring counterdemonstrations. Thousands of progovernment supporters—Salafists, Muslim Brothers, tribal elements, and others—gathered in the streets on February 21 and March 2, 2011 (Ulrichsen 2013).

The Obama administration had just backed the Egyptian uprising and called on Mubarak to depart, but there was an immediate recognition among the president's top advisers that Bahrain would necessitate a different US response given the unique military relationship and the presence of the Fifth Fleet. Likewise, in the State Department, as a top official told me, "there was just never any sense that we were going to support any movement that was going to topple the Khalifa in a violent or even a nonviolent revolution."[30] The challenge for Washington was to formulate a policy that signaled the need for reforms without jeopardizing the Fifth Fleet or access to Bahraini facilities and without further antagonizing Saudi Arabia. From the beginning of the Bahraini uprising, then, formulating a message on Bahrain was a delicate balancing act.

But Obama's inner circle also understood that they could not ignore the aspirations of the Bahraini protesters after having just validated those of protesters in Tunisia and Egypt. They were egged on by the media. "One thing about this White House," a former senior official told me, "is they were very responsive to public opinion, particularly editorials in the *Washington Post*."[31] President Obama's initial public response to the protests was a statement welcoming the king's reform plans and reaffirming the US position that Bahrain's stability could only be ensured through "respecting the universal rights of the people of Bahrain and reforms that meet the aspirations of all Bahrainis" (Obama 2011e). The White House had already moved toward greater criticism of the Bahraini monarchy than previously thought possible. Yet, from the perspective of the DoD and some NEA hands in the State Department, Obama's young White House advisers were going too far and taking a "cookie cutter" approach modeled on the response to Egypt that, they argued, could not work in the Bahraini context.[32]

Though most of the early protests were peaceful, there was also violent incitement on the part of some protesters, which the Bahraini regime then used to justify a crackdown. On February 17, 2011, security forces used rubber bullets and tear gas to clear the Pearl Roundabout. Four demonstrators were killed as police arrested over 1,600 people (including children) who had participated in or were suspected of supporting the protests (Human Rights Watch 2012c). There were reports of armed masked men, some in civilian clothes, pulling people out of their homes, cars, and workplaces and transferring them to unknown locations (Human Rights Watch 2015). Two days later, in an about-face, the regime took a more conciliatory approach and evacuated the police from Pearl Roundabout, allowing protesters to regroup. But the killings had motivated many more Bahrainis to join the protest movement, while radicalizing others. On February 25, an estimated 200,000 people participated in a prodemocracy march on the Pearl Roundabout to demand the resignation of the prime minister. Per capita, this was a turnout unprecedented in the entire Arab Spring (Lynch 2012, p. 110).

Owing to the work of individuals in the State Department and DRL (described in Chapter 3), the Obama administration had embarked on a campaign of behind-the-scenes pressure on the regime to enter into a dialogue with the opposition about their demands. In the aftermath of the February protests and the initial crackdown, a number of high-level US officials visited Bahrain, urging dialogue and signaling US displeasure with the government's response. Assistant Secretary of State for Near Eastern Affairs Jeffrey Feltman paid four visits to Manama, shuttling between the opposition and the regime to try to forge a compromise. He also conveyed US disapproval of the crackdown and the Bahraini judiciary's attempt to ban al-Wifaq. That decision was apparently overturned thanks to US pressure.[33] Defense Secretary Robert Gates, despite his realpolitik inclinations, also visited Bahrain and urged the monarchy to quickly pass meaningful reforms, telling the regime that "baby steps" were not enough (Hodge 2011).

Even then, the consensus among some senior officials was that the White House was misreading the events. One former such official told me: "You know, it was scary and it was getting scarier: burning tires, Molotov cocktails, and so on. So there was a sense that it was becoming more violent. But in the White House, it was still being perceived as kids with signs demanding their rights, so the reaction in Washington was really strong. I think, in hind sight, always the best sight, we really overreacted."[34] However, there were limits to US leverage, particularly in light of intense pressure from Saudi Arabia on the al-Khalifa family to put an end to the protests with force before they got out of hand.

The crown prince and king responded positively to US calls for dialogue with the opposition on reform. The crown prince announced a National Dialogue and called for a parliament with "full authority" and "a government that meets the will of the people" (Bassiouni et al. 2011, p. 130). King Hamad released hundreds of political prisoners and dismissed several cabinet members as a way to appease internal and external critics. But as one senior US official who worked closely with the king told me, "the king is a lovely man, but he's not always informed on things that were going on."[35] However, al-Wifaq, caught between the regime's hardening line and the radicalism of the younger protesters, chose to reject the crown prince's offer, arguing that any dialogue needed to be preceded by the resignation of the current government and elections to a new constituent assembly. Perhaps some protesters did not trust the al-Khalifa family to enact genuine political reforms, or perhaps they felt confident to adopt a more maximalist negotiating position as the protest numbers swelled. The conditions demanded by the opposition to open negotiations with the regime included the following: (1) the release of more than 90 political prisoners; (2) an investigation into protesters' deaths; (3) an end to anti-Shiite incitement in the state-run press; (4) the immediate resignation of the hard-line prime minister; and (5) the drafting of a new constitution by an elected Constituent Assembly (McEvers 2012). At the same time, the al-Wifaq leadership under Shaikh Ali Salman also tried hard to keep the protesters from going too far, imploring them to keep the roads open and confine the demonstrations to the Pearl Roundabout while staying away from the royal palace so as not to incite a violent response by the regime (Salloum 2011). Nevertheless, young demonstrators caught up in the moment decided to march on the palace, a move that was interpreted by the hard-liners as a direct provocation.

The Crackdown: Obama Responds

The Obama administration made a last-ditch effort to broker a compromise. On March 14, Feltman returned to Bahrain and tried to convince the opposition to accept the crown prince's offer. The opposition, meanwhile, demanded a new constitution, to be drafted by a popularly elected assembly. Just as it appeared that Feltman had helped the two sides reach a breakthrough, his access to the royal family was cut off (McEvers 2012):

> The agreement said that protesters would remove their barricades from streets and roads while the opposition entered a "genuine and credible" dialogue with the government. And the regime agreed to curb the activity of pro-government vigilantes, temporarily shutter state TV, release all political prisoners, and form a new government within two months. But then suddenly—at the most critical moment in the negotiations—the crown prince stopped taking Feltman's calls. So did the king.

As Kelly McEvers (2012) reports, the problem now was a deep fissure in the Bahraini ruling family:

> It's now clear that the falcons and the pigeons were pursuing two completely different solutions to the crisis. The pigeons, led by the crown prince, were pressing for reform, while the falcons, led by the prime minister and his allies in Saudi Arabia, were readying for a crackdown. The falcons plainly won out. On March 16, in a melee that left three protesters and three policemen dead, Bahraini security forces dismantled protesters' makeshift camps and scattered the demonstrators with both rubber bullets and live ammunition, effectively ending the uprising and beginning the government's strike back.

Regime hard-liners had seized on al-Wifaq's refusal to negotiate and the march on the royal palace to push for a forceful response. The al-Khalifa family had witnessed what happened in Tunisia and Egypt when protests were allowed to continue unabated. They also saw the uprising, and what they understood as US support for it, through the frame of Iraq, with the state media suggesting that a Shia takeover would destroy Bahrain.[36] Bahrain's Saudi patrons evidently had had enough, perhaps fearing that the Obama administration would not stand up for the al-Khalifa family as it had not stood up for Mubarak. On March 14, 2011, the very day Feltman left Manama, Saudi tanks and troops and a small contingent of Emirati soldiers operating under the authority of the GCC's Peninsula Shield Force rolled across the causeway into Bahrain. The crackdown, led by Bahraini security forces and hired Sunni mercenaries from countries such as Pakistan and starkly documented in the 2011 Al Jazeera English film *Shouting in the Dark,* was as brutal as any seen during the Arab Spring and resulted in nearly 100 deaths.

A state of national emergency was declared the following day, March 15. The Bahraini government began to crush any sign of dissent, detaining doctors and lawyers for treating or representing protesters, suspending opposition political societies and arresting their leaders, and detaining a founder of a major independent newspaper, *Al-Wasat,* who subsequently died in custody (Ulrichsen 2013, p. 4). The regime and its proxies also deployed tools of intimidation such as the destruction of Shiite shrines and the display of posters featuring prominent Shiite leaders with nooses around their necks. Moreover, a relentless propaganda campaign in the state media portrayed dissidents as "traitors" and incited violence against them (Ulrichsen 2013, p. 4). On March 18, in a final symbolic blow to the uprising, the regime sent bulldozers into Pearl Roundabout to destroy any vestiges of the protest movement.

The harsh crackdown immediately put US credibility on the line. Obama and his advisers were furious at the GCC intervention, apparently not being alerted by their Gulf allies that it was imminent.[37] Moreover, in May 2011 the regime launched an orchestrated attack on Ludovic Hood, the human rights officer at the US embassy (Flock 2011). These circumstances left little room for DoD to oppose a tougher response. A series of State Department and White House statements did not mince words. As Elliott Abrams (2015) writes, "the message was clear: Stability must depend on respecting the rights of the people, not on foreign troops." This public pressure on the Bahraini regime reached an apex in President Obama's May 2011 speech on the Arab Spring at the State Department, in which he said (Obama 2011b): "We have insisted both publicly and privately that mass arrests and brute force are at odds with the universal rights of Bahrain's citizens, and . . . such steps will not make legitimate calls for reform go away."

In the same speech, Obama declared that Shia "must never have their mosques destroyed in Bahrain," thereby "raising one of the most explosive aspects of how the Sunni government has attempted to suppress protests by the Shiite majority" (Abrams 2015).

In spite of being rebuffed by regime hard-liners, the administration kept up the pressure. Senior figures such as Deputy Secretary of State James Steinberg and Undersecretary of State William Burns both got involved. By May 2011 senior Obama administration officials, especially the Mattis-Posner duo described in Chapter 3, were engaged in intense diplomacy with the more moderate parts of the Bahraini regime, pushing for a negotiated solution that would allow for greater Shia representation in the security forces and other state structures.

In Manama, the US embassy was then led by a chargé d'affaires, Stephanie Williams, who took over after the departure of Ambassador Adam Ereli in January 2011. Williams worked hard to consistently deliver the Obama administration's messages on the need for reform, reconciliation, and the release of political prisoners. But she faced an uphill battle as an interim leader, especially given the rising fortunes of hard-line factions within the Bahraini regime. Moreover, the regime was counting on the acquiescence of the US military establishment, whom they tried to play off the State Department.[38] The embassy and NAVCENT command mostly spoke with one voice during this period.[39] Yet, the public messaging emanating from Washington was often inconsistent. Even as the State Department at times criticized the regime for the excessive use of force, at others it praised the monarchy for its willingness to negotiate. "We were flying by the seat of our pants in our messaging," one official who worked on Bahrain at the time told me.[40]

US engagement in the weeks after the crackdown, as well as an initial freezing of weapons sales, helped encourage the formation of the so-called Bahrain Independent Commission of Inquiry (BICI), created by a royal order on June 19, 2011. Headed by the prominent Egyptian human rights lawyer Cherif Bassiouni, BICI was tasked with determining whether the events of February and March 2011 involved violations of international human rights law and norms and to make the recommendations to remedy any abuses (Bassiouni et al. 2011, p. 1). Among other things, BICI was mandated with investigating what happened during the uprising and subsequent crackdown, including arrests, detentions, allegations of disappearances and torture, destruction of religious buildings, use of mercenaries, and instances of media harassment, dismissals, and other pressure tactics used against protesters (Bassiouni et al. 2011, pp. 3–4).

The White House had also come under substantial pressure from the Saudis and Emiratis, who feared that Obama might abandon the Khalifas as he had, in their eyes, "abandoned" Mubarak. They used every means of leverage available to them. For example, earlier in 2011, they refused to lend their support to the intervention in Libya without a guarantee that Washington would not demand far-reaching change in Bahrain that might threaten the rule of the al-Khalifa family.[41] As detailed in Chapter 5, the Saudis and Emiratis also unleashed their well-funded lobbying apparatus to convince both executive branch policymakers and members of Congress that the protesters and Bahraini opposition more generally were merely puppets of Iran.

Bahrain Beyond the Arab Spring: The US "Pause" on Weapons Sales

The state of emergency was lifted on June 1, 2011. Despite the king's announcement of a national dialogue and the formation of BICI, the implementation of reforms and accountability for the crackdown lagged, casting serious doubt on the regime's commitment to recognize the opposition's grievances. The hard-line faction in the monarchy, which included the prime minister, the head of the Royal Court, and the head of the Bahraini Defense Forces, were all major figures in this camp who blocked all attempts at a more conciliatory approach (Cockburn 2011). The disillusionment of the opposition groups only deepened.

Meanwhile, in Washington, high-level attention on Bahrain was becoming more episodic.[42] After determining that in the wake of the March 2011 crackdown US policy could not be run according to a business-as-usual logic, the question of how to operationalize democracy promotion was kicked to the bureaucracy. Discussions in interagency meetings focused on what levers the United States could use to compel reform. During Obama's September 2011 address to the UN General Assembly (UNGA), the president said that although reforms had been made, "more is required." The fact that Obama himself raised the issue at a forum such as the UN indicated that the administration had not given up on a high degree of democracy promotion in Bahrain. However, the DoD was adamantly opposed to the instrumentalization of the security relationship as a way to compel democratic reform. Nonetheless, under congressional pressure, strong advocacy from individuals in DRL (as described in Chapter 3), and buy-in from figures such as Feltman and Undersecretary of State for Political Affairs Bill Burns, in September 2011 the State Department announced publicly that the Obama administration would put a hold on $53 million in proposed US arms sales while it assessed progress by the Bahrain authorities on reforms. The hold in fact had already been agreed upon at an NSC Deputies Committee meeting in July 2011, but it was kept from the public at the time as officials agreed that quiet pressure would be more effective.

The arms hold was a significant step for the United States in the Bahrain context, given that using security conditionality as a way to push for reform had never been part of the US policy mix in Bahrain. But as with other Obama policy responses to the Arab Spring, the measures were an attempt to do something without fully committing to the issue for the long term and, critically, without applying the kind of truly tough conditionality that might have compelled the regime to undertake reforms. DoD's insistence on the centrality of the US-Bahraini security relationship and the importance of maintaining positive ties with the al-Khalifa family constrained the tools that were considered. For example, there was never any serious discussion of using conditionality such as drawing down the military presence, sanctioning members of the Bahraini regime, or downgrading relations in any way.[43] The decision to withhold crowd control equipment such as tear gas was designed to limit the symbolic damage to the US image after the crackdown. But this did not stop the regime from purchasing this same equipment from countries such as Brazil, China, and Turkey (Wehrey 2012). This fact was immediately seized upon by DoD to argue that the hold on weapons sales was a misguided policy, and that the equipment the Bahrainis were acquiring elsewhere was potentially more lethal than what the United States had sold the regime (Wehrey 2012). It was a brilliant strategy on the part of the Bahrainis too, a way to call the US bluff, since they understood how much these outside purchases would alarm the Pentagon. Bahraini embassy staff in Washington launched a campaign of lobbying to reinstate the sales, inserting themselves into the interagency process by going directly to the Pentagon in an attempt to lift the arms hold.[44]

One former official told me that the DoD had been initially deeply shocked that the United States would demand a new kind of accountability.[45] Up to that point, DoD had been accustomed to tactical accountability; for instance, ensuring that weapons and equipment sold to the Bahrainis or Egyptians were being properly used. However, the idea that the "security pipeline" to Arab allies would be subjected to democratic and human rights conditionality was deeply unsettling to the Pentagon. The large number of DoD staff charged with the day-to-day operations of the security relationship, especially the military sales program, were unhappy that they had to tell their Bahraini interlocutors that supplies were not forthcoming because of the hold, but some may have reassured their interlocutors that they could simply wait out the administration's apparent resolve.[46] As such, the institutional lines of conflict had been drawn and resembled those in Egypt after 2013: The White House and DRL were advocating well-meaning if rather weak democracy promotion in the form of limited conditionality, while the State, NEA, DoD, and CIA were arguing that conditionality, rather than having any effect, was in fact reducing channels of US influence. In the Bahraini case, however, the DoD voice was even stronger than in the case of Egypt owing to institutional interest stemming from the presence of NAVCENT.

As for the Bahraini monarchy, it was stunned and furious that its longstanding ally would reproach it at all. Ambassador Krajeski told me:

> The King reacted very strongly to [Obama's criticism at UNGA], and it was basically a shock that the Americans didn't understand that he had to do it to save his country. The King truly has a love for America, the navy and the military being the primary facets of that. He spent a year at Leavenworth, the Staff and Command College. As a young Crown Prince here, he remembers the Admirals like heroes. Every time you met him, you would have to listen to at least half an hour of admiral stories and how much he loved the admirals. So when Obama criticized him and his government so harshly, it really shocked him.[47]

Another official said:

> [Obama's remarks at UNGA] sent the Bahrainis over the edge. Because I saw the foreign minister afterwards and he was out of his mind. How could the president say that? How could the president equate the uprising against Bashar al-Assad to the Shi'a party in Bahrain protesting? The equivalency is mind-boggling and insulting to the Bahrainis.[48]

Thus, while the White House may have seen Bahrain as the sole Gulf country in which it could actually effect democratic change, the al-Khalifa monarchy saw a White House who was singling them out while endangering the bilateral security relationship.

The monarchy elected to take out its frustration with the Obama administration on Ambassador Tom Krajeski, who arrived in Manama in late 2011. Krajeski was a State Department Arabist in the archetypal mold, meaning that he did not see democracy promotion as a central mission of the diplomatic craft. One former State Department officer told me Krajeski was wary of meeting with human rights NGOs during his consultations in Washington at the risk of offending his future interlocutors in the regime.[49] In fact, Krajeski was not responsible for the pause in military sales—quite the contrary, he soon became an opponent of the policy, lobbying the White House and others from his perch in Manama to cancel it. He did not see it as effective in terms of changing Bahraini regime behavior and perceived that it was diminishing US influence in the country. His stance was a classic case of institutional and subinstitutional interest: An embassy in the field perceives that its Washington bureaucratic masters are devising policies thousands of miles away without regard to local conditions and seemingly ignorant of the way in which that policy was affecting the access and influence of diplomats on the ground.

Krajeski's position was indeed often made untenable by the Bahraini government. Even before his arrival in the country, the Bahraini press vilified Krajeski for being behind a policy of defaming the monarchy. Even though the ambassador did not personally agree with the administration's approach, he duly delivered the administration's talking points on reform and often did so in a blunt, colorful way, reflecting his personal approach. His efforts were appreciated by the Bahraini opposition figures with whom I spoke. But the US focus of democracy and human rights issues, to which the monarchy was wholly unaccustomed, enraged his Bahraini interlocutors. At one point, the Bahraini cabinet approved a parliamentary proposal to "put an end to the interference of US Ambassador Thomas Krajeski in Bahrain's internal affairs." Krajeski told me:

> I was accused of personally wielding the levers of power behind the scenes and that it was our intention to replace the al-Khalifa with a Parliamentary government and of course, after that, a government dominated by the Shi'a and Iran. There were even press articles suggesting that somehow I was involved in masterminding an Iranian-American-Israeli conspiracy to do this.[50]

And yet, Krajeski also conceded that US criticism and pressure in 2011 probably helped convince the monarchy to allow the BICI investigation and report to go forward, and to endorse its findings:

> I also think that part of this was the king learning what had happened—and it's not just the king, but other folks too, didn't fully realize what was happening on the street and they don't fully realize how violently their beloved police, military, security forces had just crushed this movement. So, as it became known to him, I do think he was genuinely appalled at what had happened and was looking for a way to recover. But an equally large motivator was a fear that the relationship with the United States was going to suffer.[51]

The Release of the BICI Report

In November 2011, the BICI released its highly anticipated report on the regime's conduct during the uprising. For a Bahraini government-commissioned report, it was surprisingly critical, citing the excessive use of force, illegal detentions, denial of medical care, and torture and implicating the BDF in the killings of protesters (Bassiouni et al. 2011, pp. 415–422). The BICI also produced twenty-six recommendations designed to serve as a roadmap for reform (Bassiouni 2011, pp. 422–426). For the Pentagon and other bureaucratic actors, the release of the BICI report was seen as a green light to return to business as usual with the al-Khalifa family. Its existence was proof that the monarchy was sincere in its stated desire to implement democratic reforms. Or, as one former official told me, perhaps it was an easy "out" for those who were uncomfortable with the policy of pressuring the regime. The same official, who worked closely on Bahrain, observed: "In the bureaucracy, it became a common understanding that BICI was an act of redemption by the king, an effort to look at what had happened. It was his way of kind of turning around the response from pure military force to something that was more consultative and at least accommodating in the smallest possible way."[52] An analyst described the BICI report as a "face-saving" measure for everyone, Bahrainis and Americans alike.[53]

It is true that the acknowledgment of the report's findings by the monarchy was a significant step—no other Gulf country had taken responsibility for state-sponsored abuses in this way. And it gave DRL Assistant Secretary Posner and others a potentially powerful tool with which to push for concrete reforms. Yet, just as the report may have been a "feel good" measure for certain parts of the US government, so was it also a means for the monarchy to placate its international critics, the United States included, without actually promoting real accountability for abuses and undertaking the kinds of reforms that would meaningfully integrate Shia Bahrainis into the state. Indeed, this view has been borne out in the years since the publication of the BICI report. While the Bahraini government has repeatedly claimed that it is implementing the mandated reforms, international NGOs, Bahraini human rights activists, and the State Department's Human Rights Reports all beg to differ (US Department of State 2019a). Some security sector reforms, such as prohibiting torture and creating a code of conduct for the police based on international best practices, were implemented. But other recommendations were routinely ignored. In 2012, the commission's chairman, Bassiouni, delivered a harsh critique of the regime's failure to undertake political or social reform (Human Rights Watch 2017).

Arms Sales Resume

By the end of 2011, and before any progress had been shown on the BICI recommendations, DoD was lobbying furiously to reinstate the military sales. Defense suppliers were also pushing the administration to change course. Officials from all agencies agreed upon the need to address Shia grievances, but DoD in particular argued that it was important to repair the relationship with the al-Khalifa family first. "When we get back to the pre-2011 relationship, we can quietly push them for more" was a line used by DoD officials at interagency meetings.[54] On January 27, 2012, a State Department press release announced that a part of the planned sale would proceed, referring to a clause in the October 2011 legislation that allowed military equipment under $1 million to be sold without congressional approval. The statement cited "initial steps" by the Bahraini government to implement the BICI's recommendations and stated that the equipment, reportedly nonlethal spare parts, would be used to "reinforce reforms in Bahrain" (Human Rights Watch 2012b). The State Department emphasized, however, that the release would not include Humvees and munitions used by Ministry of Interior forces for crowd control—the strategy, pushed by DRL and those responsible for human rights in the NSC, was to maintain a hold on 6–7 percent of the sales as a way to maintain leverage over the regime. An official who helped devise this strategy told me that the thinking was that since the initial pause had served as a catalyst for BICI, a continuing hold would perhaps help spur further and more meaningful reforms.[55] However, the decision to release any arms at all was immediately criticized by some members of Congress, such as Senator Patrick Leahy of Vermont, a powerful member of the Appropriations Committee, who had been part of a group calling for increasing scrutiny of the US-Bahrain security relationship in light of the human rights situation on the island. Some voices in Congress even called for an outright halt to all US arms sales, while others called for relocating the Fifth Fleet either to Qatar or the UAE (Pecquet 2015). On the other side of the debate, there were those who saw the continuing hold of a small percentage of the sales as the policy of a negligible group of human rights "crazies" who were willing to risk a vital security relationship just to make a point.[56]

An announcement to further restore US arms sales was made in March 2012, prior to the visit of the proreform crown prince to Washington that May. The plan was to shore up the crown prince's stature (Rogin 2012a). "We wanted to empower this guy," one former official told me, "we thought he would go back and be able to say 'we got the arms' and maybe make some changes."[57] However, by this point, the crown prince had already been marginalized in the Bahraini power structure. Moreover, as some analysts told me, rather than strengthening the reformers, the hard-line faction of the monarchy may have interpreted the renewal as a "win" and a resumption of the status quo in US-Bahrain relations and thus felt empowered to pursue further repression of the opposition. In fact, there is evidence that the king and crown prince were not even calling the shots by early 2012.[58]

The Obama administration had failed to link the arms release to progress on the implementation of BICI-mandated reforms. State Department press releases spoke of "encouraging signs," only to later say the opposite in yearly human rights reports. This ambiguity reflected a tug of war between State NEA and DoD on one side and State DRL and certain White House elements on the other. The prodemocracy camp in the NSC also continued to argue that the hold should not be lifted.[59] But at the end of the day, the DoD view, which continually emphasized the centrality and irreplaceability of the Fifth Fleet and the US-Bahrain security relationship, won the day. Moreover, the lack of clearly articulated conditions for resuming the arms sales created confusion among the US diplomats who were charged with implementing the administration's policy. While the diplomats tried to use implementation of the BICI recommendations to press their Bahraini counterparts on specific reforms, there was never a clear sense of what reforms were tied to what conditions. That, one official told me, "got lost in the interagency process."[60]

Indeed, if there was ever a critical time to implement a high degree of democracy promotion, such as conditionality, the period immediately following the issuing of the BICI report may have been such a moment. But the half-hearted weapons pause followed by a restoration of a large part of the sales may have been interpreted by hard-liners in the regime as carte blanche to redouble their campaign of repression against the opposition, clamping down on dissent, instituting media censorship, and arresting Shia clerics (Wehrey 2012). High-level officials told me that the king was sincere about reforms and that he wanted to turn his kingdom into a constitutional monarchy, in the mold of King Juan Carlos of Spain. One official who dealt with the king told me:

> He wanted to be Juan Carlos, but I don't think he understood that Juan Carlos had almost zero political power in Spain and that that's the road he was on. At one point he did say to me, "You know, I want to make sure that I have a country that I can turn over to my son." And I said, "Well, that's not exactly a ringing endorsement of parliamentary rule here."[61]

The king and crown prince may have been attempting to use the BICI report as a roadmap for reform, but the hard-line faction of the regime—which controls the instruments of censorship and repression—was resolute in its determination to silence the opposition. The parliament, lacking a real opposition, stepped up its criticism of Shia clerics. Prominent Bahraini dissidents such as Nabeel Rajab and Zaynab al-Khawaja were arrested for commentary on social media and other expressions of dissent. Human rights NGOs reported ongoing abuses by security forces (Human Rights Watch 2012c).

The resumption of US arms sales was a major disappointment for the leadership of al-Wifaq.[62] They felt that the pause would have over time compelled the regime to deliver reforms and that Washington had prematurely caved under the pressure from the Saudis, DoD, State Department, and other actors. From the perspective of the Bahraini opposition, it confirmed that the Obama administration was willing to use only large carrots and small sticks to promote democracy. Bahraini prodemocracy activists argued that the United States should put a pause on all training and assistance programs for the Bahraini military until steps were taken to integrate Shia into the security forces. In fact, this is what the Mattis-Posner engagement had tried and failed to achieve a year before. Other opposition activists told me that private Pentagon pressure simply would not work in the case of the Bahraini monarchy and that real shifts in the direction of reform have occurred only when the high-level US officials have publicly named and shamed the regime.[63] This was the view of State DRL and some White House advisers as well, but it was not shared by any of the Pentagon and State NEA officials I interviewed. In any case, the partial resumption in sales, one analyst told me, signaled that the administration was "moving the goalpost" of conditionality, thereby diminishing US leverage. The message to the Bahrainis, this analyst said, was: "If you wait long enough, the pressure will go away."[64]

The regime's uncompromising approach led the moderate opposition elements to lose ground to the more radical February 14 Youth Movement and other rejectionists in the opposition, who subsequently began to adopt a more anti-American stance. Among these tensions, discussion of a political union with Saudi Arabia further strengthened the hard-line faction (Khorrami Assl 2012). The group declared a "Week of Resisting American Arms Sales," on its Facebook page, which was emblazoned with blood-drenched shotgun shells stamped "U.S.A" (Wehrey 2012).

The End of the Arab Spring in Bahrain, 2013–2016

The situation in Bahrain moved further away from the democratic aspirations of the 2011 uprising in subsequent years. The regime pulled out all the stops to crush the opposition: revoking the citizenship of prominent Shia activists for "undermining state security" (Aboudi 2016); banning demonstrations of any size and violently dispersing any protests (Human Rights Watch 2012a); upholding lengthy prison sentences given to teachers and medical professionals for expressing their political views (Amnesty International 2012); clamping down on independent media and civil society (Dooley 2017); and in a particularly sinister policy reported by Ala'a Shehabi (2014), "nurturing and nourishing extremist groups and their sectarian ideology to counter the so-called 'Shiite threat' posed by the pro-democracy uprising."

In 2014, al-Wifaq made the fateful decision to boycott parliamentary elections, a move that the United States strongly opposed. Ambassador Krajeski told me he had spent hours drinking tea with al-Wifaq leader Ali Salman trying to convince him not to proceed with the boycott.[65] As recounted in Chapter 3, DRL Assistant Secretary Tom Malinowski (who replaced Posner in 2014), NEA Assistant Secretary Anne Patterson, and others had tried to do the same. And some of Salman's deputies also wanted to participate. But as during the uprising, Salman and al-Wifaq were caught between an impulse to compromise and the demands of a radicalized, younger group of activists. Many of its members were in jail. The voting districts had been gerrymandered in favor of Sunnis. There was a strong sense that the playing field was so uneven as to make the election meaningless. The feeling among al-Wifaq leaders was that they could not return to their supporters empty-handed.⁶⁶ But the United States saw al-Wifaq participation as crucial to its efforts, and the decision to boycott was seen by many as squandering the last, best chance for representation. In Malinowski's view, the boycott only empowered the hard-liners in the regime, giving them the ability to argue that the Shia had opted out of political participation and were disloyal. Moreover, Malinowski argues, it lessened US leverage—had al-Wifaq participated, it would have invested the United States in the process. "I understood where Ali Salman stood emotionally," said Malinowski, "but I thought he made the wrong decision."⁶⁷ Two years later, al-Wifaq was banned, dissolved, and its assets were seized by the state, while Ali Salman, considered a moderate leader in al-Wifaq, was thrown in jail and given a life sentence. Just as the Bahraini regime had several distinct factions, so did the opposition, but the monarchy lumped them all together.

Meanwhile, the Obama administration's democracy promotion agenda in Bahrain began to decline, until it was a shadow of its former self by the end of Obama's presidency. Only a year after Obama's bold and unprecedented criticism of the al-Khalifa monarchy in his speech before the UN General Assembly, the president didn't even mention Bahrain in his speech before the body in 2012. Throughout the year 2012, the White House issued only one rather weak statement regarding Bahrain, and it came from the spokesperson rather than Obama himself (Carney 2012). In 2013, the Navy announced that it was adding five more coastal patrol ships to the NAVCENT fleet (Abrams 2015). In 2014, the Obama administration proceeded with a $500 million expansion of the US presence in Bahrain. Neither of these enhancements in the security relationship had any democratic conditionality attached to it, nor was there any real effort to engage the Saudis to push their Bahraini allies to implement reform.⁶⁸ By 2015 and 2016, talking points on democracy and human rights were barely making it into the briefing documents of senior officials. As one senior State Department official told me, military officials meeting with their Bahraini counterparts rarely raised human rights, democracy, or reconciliation issues.⁶⁹

Yet despite, or perhaps because of, the administration's abandonment of a high degree of democracy promotion in Bahrain, the regime felt emboldened enough so as to make an unprecedented and extraordinary move for an ostensibly close US ally: In July 2014, the Bahraini government expelled DRL Assistant Secretary Malinowski from the country for meeting with members of the country's political opposition before seeing government ministers. Malinowski had arrived a day earlier than expected, and Ali Salman had invited him to an evening iftar to break the Ramadan fast. In fact, the purpose of Malinowski's trip was to deliver the final push on reform and to placate congressional critics before announcing a lifting of sanctions. An additional goal was to make yet another effort to convince

Salman not to boycott the upcoming elections. But the images of Malinowski happily dining with Salman were too much for the regime, while the expulsion of a senior US official was too much for even the committed realists in Washington. Secretary of State John Kerry called Bahrain's foreign minister and conveyed that the expulsion was "unacceptable." Eighteen members of Congress signed a letter to King Hamad calling on the king to invite Malinowski back. Ultimately, Bahrain reversed its position and both Malinowski and Assistant Secretary Patterson visited Bahrain later that year. But the diplomatic tussle, while provoking a period of US outrage, did little to halt the rapidly narrowing political space for free expression and dissent in Bahrain.

The War on the Islamic State and US Democracy Promotion in Bahrain

The rise of the Islamic State in 2014 and the formation of a US-led anti-ISIL coalition contributed to the decline of US democracy promotion in Bahrain. A former senior White House official told me that at some point "Obama came to the conclusion that his legacy would be defined by how he handled ISIL."[70] The imperatives of the war on ISIL in Iraq and then Syria gave DoD officials added weight in interagency debates, especially since the Gulf bases became critical to the anti-ISIL campaign.[71] They used that weight to argue that, if the administration was serious about "degrading and defeating" the terror outfit—one of its leading foreign policy goals—then, as an interviewee told me, the White House would have to lay off the already limited pressure it was putting on the Bahraini monarchy.[72]

State's Bureau of Democracy, Rights, and Labor, meanwhile, was increasingly sidelined, and senior NEA officials began pushing back on its democracy and human rights–focused additions to briefing documents on Bahrain. The DoD began to play up the contributions of the Bahrain Defense Forces to the anti-ISIL coalition, even though Bahraini pilots had carried out only a handful of air strikes. As the campaign against ISIL gained strength, Fifth Fleet–based carriers and Shaikh Isa Air Base were used to launch strikes. "It was hard to keep talking to [the commander of the BDF] about Shia integration and human rights issues when you wanted him to help on the ISIL thing," a senior official told me.[73] The same official said: "DoD people sat down with the President of the United States and his senior people and said, 'We're fighting a war. It's a really hard fight and this is a key element. The naval support activity in Bahrain is a critically important element. We need to make nice with the Bahrainis.'"[74]

Other officials, however, insist that the Bahraini assistance on ISIL was "greatly exaggerated."[75] A diplomat who worked on Bahraini issues told me that by 2014 there was a "bifurcated" message coming from DoD and the

State Department. While State officials would half-heartedly raise the BICI recommendations, DoD officials would not even mention them. Human rights were rarely, if ever, raised by visiting Pentagon officials, including the secretary of defense. A DoD official who worked on Bahrain told me that DoD and the State Department operate on "parallel but separate tracks." DoD people stick to their mission, the official noted: "We protect the Gulf. We make sure the waterways remain open, irrespective of other political realities."[76] By 2016, this same official told me, raising the BICI was "moot, like beating a dead horse." Some State officials tried to keep the BICI report alive, and the department still wrote its congressionally mandated yearly human rights reports, duly noting how little progress had been made on BICI, but these conclusions were never amplified, or used for leverage in any way.[77]

US Democracy Promotion Disappears in Bahrain

As the campaign to degrade and defeat anti-ISIL raged, the US push for much-needed reform in Bahrain had been significantly dialed back. Bahrain was the daily scene of protests met with violent responses and a growing sense among many Shia youth that they had little to no future in a Bahraini state led by the al-Khalifa family. Nevertheless, the United States fully reinstated arms sales to Bahrain in June 2015, despite continuing and credible reports of torture and other abuses and little movement on implementing the recommendations of BICI or those of a UN commission. The State Department issued a press release saying the following:

> While we do not think that the human rights situation in Bahrain is adequate—as our statement on the recent sentencing of Sheikh Ali Salman and the content of our recently-released Human Rights Report make clear—we believe it is important to recognize that the government of Bahrain has made some meaningful progress on human rights reforms and reconciliation. (US Department of State 2015)

The State Department continued to issue statements urging reform and political inclusion of the opposition. As described in Chapter 3, DRL Assistant Secretary Malinowski in partnership with NEA Assistant Secretary Patterson led the charge to ensure that US democracy promotion in Bahrain did not completely fall by the wayside. When al-Wifaq was dissolved by court order in July 2016, Secretary of State Kerry issued a strong-worded statement (Katzman 2018):

> This ruling is the latest in a series of disconcerting steps in Bahrain. . . . These actions are inconsistent with US interests and strain our partnership with Bahrain. . . . We call on the Government of Bahrain to reverse these and other recent measures, return urgently to the path of reconciliation, and work collectively to address the aspirations of all Bahrainis.

The administration again put a hold on some military sales in 2016, including attaching progress on human rights issues to the sale of nineteen F-16 fighter jets at a cost of $3 billion. But it did not take those warplanes off the list entirely, as Malinowski and others had advocated. One member of the Bahraini opposition told me that Kerry's engagement was too little, too late. "If Kerry had been engaged in 2014, when the crown prince wanted to talk to the opposition, he could have made a difference by pressuring the hard-liners," the interviewee said, emphasizing the importance of high-level US engagement on democracy promotion.[78]

Ambassador Bill Roebuck, who replaced Krajeski in January 2015, continued to reach out to the opposition (at least that part of it that was not in jail). Unlike his predecessor, Roebuck was soft-spoken and cautious. The White House may have sent him deliberately given the bad feelings toward Krajeski. Roebuck also was unwilling to push as hard on democracy and human rights as his predecessor, perhaps reflecting prevailing sentiments in the administration.[79] Instead, it was Congress who again stepped in and attempted to fill the democracy promotion void. A bipartisan group of senators led by Ron Wyden and Marco Rubio attempted in 2015 to pass a bill that would have required the State Department to certify Bahraini compliance with all twenty-six recommendations of the BICI report, but it failed to generate sufficient support. In any case, high-level US engagement with Bahraini leaders was never discontinued, and no sanctions were imposed on any Bahraini officials. US military cooperation with Bahrain continued without interruption, despite the "pause" in sales.

While one can argue about whether NAVCENT is truly "irreplaceable," as the DoD claims, even the existence of plans to move the base might have given the United States greater leverage over Bahraini reforms (Abrams 2015). But when asked if there was a "Plan B" for NAVCENT, Admiral Mark Fox, who commanded the Fifth Fleet at the time, told a congressional committee that "Option B is making sure Option A doesn't fail," which is another way of saying, as one official told me, "We're not going to talk about it." "I cannot imagine any scenario, short of a war with Iran, under which NAVCENT would move out of Bahrain," a former senior DoD official who had worked on Bahrain told me.[80] A former State Department official noted other motivations for keeping the Fifth Fleet in Bahrain:

> Bahrain was special not only because Bahrain is special, it was one of the few places in the Middle East where we could assign military officers and other personnel for one- or two-year assignments with their families and they lived on the local market, they didn't live on the base. The enlisted people lived on the base in barracks, but there were many officers who lived in the neighborhoods right near where the base is.[81]

Knowing this, why would the hard-liners in the Bahraini regime act any differently?

Discussion

The case of Bahrain demonstrates how interests framed by powerful institutions around the indispensability of a reliable ally and longstanding security relationship constrain US democracy promotion. The Obama administration encountered a number of critical moments for democracy promotion in Bahrain around the Arab Spring, among them the initial 2011 uprising and the issuing of the BICI report in November 2011. These moments took shape in a country that already had in place some of the building blocks of a democracy, including a moderate, well-organized opposition. As the Bahraini regime moved in a repressive direction, the Obama administration's response was more bark and less bite, conveying in so many ways to the hard-liners in the Bahraini regime that business as usual would continue. Yet, that there was even a bark in US policy was a testament to the individuals, starting with Obama himself, who believed that the Bahraini uprising could and should be seen through an Arab Spring framework—that is, a call for greater freedoms—rather than through a sectarian lens or exclusively in terms of short-term US interests. Thus, in 2011 and to a much lesser extent in 2012, there was a high degree of US democracy promotion in Bahrain, including the assistance pause and Obama's criticism of the regime in two high-profile speeches. But Bahrain was not Egypt or even Libya (where the United States was participating in a military intervention), and after those speeches, the debates over Bahrain policy moved to the bureaucracy, where the DoD was the kingmaker. Bahrain was not a priority for either of Obama's secretaries of state, Clinton or Kerry. Clinton worried about the Iranian angle, while Kerry mostly saw Bahrain through a broader regional context, focusing on issues such as Iran and Israeli-Palestinian peace. While he got involved at key moments in the cases of individual political prisoners and occasionally issued statements about the need for reform, Kerry was not interested in pursuing a broader and more consistent strategy of democracy promotion in Bahrain. As on Egypt after 2013, Kerry and the State Department often lined up with DoD on Bahrain policy.[82]

The DoD's continuing emphasis on the security partnership as a goal in itself fostered short-term thinking about US interests in Bahrain. The Bahraini hard-liners were well aware of the DoD stance and exploited it to their advantage. As one former senior US official noted: "The Bahrainis had a closer relationship with the admiral than [Ambassador Krajeski] because they felt the admiral understood them better and stayed in his lane. And didn't make their life difficult. So in that case I think they froze out the ambassador and cozied up to the admiral."[83] In interagency debates, DoD officials stressed the irreplaceability of NAVCENT and the need to maintain access so as to ensure cooperation. The Pentagon used other arguments to support its position, including the possibility that cutting off arms transfers or threatening to relocate the Fifth Fleet could lead the hard-liners in the regime toward even greater entrenchment and repression. This is one interpretation of the rise of the hard-liners after the first year of stepped-up US public criticism and the pause on weapons sales. Nevertheless, some of the worst repression came after the aid was mostly restored in 2015, just as another wave of repression had followed the partial reinstatement of arms sales in 2012. Moreover, in addition to making flows of security assistance conditional on changes in regime behavior, there are other democracy promotion tools available: from sanctioning the individuals who called in the hired foreign thugs to beat protesters to more closely linking specific reforms to continued assistance. But the Pentagon opposed these as well.

The fact that DoD officers working on Bahrain issues in Washington rotate frequently tends to foster myopic thinking. As an official working on Bahrain told me, "to understand the effects of leverage you have to talk about the past, but [the Pentagon officials] have recently rotated in and don't think about that past."[84] Or, as another official pointed out, one- to three-year assignments do not encourage long-term thinking about risks and deeper drivers of instability: Why would they risk their next evaluation by making waves and predicting an event that is unlikely to happen on their watch, or advocate measures that are harmful to the operational relationship in the near term?[85] One may infer that this is why DoD analysts failed to predict the Bahraini uprising in the first place.

The Bahraini uprising and the government's heavy-handed crackdown could have served as a sign that both Bahrain and the US-Bahraini relationship had entered a new era in which the status quo was unsustainable. As DRL Assistant Secretary Tom Malinowski told me, he often argued in interagency meetings, "It is not in our interest to have [Bahrain] in a permanent state of crisis, a permanent clampdown on the majority of population." For Malinowski, that was not a recipe for stability.[86] In addition to the damage to US credibility that stems from conducting business as usual in the face of repression, an argument can be made that the longer reforms are delayed in Bahrain, the harder it will be to ensure security for US naval assets. In 2013, a naval officer, Commander Rich McDaniel, wrote a think tank report arguing that in spite of Bahrain's "immense strategic and operational value" for the United States, the situation there "could deteriorate very rapidly, leaving the US without a key maritime hub in the Middle East" (McDaniel 2013). He argued for a contingency plan to move the base, but also emphasized that stability will depend on the Bahraini government's implementation of reform, noting that "the United States has a moral obligation to strongly encourage democratic reforms . . . particularly where we have such an influential relationship and significant investment" (McDaniel 2013). Some NSC officials in fact have argued that contingency plans were needed both as a form of pressure and to prepare for possible instability on the island, but this was a minority view.[87]

Yet, a longer-term, strategic view of US interests in Bahrain was crowded out of the policy debates by the end of the Obama administration. "There is no long-term view of Bahrain in the military establishment," one official who worked on Bahrain told me.[88] Instead, as another official stated, it was all about short-term security, especially after ISIL:

> Why is this place, Bahrain, important to us, the United States, and our security? Because God knows, since 9/11 especially, but even before that, security, security, security, security—it just dominates the foreign policy debate. So if our number one priority in the world is the security of the United States and its population, then our number one priority in Bahrain is that Navy base.[89]

But the same official said the following about the "habits of thinking" in DoD that prevent top military officials from thinking out of the box about security relationships:

> What I find so fascinating is that these tropes recur in case after case: Pakistan, Egypt, Saudi Arabia, Bahrain. You see it over and over again. It's "we need them more than they need us." It's "the relationship is asymmetric but to our advantage," which is crazy! We are the global freaking hegemon. The idea that we don't have options is insane. When we decided to build that base in Bahrain, that was a decision with consequences that constrain us if we allow them to.[90]

Even when and where longer-term understandings of US interests in Bahrain were articulated, they were never translated into a high degree of democracy promotion that might have changed the regime's behavior. The principled use of conditionality, Tom Malinowski told me, "would have been a very effective tool." Instead, he said, "we gave [the military equipment] away too easily." The Bahrainis, Malinowski said, "worked hard to convince us that they were making progress" and were adept at "buying time." In the end, "they were either not sincere, or the hard-line faction had completely taken over."[91]

The ironic thing about the Obama administration's half-hearted use of conditionality is that it succeeded in angering both the regime and the opposition, all while compelling few democratic reforms. Fears about diminishing the access and cooperation needed to maintain the Fifth Fleet repeatedly limited the use of conditionality. In NSC debates, DoD framed the complete resumption of US arms sales to Bahrain as central to US interests because they constituted a necessary expression of loyalty to a Gulf ally who had hosted a US naval presence for sixty years. An official who supported democracy promotion in Bahrain told me that Pentagon officials often deployed the argument that the "military relationship was deteriorating" because of the continuing hold on certain arms sales and criticism of the monarchy. This official noted that she was "unimpressed" by such arguments because the Pentagon representatives often did not have evidence to back them up—instead, they were just channeling what their Bahraini counterparts told them (and indeed had an interest in telling them so as to reduce the pressure).⁹² DoD also reiterated through multiple channels that Bahraini leaders need "sustained reassurance" that the United States stands by them. NEA, now run by a new cadre of leaders, was consumed by Saudi and Emirati pressure and the appearance of ISIL. They were also keen to engage Iran in the run-up to the JCPOA negotiations.

The fear of Iran that often grips the Washington policy establishment also contributed to the decline of US democracy promotion in Bahrain. The Fifth Fleet as an institution played a role in this. A former official explained to me how NAVCENT influenced the thinking of Washington policymakers about the situation in Bahrain:

> NAVCENT is . . . highly influenced by Bahraini Defense Forces threat assessments. In other words, they see everything and everyone [opposing the regime] as an Iranian stooge, convinced of the revisionist nature of Iranian foreign policy. They are never open to the possibility of dialogue and negotiation to settle anything. This is exactly where the [Bahraini regime] hard-liners are as well. [CENTCOM analysts in Tampa] respond to this. They take what NAVCENT says about the Gulf and this becomes Tampa's analysis of the Middle East, which then influences State NEA and other actors.⁹³

As the official noted, the Manama-based military analysts often take what their BDF counterparts tell them at face value, without any further investigation. Officials from non-DoD agencies visiting the Fifth Fleet are subjected to a "dog and pony show" in which they are shown Iranian-manufactured improvised explosive devices (IEDs) to highlight the dangers posed by Bahrain's eastern neighbor. In Washington interagency meetings, Pentagon officials "throw out the Iran bogeyman," and then leave the building, without presenting adequate evidence or arguments. "I wasn't impressed with their documentation," this official, who pushed for democracy promotion in Bahrain, told me.⁹⁴ DoD bargaining strategies contributed to shaping a narrative whereby any pressure on the Bahraini regime translates into a win for Iran, thereby lowering the propensity to promote democracy.

Paradoxically, in the face of continuing heavy-handedness by the Bahraini regime, some Shia opposition actors *have* in fact turned to Iran for support. Since the 2011 crackdown, there have been a series of smaller terrorist attacks in Bahrain, and plots for larger ones, allegedly linked to Iran, have been uncovered (Knights and Levitt 2018). This has created a vicious cycle in which evidence of Shia radicalization creates further justification for regime hard-liners to step up their crackdown and conflate the small number of radicals with the much larger, peaceful Shia opposition.

Thus, a framing of US interests around short-term security cooperation with the Bahraini regime led the United States to miss a critical moment for democracy promotion, not only because it failed to encourage reforms but also because the decimated opposition had given up. It was not only that the moment for US democracy promotion may have passed, but perhaps even the moment for stability, that much-coveted Washington policy objective. As one senior US official who worked on Bahrain said to me: "The approach has been co-opt and crush, co-opt and crush. Now they have decided to crush again. So yes [the regime] bought some stability by throwing the whole opposition leadership in jail, or exiling a few. But how many years of stability did they buy? Two? Three? Four? Maybe five? What next?"[95]

Institutions and the Limits of Democracy Promotion in Egypt

Chapter 3 described the significant influence individuals, starting with Obama himself, played in overcoming institutional resistance and implementing a moderate degree of democracy promotion in Egypt, at least until the 2013 coup. Meanwhile, other individuals who believed that US interests lie in backing the Egyptian military helped shape ambiguous messages about US policy intentions. However, as in the Libya and Bahraini cases above, institutions also had independent explanatory power over outcomes in US democracy promotion in Egypt at several key junctures. For example, Chapter 3 noted the contradictory statements coming from Secretary of State Clinton, Vice President Biden, President Obama, and other administration surrogates during the eighteen days of the 2011 Egyptian uprising. I attributed these differences to variation in individual attributes: generational factors, relationships with the Mubarak family, and socialization in established US views about the inherent stability of authoritarianism in Egypt. However, the bureaucratic politics approach might attribute these differences to varying institutional interests and organizational cultures.

Take Clinton's initially cautious approach, which emphasized a need to move slowly and reassure allies that they were not being abandoned, or her plan to put intelligence chief Suleiman in charge after Mubarak's removal. The State Department's interests lie in maintaining relationships and lines of access and influence built over many decades. Frank Wisner, Obama's temporary envoy to Mubarak, was very much socialized in this approach as a career diplomat. The State Department's organizational culture, moreover, is characterized by caution. Its powerful Near Eastern Affairs Bureau has long emphasized stability in the region and an aversion to meddling in the internal affairs of its states. Thus, when Clinton seemed to dial back some of Obama's more forward-leaning statements on democratic transition in Egypt at the February 6, 2011, Munich Security Conference, it may have been that as a relatively new secretary she was influenced by the institutional interests transmitted to her by State's career ranks. Clinton was described as a voracious consumer of the briefings materials prepared for her by the department's regional bureaus.[96] In these papers, the career diplomats were undoubtedly reminding Clinton about the benefits the United States had derived from its relationship with Mubarak and the consequences of instability in Egypt for US interests: for instance, potential threats to the 1979 peace accord between Egypt and Israel and by extension the effects on the Middle East peace process. One senior official who was a political appointee during the Egyptian uprising told me that the general reaction among NEA career officials to the White House's moves toward separating the United States from Mubarak was, "'Wow, that is how we treat a friend of thirty years?' I remember one of our NEA official's jaw was on the floor that we would do that."[97] Clinton was also under simultaneous pressure from America's Gulf allies and parts of the State Department that emphasized the importance of those alliances. These factors likely influenced Clinton to "stand" where she "sat" (that is, the State Department bureaucracy).

The perspective of many politically appointed NSC staffers may similarly have derived from their institutional perspective. NSC staff tend to look after the president's political reputation, and this in turn may condition their perspective on the "national interest." In 2011, NSC advisers such as Power, Rhodes, and McDonough were "worried that if Mr. Obama did not encourage the young people in the streets with forceful, even inspiring language, he would be accused of abandoning the ideals he expressed in his 2009 speech in Cairo" (Cooper, Landler, and Sanger 2011). These advisers "pushed Mr. Obama to challenge the assumptions of the foreign policy establishment" because "a failure to side with the protesters could be remembered with bitterness by a rising generation" (Cooper, Landler, and Sanger 2011). In other words, the young advisers were driven by views on Egypt that challenged the traditional American view of how to achieve stability in the Arab world, but as protectors of the president's reputation and legacy—an institutionally driven interest—they were also worried that a failure to back the Arab Spring uprisings would put the young president on the wrong side of history. National security adviser Donilon's caution, by contrast, may also be interpreted as driven by his institutional incentive to look after Obama's reputation, in addition to channeling the president's own inherently cautious instincts.

Institutional influence over the contours of Obama's post-Mubarak democracy promotion policy was also evident in the period between the uprising and the 2013 coup, when the United States simultaneously nudged the SCAF toward a democratic transition while continuing to see it and other vestiges of the Egyptian authoritarian apparatus—the all-powerful Interior Ministry, for instance—as the primary and legitimate interlocutors of the US-Egyptian relationship. Rhodes (2018, p. 107) writes that institutions were "hard wired to defer to the Egyptian military." For DoD and the CIA, it was largely business as usual (despite the frozen assistance), and counterterrorism cooperation, arms sales, joint trainings, and other forms of cooperation continued as before. DoD channels flowed naturally through the SCAF, since after all this was the same military with which it had always dealt. The institutional influence of DoD is literally built into the large US embassy in Cairo, where officials working on arms sales occupy entire floors, for example. These continuities were more about bureaucratic inertia than deliberate institutional thwarting of a robust democracy promotion agenda, but nonetheless they probably convinced many in the Egyptian security sector that when it came to military cooperation, nothing had changed. "Sisi is a smart actor," one former official said, "who knew they were championing him in DoD."[98]

By the end of Obama's presidency, DoD resumed its habit of arguing for a nonpunitive approach, one that would not humiliate the Sisi government. One former senior official told me: "It's not that [DoD officials] are sort of callous and don't care about human rights or democracy . . . it's just that they're looking at it from the prism of, 'okay, if we suspend assistance to a place like Egypt, this is the cost we're going to carry.'" This official noted that throughout the government, there was the feeling that military channels to the Egyptian government were the "most reliable channels" and "if you cut off the assistance you would cut off the actual channels you had to try to influence anything in a positive direction . . . it will just mean that we have fewer abilities to shape the relationship."[99] DoD argued, moreover, that withholding assistance had not had any effect on regime behavior, especially given massive infusions of assistance from Gulf states.

The State Department, and some members of Congress, continued to advocate the use of assistance conditionality. Even Congress's threats to cut funding proved useful since State officials could use the specter of reductions to try to push Sisi on human rights and democracy issues. State published its annual Human Rights Report on Egypt, detailing the deteriorating situation on many dimensions, from journalistic freedom to torture in prisons. Yet, as one official who dealt with the Egyptians told me, "it is both confusing and unhelpful when one side of the US government gives supportive messages on counterterrorism cooperation only to have those efforts highlighted in a negative context in the human rights report."[100]

The appearance of an Islamic State affiliate on Egypt's Sinai Peninsula and a rise in terrorist attacks in other parts of Egypt crystallized the sense in the White House that counterterrorism cooperation with the Egyptians must necessarily take priority over democracy promotion. Egyptian military leaders pressed visiting Pentagon officials to make weapons and equipment available to enable the fight against ISIL. The Sisi regime skillfully sought to warn the US about its security assistance cuts by using delays in granting overflight permission, a successful way to sound alarm bells among Pentagon planners accustomed to preferential treatment. This led DoD representatives at interagency meetings to argue that the use of security conditionality was hampering cooperative efforts with the Egyptian military on the anti-ISIL campaign. Many members of Congress signed on to this view.[101] Secretary of State Kerry was also pushing for a return to business as usual. As a result, the number of high-level statements and engagements focused on democracy and human rights in Egypt dropped off sharply, a trend that accelerated under the Trump administration, discussed in Chapter 6.

Notes

1. Parts of this account, especially those that are not otherwise cited, stem from my firsthand experience as a US diplomat in Libya after the fall of the Qaddafi regime.

2. Morrell (2016, p. 190) further describes his cultivation of a relationship with Abdullah al-Senussi, Qaddafi's intelligence chief. In 2011, the International Criminal Court issued an arrest warrant for Senussi in relation to his involvement in crimes against humanity.

3. Interview with Ben Fishman, Washington, DC, November 2018.

4. Interview with former US official, Washington, DC, February 2018. In leaked emails, Hillary Clinton's friend and informal adviser Sidney Blumenthal counsels her to capitalize on her role in liberating Libya.

5. Interview with Fred Wehrey, Claremont, CA, October 2018.

6. Ibid.

7. Phone interview with former US official, February 2018.

8. Phone interview with US official, May 2018. The CIA was also motivated by the fact that it had lost two officers in the Benghazi attacks.

9. Interview with former Libyan official, Tunis, November 2017.

10. Phone interview with Bill Lawrence, May 2018.

11. Interview with former US official, Washington, DC, November 2018.

12. However, some senior officials were unhappy that the US could not step up to the plate and offer US assistance, especially given the Libyan government's limitations in spending its funds. Interview with former senior US official, Washington, DC, February 2018.

13. Interview with former US official, New York, January 2018.

14. Interview with former US official, Washington, DC, October 2018.

15. Personal communication with Fred Wehrey, December 2018.

16. Interview with former US official, Washington, DC, February 2018. *Bad actors* is a favored term of US security agencies for alleged terrorists.

17. Interview with former US official, Washington, DC, October 2018.

18. Ibid.

19. Bolduc, quoted in Naylor and Turse (2019).
20. Ibid.
21. Quoted in Wroughton and Scherer (2015).
22. Interview with former US official, Washington, DC, October 2018.
23. Phone interview with Jason Pack, June 2018.
24. Interview with former US official, Washington, DC, February 2018.
25. Phone interview with member of Bahraini opposition, June 2018.
26. Interview with Tom Krajeski, Washington, DC, February 2018.
27. Political parties are illegal in Bahrain, but "political societies" operate much like parties.
28. Interview with Adam Ereli, Washington, DC, February 2018.
29. Ibid.
30. Interview with former US official, Washington, DC, February 2018.
31. Ibid.
32. Interview with former US officials, Washington, DC, and New York, February 2018.
33. Interview with former US official, New York, February 2018.
34. Interview with former US official, Washington, DC, February 2018.
35. Ibid.
36. Ibid.
37. Interview with Ben Rhodes, Claremont, CA, April 2019.
38. Interview with former US official, Washington, DC, February 2018.
39. Phone interview with US official, April 2018.
40. Interview with US official, New York, February 2018.
41. Phone interview with US official, March 2018.
42. Interview with former US official, Washington, DC, February 2018.
43. Ibid.
44. Phone interview with former US official, May 2018.
45. Interview with former US official, Washington, DC, February 2018.
46. Phone interview with Washington analyst, May 2018.
47. Interview with Tom Krajeski, Washington, DC, February 2018.
48. Interview with former US official, Washington, DC, February 2018.
49. Phone interview with former US official, March 2018.
50. Interview with Tom Krajeski, Washington, DC, February 2018.
51. Ibid.
52. Interview with former US official, Washington, DC, February 2018.
53. Phone interview with analyst, April 2018.
54. Interview with former US official, Washington, DC, February 2018.
55. Ibid. Interestingly, a former official admitted that at first the Bahrainis were not even aware that they were still being "punished." The continuing hold only became apparent when the media seized upon it later.
56. Ibid.
57. Ibid.
58. Ibid.
59. Ibid.
60. Phone interview with analyst, April 2018.
61. Interview with former US official, Washington, DC, February 2018.
62. Phone interview with Bahraini activists, May 2018.
63. Phone interview with member of Bahraini opposition, April 2018.
64. Ibid.
65. Interview with Tom Krajeski, Washington, DC, February 2018.

66. Phone interview with member of Bahraini opposition, April 2018.
67. Phone interview with Tom Malinowski, June 2018.
68. Interview with former US official, Washington, DC, February 2018.
69. Phone interview with Tom Malinowski, February 2018.
70. Interview with former US official, Washington, DC, February 2018.
71. Interview with Emma Ashford, Washington, DC, February 2018.
72. Interview with former US official, Washington, DC, February 2018.
73. Interview with US official, Washington, DC, February 2018.
74. Ibid.
75. Phone interview with former US official, June 2018.
76. Interview with US official, New York, February 2018.
77. Phone interview with US official, May 2018.
78. Phone interview with Bahraini opposition activist, May 2018.
79. Interview with former US official, Washington, DC, February 2018.
80. Phone interview with former US official, April 2018.
81. Interview with former US official, Washington, DC, February 2018.
82. Phone interview with Washington-based analyst, May 2018.
83. Interview with former US official, Washington, DC, February 2018.
84. Ibid.
85. Phone interview with Tom Malinowski, June 2018.
86. Ibid.
87. Ibid.
88. Ibid.
89. Interview with former US official, Washington, DC, February 2018.
90. Ibid.
91. Phone interview with Tom Malinowski, June 2018.
92. Ibid.
93. Interview with former US official, Washington, DC, February 2018.
94. Ibid.
95. Ibid.
96. Ibid.
97. Ibid.
98. Ibid.
99. Interview with former US official, Washington, DC, October 2018.
100. Ibid.
101. Interview with Steve Cook, Washington, DC, February 2018.

5

Challengers

It is hard to overstate the extent to which the events of the Arab Spring shook the Gulf Arab monarchies, which are organized in the Gulf Cooperation Council (GCC). Seen from Riyadh or Abu Dhabi, capitals of the largest and most influential GCC countries, the Arab uprisings created a perfect storm, threatening interests such as regime survival and countering Iran. The Saudi regime, in fact, refers to the 2011 uprising not as the Arab Spring but as the "Arab troubles" (Wehrey 2015, p. 72). For the Saudis and other Gulf monarchies, 2011 was a continuation of the *fitna* (strife, chaos) unleashed by the American attempt to install "democracy" in Iraq: state breakdown, the rise of militias and jihadist terror, sectarianism, and the expansion of Iranian influence (Wehrey 2015, p. 79). The fact that the Obama administration adopted a policy of rallying behind the Arab Spring protesters sent further shock waves through the royal palaces of the Gulf. Ben Rhodes (2018, p. 102) recalls that on January 29, 2011, days before the US president asked Mubarak to step down,

> Obama got a call from King Abdullah of Saudi Arabia, who complained that our statements were too forward-leaning. In a sign of how closely our words were being watched, he took exception to statements [White House Press Secretary Robert Gibbs] had made in his briefings supporting the protestors. He dismissed the people in the streets as nothing more than the Muslim Brotherhood, Hizbollah, al Qaeda, and Hamas. This was their view of who was protesting in Egypt: terrorists.

A former senior DoD official told me that the Saudis and Emiratis (and Israelis) thought "we were insane" to "even contemplate" asking Hosni Mubarak to resign, speaking with Morsi, or cutting off aid from Sisi. This same official quoted above added that after that, he spent much of his time in the Obama administration defending it before the Gulf's "endless barrage of criticism."[1] After Mubarak's departure, Saudi King Abdullah told then undersecretary of state William Burns: "You abandoned your best friend" (Burns 2019, p. 302).

From the Gulf Arab perspective, Obama's withdrawal of support for Mubarak was an unforgiveable transgression, since the former Egyptian president was an ally of both Washington and the GCC. The GCC states concluded that the Obama administration could not be trusted to stand by its friends, and from that point on, the Gulf royals decided to take a more muscular approach to protecting their interests. In allies such as Egypt, as well as in allied conservative monarchies such as Bahrain, Morocco, Oman, and Jordan, these interests lay decisively in preserving the authoritarian, military-led status quo. The GCC lent financial support to less prosperous Arab monarchies such as Morocco, Jordan, and Oman to help them weather the protests. However, in Egypt, GCC member state interests diverged. Qatar decided to throw its weight behind the protesters in Egypt, perhaps due to realist calculations but perhaps also due to a desire to "do the right thing" (Kamrava 2015, p. 63). Later, Qatar became a financial backer of the government of Brotherhood president Mohamed Morsi.

Unlike Iran, Saudi Arabia and the other Gulf states do not limit their support to one kind of political group in terms of ideological orientation. For example, the Saudis have supported Salafists in Egypt and Libya, the Nasserite military in Egypt, and a Sunni monarchy in Bahrain. All of these groups, however, have in common the counterrevolutionary roles they have played after the Arab Spring. Thus, in the context of the Arab world, Gulf strategic concerns and fears about the consequences of a more pluralistic political order converge. As I will show, the effect of GCC policies has been unmistakably counterdemocratic in Egypt, Bahrain, and Libya.

Domestic Insecurities

The Gulf states examined here—Saudi Arabia, the United Arab Emirates, and Qatar—are an anachronism in today's world: hereditary, absolutist monarchies run by extended families who effectively "own" their countries and their extensive natural resources. Saudi Arabia, in addition, is a theocratic state built on a fundamentalist interpretation of Islam. The main preoccupation of the Gulf royal families is to survive and maintain their privileges in a globalized, wired world, acutely conscious that their youthful populations have tasted greater political freedoms, economic opportunities, and social freedoms outside their borders. In their pursuit of regime survival, the ruling Gulf monarchies spread their mind-boggling hydrocarbon wealth broadly, both at home and abroad.

The GCC states are significant global economic and diplomatic players. Saudi Arabia, the largest and most influential Gulf state, maintains economic ties and linkages with Muslim communities in many parts of the world. Despite its global reach and assertive foreign policy, Saudi Arabia often acts from a position of deep insecurity, starting with economic concerns. Saudi Arabia is dependent on oil for 90 percent of its budget revenue. A growing population, declining oil prices, and competition from shale-oil producers strain its policies of housing and other subsidies, as well as regional assistance and lavish stipends for members of the royal family. This is exacerbated by the fact that unlike Qatar and UAE, with small citizen populations, 70 percent of Saudi Arabia's people are citizens. The younger generation of Saudis is unlikely to receive the welfare benefits their parents enjoyed. Official estimates put the Saudi unemployment rate at nearly 13 percent in 2018, with a large part of the job seekers in their twenties and thirties. For Saudi women, the unemployment rate was over 31 percent that same year (General Authority for Statistics of the Kingdom of Saudi Arabia 2018). About 70 percent of working people are employed in the public sector. The Saudi working-age population is expected to increase to nearly 18 million by 2025, meaning 226,000 new Saudi workers will enter the labor force each year (Dutt D'Cunha 2017). The public sector simply cannot absorb so many workers. As a result, over the past two decades Saudi leaders have introduced reforms to diversify the Saudi economy and increase employment opportunities (Hertog 2006, p. 74). Crown Prince Mohammed bin Salman's proposals to modernize the Saudi economy are the latest and most dramatic example (*The Economist* 2018), but reform in the kingdom is difficult owing to entrenched religious and economic interests.

But it is by no means certain that these reforms will be enough to buy social peace. In addition to instability resulting from a large population of unemployed and disaffected youth, Saudi Arabia could face succession crises owing to the large number of potential royal heirs combined with decreasing resources. Other challenges to the regime could come from Saudi Arabia's clerical establishment, or from extremist Sunni organizations. In addition to all of this, Saudi Arabia and other Gulf monarchies worry about the destabilizing influence of their Shia citizens. Besides using their immense wealth to buy political acquiescence, the primary solution to containing such threats in Saudi Arabia and other GCC states has been unbridled authoritarianism: a suppression of free speech, civil society, opposition groups, and independent media. The Arab uprisings thus directly challenged not only the strategic context, but also the logic of authoritarianism in the Gulf.

Gulf Views of the Egyptian, Bahraini, and Libyan Uprisings: The Strategic Context

The Bahraini uprising played directly into Saudi and broader Gulf domestic insecurities because the prospect of greater democratization signaled Shia empowerment, potentially leading to a spillover into the kingdom's oil-rich Eastern Province, where there is a sizeable Shia population (Ulrichsen 2013, p. 8). Shia empowerment is closely linked in the minds of Saudi elites with the influence of its ideological, sectarian, and geopolitical foe, Iran. Invoking the Iranian threat also goes far in helping the Saudis rally support from other GCC member states, especially the Emiratis. In fact, the only protests that took place in Saudi Arabia during the Arab Spring were in the Eastern Province, giving the regime an easy excuse to frame the protesters' grievances in sectarian terms (Wehrey 2013b). Beyond the Shia–Bahrain–Iran–Eastern Province nexus, Saudis see themselves as Bahrain's "big brother," protector, and benefactor, a mentality that certainly plays into fears about reforms that could threaten the power of the Bahraini al-Khalifa ruling family.[2]

As the largest and historically most important Arab state from which it is separated by the narrow Red Sea, the stability and economic viability of Egypt has always been important to the Saudis. But Egypt matters to Riyadh in ways that go beyond this. If Bahrain was seen by the Saudis as a front in the geopolitical struggle against Iran, "then Egypt is the main front in the political and ideological struggle against the Muslim Brotherhood" (Wehrey 2015, p. 76). Hosni Mubarak's fall in early 2011, Wehrey (p. 76) writes, "hit the Saudi royals like an earthquake—in one stroke, they lost an authoritarian bulwark against both Iran and the Brotherhood." While the 2011 Egyptian revolution and the resulting loss of the anti-Brotherhood and anti-Iran Mubarak was a shock, the rise to power of Muslim Brotherhood president Mohamed Morsi was a step too far for both the Saudi and Emirati monarchies. To understand why, we must look to the Muslim Brotherhood's ideology, and the threat that poses to both Saudi Arabia's religiously legitimized political elite and the UAE's "secular" one. In the former case, Morsi's victory created a "democratically elected Islamist rival to claims of Saudi Arabia being the protector of Islam, and offered a potentially dangerous exemplar in the region that could well have undermined the kingdom's legitimacy in the long term" (Hassan 2015, p. 486).

The Egyptian Muslim Brotherhood openly questions the rule of the Gulf monarchies, and thus its rise is seen as a serious ideological threat by the royal families of the region. Though the Brothers once found safe haven in Saudi Arabia during Gamal Abdel Nasser's presidency (1956–1970), the welcome ended once it became clear that the group's activist ideology threatened the kingdom's quietist form of Salafism (Wehrey 2012). But the presence of the Brotherhood inspired some Saudi clerics who launched a campaign of criticism against the monarchy in the 1990s, with some even turning to al-Qaeda. "A desire to prevent a repeat of this scenario," writes Wehrey (2015, p. 72), "has factored heavily into Saudi Arabia's post-2011 policies toward the Brotherhood." The fear of the Brotherhood mingling with al-Qaeda as a violent challenger to monarchical rule may also help explain the UAE's fervent opposition to political Islam, and its penchant for grouping all Islamists together as "terrorists." Indeed, it was the UAE that became the driving force behind the anti-Brotherhood campaign, though the Saudis threw their "considerable weight behind it" (Lynch 2016, p. 159). As one senior official who worked extensively with the Emiratis told me, the anti-Brotherhood bias is "hard-wired into the DNA" of the Emirati ruling family.[3]

Gulf views of the Arab Spring in Libya and Syria were more complicated. Libya was a special case: The Qaddafi regime might have actually been useful to the Gulf states had the Libyan dictator not alienated many Arab rulers as a result of his capricious behavior, which included insulting the Saudi monarch personally at an Arab League meeting and hatching a plot to assassinate him (Tyler 2004). Thus, the GCC monarchies mostly saw Qaddafi as an erratic thorn in their side and were happy to use the Arab League to pave the way for a military intervention. Syria, by contrast, was seen through the sectarian and Iranian lens, since Assad was an ally of Tehran. As in Libya, the GCC used the Arab League to increase pressure on Assad and later channeled support to anti-Assad proxy militias (Perry and al-Khalidi 2017). After Qaddafi's demise, Saudi and Emirati attention in Libya turned to countering the Brotherhood and containing the brand of violent jihadism that could constitute a threat not only to the GCC monarchies, but also to their Egyptian military allies. By contrast, for ideological reasons and to compete with its Saudi rivals, Qatar sought to support rising Libyan Islamist groups.

The Threat of Democratization

The possibility for an opened political space in allied Arab regimes struck fear in the hearts of rulers in Riyadh and Abu Dhabi. Political pluralism threatened not only their absolutist rule, but also economic privileges. Moreover, democratization in Bahrain or Egypt in particular might have been too close for comfort, threatening the Emirati monarchies with the kind of "contagion" or "democratic diffusion" identified in the literature on the international dimension of democratization (Whitehead 2001). In accordance with such fears, writes Wehrey (2015, p. 78), Saudi Arabia initiated new GCC integration initiatives focusing on the internal security of member states with the intention "to make each state's domestic stability the biggest concern of all, as well as to ease the task of policing dissent."

Meanwhile, the rising fortunes of political Islam after the Arab Spring not only presented a religiously rooted ideological challenge to continued absolutist rule, but also a governance-rooted one. This is because the Muslim Brothers in Egypt and other countries claim to support a model of state and society in which an "Islamic" government can and should be a democratic one (Al-Rasheed 2013). By contrast, Saudi-style Salafism dictates obedience to the existing ruler as long as they are Muslim (*The Economist* 2018).

Thus, fears of democracy might be a greater driver of Saudi and Emirati responses to the Arab Spring than fears of Iran. As Wehrey writes in his analysis of Saudi policy in Bahrain, "hyperbole about the Iranian threat is useful, however, both as a distraction from the Khalifa family's governance failings and corruption, and as a way of maintaining the support of the United States, which bases its Fifth Fleet on the island" (Wehrey 2015, p. 78). The GCC, like the Americans, had grown accustomed to dealing with pliant Arab rulers and autocratic regimes to whom they had to make only one phone call to get things done, and could not imagine an alternate scenario.

Financing Authoritarian Retrenchment

After the 2011 Arab Spring uprising in Egypt, Saudi Arabia embarked on a determined campaign to shape the Egyptian transition in favor of continued autocratic military rule. To accomplish this, the Saudis deployed their immense wealth. Between early 2011 and 2014, Saudi Arabia and its GCC allies pledged a staggering $23 billion in aid to Egypt and other countries in the region (Wehrey 2015, p. 72), far more than the West was willing and able to contribute. In multiple interviews with US officials who worked on Egypt policy during and after the Arab Spring, I heard the same refrain: The Gulf willingness (led by the Saudis) to buy influence in Egypt directly and consequentially challenged US leverage over the transition.

After the fall of Mubarak, the interim Egyptian authorities quickly reaffirmed bilateral relations with the Gulf states (Dickinson 2012). Prime Minister Essam Sharaf, appointed by the Supreme Council of the Armed Forces (SCAF) in March 2011, stated that "we are tied with the GCC countries by historic relations and interference in their affairs is a red line."[4] While the SCAF allowed two Iranian war ships to pass through the Suez Canal in February 2011, it also vowed that this limited rapprochement with Tehran would not interfere with Egyptian-GCC relations (Hassan 2015, p. 486). Egyptian-GCC military cooperation continued, and the Saudis and other Gulf states offered the SCAF a $500 million grant to support the Egyptian budget, a pledge of $3.75 billion in aid, and 48,000 tons of liquefied petroleum gas (p. 486).

There were reports that the Saudis also channeled money to the Salafist al-Nour party during the 2011–2012 parliamentary elections as a way to counteract the influence of the Muslim Brotherhood (Wehrey 2015, p. 76). In other words, at a time when the United States had pledged rhetorical support for Egyptian democracy, the Saudis had already stepped in with financial power (and thus leverage) that eclipsed whatever the Americans could offer. Since the United States had also accepted the SCAF as the legitimate Egyptian transitional government in part to protect its own interests, the Saudi assistance was not yet countervailing to democracy promotion. But it set the stage for subsequent infusions of cash and influence that did challenge US democracy promotion in a direct and determining way.

In Chapter 3, I described the second round of the Egyptian presidential election in June 2012 as a high point for US democracy promotion. Working through Ambassador Anne Patterson, Washington pressed the interim military government to recognize the legitimate winner in spite of Gulf pressure to rig the election in favor of the military-friendly candidate, Ahmed Shafik. It was at this point that the Obama administration also successfully lobbied the GCC states to not take actions that would undermine the integrity of the election. This effort was a success, but a short-lived one. The existence of the SCAF had been a reassurance to the Gulf states that their interests would be respected; but now the SCAF was no more. Instead, Mohamed Morsi of the Muslim Brotherhood, the ideological foe of the Saudis and Emiratis, was now president of Egypt.

While Morsi sent the right signal by making his first foreign visit to Riyadh the month he took office, he also visited Tehran the following month to attend a summit of the Non-Aligned Conference, becoming the first Egyptian leader to visit Iran since relations were cut off in 1980. The visit immediately sounded alarm bells in Gulf capitals, even though Morsi took no actual steps to realign Egypt with Iran (Lynch 2016, p. 148). In May 2013, he hosted a conference in Cairo featuring the hard-line preacher Yusuf al-Qaradawi, an Egyptian long exiled in Qatar because of his alignment with the Brotherhood. At the conference, al-Qaradawi called for a jihad in Syria in overtly sectarian terms, raising eyebrows in Washington and the GCC. Riyadh and Abu Dhabi instinctively already distrusted Morsi, and moves such as those just described helped convince them to cut off badly needed assistance. Both the Saudis and Emiratis began plotting how they could undermine Morsi's government, even as the Obama White House searched for ways to bolster and work with the democratically elected Egyptian president. The Qataris, who saw the Muslim Brotherhood as an ally, eventually stepped in with $5 billion to replace much of the lost Saudi aid (Daragahi 2014), thereby reflecting a pattern by which Gulf money became a vehicle to prop up favored proxies rather than support a democratic transition.

Morsi in fact maneuvered shrewdly between the Gulf, the United States, his conservative base, the military, and other constituencies. When the US embassy in Cairo was attacked in September 2012 by protesters angry over an anti-Islamic YouTube video produced in the United States, Morsi acted responsibly to protect the embassy, in spite of pressure from his Islamist base to stand with the protesters. That fall, Morsi helped broker a ceasefire between Israel and Hamas after a flare-up of violence, thereby demonstrating his pragmatic and moderate credentials in the eyes of Washington and the Gulf (Lynch 2016, pp. 149–150).

Financing the 2013 Coup

While Sisi claimed that the anti-Morsi Tamarrod movement had pushed him to carry out the coup, we now know that the more likely scenario is that the Egyptian Defense Ministry backed the movement with Emirati money. In 2015, an anti-Sisi media outlet in Turkey released secret recordings in which top Egyptian defense officials discuss transferring UAE funds to Tamarrod, substantiating earlier rumors of *mokhabarat* (secret police) figures milling about Tamarrod offices (Kirkpatrick 2018, p. 217). This is not to suggest that there wasn't broad popular dissatisfaction with Morsi at the time Tamarrod was organized. But the fact that the Egyptian deep state collaborated with a foreign power to undermine a democratically elected president, however flawed, put a permanent dark cloud over the legitimacy of Sisi's narrative of a "popular" coup. Moreover, such collaboration undermined US efforts to discourage a coup and find a negotiated solution to Egypt's political impasse. At the time, however, US officials had no idea of the extent of Gulf involvement. One former official said, "we suspected that Gulf money was flooding into the anti-Morsi opposition, but we did not know how much."[5]

In the spring of 2013, Emirati- and Saudi-based pan-Arab satellite networks were going after not only Morsi, but also after the Obama administration and Ambassador Patterson, both supposedly part of a conspiracy to bring the Brotherhood to power. Kirkpatrick (2018, p. 208) writes: "The Gulf-based satellite networks were full of accusations that [Patterson] was a Brotherhood 'lackey,' 'an old hag,' or 'an ogre' who worked to rig the election in favor of Morsi as a part of an American plot to weaken Egypt." Rhodes (2018, p. 203) recalls this campaign in his memoir: "It was a way to apply pressure on us, to demonstrate that this time they weren't going to yield in their intention to see the type of government they wanted to see in Cairo just because of America's views." Rhodes (p. 203) also describes how the Emirati ambassador to the United States, Yousef al-Otaiba, in a "brazen" act sent him a photo of a poster that caricatured Patterson as a lackey of the Brotherhood. For Rhodes, this was all too much:

> They essentially ran a plan to denigrate any nonmilitary Egyptian government, denigrate our ambassador, and denigrate our policy. . . . Allies of the United States funded a denigration campaign against the United States ambassador in a country that is one of the largest recipients of U.S. assistance, to overturn the democratically elected government of that country. It was extraordinary, really . . . constant, incessant, and effective.[6]

Following the July 3, 2013, military coup, the GCC stepped in with financial guarantees to support the military junta. Just a few days after Morsi's ouster, Saudi Arabia announced a $5 billion aid package, along with an additional $3 billion from the UAE and $4 billion from Kuwait (Hassan 2015, p. 486).[7] In all, the Gulf powers contributed over $20 billion to keep Egypt afloat and provide "essential political protection from American pressure for reconciliation" (Lynch 2016, p. 157). Qatar, which had supported Morsi, did not join its fellow GCC donors. The Saudis also declared their strong support for Sisi and his crackdown on the Muslim Brotherhood. They financed media outlets supportive of the coup and Sisi, as well as the Salafi groups who jumped on the pro-coup bandwagon (Lacroix 2016). Like Sisi, they labeled the Muslim Brothers as "terrorists." Saudi King Abdullah, besides declaring that Sisi had "saved" Egypt, followed up by issuing a thinly veiled rebuke to Western powers who might try and undermine the coup, warning "against those who try to tamper with Egypt's domestic affairs."[8] Kirkpatrick (2018, p. 265) further quotes Rhodes as saying: "[The Gulf powers] celebrated the military takeover, and yet there was no questioning of that in Washington."[9]

The immense sums of money pledged by the GCC states to help consolidate Sisi's coup were frequently cited in my interviews as constraining Washington's options on how to respond to the military takeover. But the GCC actions also likely reinforced Obama's preexisting sense of American powerlessness over events in the region. Moreover, by this point the Obama administration had its eyes on another prize: the nuclear deal with Iran, which was ruffling GCC feathers even further. According to some, Obama did not want to pick any more fights with the Gulf monarchs.[10]

At first glance, Gulf policies did not seem to directly challenge the numerous democracy assistance and development programs the United States had established in Egypt under MEPI and other mechanisms since the George W. Bush administration. Oz Hassan (2015, p. 485) notes that there is yet another, more subtle way in which Gulf money countered US democracy promotion efforts in Egypt:

> External democracy promotion strategies seek to create an independent middle class, which in turn sets into motion wider political and economic modernization processes. With this form of modernization thesis underlying both the US and EU external democracy promotion strategies

in the MENA, Saudi Arabia's willingness to financially support the Egyptian state can be seen to undercut these efforts. That is to say, that to stymie transatlantic democracy promotion's long-term efforts of promoting democracy, Saudi Arabia targets these modernization processes. Saudi Arabia's ability to undercut the US and EU's economic leverage, and plans to promote modernization, are therefore a direct challenge to the transatlantic external democracy promotion agenda.

Financing with no strings attached was just one part of the Gulf strategy to support authoritarian retrenchment in Egypt. The other, as I will describe below, was less tangible, but equally potent: a campaign to get the key US policymakers on its side.

Bankrolling Authoritarianism in Libya and Bahrain

The Gulf policy of offering financial aid to allied autocrats went beyond Egypt. In Libya, even before the 2011 uprisings, Saudi money helped support a rehabilitation program for anti-Qaddafi jihadists that aimed to school them in the Saudi model of politically acquiescent Islamism (Wehrey 2012). Unsurprisingly, years later, as Libya fragmented into two governments, the Saudis (working through the UAE, and in cooperation with Egypt) lent material support to *madhkhali* quietist Salafi militias fighting under the umbrella of anti-Brotherhood "Libyan National Army" commander Khalifa Haftar, who has barely tried to hide his autocratic impulses. The "broader, unstated goal," writes Wehrey (2015, p. 77), "is to shut political Islamists and especially the Muslim Brothers out of Libyan politics." Along with Emirati and Egyptian support, another challenger, Russia, stepped in to provide Haftar with billions of counterfeit dinars in the spring of 2016, which Obama's former Special Envoy for Libya, Jonathan Winer, described to me as playing a "huge role" in countering the momentum toward a lasting political settlement.[11]

In response to the Arab Spring uprisings in Bahrain and Oman, Riyadh announced an initiative to strengthen the GCC, which included pledges of $10 billion to each country over the next decade. More immediately, following its military incursion into Bahrain (see later section on Military Intervention) Saudi Arabia provided $500 million to boost the Bahraini economy, as well as announcing plans for a closer political and military union with the Bahraini royal family (Wehrey 2012). In addition, to counter the influence of Bahrain's Shia population, Riyadh funded deeply sectarian Sunni elements such as the al-Asala Islamic Society, the National Unity Gathering, and the Sahwat al-Fatih movement (Wehrey 2015, p. 78). While this infusion of assistance and political support did not counter US leverage to the same degree as Saudi tanks rolling across the King Fahd Causeway that March, it did lessen the impact of any potential democratic leverage the United States might have derived from using assistance conditionality.

Discussion

The financial tools used by Saudi Arabia and other Gulf states to undermine the gains of the Arab Spring in pursuit of their interests were especially potent given that both the United States and European Union faced severe fiscal constraints at the time owing to the global recession. Egyptians, Libyans, and Bahrainis with a local political agenda were only too happy to accept these funds and align themselves with Gulf interests. Counterleverage in the form of financial support was particularly effective in Egypt, helping to bring down the democratically elected president, Morsi, and giving Sisi the confidence and funding to carry out and consolidate his military takeover. Much more so than in Bahrain, the GCC financing left the United States with weakened conditionality tools with which to pursue democracy promotion in Egypt. At the same time, as Chapter 3 showed, US views on the 2013 coup were hardly unified. To the extent that certain figures and institutions in Washington were happy to see Morsi go, the Saudi policies only reinforced their preferences.

Military Intervention

In Bahrain, the Saudis and their Gulf allies demonstrated that they were willing to move beyond softer tools such as diplomatic engagement and financial backing and turned to the "hard power" of military intervention. The Saudis' willingness to put down the Bahraini uprising by force just a month after it appeared showed how much the arrival of the Arab Spring in its tiny island neighbor was perceived as a threat. Needless to say, the toppling of Mubarak and Ben Ali provided proof that the Arab Spring was a game-changing force and required a determined response. An analyst with intimate knowledge of Saudi decisionmaking told me that Riyadh, still shocked and furious that the Obama administration refused to stand behind Mubarak, likely wanted to send a message to Washington that it would not tolerate any further threats against allied autocratic regimes.[12] In this case, America's own perceived interests in preserving the al-Khalifa monarchy converged with those of the Saudis (Hassan 2015). The same analyst stated his belief that the Saudi crackdown in Bahrain more than anything else was the symbolic and early end of the Arab Spring—not only because a mostly peaceful protest movement was brutally suppressed, but because the United States had shown that it was not willing or able to stop the Gulf states from thwarting democratization in the region.[13]

On March 14, 2011, 1,200 Saudi troops riding in armored vehicles came across the causeway that links Saudi Arabia to Bahrain under the banner of the GCC Peninsula Shield Force. They were backed by UAE forces and much smaller contingents from Kuwait and Qatar, both of whom were ambivalent about the intervention. The UAE foreign minister at the time emphasized the broader implications of the Bahraini uprising: "What is happening in Bahrain is going to have an impact on all GCC countries, and we must work together from now on."[14] Meanwhile, a Saudi newspaper commentary spoke to the threat felt by Bahrain's Gulf neighbors: "We have been in the eye of the hurricane since protests and sit-ins against the authorities in Bahrain took on a critical juncture by defying the nature of the state, demanding the establishment of a republic and the abolition of the existing monarchy."[15]

Saudi soldiers took over security in the city, freeing up Bahraini security forces to go after the protesters. As Chapter 4 described, the crackdown was brutal and decisive. Bahraini security forces and hired Sunni thugs attacked protesters and dismantled the Pearl Roundabout encampment for the last time. Meanwhile, Bahraini officials justified the incursion saying that the Peninsula Shield Force was protecting government facilities, rather than intruding in the internal affairs of the country itself (Asharq Al-Awsat 2011). But the foreign troops remained on the island long after the protests were put down, reminding Bahrainis and the world that the Saudis would not tolerate meaningful change in the country.

While the United States may have shared the Saudi goal of preserving the Bahraini regime, prior to the March 14 intervention and squelching of the protests, the Obama administration had also engaged in direct diplomatic pressure to urge Bahraini security forces not to use lethal force against protesters and to encourage the regime to offer concessions and maintain a dialogue with the opposition. As Hassan (2015, p. 490) writes, "the tension between the U.S. and Saudi Arabian foreign policy, therefore, is over how the status quo in Bahrain is maintained whilst observing human rights norms, and not if the regime should be maintained." The Saudi and GCC intervention directly challenged the US approach. On that point there is little disagreement among the former Obama administration officials I interviewed. There is less agreement on the question of whether the United States could have prevented, stood up to, or punished the Saudis for their interference. Some officials who worked on human rights issues in the administration are of the mind that Washington never mustered the will to call the Saudis out, while other White House officials point out that the administration had no advance knowledge of the Saudi action and thus little power to stop it. Thus, while it is undeniable that the Saudis and the GCC aimed to prevent the emergence of democracy in Bahrain with their incursion, it is less clear whether the United States had the ability to influence their Gulf allies.

Intervention in Libya

After Libya split into two competing governments in the summer of 2014, the Gulf states were quick to take sides. The Emiratis and Qataris had previously gotten involved in the Libyan revolution and subsequent struggle for power, supporting rival commanders and their militias. However, the 2014 Libyan conflict between "Islamist" Misratan militias and the anti-Islamist "Dignity" coalition of strongman Khalifa Haftar presented a clear choice for the virulently anti-Islamist Emiratis. Starting on August 18, 2014, a series of precision air strikes targeted "Libya Dawn" positions in Tripoli, killing twenty mostly Misratan fighters (Wehrey 2018, p. 192). Initially Haftar and Dignity claimed responsibility, but Wehrey (2018, p. 192) notes that this was seen as highly unlikely from the outset given the precision of the air strikes contrasted with Haftar's aging Russian-made fleet of warplanes. Soon afterward, Dawn fighters recovered the remains of an advanced, laser-guided American-made weapon, which only the Emiratis could have possessed. Wehrey (2018, p. 192) writes: "The Emiratis had meddled in Libya during and after the revolution, but not like this. . . . This was brazen interference that worsened a civil war." US officials said that they had detected the imminent strikes and tried to stop the Emiratis from carrying them out, but to no avail (Wehrey 2018, p. 192).

Here was another example of US Gulf allies acting in a way that undercut US policy, in this case using America's own weapons. The absurdity of the situation was not lost on State Department diplomats, but the feeling among many in the Obama administration was that there was little the US could do to stop or punish the Emiratis. Unlike Bahrain, where US and Gulf goals overlapped in that neither wanted to see the al-Khalifa monarchy toppled, in the Libyan case the Obama administration policy was that an inclusive, dialogue-based approach was necessary to prevent the country's ongoing fragmentation. The US democracy promotion effort in Libya by this point was limited, but at least it had moved beyond a purely counterterrorism-focused approach. The Emirati approach was to deal with the conflict by labeling the entire opposing side as "terrorists" and eliminating them through the use of military force. And yet, as in the case of Saudi meddling in Bahrain, it is hard to conclude that the United States had no leverage over its Gulf allies, as many Obama administration officials like to emphasize. The more accurate conclusion may be that there were too many reasons why Washington was not willing to test whether such leverage could actually work given the perceived need for Emirati support on other issues.

It was not just the Emiratis and their air strikes that undermined US democracy promotion in Libya, however. The Emiratis had worked with the Saudis, Jordanians, and Sisi's Egypt to support Haftar's August 2014 campaign. Later, Egypt became even more actively involved in supporting Haftar ('Arafa and Boduszyński 2017), shipping him arms and providing logistical support. Qatar, too, entered the fray and worked with Turkey and Sudan to funnel arms to its allies, the Dawn militias, though it never became as involved as the UAE and Egypt in Libya (Wehrey 2018, p. 193). Both the military strikes and arms shipments violated the UN arms embargo and no-fly zone still in place (Wehrey 2018, p. 193). For all the other Gulf powers meddling in Libya, it was less important that democracy was surviving than that one's side was winning (Lynch 2016, p. 104). Speaking about the Gulf meddling and Qatari-Emirati rivalry, one UN official told Wehrey (2018, p. 193): "They didn't give a damn about Libya, they were always worried that the other would come out on top."

Influence on US Policymakers

As Max Fisher (2016) observes, "though American and Gulf interests have seemingly drifted further apart since 2011, Washington's pro-Gulf consensus has proven strangely resilient." He offers one answer to why this is the case, describing Washington's foreign policy community as "deeply, viscerally committed to defending and advocating for the Kingdom of Saudi Arabia, a country whose authoritarian government, ultra-conservative values, and extremist-promoting foreign policy would seem like an unusual passion project for American foreign policy professionals." During and after 2011, even as Gulf countries intervened to protect their interests and suppress democracy in Arab Spring countries, they mobilized their extensive influence apparatus in Washington, DC, with the goal of convincing powerful US actors to back their policies in Bahrain, Egypt, Libya, and other states. GCC influence runs broad and deep in Washington, from the policy think tanks funded with Saudi, Emirati, or Qatari money (Lipton, Williams, and Confessore 2014) to extensive and longstanding relationships with prominent US foreign policy makers and legislators. Sections housing "Congress-watchers" are often among the largest at GCC embassies in Washington.[16] The GCC's ability to sway US policymakers also rests on the military and defense industry ties described in Chapter 1. Moreover, it rests on shared frames emphasizing Arab autocratic stability, the irreplaceability of US-Gulf security partnerships, the existential threat posed by Iran, and the dangers of political Islam. The UAE in particular enjoys additional leverage based on the assistance it has offered to many critical US military missions around the world, and from housing State Department offices focused on engagement with Iran, and ironically, democratization in the Middle East.

In this sense, the Gulf Arab lobbying machine did not have to work too hard to persuade US policymakers to accept their perspective on the

Arab Spring: It only had to reinforce their existing beliefs, which saw democracy in the Arab world as secondary to issues such as containing Iran and fighting terrorists.

Post–Arab Spring developments only aided the GCC cause in Washington. The rise of the Islamic State in 2014 helped add a convincing argument to the talking points of Gulf lobbyists and diplomats: The collapse of existing authoritarian regimes can only lead to jihadism and chaos. These diplomats and lobbyists understood, of course, that the fear of terrorism was a touchstone and rallying point in American public opinion and thus a topic that would easily resonate among the Washington foreign policy establishment. Gulf officials also inserted themselves into US partisan and interagency divisions. They appealed to both Republican and Pentagon fears of the Muslim Brotherhood and Iran, for example.[17] With an extensive contact base in the US government, they most certainly were aware of the discord among US policymakers and policymaking institutions on how to respond to the Arab Spring. But it was on Egypt policy around the 2013 coup that the Saudis and Emiratis undertook the most concerted influence campaign.

The UAE and the Egyptian Coup

As noted above, the UAE and Saudi Arabia adamantly opposed both the Arab Spring and the rise of the Muslim Brotherhood because of the perceived threat both posed to continued absolutist monarchical rule in the Gulf. Egypt represented a confluence of both threats in a pivotal Arab country. As such, not long after Mubarak's fall, the Saudis and Emiratis began spreading the message that Obama had abandoned longstanding US allies by forcing Mubarak out, and that he had been badly advised to do so by Obama's younger advisers such as Ben Rhodes (Rhodes 2018, p. 106). "It was the beginning of a multiyear effort," writes Rhodes (2018, p. 106), "to restore a dictatorship in Egypt." Using direct diplomacy, the media, think tanks, and lobbying, they launched a campaign of deliberate fear-mongering about the threat and inherently undemocratic nature of the Egyptian Muslim Brotherhood. Their ability to reach powerful people, and the success of their message, writes Fisher (2016), was based on deep, institutionalized and personal relationships:

> Virtually anyone who has worked in the US government on Middle East policy has probably, at some point, worked alongside a Saudi counterpart on a shared policy goal of some kind. This means that Washington's foreign policy establishment is filled with people who have developed a comforting familiarity with the Saudis, who are well-attuned to Saudi views and concerns, and often who maintain personal relationships with those counterparts.

Yousef al-Otaiba, the Emirati ambassador in Washington, embodies how such relationships are used to build support for GCC policy preferences. David Kirkpatrick (2018, pp. 206–208) provides a colorful description of Otaiba and his engagement in Washington. The son of one of his father's four wives (who happened to be Egyptian), Otaiba had grown up with immense privilege in Cairo and married an Egyptian woman himself. This, he claimed, gave him special insight into the Egyptian mentality. Otaiba had attended the American University in Cairo, and "looked and sounded American," which gave him increased access to Washington elites. The long tenures of GCC ambassadors such as Otaiba, who has been in Washington since 2008, provide them with deep local knowledge and a broad contact base. One former high-level Pentagon official described to me how he could trust Otaiba and his views because of his "Western" mentality. In fact, Otaiba is seen as a friend and confidant by many in the male-dominated Washington establishment, which affectionately calls him "Bro-taiba" (Kirkpatrick 2018, p. 206). It helps that Otaiba lives in a Virginia mansion on the banks of the Potomac, hires Wolfgang Puck to cook for dinner parties, and maintains a "legendary" wine collection (Kirkpatrick 2018, p. 206).

The UAE spent over $21 million on lobbying in Washington in 2017 (Massoglia and West 2018). This is in addition to donations it frequently makes to well-regarded think tanks such as the Center for Strategic and International Studies, advertisements in influential media venues, and charitable gifts to hospitals and foundations, including the $3 million it gave to the Clinton Foundation (Kirkpatrick 2018, p. 207). Leaked emails indicate that Otaiba paid the Center for a New American Security $250,000 to help the UAE obtain military-grade drones and the Middle East Institute $20 million to hire scholars with views sympathetic to Emirati interests (Kirkpatrick 2018, p. 207). A party Otaiba hosted for a New York cancer institute included performances by Beyoncé, Alicia Keys, and Ludacris (Kirkpatrick 2018, p. 207).

Otaiba and his Saudi counterpart, Adel al-Jubeir, writes Kirkpatrick (2018, p. 207), "transcended the roles of mere envoys." Otaiba was one of the few ambassadors invited to confidential meetings at the Pentagon (p. 207). Among foreign envoys in Washington, Otaiba's connections, writes Kirkpatrick (p. 207), are "unrivaled." Former CENTCOM commander and defense secretary Mattis called Otaiba "a friend and tremendous ally through some very difficult times" (p. 207). Mattis even briefly worked as a military consultant to the UAE after retiring and before becoming Trump's secretary of defense (Herb 2017). Republican Senator Richard Burr of the Senate Intelligence Committee once said in an interview that he has "spent probably more time with Yousef than I have anybody" (Kirkpatrick 2018, p. 207). About Jubeir, Mattis said: "Adel was always one of my best advisers" (Kirkpatrick 2018, p. 207). Former CIA director Hayden (2016, p. 320) writes that Jubeir was "always a welcome guest at CIA for tea and conversation." Secretary of State John Kerry, as noted in Chapter 3, maintained similarly close ties with Gulf envoys and royals.

Summing up their role, Rhodes said to Kirkpatrick (2018, p. 207): "Yousef and Adel have gained this status in Washington where they aren't seen as representatives of foreign governments; they are seen as advisors on Middle East issues." "When you have Yousef al-Otaiba actively promoting a particular agenda, it carries weight," one official told me.[18] Another analyst added: "Otaiba saw paralysis in the US government and used it to push his agenda."[19]

One former senior official in the Obama administration described to me another way that the Saudis and Emiratis constrained US democracy promotion through direct diplomacy. In the latter part of the Obama presidency, Saudi and Emirati officials would never tire of reminding their American counterparts that it was the United States that had produced the Arab Spring and all the chaos that followed. They pointed to the White House's opening of channels to the Muslim Brotherhood to prove that it was Washington that brought Morsi to power in Egypt. Moreover, they hammered home the message that the Americans had thrown their close ally, Mubarak, under the bus. The irony of course was that before 2011 the United States had worked to keep Mubarak in power. Nevertheless, the official observed that this approach continually put the United States on the defensive. "It was hard to get to our talking points on democracy and human rights, because it sounded as if we were confirming what the Saudis and Emiratis were accusing us of."[20] The Saudi and Emirati strategy in Washington was a thorn in the side of the State Department's Bureau of Near Eastern Affairs for the remainder of the Obama administration. It was effective with a president who despised the idea of interfering and put him in a position where he felt he had to prove his loyalty to GCC allies, which in turn made Obama wary of making proactive statements or pushing too hard on the Gulf monarchies. In this sense, the Gulf states not only countervailed US democracy promotion, but also increased their leverage in Washington over a host of issues. A Washington-based analyst of the region said: "The UAE and other countries know how to conquer and infiltrate our interagency process. We let them run roughshod over our interests while advancing theirs."[21]

Why couldn't the Obama administration have pushed back more on close allies to whom it provides a security umbrella? It is a question I have put to many inside and outside of the US government. The answers are rarely convincing. Derek Chollet, a former senior official in the White House and State and Defense Departments, offered the following as an explanation:

If you're only looking at what's good for the US in Libya, then it may make sense to put it all on the table to pressure Qatar to work with us on Libya. But that's not the only thing you're doing. You're also worried about Iran, you're trying to build a pressure campaign against Iran to get leverage in the nuclear negotiations. You're also worried about Qatar's support in Gaza, if you're also worried about access that you're providing for troops in Afghanistan and the Doha channel for Afghanistan, so it's got to fit within a broader context and that's one of the challenges in government, it's one of the challenges for scholars and historians looking in from the outside. You can look through the soda straw of whatever issue it is and tell the story just looking at that, but you've also got to look at it within the broader context and that's the great challenge for decision-makers is how they manage those trade-offs.[22]

Discussion: Challengers and US Democracy Promotion in the Arab World

Chapter 1 highlighted debates in the relatively new scholarly literature about the motivations of autocracy promoters. There is an argument to be made that the Gulf powers are not necessarily driven by the desire to spread their own nondemocratic model of governance around the world. The Saudis have shown that they are willing and able to push for a very limited democratic opening when their interests are not threatened, or when those interests can be advanced. For example, in Bahrain, Riyadh in the past has counseled the al-Khalifa monarchy to adopt a national dialogue as a pressure-release tactic, but without allowing for meaningful political participation. In Yemen, the GCC helped negotiate Ali Abdullah Saleh's exit from power in 2011 while ensuring that his successor was friendly to Saudi interests. In contexts such as South Asia, Saudi and Emirati foreign policy has not been uniformly opposed to democracy (Wehrey 2015).

Motivations notwithstanding, Gulf interests have generally lined up with the promotion of an exclusionary and autocratic mode of governance in the Middle East. Electoral democracy is simply not on the table. As a senior official told me: "It is simple: after the Arab Spring the Gulf wanted to put democracy back in the box, permanently."[23] Indeed, the preceding analysis has clearly shown that Saudi, Emirati, and to a lesser extent, Qatari, financial, diplomatic, military, and propaganda power at key junctures contributed to authoritarian retrenchment in Egypt and Bahrain and state fragmentation in Libya. In so doing, the GCC countries directly challenged the Obama administration's already limited democracy promotion efforts and raised the costs of future such efforts, reducing the will of US policymakers to carry them out. A key part of the Emirati and Saudi strategy was to influence key policy elites in Washington, "amplifying preexisting norms and habits" (Fisher 2016) and playing on their fears and prejudices about the consequences of democratization in the Arab world. It should be said that other challengers to democracy promotion also mattered, notably Israel, which also exerts strong influence over Washington policymakers through a well-organized lobby. As one former official said to me, "the Israelis lobby extremely well for the Egyptians in Washington."[24]

Gulf interventions in the post–Arab Spring had unintended consequences. Libyans, for example, became fed up with Gulf meddling and its role in destroying their country. Libyans have in the past demonstrated against the policies of Qatar and other Gulf powers. Sisi faced a nationalist backlash in 2016 after announcing the transfer of two empty islands to his patrons in Saudi Arabia. When protests erupted, the Egyptian police, writes Kirkpatrick (2018, p. 326), "started arresting and shooting [protestors] as if they had been Islamists." Moreover, Sisi's Gulf benefactors soon found out, as the Americans already knew, that "Egypt was not an easy client state" (Lynch 2016, p. 157).

Notes

1. Interview with former US official, Washington, DC, November 2018.
2. In a May 2013 GCC meeting the idea of a merger between Saudi Arabia and Bahrain received an endorsement from both sides, though other GCC governments were skeptical. In 2011, pro-Khalifa hard-line Sunni groups marching against the uprising had also called for such a merger. Shia activists, meanwhile, note the irony that they are often accused of undermining Bahrain's sovereignty because of alleged ties to Iran (Wehrey 2015, p. 79).
3. Phone interview with former US official, May 2018.
4. Quoted in Hassan (2015, p. 486).
5. Interview with former US official, New York, February 2018.
6. Quoted in Kirkpatrick (2018, p. 208).
7. Wehrey (2015, p. 76) points out that Saudi backing of Morsi's ouster caused substantial anger among parts of Saudi society and its clerical establishment.
8. King Abdullah, quoted in Hassan (2015, p. 486).
9. Later, a song was recorded in Egypt thanking the Emiratis and Saudis for helping to facilitate the coup (Kirkpatrick 2018, p. 261).
10. Interview with former US official, Washington, DC, February 2018.
11. Interview with Jonathan Winer, Washington, DC, October 2018. Winer told me that in 2016 the Russians were worse than the Emiratis in terms of their meddling in Libya.
12. Interview with analyst, Paris, October 2017.
13. Ibid.
14. Quoted in Wehrey (2015).
15. Ibid.
16. Phone interview with US official, May 2018.
17. Interview with former Obama administration official, Washington, February 2018.
18. Interview with US official, Washington, DC, February 2018.

19. Interview with Middle East analyst, Washington, DC, February 2018.
20. Interview with former US official, Washington, DC, February 2018.
21. Interview with Middle East analyst, Washington, DC, February 2018.
22. Interview with Derek Chollet, Washington, DC, November 2018.
23. Interview with US official, Washington, DC, February 2018.
24. Interview with former US official, Washington, DC, October 2018.

6
Trump and the Demise of US Democracy Promotion

By the end of Obama's presidency, US democracy promotion in the Arab world was swallowed up by a new war on terror, an interventionist Gulf, and the disillusionment of Obama and his closest advisers with the gloomy aftermath of the Arab Spring. In early 2011, Obama the former community organizer, the believer in change from below, wanted the young people in Tahrir Square to win. He also wanted to be on the right side of history, as some in his inner circle advised. In an interview later that year, Obama listed the Arab Spring among the most important events in his lifetime, along with the civil rights movement, the end of the Cold War, and the release of Nelson Mandela (McFaul 2018, p. 216). "At least in the spring and summer of 2011," then White House adviser Michael McFaul (2018, p. 216) writes, "Obama understood the magnitude of what was happening in the Middle East. He wanted to be a part of it." But over time Obama the pragmatist and realist wanted other things in foreign policy too: the pivot to Asia, the Iranian deal, and the rapprochement with Cuba. The Arab Spring, McFaul (2018, p. 209) explained, was a "giant unwanted crisis, distracting us from other objectives." William Burns (2019, p. 295), Obama's deputy secretary of state, writes in his memoirs that the Arab Spring "was inexorably tugging [Obama] back to the crisis-driven Middle East focus that he had hoped so much to escape."

The result of these competing impulses might be described as a series of half measures. Obama supported a democratic transition in Egypt, but did not want to go "all in" with assistance and pressure. He wanted to punish those who carried out the 2013 coup in Egypt and killed peaceful protesters in its wake, but he did not want to completely rupture relations with the Egyptian military. He helped the Libyan rebels with US military power and was happy to see Qaddafi overthrown, but did not want to invest in the subsequent transition. He condemned the violence of the Bahraini regime against protesters and called for democratic reforms while reaffirming the closeness of Washington's relationship with the al-Khalifa monarchy. In Syria, he assisted the rebels to some degree, but not enough to enable a decisive victory over Bashar al-Assad. In Yemen, he supported a negotiated exit for a longtime strongman, Ali Abdullah Saleh, but then surrendered policy to the Saudis after ensuring that US counterterror operations could continue in the country. Even in Tunisia, the one bright spot in the post–Arab Spring, Obama took a restrained approach, never visiting the country despite being encouraged by Ben Rhodes to do so.[1]

The Obama administration, moreover, was only willing and able to offer modest amounts of economic assistance to the post–Arab Spring transitions. A year and a half after the uprisings, the United States had only allocated or proposed $2.2 billion in new aid to Arab Spring countries. By comparison, the United States committed $128 billion in today's dollars to Europe during the first four years of the Marshall Plan (Hamid 2015). While some of Obama's advisers pushed him to seize the historic moment for change in the Arab world, others wondered why, with American public opinion focused on the economy, Obama was preoccupied by the Arab Spring (Rhodes 2018, p. 111). "No one had voted for Obama so that he'd do something about Libya," writes Rhodes (p. 111).

Thus, Obama was never willing to commit major resources or expend large amounts of political capital on democracy promotion in the Arab world. For believers in US democracy promotion, and for believers in the idea that Arabs deserve better than to have to choose between chaos and autocracy, Obama's response to the Arab Spring was a disappointment. The policies were tepid, even as the May 2011 rhetoric was soaring. The words had no clear policy, strategy, or financial weight behind them, and foreign policy institutions were unwilling or unable to operationalize Obama's stated goals. One senior Obama official told me:

> After the earthquake of the Arab Spring, there was no full interagency pause that said, "let's take a look at what just happened. Let's bring our best and brightest together and ask, what are our opportunities?" Instead, the approach was, let's pump some more money in. The bureaucracy's response was basically, "let's do what we were already doing."[2]

Ironically, many career foreign policy bureaucrats criticized Obama and his young advisers for going too far, too fast in throwing US weight behind the uprisings. The career people thought that "democratic vision" was overrated in an uncertain situation and in countries with no history of democracy or opposition. They saw the young White House operatives as hopelessly naive and unable to see each Arab country through its proper unique context. One former senior career official, speaking about Bahrain, put it this way:

> But, oh by the way, yes it might be a little bit slow in reform—not slower than Saudi Arabia for God's sake—and oh by the way they do have a legitimate fear of Iran and subversion, they're making it worse through some of their repressive policies but the Bahraini interior services are not the same as the Egyptian interior services or the Tunisian interior services and I think that the White House lumped them all together as repressive knuckle-dragging autocrats.

Another career official told me that "building a Rolodex" takes time, pointing out that Obama and his progressive advisers did not even know who the "opposition" was when they chose to back the Arab Spring uprisings. This official invoked Ahmed Chelabi of Iraq as a cautionary tale of embracing opposition figures without appropriate scrutiny. In Iraq, the United States had thrown its support behind a questionable exile who turned out not to be a great democrat.[3] By contrast, many career officials succumbed to what one of my interviewees called the "soft bigotry of low expectations" vis-à-vis the Arab world.[4] By the end of the Obama presidency, few individuals, and virtually no institutions, were arguing that US ideals and US interests in the Arab world were synonymous.

Obama and the Lack of Faith in US Leverage

US democracy promotion in the Arab world under Obama was further weakened by the president's ongoing ambivalence about the region and the potential for US leverage there. His views had always been informed by Iraq, and after 2012, the unravelling of Libya was added to that script. As one former senior official observed about the "Libya effect," the voices inside the administration wanting to take more decisive action on issues from Syria to Sisi had a "harder time" after the killing of Ambassador Stevens because there was "pushback saying, 'well, wait, okay, you know what this is going to lead to.'"[5] One official who had served in a number of senior positions across the interagency said that with regard to Libya, "I think we were probably seduced by the view that we could be more in control of events than it turned out to be."[6]

This dim view of US leverage was ultimately seized upon by many institutional actors who had always been skeptical of democracy promotion. There are no four words that I heard more frequently in my dozens of interviews with administration officials than "we had no leverage." On some level, I am sympathetic. I witnessed multiple "damned if you do, damned if you don't" moments while working in and on the region at the State

Department. We opened a dialogue with the Egyptian Muslim Brotherhood only to be attacked for being "in bed" with the group a year later. We supported Egyptian civil society only to have a vicious anti-American campaign directed against us for doing so. In Libya, we tried to assist the transition to a modest degree but were often thwarted by weak and dysfunctional institutions that were unwilling or unable to serve as partners (Chollet and Fishman 2015).

Obama also repeatedly found himself in "damned if you do, damned if you don't" situations owing to domestic politics in the United States. For instance, pundits and Republicans first condemned the president for being weak on Libya when he did not advocate military intervention right away, and then criticized him for "leading from behind" once he decided on US involvement.[7] Some members of Congress, such as Senator Marco Rubio, criticized Obama for a drawn-out intervention in Libya without the necessary legislative authorization only to later attack him for not intervening in Syria. Then, when Obama sought congressional support for a possible strike in Syria, Congressional leaders balked, with Rubio arguing that it was "too late" (Kerry 2018, p. 535). Rhodes (2018, p. 123) writes: "The Arab Spring was upending a rooted, corrupt, authoritarian order in the Middle East, and yet the debate about these seismic events in Washington was an extension of our own partisan, diminished discourse."

On another level, however, the hypothesis that the United States had no influence at these key moments is hard to accept because the Obama administration was often unwilling to meaningfully test whether it had its leverage. What if the United States had maintained the hold on arms sales to Bahrain for longer than just a few months, even if the regime complained bitterly to the Pentagon? Perhaps after a year they would have seen that the United States was serious about its calls for reform and embarked on a path of greater inclusion. What if the United States had been firmer in its resolve to withhold assistance to the SCAF and Morsi in Egypt until an inclusive constitution was written and the issue of US funding for Egyptian NGOs was resolved in a just way? What if the United States had cajoled the Libyan factions toward a sustainable settlement by attempting to block access to Libya's central bank reserves until they came to the negotiation table? The inherent limitations of counterfactual reasoning need not become an excuse for the lack of US resolve.

The "we had no leverage" argument mirrors another one made by many former officials who worked on the US response to the Arab Spring: that the deployment of security assistance conditionality as a tool of democracy promotion was ultimately futile. The foreign policy bureaucracies were skeptical of its use from the beginning, with the DoD openly hostile to its application. The State Department was split between the Near Eastern Affairs Bureau, which—fearful of losing channels of access—often shared

DoD's skepticism, and the Bureau of Democracy, Rights, and Labor, which advocated it wholeheartedly. In fact, at several points it was Congress, perhaps finally waking up to its constitutionally mandated oversight role, that pushed to impose conditions on the restoration of assistance to Bahrain, Egypt, and eventually Saudi Arabia over concerns about the kingdom's use of indiscriminate bombing, which has killed scores of civilians in the Yemen war.[8] And yet, in almost all cases congressionally imposed conditions included a national security waiver clause, which Obama invoked on several occasions. As one keen observer of Congress put it, "why should Congress take ownership of these issues when you can make the White House own them?"[9]

By contrast, those who advocated for using security assistance as a lever today argue that when deployed, it actually did work. They point out that the worst repression and abuses in Bahrain and Egypt occurred after freezes in assistance were lifted. Such evidence notwithstanding, many career military officials and diplomats oppose using security assistance as a tool of democratic leverage, arguing that in the end autocrats will act in their own interest, doing whatever it takes to maintain their grip on power. These officials, furthermore, often express skepticism of the democratic credentials of the opposition. One former career official expressed such sentiments to me in candidly colorful terms, speaking about the uprising in Bahrain:

> If it's an existential thing, why would Bahrain accommodate the United States if it means they lose their heads? Right? So it's like, we're going to keep our heads, we're going to do the right thing. [The king and crown prince] don't stay up at night thinking: "how can I kill my own people? But I'm under threat. And these are not a bunch of Thomas Jeffersons over here rebelling against King George III. So, I'm going to do the right thing, maybe the wrong way, but I'm going to do the right thing, I'm going to make mistakes, you can either help me or try to stand in my way but you're not going to stop me."[10]

Those opposed to attaching conditions to security assistance also point out the ability of the Gulf states, China, Russia, and other countries to replenish lost assistance and supplies with even bigger infusions of cash and their own military equipment. Yet, others counter that Gulf monarchies would be unlikely to do so given the quality of US equipment and its compatibility with existing hardware. But even assuming they did turn to Russia or China, as one former senior DoD official, Derek Chollet, pointed out to me, the US defense industry and the Pentagon could adjust—it does not have to be "devastating," Chollet said. DoD, Chollet added, "tends to overstate the damage that withholding military assistance would have on our security interests."[11] And it is important to note that in both Egypt and Bahrain, at no point was aid *completely* cut off. Even when and where there was a suspension of assistance, it largely applied to the big-ticket items. Many other assistance mechanisms continued to disburse aid and sell arms. This fact only lends further support to the argument that it is impossible to say that security assistance conditionality would not work as leverage, since it was never meaningfully attempted.

Enter Trump, Exit Democracy Promotion

While Obama gradually lowered the importance assigned to democracy promotion in the Arab world over the course of his presidency, Donald Trump delivered the final blow to its pursuit in Arab Spring countries. In the first two years of his presidential administration, Trump has not just accelerated the rollback of US democracy promotion in the Arab world, but has also openly glorified autocracy and autocrats around the world. Indeed, no president has shown such open disdain for the well-established traditions of US democracy and human rights promotion and for US leadership of the liberal world order more generally. While previous US presidents have worked closely with nondemocratic leaders in the pursuit of security and economic interests, Trump "has moved with unprecedented alacrity, even enthusiasm, to embrace autocrats, many of whom were previously given at least a partial cold shoulder by the United States" (Carothers 2017).

Carothers (2017) notes that during the 2016 presidential election campaign, "Trump repeatedly signaled a lack of interest in or concern about violations of democratic norms and rights in other countries, a strong disinclination to prioritize democracy support in US foreign policy, and an admiration for repressive strongmen, from Russia's Vladimir Putin to Iraq's Saddam Hussein." Trump dubbed his foreign policy platform "America First," which he defined in zero-sum terms: A focus on America's security and economic interests could not be compatible with the promotion of democracy and human rights.[12] "America First" is, at its heart, transactional. As Thomas Friedman (2018) put it,

> Everything is a transaction: What have you done for *me* today? The notion of America as the upholder of last resort of global rules and human rights—which occasionally forgoes small economic advantages to strengthen democratic societies so we can enjoy the much larger benefits of a world of healthy, free-market democracies—is over.

While "America First" was never translated into a coherent doctrine during the campaign, after his inauguration, Trump's early cohort of advisers attempted to turn the slogan into something foreign policy experts could recognize as a strategy. In Trump's first National Security Strategy (NSS), released in December 2017, "America First" is situated within existing US foreign policy traditions:

> An America First National Security Strategy is based on American principles, a clear-eyed assessment of U.S. interests, and a determination to tackle the challenges that we face. It is a strategy of principled realism that is guided by outcomes, not ideology. It is based upon the view that peace, security, and prosperity depend on strong, sovereign nations that respect their citizens at home and cooperate to advance peace abroad. And it is grounded in the realization that American principles are a lasting force for good in the world. (White House 2017)

In noting that "American principles are a lasting force for good," Trump's NSS does not abandon the Wilsonian tradition of democracy promotion outright. However, it does not go beyond an abstract commitment to the concept, never elaborating how human rights and democracy promotion will be operationalized in US foreign policy. The section on the Middle East is explicit in prioritizing short-term interests over democracy and human rights, declaring that the United States "will . . . advance security through stability. Whenever possible, we will encourage gradual reforms" (White House 2017, p. 49). "Security through stability" clearly signals a return to pre–Freedom Agenda conceptions of US interests in the Arab world, providing the strategic framework to understand the Trump administration's close relationships with Arab strongmen and absolute monarchs. Carothers (2017) argues that Trump's lack of interest in democracy promotion "is an integral part of his larger discomfort with the long-standing U.S. commitment to an international liberal order." According to Carothers (2017), "it fits with his questioning of an international system of free trade, core alliance relationships, and major multilateral institutions, such as the United Nations, and his broader belief that the very idea of a positive-sum approach to international order is basically a sucker's game."

There are those who have argued that Trump is in fact a democracy promoter.[13] One could point to his forceful statements about human rights in Cuba or Iran, for example. But these are politically expedient. By harshly criticizing the Cuban or Iranian regime's human rights record, he is also distinguishing himself from Obama, and in the case of Cuba, appealing to the hard-line Cuban émigrés who voted for him. Venezuela is another case in which the Trump administration speaks frequently of democratization. In January 2019, the administration issued a statement demanding democracy for the people of Venezuela and calling for the removal of strongman Nicolás Maduro following a rigged 2018 presidential election. Working in concert with other nations, the administration also took the bold step of recognizing opposition leader Juan Guaidó as interim president. Even Democratic foreign policy stalwarts argued that this was a welcome policy (Murphy and

Rhodes 2019). However, just as contradictions and inconsistencies in the implementations of George W. Bush's Freedom Agenda lower the credibility of his democracy promotion agenda, so does Trump's record of showering praise on allied autocratic leaders adversely affect the credibility of his Venezuela policy. Carothers (2017) writes:

> Furthermore, what little attention Trump and his team have devoted to democracy abroad has been directed most pointedly to countries the United States considers hostile in a broader geostrategic sense. Democracy concerns do not appear to be asserted out of some serious attachment to principle, but rather as a club to beat up on disfavored governments. Trump's philosophy on democracy thus appears to skeptical foreign observers as profoundly cynical—for my antidemocratic friends, anything; for my enemies, democracy.

In what follows, I apply the individuals-institutions-challengers framework used throughout the book to examine more closely the forces that have shaped the abandonment of democracy promotion in the first two years of the Trump administration.

Individuals

Joshua Muravchik, a former adviser to Bill Clinton, emphasizes that in order for democracy promotion to make it on the foreign policy agenda, a president has to be seen by all levels of the administration as caring about it.[14] Moreover, the president and his top advisers have to *believe* in democracy in order for the United States to be its credible promoter. Despite the chaotic and unpredictable approach to decisionmaking that Trump seems to relish, it is possible to identify a core set of beliefs held by the president and some of his most influential advisers and evaluate the compatibility of these beliefs with democracy promotion.

Trump's praise for strongmen around the world has been so consistent and effusive that it is hard to believe that the president does not genuinely admire autocratic rule to some degree. Given that Trump has been more than willing to take a hard-line approach with traditional democratic allies from Canada to Germany on issues such as trade, his praise for authoritarian regimes is all the more striking. As Ben Rhodes pointed out to me, every time Trump sits down with the leader of a democratic allied state, there is some drama or slight, while his encounters with autocrats go swimmingly well.[15]

Although the brutality of Philippine president Rodrigo Duterte's war on drugs has earned the condemnation of most Western governments and human rights groups, Trump said that Duterte was doing "an unbelievable job" on the drug issue (Nelson 2017). In comments about the North Korean dictator Kim Jong-un following a historic summit in Singapore in June 2018, Trump said, "He speaks, and his people sit at attention. I want my people to do the same."[16] Such comments, even if motivated by an attempt at humor, as Trump later claimed, have contributed to a narrative casting doubt on Trump's commitment to democracy and human rights at home and abroad. However, Trump's silence in the face of democratic backsliding and autocracy cannot be explained by humor. This silence extends beyond encounters with autocratic Arab allies such as Sisi and Mohammed Bin Salman. During a July 2017 visit to Poland at a critical moment of "worrisome democratic backsliding," Trump did not raise issues of democracy and "instead joined the Polish government in attacking the free press" (Carothers 2017). Current officials with whom I spoke maintain that in cases such as Hungary and Poland, quiet criticism will be much more effective than public "naming and shaming." Democracy promotion experts, by contrast, see Trump's reluctance to call out nondemocratic behavior in regimes he perceives as friendly to the United States as setting a dangerous precedent and providing *carte blanche* to authoritarian populists with which to continue their attacks on democratic institutions.[17]

Trump's comfort with authoritarianism in the Arab world has lined up with his focus on Islamic extremism and his fear of Islamist parties. This has further increased his penchant to ally with leaders such as Egypt's Sisi, as well as the Emirati and Saudi royal families. Trump embraced Sisi and promised that jointly, "we will fight terrorism . . . and we're going to be friends for a long, long period of time" (Friedman 2017). The fixation on "radical Islam" and support for Sisi, the UAE, and Saudi Arabia has also been driven by other key individuals in his inner circle, some of whom were introduced earlier in the book. For example, Trump chose General James Mattis as his defense secretary and General Mike Flynn as his first national security adviser, "both eager supporters of General Sisi and relentless foes of the Muslim Brotherhood" (Kirkpatrick 2018, p. 332). Ambassador Yousef al-Otaiba of the UAE, meanwhile, tutored Jared Kushner, senior adviser to the president, on Middle East issues (Kirkpatrick 2018, p. 332), undoubtedly transmitting the uncompromising Emirati view of the Arab Spring.

Trump's words send an unmistakable signal of support to autocrats around the world, and a host of evidence suggests that strongmen rulers from the Philippines to Turkey and Hungary to Saudi Arabia have been empowered by Trump's apparent affinity for authoritarianism. But Trump's "strongman envy" also might be "seen by these same strongmen as evidence of his weakness and manipulability."[18] The autocracy-reinforcing potential of Trump's rhetoric is often indirect and not immediately evident. For example, Trump's fixation on what he calls "fake news" and his attacks on the media help reinforce the legal strategies and other methods autocrats use to quell free speech, especially by persecuting journalists and the independent media (Beiser 2017). Ben Rhodes asks, "what autocrat have you not heard use the term 'fake news' over the past two years?"[19]

The Economist (2017) made a telling observation about how Trump's rhetoric can reinforce the impulses of nondemocratic leaders, using the case of Cambodia:

> Hun Sen, Cambodia's prime minister, pounced on the humbling of reporters by the White House, declaring with approval on February 27th that Mr. Trump, like him, sees the press causing "anarchy." The gloating did not stop there. Denouncing a CNN report on sex trafficking in Cambodia in August, Hun Sen grumbled that "President Trump is right: U.S. media is very tricky."

Michael Posner, the former assistant secretary of state for democracy, human rights, and labor, who was featured in the sections of this book on Bahrain, has said that the Trump threat is not so much to US democracy but to states with much weaker democratic institutions where, for decades, activists have looked to the United States to warn regimes, sometimes publicly and sometimes quietly, that there are "consequences for [their] relations with the U.S.—trade, aid, military, investment—if [they] crush peaceful dissent."[20] Or, as Thomas Friedman (2018) observes, in the era of Trump, authoritarian governments around the world no longer think that the "Americans will never let us get away with that."

Trump has surrounded himself with individuals who share his commitment to a narrowly interest-centered and military-first foreign policy. A few months into the new administration, current or retired soldiers occupied roughly 40 percent of senior leadership positions on the National Security Council (Farrow 2018, p. 156). Reflecting the White House's preferences, the State Department stopped detailing its officials to the NSC (Farrow 2018, p. 156). Two of Trump's first three national security advisers, Flynn and H. R. McMaster, were military generals. Although his third national security adviser, John Bolton, never served in the armed forces, his preference for military solutions and distrust of international organizations are well known. While at times labeled a neoconservative, Bolton should more accurately be seen as a radical nationalist within the Republican foreign policy establishment. Radical nationalists, writes Heer (2018), "share the neoconservative disdain for international institutions but have no real interest in democracy promotion." The presence of so many military officers in top foreign policy positions means that the DoD perspective, which rarely emphasizes democracy promotion, dominates.

Trump's two secretaries of state also clearly shared his aversion to democracy and human rights promotion. In his first major policy speech, former secretary of state Rex Tillerson stressed the following:

> I think it is really important that all of us understand the difference between policy and values. Our values around freedom, human dignity, the way people are treated—those are our values. Those are not our policies. In some circumstances, if you condition our national security efforts on someone adopting our values, we probably can't achieve our national security goals. If we condition too heavily that others just adopt this value we have come to over a long history of our own, it really creates obstacles to our ability to advance our national security interests or economic interests.[21]

Early on, Tillerson ordered State officials to remove allusions to democracy promotion from the department's core mission statements (Rogin 2017), and his congratulatory messages on the national days of several countries did not mention democracy as prominently as those of his predecessor, Kerry (Bhatia 2017). Tillerson's successor, Mike Pompeo, has only selectively emphasized human rights and democracy promotion, while lavishing praise on autocratic allies such as Egypt's Sisi. Pompeo's speeches have contained sporadic mentions of religious freedom, protection for the LGBT community, and Venezuela. His background as a Tea Party–affiliated member of Congress, his previous dabbling in Islamophobia, and the fact that he shares with Trump an obsession with "radical Islam," suggests that he will be an unlikely democracy promoter. As CIA director, he once said, "you don't find many Thomas Jeffersons" in the Middle East.[22] Once you accept that, he continued, "the line needs to be drawn [between] those who are on the side of extremism and those who are fighting it."[23] Pompeo is also a former military man who supports a military-centered approach: In January 2019 he announced the expansion of the al-Udeid air base in Qatar (Diehl 2019). Noting Pompeo's alienation of career staff and many legislators, Jackson Diehl (2018) of the *Washington Post* opined in late 2018 that Pompeo's "only satisfied customer may be President Trump." Neither is Gina Haspel, who in May 2018 replaced Pompeo as CIA director, likely to be a strong advocate of democracy promotion. Haspel was previously involved in designing and carrying out the agency's rendition and torture programs. Other domestic advisers in the president's inner circle include nationalists such as Stephen Miller. Miller wields significant power over issues such as refugee policy and thus steers Trump further away from democracy and human rights issues (Thrush and Steinhauer 2017).

As telling as how Trump has chosen to fill key positions in the US foreign policy apparatus is what positions he has not filled, starting with key ambassadorial posts. Ambassadors, as previous chapters have noted, are not always ideal democracy promoters, but at the very least they can credibly deliver quiet messages on the need for reform in a way that interim chargés d'affaires cannot. As of mid 2019, the post of assistant secretary of state for democracy, human rights, and labor—a critical voice on democracy promotion issues—

remains vacant. Instead, there is a "senior bureau official" with little political clout. Tillerson had previously eliminated the post of senior adviser for civil society and emerging democracy, a post created by Hillary Clinton. As one democracy promotion advocate who served multiple presidents told me when discussing the Trump administration and democracy promotion, "With respect to President Trump, the question I would ask is, is there any one making the argument [for democracy promotion]? You're not going to get there if no one on the inside is trying."[24]

That left US ambassador to the UN Nikki Haley as the only high-level voice on democracy and human rights issues in the Trump administration until her resignation in December 2018. Though she had little prior foreign policy experience, Haley was the senior Trump official most frequently condemning human rights violations on issues such as South Sudan, Burma, and Nicaragua.[25] Though she was known for her consistent advocacy on behalf of Israel, she is also remembered for her aggressive condemnation of Russian support for the Assad regime and Russia's decision to veto resolutions in the wake of the Assad regime's chemical weapon attacks on Syrian civilians (Haley 2018b). However, it was unclear whether world leaders saw her as speaking for Trump, thereby reducing her influence over democracy and human rights issues. And she rarely raised human rights violations in the Arab world beyond Syria. It is unlikely that Kelly Knight Craft, who has been nominated to replace Haley as US permanent representative, will be a strong voice on such issues, especially since it is doubtful that she will be given cabinet-level status like her predecessor (Rucker and Gearan 2019).

Institutions

Even as Trump and his top surrogates have expressed unfavorable views of democracy promotion, "the Trump White House is far too chaotic, riven by infighting and buffeted by the impulses of the president, to have clear doctrines about democracy promotion, or many other weighty questions of geopolitics" (*The Economist* 2017). This is where institutions enter the picture and fill some of the policy voids left by the Trump White House. The Pentagon and intelligence communities, rarely at the forefront of democracy promotion at the best of times, have been troubled by Trump's verbal attacks on US allies and the liberal international order and pushed back on Trump's impulses to dismiss NATO or to wash America's hands of its Middle East commitments. In late 2018, when Trump suddenly announced the complete withdrawal of US troops from Syria, the DoD, fearing for the fate of its Kurdish and other allies, found ways to slow-roll the process (Tapper 2019). But DoD and the intelligence community are nonetheless satisfied with the increased autonomy they have enjoyed under the Trump administration on counterterrorism. The further empowerment of the DoD and CIA with a parallel decline in the power of the State Department has only intensified trends in place since 9/11 by which the State Department has lost bargaining power in the interagency process (Farrow 2018), thereby decreasing the chances that democracy promotion is incorporated into US foreign policy.

The State Department has at times contradicted Trump's statements and carried out policies indicative of a continuing commitment to democracy promotion. Many career diplomats I spoke with in 2018 and 2019 were continuing policies established under previous administrations, including the implementation of numerous democracy assistance programs around the world. Moreover, in specific cases the State Department issued statements or carried out democracy promotion policies despite silence from the White House. For example, in the Cambodia case mentioned above, in spite of Trump's apparent affinity for strongman Hun Sen, the White House itself issued a statement expressing "grave concern" after Cambodia's highest court dissolved the main opposition party and warning of "concrete steps" in response (*The Economist* 2017). This is because, as *The Economist* (2017) notes, "with a small country like Cambodia, policy remains broadly set by career foreign service officers (among them the American ambassador), by staff in the National Security Council and by members of Congress sincerely aggrieved by Hun Sen's assaults on democracy and news outlets." *The Economist* adds that "foreign autocrats are also learning that America's president does not rule alone." In another example cited by Carothers (2017), a career US ambassador, Patricia Alsup, worked during a critical moment in early 2017 to help the Gambia get through a troubled election. Carothers notes that State Department efforts in the Gambia "included rapid mobilization of democracy funds, support for the pro-democratic role by the Economic Community of West African States, and nuanced diplomacy with key Gambian political actors." Given Trump's lack of regard for and attention to Africa, working levels of the State Department play a leading role in policy formulation and can preserve democracy promotion without interference from the White House.

However, as Carothers (2017) also observes, "if such efforts do not receive general encouragement as well as specific backing at key moments from the top levels of the State Department and the White House, they will diminish in frequency and impact over time." He adds: "And if adequate resources are not available for timely injections of assistance or the tactical use of democracy assistance programming, they will suffer further."

To some degree, Congress as an institution has also stepped up to the plate as a democracy promoter. In March 2019, Congress passed a bipartisan measure to end US military support for the Saudi war in Yemen, which Trump promptly vetoed. Prominent individual members of Congress,

Republicans included, have challenged the relationship and the Saudi ruler in unusually strong terms. Senator Lindsey Graham of South Carolina, a close ally of President Trump, told reporters that "there's not a smoking gun, there's a smoking saw" connecting Mohammed bin Salman to Khashoggi's murder. After hearing an intelligence briefing on the Khashoggi murder, Graham said:

> The crown prince is a wrecking ball. I think he's complicit in the murder of Mr. Khashoggi to the highest level possible. I think his behavior before the Khashoggi murder was beyond disturbing. And I cannot see him being a reliable partner to the United States. If the Saudi government is going to be in the hands of this man for a long time to come, I find it very difficult to be able to do business because I think he's crazy, I think he is dangerous, and he has put the relationship at risk. I cannot support arms sales to Saudi Arabia as long as he's gonna be in charge of this country. You have to be willfully blind not to come to the conclusion that this was orchestrated and organized by people under the command of MBS and that he was intricately involved in the demise of Mr. Khashoggi.[26]

While human rights activists might welcome the pushback on Trump, such congressional statements have reflected a condemnation of an individual Saudi ruler rather than the entire repressive Saudi system of governance or the US relationship with the kingdom. Tom Malinowski, the former DRL assistant secretary who appeared in the sections on Bahrain and is now a member of Congress from New Jersey, went further in this regard: "If the administration will not do what is right, Congress can, and I think Congress will," he said. "We can and we should wipe the smug smile of impunity off of Mohammed bin Salman's face, and restore proper balance to our relationship with Saudi Arabia."[27] But Malinowski is hardly in the mainstream on this issue, and Congress has not yet passed legislation that would censure Saudi Arabia without giving the White House the possibility of a national security waiver.

Moreover, the fact that many democracy assistance mechanisms continue on autopilot, shielded by multiyear budgets and institutionalized in bureaucracies, might at first glance give some comfort to those proponents of democracy promotion terrified by positions Trump took during the campaign. Yet, many of their worst fears were confirmed with the announcement of the administration's first two proposed budgets, which called for massive cuts to the State Department. Within those budgets, the prospects for democracy and human rights promotion programs were especially dim. In his first budget, Trump proposed a 39 percent cut to the National Endowment for Democracy (NED) and a 24 percent cut to the Bureau of Democracy, Human Rights, and Labor, which administers many democracy assistance programs (Hill 2018). Institutions pushed back. The international affairs portion of Trump's budget was dead on arrival in the Congress. Senate Foreign Relations Committee Chair Bob Corker reportedly thought reviewing the budget was "a waste of time" and his Democratic counterpart, Ben Cardin, told Rex Tillerson in the Senate budget hearing, "we will write our own budget" (Farrow 2018, pp. 271–272). Cardin continued: "My concern today, quite frankly, is that your Administration will go down in the history books as being 'present at the destruction' of that order we have worked so hard to support—and that has so benefited our security and prosperity and ideals." Congress ultimately approved—and Trump signed—a budget with only a 0.67 percent cut to the NED and 4.5 percent increase for DRL (Hill 2018).

This did not stop Trump from proposing a budget with similar cuts for Fiscal Year 2019. The budget request proposed to cut funding for democracy programs by nearly 40 percent, including a 60 percent cut to the NED. In the budget category called "Governing Justly and Democratically," which includes many democracy assistance programs, the administration proposed a significant cut of over 30 percent. The request shows a preference for good governance, security, and economic opportunity activities and away from rule of law, human rights, political competition, and civil society support (Lawson and Epstein 2019). While continuing congressional pushback suggests that this budget will probably not become law, the priorities of the Trump administration are quite clear.

While significant will, commitment, determination, and an enormous reservoir of knowledge and experience exist among other individuals working on democracy promotion, the fact that there is little commitment at the top of the government hierarchy is disheartening to them. As Carothers (2017) argues, these professionals need a great deal of "determination and persistence to survive and ultimately overcome the negative currents at home."

Challengers

Trump's seemingly unconditional embrace of Saudi Arabia and the United Arab Emirates, the two states who have served as the most formidable challengers to US democracy in the Arab world since the uprisings of 2011, is yet another clear signal that the Trump administration had abandoned US democracy promotion in the Middle East and North Africa. "The rulers of Saudi Arabia and the United Arab Emirates were just as delighted with Trump as Sisi was," writes Kirkpatrick (2018, p. 332). The election of Trump to the presidency only emboldened Gulf influence operations in Washington, which include financial entanglements with the president's business empire. Ashford (2018a) writes about the "well-documented web of money linking the Saudis and Emiratis to the administration, its close backers, and the Trump family." Some of these linkages consist of legitimate business activity with the Gulf states through which Trump had made millions. During the presidential campaign, Trump bragged that he gets along with the Saudis brilliantly since they buy apartments from him, spending tens of millions (Farenthold and O'Connell 2018). The Gulf states have also spent generously at Trump's hotels and resorts since he was elected (Ashford 2018a).

In contrast to many presidents who used their first overseas trip to pay their respects to a democratic ally, Trump went to Saudi Arabia, where he received a lavish welcome. During the visit, he brokered a $110 billion arms deal (Liptak 2017). He told the Gulf leaders: "America is a sovereign nation and our first priority is always the safety and security of our citizens. We are not here to lecture, we are not here to tell other people how to live," sending another clear signal that the Trump administration would not be one to interfere with their authoritarian designs on the Arab Spring. Since then, the Trump administration has supported a more assertive Saudi role in the Middle East. Even as the humanitarian disaster in Yemen was worsening (Watkins and Walsh 2018), Trump pushed ahead a major weapons deal with Saudi Arabia in April 2018, approving the sale of $1.3 billion worth of artillery (Lederman 2018). While this amount is much smaller than the one announced in 2017, the arms sold—artillery—make for an odd choice given the Saudi-led coalition's indiscriminate use of artillery and air strikes.

The personal affinity between members of Trump's inner circle and Gulf royals are even more striking. Trump's son-in-law and adviser, Jared Kushner, seems to have forged a particularly close relationship with the Emirati and Saudi rulers (Kirkpatrick et al. 2018). At the same time, he has expressed disdain for their rivals, the Qataris. Some speculate that this may have something to do with the Kushner family's failure to secure Doha's funding for their real estate business (Ashford 2018a). At first glance, Trump's open Islamophobia would seem to preempt such an alliance, and indeed there was some worry on the part of Gulf monarchs after Trump won the Republican nomination. But operatives such as George Nader helped convince the Saudis and Emiratis that Trump would, in fact, act in their interests, fiercely opposing Iran (including tearing up the Iran nuclear deal) and the Muslim Brotherhood (Kirkpatrick and Mazzetti 2018).

Full Circle: Trump and US Democracy Promotion in the Arab World

While to some extent Trump has followed almost Obama-like instincts in seeking to disengage from the Arab world, he has also brought US policy full circle, back to the pre-9/11 days of unbridled support for authoritarianism in the region. "We are seeing a growing sense of impunity among Arab autocrats, a sense that they can do what they want no matter how many human rights violations they commit," said Maha Yahya, director of the Carnegie Middle East Center.[28] As Karlin and Wittes (2019) eloquently note, the combination of

Obama's reticence and Trump's embrace of autocracy leaves the United States now in a "worst-of-both-worlds" scenario in the Middle East:

> The United States thus exists in a kind of Middle Eastern purgatory—too distracted by regional crises to pivot to other global priorities but not invested enough to move the region in a better direction. This worst-of-both-worlds approach exacts a heavy price. It sows uncertainty among Washington's Middle Eastern partners, which encourages them to act in risky and aggressive ways. . . . It deepens the American public's frustration with the region's endless turmoil, as well as with U.S. efforts to address it. It diverts resources that could otherwise be devoted to confronting a rising China and a revanchist Russia. And all the while, by remaining unclear about the limits of its commitments, the United States risks getting dragged into yet another Middle Eastern conflict.

In what follows, I briefly survey the first two years of the Trump administration's policies toward the three countries highlighted in the book.

Bahrain

In a press conference after a May 2017 meeting with the Bahraini monarch, Trump sent yet another signal of his intention to downgrade, if not eliminate, the promotion of democracy and human rights, saying "our countries have a wonderful relationship, but there has been a little strain, but there won't be strain with this administration" (Reuters 2017). It is no coincidence, a Bahraini opposition figure told me, that almost immediately afterward the Bahraini security services carried out further crackdowns. The oppositionist added that if the regime knew that they were likely to pay a small cost under Obama for such repression, they knew that they would certainly pay no price under Trump. "Obama could have done a lot more," the person told me, "but Trump has done nothing, and only encouraged the hard-liners in the regime."[29] Other Bahraini opposition figures with whom I spoke in 2018 told me that US engagement on human rights, reconciliation, and democracy-related issues has disappeared since Trump took office. "The US embassy continues to meet with us to solicit input for the Human Rights Report," one such figure told me, "but they have given up on any advocacy activities."[30] This interviewee added that visiting senior US officials have not met with the Bahraini opposition since Trump came into office.

In March 2017, just two months after the inauguration, the Trump administration announced that it was lifting all Obama-era human rights conditions on the sale of F-16 fighter jets and other arms to Bahrain (Sanger and Schmitt 2017). In April 2018, the Department of State approved a potential new sale of attack helicopters and munitions to Bahrain's military, adding to the nearly $4 billion arms package notified for Bahrain in 2017, which included the F-16s (Americans for Democracy and Human Rights in

Bahrain 2018). The Bahraini opposition figures with whom I spoke noted that this would surely be interpreted by the regime as a green light to continue their crackdown. But it is doubtful that the hard-liners in Bahrain needed such a signal from the Trump administration in order to continue their repression. Even before the sales had been approved, at about the same time as Trump's inauguration, the Bahraini government reversed one of the few previously implemented recommendations of the Bahrain Independent Commission of Inquiry (BICI), restoring arrest and investigation powers to the National Security Agency, despite its record of using torture during interrogations. In April 2017, Bahrain's ruler reversed progress on another BICI recommendation by signing legislation authorizing civilian trials in military courts, a provision that contravenes international law.

Meanwhile, as Human Rights Watch (2018) documented, the Bahraini government continued its crackdown in countless other ways. The country's preeminent human rights defenders are either in prison or exile, indicted in trials that did not meet basic due process standards. Authorities regularly use excessive and deadly force to disperse peaceful protests and have forcibly disappeared people, holding them in incommunicado detention. The regime has arbitrarily revoked the citizenship of hundreds of dissident activists, sometimes in mass trials, a practice that UN High Commissioner for Human Rights Michelle Bachelet sharply criticized in April 2019 (Chick 2017; Altaher 2019). In 2017, Bahraini authorities again shut down the country's only independent newspaper and suspended the activities of the leading secular-left opposition political society, Wa'ad. In May 2018, Bahrain's parliament passed a law barring members of dissolved opposition groups from running in general elections planned for the end of that year. The Trump administration has barely reacted to the worsening human rights climate, other than expressing "concern" at the jailing of activist Nabeel Rajab in early 2018 (Reuters 2018).

Not surprisingly, the Pentagon does not object to the new policy approach. Under the Obama administration, the DoD had staunchly opposed transforming the security relationship into a tool of conditionality and publicly criticizing the monarchy. At the International Institute for Strategic Studies Manama Dialogue hosted in Bahrain in late October 2018, then secretary of defense Mattis stressed the US commitment to multilateral efforts to establish "sustainable peace" within the region, which include maintenance of the Fifth Fleet and opposition to Iran's proliferation (US Department of Defense 2018). Mattis discussed the bilateral defense relationship at length and pushed for "Gulf unity as a bulwark against these shared threats" during a meeting with King Hamad bin Isa Al-Khalifa (US Embassy in Bahrain 2018). The readouts of Mattis's meetings did not mention democracy and human rights.

During the Obama administration, it was top State Department officials that often delivered the tough talking points. However, under the Trump administration, the State Department appears unwilling to engage the

Bahrainis on democracy and human rights issues. In a January 2019 meeting between Secretary Pompeo and Bahraini leaders, the emphasis was entirely on security cooperation (US Department of State 2019a). Congress, meanwhile, has made some, largely unsuccessful, efforts to push the administration toward a democracy promotion stance in Bahrain. In November 2018, Senator Rand Paul unsuccessfully attempted to block a $300 million arms sale to Bahrain to protest its membership in the Saudi-led coalition waging a military campaign in Yemen.

Egypt

During the 2016 campaign, Trump praised Egypt's strongman Abdel Fatah al-Sisi as a "fantastic guy" doing a "fantastic job" under difficult circumstances. He made these comments even as the State Department was preparing a memorandum to Congress accusing Egyptian authorities of arbitrary arrests, detentions, disappearances, and reported extrajudicial killings (*The Economist* 2017). The Project on Middle East Democracy has called Sisi's Egypt "the most repressive political environment in Egypt's modern history" (POMED 2018). In a January 2018 visit I made to Cairo, my Egyptian friends reduced their voices to whispers on crowded streets when talking about politics. Nevertheless, barely three months after taking office, Trump invited Sisi to the White House, where he was received warmly. The scene was repeated in April 2019. The pictures of the two men sitting and laughing together in the Oval Office spoke a thousand words about the new administration's Egypt policy. Opposition figures in Egypt told me that the meeting sent a powerful signal to democracy and human rights activists throughout the region. "While Obama wasn't always with us, he tried at times," one activist told me. "When we saw Sisi at the White House, we knew Trump was not going to try."[31]

Some of Trump's appointments to top foreign policy jobs were all declared Sisi fans. Sebastian Gorka, chosen as a counterterrorism adviser to the president, had "characterized Sisi's removal of the Muslim Brotherhood–led government not as a military coup, but as a bold attempt to modernize Islam and separate religion from politics in the Muslim world" (Friedman 2017). Trump's former defense secretary, Mattis, previously stated that the United States should throw its support behind Sisi, saying, improbably: "Right now the only way to support Egypt's maturation as a country with civil society, with democracy, is to support President al-Sisi."[32] Secretary of State Pompeo visited Cairo in January 2019 and lavished praise on Sisi for his fight against terrorism, while barely mentioning human rights or democracy. He and some of his congressional allies see Sisi as a bulwark against terrorism, even though there is no evidence that his repression and human rights abuses have yielded any gains in the fight against terrorist groups. Instead, experts agree that the Egyptian regime's heavy-handed approach only creates more terrorists (Albouy 2017). As Tom Malinowski told the *New York Times,* "We've given Egypt $70 billion over the years, and last I checked there are no Egyptian F-16s helping us fight ISIS over Raqqa or Mosul. . . . All we get from the Egyptians is political repression that radicalizes its youth and gives terrorist groups new life."[33]

While the State Department has continued to document Sisi's abuses in its annual human rights report, there has been minimal effort under the Trump administration to translate its findings into meaningful and consistent pressure on the Egyptian government. The March 2018 presidential election, which Sisi won with 97 percent of the vote, was declared a farce by international monitors. Rather than joining the chorus of criticism about the conduct of the elections, Trump immediately called to congratulate Sisi, and the White House subsequently followed up with a readout statement that said that "the two leaders affirmed the strategic partnership between the United States and Egypt, and noted that they look forward to advancing this partnership and addressing common challenges" (White House 2018a). There was no mention of the fact that the election was deeply flawed. The State Department spokesperson, Heather Nauert, struck a different, though hardly forceful, tone: "We have noted reports of constraints on freedoms of expression and association in the run-up to the elections. We will continue to encourage a broadening of opportunities for political participation for Egyptians, and emphasize the importance of the protection of human rights and the vital role of civil society in Egypt" (Nauert 2018a).

In 2019, the Egyptian parliament passed a series of constitutional amendments designed to guarantee Sisi's rule until at least 2030. The White House has remained silent on Sisi's attempts to prolong his rule, including during the Egyptian president's White House visit in April of that year (Landler 2019). Mixed messages on Egypt policy were not uncommon in the Obama administration. However, the White House, ultimately the most important foreign policy messenger, was also generally the institution issuing the most forward-leaning messages on democracy and human rights issues, while at times State, and occasionally DoD, would issue weaker ones. In the Trump administration, the situation has been reversed. If the president of the United States is congratulating the winner of a facade election who has presided over some of the worst human rights abuses in Egyptian history, why would anyone heed what the State Department has to say? As I noted earlier, the State Department's Near Eastern Affairs Bureau has rarely been a strong democracy promotion advocate. But given a president who seems to so blatantly disregard even the most egregious cases of abuse against human rights and democratic norms, even NEA feels obligated to protect a long tradition of incorporating values into US foreign policy.

Yet, the Trump White House has taken some strong actions vis-à-vis Egypt. In August 2017, the administration froze nearly $300 million in military and economic aid to Cairo (*The Economist* 2017). The official explanation was human rights concerns, but observers with contacts in the administration say that the real reason was White House anger over Egypt's dealings with North Korea, and secondarily, unresolved issues relating to the 2011–2012 NGO trials described in Chapter 3.[34] In April 2017, Trump convinced the Sisi regime to free Aya Hijazi, an Egyptian American jailed on politically motivated charges in Cairo. Trump hailed Hijazi's release—and his role in it—with great fanfare, inviting her to the White House. However, like the freeze in assistance, Trump's motives may have had much less to do with human rights and democracy concerns, and much more to do with Trump's desire to be seen as a successful dealmaker. Administration officials point to these accomplishments as evidence of the appropriateness of Trump's transactional approach, which they argue works better than high-profile shaming of autocrats.[35] However, while such an approach may result in the freeing of a few lucky prisoners, there is little evidence that this has had or will have any effect on the Sisi regime's ongoing repression, especially if the president himself has no interest in pushing Sisi to change his autocratic behavior. Most of the withheld military assistance was restored in July 2018.[36]

Mostly, however, the Trump administration's Egypt policy has been focused on counterterrorism and countering Iran. In July 2018, the White House announced that Egypt was among the members of a new Middle East Strategic Alliance, meant to "serve as a bulwark against Iranian aggression, terrorism, extremism, and will bring stability to the Middle East" (Bayoumy 2018). After President Trump's meeting with Sisi at the UN General Assembly in September 2018, he praised successful joint military operations as well as a strong bilateral relationship "on many different fronts, including military and trade" (White House 2018b), a message he repeated during Sisi's April 2019 visit to the White House.

Libya

Washington insiders have told me that at the beginning of Trump's presidency, some advisers tried to get him interested in Libya, telling him that a big policy win there would be a way to make Hillary Clinton and Obama look bad. The president did not appear interested.[37] Instead, he largely avoided formulating any policy strategy on Libya. His administration did not appoint a replacement for Jonathan Winer, Obama's special envoy to Libya, and as of spring 2019, there is no accredited ambassador at the US mission to Libya, which is still based in Tunis. In April 2018, Trump announced that he had no intention of ramping up US engagement: "I do not see a role in Libya. I think the United States has, right now, enough roles," he told the Italian prime minister.[38] During the same remarks, Trump said, "We are effectively ridding the world of ISIL. . . . I see that as a primary role, and that's what we're going to do whether it's in Iraq or in Libya or anywhere else."[39] Accordingly, under the Trump administration all limited democracy assistance programs in Libya must be justified by their "contribution to countering violent extremism."[40]

Thus, the counterterrorism-focused approach to Libya has only been strengthened to the detriment of democracy promotion. In 2017, reports suggested that the Trump administration was planning to increase the involvement and presence of US military and intelligence personnel in Libya based on an approach used in Somalia (Starr 2017). The administration also stepped up air strikes against the Islamic State and other targets in the country. In the period between January 2017 and March 2018, the United States carried out at least eight strikes in the country (Pearson 2018), and further air strikes were confirmed in August and December 2018. Moreover, the Pentagon, and especially the AFRICOM command based in Stuttgart, Germany, have a larger scope of autonomy vis-à-vis Libya policy. This has been accentuated by gaps in appointments at the State Department on the Libya portfolio. "AFRICOM is taking the lead on Libya," an interviewee told me.[41] Meanwhile, the CIA has bolstered its drone capabilities in northeastern Niger as a means of attacking Islamic militants, especially in southern Libya (Penney et al. 2018). With AFRICOM and CIA in leading roles, democracy and human rights issues are only likely to get further sidelined.

From the institutional perspective, Trump's disinterest in Libya has also had unintended positive consequences for democracy promotion in terms of leaving in place some Obama policies that focused on a balanced approach to dealing with the various factions while resisting the temptation to throw US support behind Khalifa Haftar, the commander of the Libyan National Army. Some observers I spoke with early in Trump's presidency expected the new administration to declare its backing for Haftar. White House insiders such as the national security adviser Michael Flynn and senior adviser Jared Kushner advocated such a policy. Haftar, after all, was a hard-line anti-Islamist strongman allied with the UAE, Egypt, and Saudi Arabia, a perfect combination from the White House's point of view. But Trump's failure to meaningfully engage with Libya has left day-to-day US policy implementation in the hands of the bureaucracies. While AFRICOM may be influential in pushing a counterterrorism agenda in Libya, on the issue of taking sides among the Libyan factions, the State Department—along with inertia—carried the day for the first two years of Trump's presidency, despite DoD and CIA calls to lend greater support to Haftar.[42]

And then, on April 19, 2019, in the midst of an attack on Tripoli by Khalifa Haftar's militias, Trump seemingly threw US policy toward Libya into disarray during a phone call with the strongman. According to an official readout of the call, Trump "recognized Field Marshal Haftar's significant role in fighting terrorism and securing Libya's oil resources, and the two discussed a shared vision for Libya's transition to a stable, democratic political system" (DeYoung and Ryan 2019). Just a few days before, Secretary of State Mike Pompeo had urged "the immediate halt to [Haftar's] military operations" against militias defending Tripoli and the United Nations–backed Government of National Accord (GNA). In fact, Pompeo was articulating what has been US policy since 2015: backing the GNA, formed as part of the December 2015 Libyan Political Agreement. Fayez al-Sarraj, the prime minister of the GNA, had traveled to Washington and met with Trump at the White House in December 2017, a small victory for those who continued to advocate for US diplomatic engagement in Libya that goes beyond counterterrorism. In December 2018, Secretary of State Pompeo met Prime Minister al-Sarraj in Brussels and affirmed Washington's "strong partnership" with the GNA on counterterrorism and other issues (Nauert 2018b). As this book went to press in summer 2019, it was unclear whether the president's call with Haftar signaled a significant break with this policy, but if so, it would be entirely in line with Trump's worldview.

Beyond this, the United States and its Western partners have shown little will to respond to ongoing human rights issues in Libya (Youssef and Walsh 2017). The country in which the international community came together in an extraordinary show of unity in support of human rights in 2011 is now a place where human rights abuses are rampant. As in Egypt and Bahrain, the situation is worse than it was before 2011. Whereas in Bahrain and Egypt the violations are carried out by repressive state structures, in Libya the perpetrators are extrastate militias. A UN report published in April 2018 documents thousands of incidents of human rights violations carried out by militias in Libya (UNHCHR 2018). Militias, the report notes, hold thousands of people in prolonged arbitrary and unlawful detention and submit them to torture and other abuses. Libyans are often arbitrarily detained based on their tribal or family links and perceived political affiliations. Victims have little or no recourse to justice because of a nonfunctioning judicial system, while members of armed groups enjoy total impunity. All of this is only six years away, but at the same time light-years removed, from the Libya I witnessed in 2012, when both Libyans and the United States hoped and worked for a future of greater freedom, justice, and dignity.

Notes

1. Interview with Ben Rhodes, Claremont, CA, April 2019.
2. Interview with former US official, Washington, DC, October 2018.
3. Phone interview with US official, May 2018.
4. Interview with former US official, Washington, DC, October 2018.
5. Ibid.
6. Ibid.

7. Interview with Ben Rhodes, Claremont, CA, April 2019.
8. One former official told me that "perhaps the best thing we did in the Obama administration" was to make Congress more activist in its oversight role of human rights issues in particular.
9. Interview with Derek Chollet, Washington, DC, November 2018.
10. Interview with former US official, Washington, DC, February 2018.
11. Ibid.
12. Some Trump officials have defined the president's foreign policy doctrine as, "We're America, Bitch." See Goldberg (2018).
13. For example, Shelton (2017) points to Trump's support for democracy in Cuba.
14. Muravchik, quoted in Bouchet (2015, p. 56).
15. Interview with Ben Rhodes, Claremont, CA, April 2019.
16. Trump, quoted in Friedman (2018).
17. Interview with US official, Washington, DC, November 2018.
18. William Burns, quoted in Landler (2019).
19. Interview with Ben Rhodes, Claremont, CA, April 2019.
20. Posner, quoted in Friedman (2018).
21. Tillerson, quoted in Borger (2017). A political appointee and Tillerson advisor, Antholis (2019), notes, subsequently argued in an internal memo, that the United States should use human rights as leverage with adversaries, but not allies.
22. Pompeo, quoted in Friedman (2017).
23. Ibid.
24. Interview with US official, Washington, DC, February 2018.
25. For example, see Haley (2018a).
26. Quoted in Breuninger (2018).
27. Quoted in Rogin (2019).
28. Yahya, quoted in Hubbard (2019).
29. Phone interview with Bahraini opposition figure, May 2018.
30. Phone interview with Bahraini opposition figure, September 2018.
31. Interview with Egyptian activist, Cairo, January 2018.
32. Mattis, quoted in Friedman (2017).
33. Malinowski, quoted in Baker (2017).
34. Interview with Egypt analyst, Washington, DC, February 2018.
35. Interview with US official, Washington, DC, November 2018.
36. On July 25, 2018, Secretary of State Pompeo "released $195 million in military assistance, which had been frozen since last August," even though Egypt had not fully met the three conditions set by former Secretary of State Tillerson. These conditions were "the resolution of a 2013 trial involving 43 employees of various nongovernmental organizations, including 17 Americans, who were convicted on politicized charges of operating without licenses and receiving illegal foreign funding; the repeal or wholesale revision of Egypt's draconian 2017 NGO law; and the discontinuation of Egypt's diplomatic, military, and economic cooperation with North Korea" (Miller 2018).
37. Phone interview with Washington, DC, analyst, July 2018.
38. Trump, quoted in Fishman (2017). The Italians and French have urged the Trump administration to be more engaged on Libya, but mostly without success.
39. Trump, quoted in Pearson (2018).
40. Interview with US official, Tunis, January 2019.
41. Interview with US official, Tunis, February 2018.
42. Interview with US official, Tunis, March 2019.

Appendix:
Foreign Policy Institutions and Their Stake in Democracy Promotion

National Security Council (NSC)

The NSC is the cadre of advisers attached to the White House who manage the foreign-policy-making process on a daily basis.[1] Led by the national security adviser, the NSC has grown precipitously in recent decades, from 40 staff in 1991 to around 400 persons in the Obama administration (Cancian 2016). Many of the senior directors are political appointees, while working-level staff are borrowed from the foreign affairs agencies for one- or two-year assignments on the NSC. As outlined by the 1947 National Security Act, the NSC's role is to advise the president on foreign affairs and act as a convener and arbiter of the larger foreign policy bureaucracy. The NSC seeks maximum flexibility and political protection for presidents, looking after their agenda and legacy. In recent years, the NSC has been criticized for becoming too operational and too prone to micromanaging the bureaucracy. The NSC, like the State Department, has sections responsible for both functional and geographic issues. The latter are more established and dominant and, like their State counterparts, tend to emphasize the maintenance of relations over "stirring the pot" with contentious issues such as democracy promotion. However, functional offices, of which democracy and human rights is one, can also have a policy impact under influential and forceful leadership.

The NSC has the authority to call interagency policy meetings at various levels that are responsible for hashing out policy options and making recommendations. It takes the lead in drafting the memoranda that go to the president for a decision. Moreover, as the foreign policy institution closest to the president, and one whose leadership and staff is not subject to Senate confirmation, the NSC can most credibly claim to represent the president's preferences. The opposite is also true: Due to its proximity and access to informal action channels, the NSC can most easily influence the president's thinking. In past decades, presidents would not make foreign policy decisions without consulting cabinet members. However, by the turn of the twenty-first century, presidents were much more willing to act on the advice of the national security adviser alone (Halperin and Clapp 2006, p. 110). The views of other NSC members who are selected based on their political loyalty can carry significant weight owing to direct access to the president. It is for these reasons of proximity and loyalty that at times presidents will bypass the bureaucracy altogether and rely on key NSC staff to carry out the most sensitive diplomatic tasks.[2]

While the NSC by itself has few tools with which to promote democracy, its ability to deploy the president to pursue it at the highest levels and its parallel capacity to compel the larger bureaucracy to get on board with a democracy promotion agenda is vital. Yet, the NSC also referees among policy preferences, which at times might dilute democracy promotion. The NSC can also become a backer of democracy promotion if it perceives that a president politically benefits from pursuing it. NSC staff, furthermore, can more quickly move policy in the direction of democracy promotion by relying on ad hoc but highly effective action channels, directly communicating key facts to the president. Moreover, the organizational culture of the NSC can be less risk-averse than bureaucratic actors such as the State Department or Department of Defense, which may lead it to more readily "make waves" in a bilateral relationship and thus make bolder moves on democracy promotion than other bureaucratic actors.

State Department (State)

The State Department is the primary diplomatic organ of the US government and the day-to-day manager of relations with foreign countries. State represents the US overseas, reporting on the activities of foreign governments, engaging in negotiations, and protecting American citizens. Owing to its diplomatic mission, State prefers engagement over isolation and sanctions, which at key moments can run counter to democracy promotion goals. State diplomats are traditionally uncomfortable about exerting pressure to influence domestic politics, but are much more willing to use such pressure in order to secure cooperation on traditional diplomatic issues such as arms control.

Lacking a domestic base of support and the massive resources of the military and intelligence establishments, State's institutional power in the interagency process rests on its reservoir of specialized knowledge of other countries and certain functional issues. State can wield its influence over democracy promotion by "taking the pen" on key briefing documents that get passed through the interagency process and become the basis for policy debates and decisions. In this regard, State may have particular influence over policy toward countries that are not high profile in terms of media, presidential, or interest group attention. State's power is also based on its proximity to foreign officials and institutions. Physical presence in the field gives State Department diplomats ready access to information that they transmit to Washington in the form of reporting cables that NSC staff and others use to formulate policy.

State prefers carrots over sticks as a way of compelling other governments to do what it wants, though it has limited carrots and sticks to use on its own. It can engage in private diplomacy and public shaming in the pursuit of democracy promotion, but these tools have little leverage once target governments learn that its rhetoric is not tied to the material support or sanctions needed to induce changes in regime behavior (Spence 2005). However, State manages approximately 50 percent of the US government's security sector assistance (Kaidanow 2017), including the Foreign Military Financing program. This power to set policy on security assistance gives State the potential to use it as a form of democratic conditionality, though it rarely chooses to do so without support from the Department of Defense.[3]

State is also characterized by substantial internal differentiation, so much so that "it's often very hard to get a single opinion in the interagency process from the State Department."[4] One internal division of consequence for democracy promotion is between regional bureaus (charged with managing bilateral relations) and functional bureaus (responsible for transnational issues). Regional bureaus tend to be less engaged on democracy promotion, especially in allied countries, where they don't want to "break glass."[5] Regional bureaus, one official told me, like maintaining lines of access "to feel like even if you're making only a little bit of difference you're making a difference."[6] The most prominent functional unit dealing with democracy and human rights issues is the Bureau of Democracy, Rights, and Labor (DRL), led by an assistant secretary who is often the moral conscience of the interagency process. DRL manages the human rights vetting for security assistance programs and oversees the writing and rollout of the annual State Department Human Rights Reports. However, not only is DRL weaker than the regional bureaus, but also it is often viewed as meddlesome and out of touch with reality. Yet, skilled DRL assistant secretaries can build alliances with regional bureau leaders and others across the interagency to advance a democracy promotion agenda (Bouchet 2015, pp. 54–55).

Another internal cleavage with salience for democracy promotion is the division between State's Washington headquarters and its 300 embassies and consulates around the world. Embassies and consulates typically seek the freedom and flexibility to manage day-to-day relations with foreign countries as they see fit. They resent micromanagement by Washington bureaucrats, whom they see as out of touch with the reality "on the ground." Diplomats' antipathy toward Washington directives is well known by senior policymakers, and over time Washington might defer to ambassadors' preferences, thereby giving them more power over policy formulation, implementation, and management.

A popular adage notes that no diplomat wants to get sent to the field to downgrade a bilateral relationship. Officials in the field are usually convinced that improving relations with their host country is a vital US interest, whereas priorities decided on in Washington appear out of touch with the diplomat's daily reality. Diplomats' interests lie in retaining lines of access and influence to gain access to information for reporting cables and assuring a hospitable environment for everything from assistance programs to US businesses operating in the country. Delivering tough messages on political reform or using "sticks" to compel change may prove to be in tension with these interests. As a consequence, ambassadors often "water down" tough messages or "wait out" current administrations' democracy promotion agendas. Or, they may deliberately make a move without seeking permission as a way to later box their Washington superiors into a particular policy (Halperin and Clapp 2006, p. 290).

Career State officials tend to be cautious, deferential, and focused on advancement, which means that they are unlikely to take the long view with regard to advocating any bold policy initiatives that may hurt them if things go awry. Yearly performance evaluations and relatively short assignments also condition short-term thinking about more modest, measurable goals. Bold ideas vis-à-vis democracy promotion often are not compatible with the logic of career promotion. State's political appointees, by contrast, are uncommitted to the institution in the same way and have more room and motivation to take risky moves, at times making them better agents of democracy promotion. However, as one senior career official pointed out to me, political appointees can also be motivated mainly by achieving "deliverables" to serve the president's legacy, which can foster shortsighted thinking.[7] Career officials often express disdain toward political appointees—who enter the department with little knowledge of its culture and processes—and bristle at having to "clean up" after brazen and misguided appointees damage bilateral relations.

Department of Defense (DoD)

DoD commands an enormous workforce and budget and maintains bases and other military installations throughout the United States and around the globe as part of its mission to defend the United States from foreign enemies. DoD's core interests include the retention of resources, budgets, and property (especially bases) and the maintenance of forces that it believes are necessary for various defense contingencies. It favors strategies that presume that those forces will be used in the event of hostilities (Halperin and Clapp 2006, p. 58). The DoD also favors the development of new technology and the procurement of new equipment, even if the equipment and technology cannot always be justified by current needs and plans (Fallows 2015). Military officers are deeply suspicious of using force toward achieving political, "nation-building," and humanitarian goals in particular. While opposing interventions, especially those with unclear goals and timelines, once such commitments are authorized by the political leadership, the DoD will push for maximum flexibility, autonomy, and authority to carry out the operation (Halperin and Clapp 2006, p. 59).

While DoD has the conditionality and coercion tools of democracy promotion, Pentagon officials do not like to publicly lecture countries to democratize but instead prefer private engagement backed by good relationships (Spence 2005). DoD officials advocate working closely with partner militaries "to model proper behavior of how the armed forces should function in a democracy" (Spence 2005). The DoD is reluctant to cut military assistance to partner countries, even when those countries engage in questionable behavior, fearing that critical lines of access and influence will be lost. In the interagency and in its interactions with foreign governments, the DoD "speaks with the loudest voice about security issues" while usually downplaying concerns about democracy (Spence 2005).

Even before 9/11, DoD enjoyed influence in Washington owing to strong congressional budgetary support, its connection to a vast military-industrial complex, the network of overseas bases and partnerships, and broad public support for its mission. Since 9/11, DoD has garnered enormous resources and institutional power over foreign policy attacks because of its role in the Iraq and Afghanistan wars, the war on terror, and its expanded functions. Public and political displays of military "worship" have only increased since 9/11 (Fallows 2015). All of these factors translate into significant bargaining advantages for DoD in interagency debates over whether and how much to pursue democracy promotion.

The DoD approaches bilateral military relationships first and foremost based on operational and tactical considerations. Democracy and human rights issues are only secondary. Once a bilateral security relationship is established, it often becomes personalized because of the common shared bond and cultural identity of being soldiers, whether from the United States or the partner country, and regardless of political persuasion and system of government. These relationships are sustained over many years as both sides progress through their ranks: For example, US and foreign officer cadets who attended the same training program and institution often retain those relationships as they progress through their careers and can harness them as a "back door" channel for communication.

Like State Department career officials, military officers are reluctant to "make waves" beyond war planning and execution lest they make mistakes that derail their plans for promotion. Military command in the field sees the national interest not only in terms of the interests of their institution, but also their own interest in promotion. And the key to promotion lies with their DoD superiors in Washington. Like State ambassadors, DoD officials in the field resent micromanagement by the Pentagon because of their belief that they know better than Washington what should be done.

The DoD is a bureaucratic behemoth, and there are significant differences among its subunits in terms of both institutional interest and organizational culture. Defense officials within particular units often develop their position "largely by calculating the national interest in terms of the organizational interests of the career service to which they belong" (Halperin and Clapp 2006, p. 61). For example, officials in the Defense Security Cooperation Agency are first and foremost interested in continuing the relationships that facilitate sales to partner militaries. Their interests are driven, in turn, by the defense industry that manufactures the weapons systems purchased by foreign governments. Base commanders in the field are above all concerned with force protection and the daily cooperation with host country officials. Pentagon-based officials charged with policy portfolios, by contrast, might be more focused on long-term strategic issues.

Central Intelligence Agency (CIA)

The CIA, the most powerful actor in the intelligence community, is charged with collecting and disseminating intelligence. In theory, the CIA is meant to inform policymakers rather than advocate policy, but in practice it influences foreign policy outcomes as well. The CIA seeks to preserve a maximum degree of autonomy and shuns political influence in its operations. As a bureaucratic actor whose power derives from its privileged access to information, it jealously guards its secrets. Consummate with its growing counterterrorism role after 9/11, the CIA cultivated closer relations with intelligence services around the globe. Like the DoD's relationships with allied militaries, it is a tall order to ask the CIA to downgrade these relations.

The CIA's access to information is a major source of its institutional power. CIA analysts are the first to speak at interagency meetings in Washington, a critical role that helps frame the agenda and delimit policy options. The CIA and other parts of the intelligence community also review drafts of presidential speeches and those of other senior officials, a measure that was introduced after the scandals surrounding the politicization of intelligence on Iraq in the George W. Bush administration (Rhodes 2018, p. 50). But this has also given the intelligence community an added veto point on policy.[8] The CIA's need for extreme secrecy has been an additional source of power, as it can invoke national security imperatives to keep most of its activities out of the public eye. Ambassadors, for instance, are not always informed of the full range of activities conducted by their CIA station.

Since 9/11, the CIA has developed a more powerful set of institutional prerogatives and interests and draws on them to exert influence over policy outcomes. Its covert operations branch was revived after 9/11, and the agency was made the tip of the spear in the war on terror (Mazzetti 2013). Upon assuming the role of CIA director in the first Obama term, Leon Panetta was told that he would be the "combatant commander in the war on terrorism" (Panetta 2014, p. 205). The intense focus of the public and policymakers on terrorism has given the CIA broad leverage and institutional power in Washington. This power derives not only from the CIA's traditional intelligence-gathering capabilities but also from its covert capabilities, such as armed drone strikes and paramilitary operations, often conducted jointly with DoD (Mazzetti 2013). The CIA provides presidents with the tools to address the public's preoccupation with terrorism in a way that is also politically popular: that is, without deploying conventional forces, which might lead to American deaths.

The functions of CIA subunits point to competing interests. The analyst side of the CIA "house" values facts and rigorous analysis and is also most likely to perceive the longer-term consequences of political repression. This analysis group believes that the CIA should not advocate policy but rather be an impartial purveyor of objective analysis to inform that policy. It worries that covert operations only jeopardize the CIA's claim to impartiality (Halperin and Clapp 2006, p. 34). However, the operations perspective, especially when it comes to counterterrorism, often wins out over the analyst one. As one former official put it, "to ask someone who is biased to present their unbiased perspective is unrealistic."[9] This is why some advocate for the separation of the clandestine service and the analysts, "believing that intelligence analysis will never capture the attention of the top leadership of the agency as long as the agency is engaged in clandestine operations" (Halperin and Clapp 2006, p. 35).

Congress

The US Congress consists of two houses, the Senate and House of Representatives, with the former playing an especially important role in funding US foreign policy operations, approving military deployments, and providing oversight to foreign policy institutions. Over the past four decades, Congress has inserted itself more formally into the foreign policy decision-making process through legislation, a growing professional committee staff, and the direct engagement of some members with foreign countries. Like the institutions described above, Congress also has units and actors in "different positions who see different faces of an issue and compete to affect outcomes" (Halperin and Clapp 2006, p. 38). Congress can create and reorganize the structure of the federal government, such as when it created the Bureau of Democracy and Human Rights at State during the Carter administration or mandated the position of director of national intelligence and the Department of Homeland Security after 9/11. Such changes in structure can directly affect the weight given to democracy promotion by changing the balance of power among institutional actors. The Senate has the power to approve or reject presidential appointments to key foreign policy positions and can thus help empower individuals with a democracy promotion agenda. Congress, moreover, can shape the perception of the national interest held by the bureaucracy and can influence shared images of foreign policy priorities. Congressional legislation can be used to advance a democracy and human rights agenda by mandating reporting, creating vetting mechanisms, or establishing new bureaucratic positions focused on such issues.

Congress also controls the purse strings, which gives it the power to directly shape democracy promotion. For example, congressional authorizing committees affect the capabilities of the executive branch agencies to use democratic conditionality by funding programs and by prescribing rules for their conduct. The foreign relations committees, for example, authorize specific democracy assistance programs to a country or region. Appropriations committees can also pass through riders, earmarks, and limitations that directly address human rights and democracy issues. However, if the large defense and intelligence budgets approved by Congress are key to the bureaucratic power of those institutions, they are also the most difficult to change. No member of Congress wants to be the one who makes funding cuts to agencies designed to protect their constituents from terrorism and other threats, just as no member of Congress wants to be seen denying the military needed resources. And no member of Congress wants to cut DoD programs that generate jobs domestically.

Individual members of Congress may be motivated by their personal commitment to democracy promotion and use their leadership positions on committees to raise its profile, push and prod executive branch officials to take it more seriously, or engage in direct diplomacy around democracy promotion issues through congressional delegations (CODELs). But the opposite can also be true: Some members may favor a realpolitik approach and send mixed signals to foreign governments on overseas visits.

In addition to fierce partisan loyalties, members of Congress are highly sensitized to public opinion and constituent preferences. Insofar as voters care little about democracy promotion or foreign assistance, there is little appetite in Congress for democracy promotion in general. The same is true with foreign assistance: Congressional members often have to sell it in terms of constituent interests. As such, US foreign aid policies sometimes reflected the efforts of ethnic diaspora lobbies, interest group constituencies, and attempts to win over American farmers (Spence 2005).

Subunits within the congressional structure influence how various actors see foreign policy issues such as democracy promotion. Halperin and Clapp (2006, p. 324) write: "Since committee interests and influence are intricately linked with the welfare of the agencies that they oversee, committees come to equate their welfare with the welfare of these agencies." Thus, members of the Foreign Relations Committee prefer diplomacy and foreign assistance programs, while members of the Armed Services Committee prefer larger appropriations for the armed services. The compromise struck among the committees has shaped a system in which funds are authorized by the foreign affairs committees and then transferred by the State Department to the Defense Department, which manages the program consistent with policy laid down by the foreign affairs committees. This has allowed the foreign affairs committees to impose human rights conditions and exclude certain countries from assistance because of their poor human rights record (Halperin and Clapp 2006, p. 330). But the compromise has also often frustrated the defense committees, who attempt to minimize the restrictions, caring mostly about the interoperability of foreign forces with the United States and their ability to assist in combat. They also argue that exposure to US values is the best way to foster military leaders who will respect human rights and democratic norms (Halperin and Clapp 2006, p. 331). Over time, the defense committees have succeeded in wresting control over more programs from their foreign affairs counterparts, giving regional military commanders more autonomy to pursue cooperative programs, especially those dealing with counterterrorism.

Other Institutional Actors

Other institutional actors play a role in formulating and executing US policies related to democracy promotion, including the US Agency for International Development (USAID), the Treasury Department, and the Department of Homeland Security (DHS). USAID provides funding for democracy assistance in areas such as elections and political party development, rule of law and human rights, civil society, and good governance. USAID does not, however, have a powerful voice at the policymaking table or tools such as carrots and sticks to induce deeper reforms and change regime behavior. At the field level, USAID mission directors are often just as motivated by maintaining access to ruling elites as other institutional actors.

The Treasury Department, by contrast, can deploy multiple carrots and sticks related to democracy promotion—namely, the power to turn on or off the spigot of billions of dollars in International Monetary Fund and World Bank assistance and the ability to impose sanctions. Treasury mostly deploys these tools to support goals in the realm of economic rather than political reform, or to punish the behavior of "rogue states" such as Iran and North Korea for their nuclear programs. Yet, targeted sanctions announced by Treasury's Office of Foreign Assets Control can also be an effective tool used to punish human rights abusers. After 9/11, the newly created DHS became a player in foreign policy debates. The presence of DHS at interagency debates can swing the pendulum toward counterterrorism concerns and away from democracy promotion.

Notes

1. One of the best accounts of NSC inner workings is Rothkopf (2006).
2. For example, Obama relied on two young NSC staffers to carry out the secret negotiations leading to the rapprochement with Cuba (Rhodes 2018).
3. Interview with US official, Washington, DC, February 2018.
4. Interview with former US official, Washington, DC, October 2018.
5. Ibid.
6. Ibid.
7. Phone interview with US official, May 2018.
8. Rhodes (2018, pp. 50–51) recounts how the intelligence community refused to clear a line in one of Obama's speeches describing Guantanamo detainees as being in a "legal black hole."
9. Interview with former US official, Washington, DC, October 2018.

References

Abdallah, Nayera. 2019. "Trump and Egypt's Sisi Discuss Middle East in Phone Call." *U.S. News & World Report,* January 1.
Abe, Nicola, and Matthias Gebauer. 2012. "Muslim Brotherhood Metes Out Vigilante Justice." *Spiegel,* December 11.
Abelson, Robert P. 1981. "The Psychological Status of the Script Concept." *American Psychologist* 36, no. 7: 715–729.
Aboudi, Sami. 2016. "Bahrain Strips Top Shi'ite Muslim Cleric of Citizenship." *Reuters,* June 20.
Abrams, Elliott. 2015. "How Obama Caved on Bahrain." *Foreign Policy,* February 27.
———. 2017. *Realism and Democracy: American Foreign Policy After the Arab Spring.* New York: Cambridge University Press.
Albouy, Pierre. 2017. "U.N. Rights Boss Says Egypt Crackdown 'Facilitates Radicalisation.'" Reuters, May 1.
Alhasan, Tariq Hasan. 2011. "The Role of Iran in the Failed Coup of 1981: The IFLB in Bahrain." *The Middle East Journal* 65, no. 4: 603–617.
Altaher, Nada. 2019. "Bahrain Revokes Citizenship of 138 People in Mass Trial." *CNN.* April 17. https://www.cnn.com/2019/04/16/middleeast/bahrain-mass-trial-intl/index.html.
Al Jazeera. 2017. "What Is the Muslim Brotherhood?" Al Jazeera, June 18.
Allaire, Yvan, and Mihaela E. Firsirotu. 1984. "Theories of Organizational Culture." *Organization Studies* 5, no. 3: 193–226.
Allison, Graham T. 1971. *Essence of Decision: Explaining the Cuban Missile Crisis.* Boston: Little, Brown.
Al-Rasheed, Madawi. 2013. "Saudi Arabia Pleased with Morsi's Fall." *Al-Monitor,* July 4.
Americans for Democracy and Human Rights in Bahrain. 2018. "Trump Administration Approves New Arms Sales to Bahrain Despite Military Abuses." May 1. https://www.adhrb.org/2018/05/trump-administration-approves-new-arms-sales-to-bahrain-despite-military-abuses.
Amnesty International. 2012. "Bahraini Teachers Face Further Jail Time After 'Nightmare' Verdict." Press release, October 24. https://www.amnesty.org.uk/press-releases/bahraini-teachers-face-further-jail-time-after-nightmare-verdict.

Anderson, Jon Lee. 2015. "The Unraveling." *The Atlantic,* February 23.
Antholis, William J. 2019. "Values in US Foreign Policy: 'America First' Meets the Pro-Democracy State." In Krishnan Srinivasan, James Mayall, and Sanja Pulipaka, eds. *Values in Foreign Policy: Investigating Ideals and Interests.* London: Rowman & Littlefield.
'Arafa, Mohammed, and Mieczysław P. Boduszyński. 2017. "Understanding Egyptian Policy Toward Libya." Tahrir Institute for Middle East Policy, Analysis, March 28. https://timep.org/commentary/analysis/understanding-egyptian-policy-toward-libya.
Asharq Al-Awsat. 2011. "A Talk with Peninsula Shield Force Commander Mutlaq Bin Salem al-Azima." March 28. https://eng-archive.aawsat.com/theaawsat/interviews/a-talk-with-peninsula-shield-force-commander-mutlaq-bin-salem-al-azima.
Ashford, Emma. 2018a. "A Guide to Saudi Arabia's Influence in Washington." *New Republic,* December 6.
———. 2018b. "Unbalanced: Rethinking America's Commitment to the Middle East." *Strategic Studies Quarterly* 12, no. 1 (Spring): 127–148.
Awad, Marwa, and Sherine El Madany. 2011. "Egypt Police Raid U.S.-Backed Pro-Democracy Groups." Reuters, December 29.
Bader, Julia, Jörn Grävingholt, and Antje Kästner. 2010. "Would Autocracies Promote Autocracy? A Political Economy Perspective on Regime-Type Export in Regional Neighborhoods." *Contemporary Politics* 16, no. 1: 81–100.
Baker, Peter. 2017. "In a Shift, Trump Will Move Egypt's Rights Record to the Sidelines." *New York Times,* March 31.
Balfour, Rosa. 2012. *EU Conditionality After the Arab Spring.* Barcelona: IEMed.
Baroudos, Constance. 2016. "Chaos in Libya: The Rising ISIS Threat to Europe." *National Interest,* April 15. http://nationalinterest.org/blog/chaos-libya-the-rising-isis-threaten-europe-15801.
Bassiouni, Mahmoud Cherif, Nigel Rodley, Badria Al-Awadhi, Philippe Kirsch, and Mahnoush H. Arsanjani. 2011. "Report of the Bahrain Independent Commission of Inquiry." Bahrain Independent Commission of Inquiry, November 23. http://files.bici.org.bh/BICIreportEN.pdf.
Bayoumy, Yara. 2018. "Trump Seeks to Revive 'Arab NATO' to Confront Iran." Reuters, July 28.
BBC. 2011. "Libya: White House Dashes Rebel Hopes of Recognition." *BBC News,* May 14.
Beaumont, Peter. 2013. "Yes, the UN Has a Duty to Intervene. But When, Where and How?" *The Guardian,* May 4.
Becker, Jo, and Scott Shane. 2016. "Hillary Clinton, 'Smart Power' and a Dictator's Fall." *New York Times,* February 27.
Beiser, Elana. 2017. "Record Number of Journalists Jailed as Turkey, China, Egypt Pay Scant Price for Repression." *Committee to Protect Journalists,* December 13. https://cpj.org/reports/2017/12/journalists-prison-jail-record-number-turkey-china-egypt.php.
Benaim, Daniel, Mokhtar Awad, and Brian Katulis. 2017. "Setting the Terms for U.S.-Egypt Relations." *Center for American Progress,* February 21. https://www.americanprogress.org/issues/security/reports/2017/02/21/426654/setting-the-terms-for-u-s-egypt-relations.
Benstead, Lindsay J., and Mieczysław P. Boduszyński. 2017. "Public Opinion & the Demise of U.S. Public Diplomacy in Libya." *USC Center for Public Diplomacy,* December 14. https://uscpublicdiplomacy.org/blog/public-opinion-demise-us-public-diplomacy-libya.
Bhatia, Rukmani. 2017. "Quietly Erasing Democracy Promotion at the U.S. State Department." *Freedom House,* August 8. https://freedomhouse.org/blog/quietly-erasing-democracy-promotion-us-state-department.

Blomdahl, Mikael. 2016. "Bureaucratic Roles and Positions: Explaining the United States Libya Decision." *Diplomacy & Statecraft* 27, no. 1: 142–161.

Boduszyński, Mieczysław P. 2013. "The Benghazi Syndrome." *Los Angeles Times*, December 1.

———. 2015. "The External Dimension of Libya's Troubled Transition: The International Community and 'Democratic Knowledge' Transfer." *Journal of North African Studies* 20, no. 5: 735–753.

Boduszyński, Mieczysław P., and Marieke Wierda. 2017. "Political Exclusion and Transitional Justice: A Case Study of Libya." In *Transitional Justice in the Middle East and North Africa*, edited by Chandra Lekha Sriram. New York: Oxford University Press.

Boduszyński, Mieczysław P, Kristin Fabbe, and Christopher Lamont. 2015. "After the Arab Spring: Are Secular Parties the Answer?" *Journal of Democracy* 26, no. 4 (October): 125–139.

Borger, Julian. 2011. "The Egyptian Crisis: Another Day, Another Two U.S. Policies." *The Guardian*, February 6.

———. 2017. "Rex Tillerson: 'America First' Means Divorcing Our Policy from Our Values." *The Guardian*, May 3. https://www.theguardian.com/us-news/2017/may/03/rex-tillerson-america-first-speech-trump-policy.

Bouchet, Nicolas. 2015. *Democracy Promotion as US Foreign Policy: Bill Clinton and Democratic Enlargement.* Routledge Studies in US Foreign Policy. London: Routledge.

Breuninger, Kevin. 2018. "'A Smoking Saw': Senators Say Saudi Crown Prince Was 'Complicit' in Journalist Jamal Khashoggi's Killing After CIA Briefing." *CNBC*, December 4. https://www.cnbc.com/2018/12/04/senators-say-saudi-crown-prince-complicit-in-khashoggi-killing-after-cia-briefing.html.

Brooke, Steven. 2015. "U.S. Policy and the Muslim Brotherhood." Al Mesbar Studies and Research Center, January 19. http://mesbar.org/u-s-policy-muslim-brotherhood.

Brownlee, Jason. 2012. *Democracy Prevention: The Politics of the U.S.-Egyptian Alliance.* Cambridge: Cambridge University Press.

Brumberg, Daniel. 2002. "The Trap of Liberalized Autocracy." *Journal of Democracy* 13, no. 4 (October): 56–68.

Burns. William J. 2019. *The Back Channel: A Memoir of American Diplomacy and the Case for Its Renewal.* New York: Random House.

Bush, George W. 2003. "President Discusses the Future of Iraq." The White House Office of the Press Secretary, February 26. https://georgewbush-whitehouse.archives.gov/news/releases/2003/02/20030226-11.html.

———. 2005. "The Second Inaugural Address." https://georgewbushwhitehouse.archives.gov/infocus/bushrecord/documents/Selected_Speeches_George_W_Bush.pdf.

Bush, Sarah Sunn. 2015. *The Taming of Democracy Assistance: Why Democracy Promotion Does Not Confront Dictators.* Cambridge: Cambridge University Press.

Cancian, Mark F. 2016. "Limiting Size of NSC Staff: Assessing Defense Reform Series." Center for Strategic and International Studies Report, July 1. https://www.csis.org/analysis/limiting-size-nsc-staff.

Carney, Jay. 2012. "Statement by the Press Secretary on the Situation in Bahrain." The White House Office of the Press Secretary, April 11. https://obamawhitehouse.archives.gov/the-press-office/2012/04/11/statement-press-secretary-situation-bahrain.

Carothers, Thomas. 1999. *Aiding Democracy Abroad: The Learning Curve.* Washington, DC: Carnegie Endowment for International Peace.

———. 2004. *Critical Mission: Essays on Democracy Promotion.* Washington, DC: Carnegie Endowment for International Peace.

———. 2012. *Democracy Policy Under Obama: Revitalization or Retreat?* Washington, DC: Carnegie Endowment for International Peace.
———. 2017. "Democracy Promotion Under Trump: What Has Been Lost? What Remains?" Washington, DC: Carnegie Endowment for International Peace, September 6.
Chick, Kristen. 2017. "Bahrain Is Stripping Dissidents of Their Citizenship, and the U.S. Is Silent." *Washington Post,* July 8.
Childress, Sarah. 2013. "The Deep State: How Egypt's Shadow State Won Out." *Frontline,* September 17. https://www.pbs.org/wgbh/frontline/article/the-deep-state-how-egypts-shadow-state-won-out.
Chollet, Derek. 2016. *The Long Game: How Obama Defied Washington and Redfined America's Role in the World.* New York: PublicAffairs.
Chollet, Derek, and Ben Fishman. 2015. "Who Lost Libya? Obama's Intervention in Retrospect." *Foreign Affairs,* May/June.
Clapper, James R. 2018. *Facts and Fears: Hard Truths from a Life in Intelligence.* New York: Viking.
Clarke, Michael, and Anthony Ricketts. 2017. "U.S. Grand Strategy and National Security: The Dilemmas of Primacy, Decline and Denial." *Australian Journal of International Affairs* 71, no. 5: 479–498.
Cockburn, Patrick. 2011. "Power Struggle Deepens Divisions Among Bahraini Royal Family." *Independent,* September 27.
Cohen, Roger. 2018. "The Prince Who Would Remake the World." *New York Times,* June 21.
Cooper, Helene, Mark Landler, and David E. Sanger. 2011. "In U.S. Signals to Egypt, Obama Straddled a Rift." *New York Times,* February 12.
Cox, Michael, G. John Ikenberry, and Takashi Inoguchi, eds. 2000. *American Democracy Promotion: Impulses, Strategies, and Impacts.* Oxford: Oxford University Press.
Crowley, Michael. 2016. "'We Caved.'" *Politico,* January 17.
Daragahi, Borzou. 2014. "Voices from Libya's Armed Struggle." *Financial Times,* July 27.
Defense Security Cooperation Agency (DSCA). 2012. "United Arab Emirates—Terminal High Altitude Area Defense System Missiles (THAAD)." *DSCA News Release,* November 5. http://www.dsca.mil/sites/default/files/mas/uae_12-40_0.pdf.
DeYoung, Karen, and Missy Ryan. 2019. "Trump's Call with Renegade Libyan General Could Signal a Shift in U.S. Policy." *Washington Post,* April 19.
Diamond, Larry, and Marc Plattner, eds. 2014. *Democratization and Authoritarianism in the Arab World.* Baltimore: Johns Hopkins University Press.
Dickinson, Beth. 2012. "Morsi Enters the World Stage with Saudi Arabia Trip." *The National,* July 13.
Diehl, Jackson. 2018. "Mike Pompeo Swaggers His Way to Failure." *Washington Post,* December 9.
———. 2019. "How Far Can the U.S. Really Retreat from the Middle East?" *Washington Post,* January 18.
Dooley, Brian. 2017. "Another Light Goes Out in Bahrain as al-Wasat Closes." *Huffington Post,* June 26.
Drezner, Daniel. 2011. "Does Obama Have a Grand Strategy? Why We Need Doctrines in Uncertain Times." *Foreign Affairs* 90, no. 4: 57–68.
Dutt D'Cunha, Suparna. 2017. "Plagued by a 30% Unemployment Rate, Arabian Youth Turn to Startups for a Lifeline." *Forbes,* May 11.
Dyer, Geoff, and Heba Saleh. 2016. "Clinton and Obama: An American Rift over an Egyptian Despot." *Financial Times,* October 27.
The Economist. 2017. "Donald Trump's Administration Is Promoting Democracy and Human Rights." December 6.

———. 2018. "Muslims but Not Brothers: Saudi Arabia Turns Against Political Islam." June 23.

Edmondson, Catie. 2019. "US Role in Yemen War Will End Unless Trump Issues Second Veto." *New York Times,* April 4.

Epstein, Jennifer. 2011. "Libya Rebels to Open D.C. Office." *Politico,* May 24.

Essam El-Din, Gamal. 2011. "U.S. Aid to Egypt's Civil Society: A Need, a Blessing and a Curse." *Ahram Online,* August 5. http://english.ahram.org.eg/NewsContent/P/1/17749/Egypt/US-aid-to-Egypts-civil-society-a-need,-a-blessing-.aspx.

Fadel, Leila, and William Wan. 2012. "NGO Workers Under Criminal Investigation in Egypt Leave Country After Bail Is Paid." *Washington Post,* March 1.

Fahrenthold, David A., and Jonathan O'Connell. 2018. "'I Like Them Very Much': Trump Has Long-Standing Business Ties with Saudis, Who Have Boosted His Hotels Since He Took Office." *Washington Post,* October 11.

Fallows, James. 2015. "The Tragedy of the American Military." *The Atlantic,* January/February.

Farrow, Ronan. 2018. *The War on Peace: The End of Diplomacy and the Decline of American Influence.* New York: W. W. Norton & Company.

Fifield, Anna, and Camilla Hall. 2011. "U.S. and Bahrain Secretly Extended Defense Deal." *Financial Times,* September 1.

Fisher, Max. 2016. "How Saudi Arabia captured Washington." *Vox,* March 21, 2016. https://www.vox.com/2016/3/21/11275354/saudi-arabia-gulf-washington.

———. 2018. "A Saudi Prince's Quest to Remake the Middle East." *New Yorker,* April 9.

Fishman, Ben. 2017. "The Trump Administration and Libya: The Necessity for Engagement." Washington Institute for Near East Policy, *Policy Notes* 40. http://www.washingtoninstitute.org/uploads/Documents/pubs/PolicyNote40-Fishman.pdf.

Flock, Elizabeth. 2011. "Bahrain Diplomat Brought Home Because of Threats, Ethnic Slurs." *Washington Post,* June 1.

Forsythe, David P., and Patrice C. McMahon. 2017. *American Exceptionalism Reconsidered: U.S. Foreign Policy, Human Rights, and World Order.* New York: Routledge.

Fraihat, Ibrahim. 2019. "Palestine and the Israel–Saudi Arabia Alliance." *Al-Shabaka,* February 7. https://al-shabaka.org/commentaries/palestine-and-the-israel-saudi-arabia-alliance/.

Freedom House. 2009. "Freedom in the World 2009." https://freedomhouse.org/report/freedom-world/freedom-world-2009.

Friedersdorf, Conor. 2016. "Obama's Weak Defense of His Record on Drone Killings." *The Atlantic,* December 23.

Friedman, Thomas L. 2018. "Trump to Dictators: Have a Nice Day." *New York Times,* June 19.

Friedman, Uri. 2017. "Trump and the Cycle of Democracy Promotion." *The Atlantic,* April 3.

Gates, Robert Michael. 2014. *Duty: Memoirs of a Secretary at War.* Kindle edition. New York: Alfred A. Knopf.

General Authority for Statistics of the Kingdom of Saudi Arabia. 2018. "Unemployment Rate 2018." https://www.stats.gov.sa/en/820.

George, Alexander L. 1980. *Presidential Decision-making in Foreign Policy: The Effective Use of Information and Advice.* Boulder: Westview Press.

Gholz, Eugene, and Daryl G. Press. 2010. "Protecting 'the Prize': Oil and the U.S. National Interest." *Security Studies* 19, no. 3: 453–485.

Gilley, Bruce. 2013. "Did Bush Democratize the Middle East? The Effects of External-Internal Linkages." *Political Science Quarterly* 128, no. 4: 653–685.

Gleditsch, Kristian Skrede, and Michael D. Ward. 2006. "Diffusion and the International Context of Democratization." *International Organization* 60, no. 4: 911–933.

Glenn, Cameron. 2017. "Libya's Islamists: Who They Are—And What They Want." *The Wilson Center,* August 8. https://www.wilsoncenter.org/article/libyas-islamists-who-they-are-and-what-they-want.

Goldberg, Jeffrey. 2016. "The Obama Doctrine." *The Atlantic,* April.

———. 2018. "A Senior White House Official Defines the Trump Doctrine: 'We're America, Bitch.'" *The Atlantic,* June 11.

Gordon, Michael R., and Kareem Fahim. 2013. "Kerry Says Egypt's Military Was 'Restoring Democracy' in Ousting Morsi." *New York Times,* August 1.

Graham, Lindsey, and John McCain. 2013. "John McCain and Lindsey Graham: Cut Off Aid to Egypt." *Washington Post,* July 12.

Hachigian, Nina, and David Shorr. 2013. "The Responsibility Doctrine." *Washington Quarterly* 36, no. 1 (Winter): 73–91.

Haley, Nikki. 2018a. "Explanation of Vote Before the Adoption of UN Security Council Resolution 2418 Extending South Sudan Sanctions." US Mission to the United Nations. May 31. https://usun.state.gov/remarks/8456.

———. 2018b. "Remarks at an Emergency UN Security Council Meeting on Syria and Unilateral Threats to International Peace and Security." US Mission to the United Nations. April 13. https://usun.state.gov/remarks/8385.

Halime, Farah. 2013. "From Washington, with a Slap." *Egypt Independent,* October 14.

Halperin, Morton H., and Priscilla Clapp, with Arnold Kanter. 2006. *Bureaucratic Politics and Foreign Policy.* Washington, DC: Brookings Institution Press.

Hamid, Shadi. 2015. "Islamism, the Arab Spring, and the Failure of America's Do-Nothing Policy in the Middle East." *The Atlantic,* October 9.

———. 2016. "How Iraq Warped Obama's Worldview." *The Atlantic,* March 11.

Hanly, Ken. 2016. "Mayor and Council of Benghazi Replaced by Libyan Military Colonel." *Digital Journal,* August 12.

Hanna, Michael Wahid. 2015. "Getting Over Egypt." *Foreign Affairs,* November/December.

Hashem, Ali. 2012. Interviewed by Paul Jay. *Real News Network,* March 21. http://openanthropology.org/libya/News%20Libya%20Benghazi%20Protests.pdf.

Hassan, Oz. 2015. "Undermining the Transatlantic Democracy Agenda? The Arab Spring and Saudi Arabia's Counteracting Democracy Strategy." *Democratization* 22, no. 3: 479–495.

Hawthorne, Amy. 2005. "The New Reform Ferment." In *Uncharted Journey: Promoting Democracy in the Middle East,* edited by Thomas Carothers and Marina Ottaway, 63. Washington, DC: Carnegie Endowment for International Peace.

Hayden, Michael V. 2016. *Playing to the Edge: American Intelligence in the Age of Terror.* New York: Penguin.

Heer, Jeet. 2018. "Scarier Than a Neoconservative." *New Republic,* March 23.

Henderson, Simon. 2014. "Royal Rivalry: Bahrain's Ruling Family and the Island's Political Crisis." Washington Institute for Near East Policy, Policywatch 2198, January 24. http://www.washingtoninstitute.org/policy-analysis/view/royal-rivalry-bahrains-ruling-family-and-the-islands-political-crisis.

Herb, Jeremy. 2017. "Mattis Advised UAE Military Before Joining Trump Administration." *CNN,* August 2.

Hertog, Steffen. 2006. "Modernizing Without Democratizing? The Introduction of Formal Politics in Saudi Arabia." *Internationale Politik und Gesellschaft* 3: 65–78.

Hill, Thomas. 2018. "What Trump's Budget Would Mean for the State Department—Snap Judgments." Brookings Institution, February 13. https://www.brookings.edu/blog/fixgov/2018/02/13/what-trumps-budget-would-mean-for-the-state-department-snap-judgments.

Hinnebusch, Raymond. 2014. "The Arab Uprisings: Alignments and Regional Power Balance." In *The Arab Uprisings: Catalysts, Dynamics, and Trajectories,*

edited by Fahed al-Sumait, Nele Lenze, and Michael C. Hudson London: Rowman & Littlefield.
Hobson, Christopher, and Milja Kurki, eds. 2012. *The Conceptual Politics of Democracy Promotion.* Democratization Studies 20. New York: Routledge.
Hodge, Nathan. 2011. "Gates Calls Bahrain Reforms Insufficient." *Wall Street Journal,* March 12.
Holsti, Kalevi J. 1970. "National Role Conceptions in the Study of Foreign Policy." *International Studies Quarterly* 14, no. 3: 233–309.
Holsti, Ole R. 1976. "Cognitive Process Approaches to Decision-Making: Foreign Policy Actors Viewed Psychologically." *American Behavioral Scientist* 20, no. 1: 11–32.
Hosenball, Mark. 2011. "Exclusive: Obama Authorizes Secret Help for Libya Rebels." Reuters, March 30.
Houghton, David Patrick. 2013. *The Decision Point: Six Cases in U.S. Foreign Policy Decision Making.* New York: Oxford University Press.
Hubbard, Ben. 2019. "As U.S. Exits Syria, Mideast Faces a Post-American Era." *New York Times,* January 11.
Huber, Daniela. 2008. "Democracy Assistance in the Middle East and North Africa: A Comparison of US and EU Policies." *Mediterranean Politics* 13: 143–162.
———. 2015. *Democracy Promotion and Foreign Policy: Identity and Interests in U.S., EU, and Non-Western Democracies.* London: Palgrave Macmillan.
Human Rights Watch. 2012a. "Bahrain: Police Attack Peaceful Protest." June 27. https://www.hrw.org/news/2012/06/27/bahrain-police-attack-peaceful-protest.
———. 2012b. "U.S.: Wrong Time for Bahrain Arms Sales." February 8. https://www.hrw.org/news/2012/02/08/us-wrong-time-bahrain-arms-deal.
———. 2012c. "World Report 2012: Bahrain Events of 2011." January. https://www.hrw.org/world-report/2012/country-chapters/bahrain.
———. 2015. "The Blood of People Who Don't Cooperate." November 22. https://www.hrw.org/report/2015/11/22/blood-people-who-dont-cooperate/continuing-torture-and-mistreatment-detainees.
———. 2017. "Bahrain: Events of 2016." January. https://www.hrw.org/world-report/2017/country-chapters/bahrain.
———. 2018. "Bahrain: Hundreds Stripped of Citizenship." July 27. https://www.hrw.org/news/2018/07/27/bahrain-hundreds-stripped-citizenship.
Huntington, Samuel P. 1993. *The Third Wave: Democratization in the Late Twentieth Century.* Julian J. Rothbaum Distinguished Lecture Series, Volume 4. Norman: University of Oklahoma Press.
Ibrahim, Raymond. 2013. "U.S. Ambassador to Egypt: 'Muslim Brotherhood's Lackey.'" *Gatestone Institute,* July 17. https://www.gatestoneinstitute.org/3855/us-ambassador-egypt.
International Atomic Energy Agency. 2018. "Verification and Monitoring in the Islamic Republic of Iran in Light of United Nations Security Council Resolution 2231." May 24. https://www.iaea.org/sites/default/files/18/06/gov2018-24.pdf.
International Crisis Group. 2011. "Popular Protest in North Africa and Middle East (VIII): Bahrain's Rocky Road to Reform." *Middle East/North Africa Report,* no. 111, July 28. https://d2071andvip0wj.cloudfront.net/111-popular-protest-in-north-africa-and-the-middle-east-viii-bahrain-s-rocky-road-to-reform.pdf.
———. 2013. "Trial by Error: Justice in Post-Qadhafi Libya." Middle East and North Africa Report, no. 240. April 17. https://www.crisisgroup.org/middle-east-north-africa/north-africa/libya/trial-error-justice-post-qadhafi-libya.
———. 2016. "The Libyan Political Agreement: Time for a Reset." Brussels: ICG Middle East and North Africa Report, no. 170. November 4. https://d2071andvip0wj.cloudfront.net/170-the-libyan-political-agreement.pdf.

Janis, Irving L. 1972. *Victims of Groupthink: A Psychological Study of Foreign-Policy Decisions and Fiascoes.* Boston: Houghton Mifflin.

Janis, I., and L. Mann. 1979. *Decision Making. A Psychological Analysis of Conflict, Choice, and Commitment.* New York: The Free Press.

Jones, Toby C. 2011a. "The Siege of Bahrain." *Foreign Policy,* February 18.

———. 2011b. "Time to Disband the Bahrain-Based U.S. Fifth Fleet." *The Atlantic,* June 10.

Kaidanow, Tina S. 2017. "Opening Statement to the Committee on Foreign Relations United States Senate." September 26. https://www.foreign.senate.gov/imo/media/doc/092617_Kaidanow_Testimony.pdf.

Kamola, Isaac A. 2018. "The Arab Spring, U.S. Intervention in Libya, and the Lingering Politics of Rwanda Remorse." In *U.S. Approaches to the Arab Uprisings: International Relations and Democracy Promotion,* edited by Amentahru Wahlrab and Michael J. McNeal. Kindle edition. London: I. B. Tauris.

Kamrava, Mehran. 2015. *Qatar: Small State, Big Politics.* Ithaca: Cornell University Press.

Kaplan, Robert D. 2013. "The Tragedy of U.S. Foreign Policy." *National Interest,* August 1. http://nationalinterest.org/commentary/the-tragedy-us-foreign-policy-8810.

Karlin, Mara. 2017. "Why Military Assistance Programs Disappoint: Minor Tools Can't Solve Major Problems." Brookings Institution, November/December. https://www.brookings.edu/articles/why-military-assistance-programs-disappoint.

Karlin, Mara, and Tamara Cofman Wittes. 2019. "America's Middle East Purgatory: The Case for Doing Less." *Foreign Affairs,* January/February.

Katzman, Kenneth. 2010. "Bahrain: Reform, Security, and U.S. Policy." Congressional Research Service, April 26. https://www.everycrsreport.com/files/20100929_95-1013_e9c24e9229ea529b7df0adcce0b3c284ae976818.pdf.

———. 2017. "Bahrain: Reform, Security, and U.S. Policy." Congressional Research Service, September 29. http://www.refworld.org/docid/59e882f84.html.

———. 2018. "Bahrain: Reform, Security, and U.S. Policy." Congressional Research Service, February 15. https://fas.org/sgp/crs/mideast/95-1013.pdf.

Kerry, John. 2014. "Remarks with Egyptian Foreign Minister Shoukry After Their Meeting." Cairo, Egypt. US Department of State, June 22. https://2009-2017.state.gov/secretary/remarks/2014/06/228234.htm.

———. 2015. "Remarks by John Kerry." Rome, Italy. US Department of State, December 12. https://2009-2017.state.gov/secretary/remarks/2015/12/250599.htm.

———. 2018. *Every Day Is Extra.* New York: Simon and Schuster.

Khorrami Assl, Nima. 2012. "The Kingdoms United?" Washington, DC: Carnegie Endowment for International Peace, May 22. http://carnegieendowment.org/sada/48204.

Kilcullen, David. 2016. *Blood Year: The Unraveling of Western Counterterrorism.* New York: Oxford.

Kingsley, Patrick. 2013. "Who Are the Muslim Brotherhood?" *The Guardian,* April 2.

Kirchgaessner, Stephanie, and Ruth Michaelson. 2017. "General Accused of War Crimes Courted by West in Libya." *The Guardian,* September 25.

Kirkpatrick, David D. 2012. "Egyptian Official Vexes Ruling Generals and U.S. by Pressing Investigation." *New York Times,* February 14.

———. 2018. *Into the Hands of the Soldiers: Freedom and Chaos in Egypt and the Middle East.* Kindle edition. New York: Viking.

Kirkpatrick, David D., Ben Hubbard, Mark Landler, and Mark Mazzetti. 2018. "The Wooing of Jared Kushner: How the Saudis Got a Friend in the White House." *New York Times,* December 8.

Kirkpatrick, David D., and Mark Mazzetti. 2018. "How 2 Gulf Monarchies Sought to Influence the White House." *New York Times,* March 21.

Knights, Michael, and Matthew Levitt. 2018. "The Evolution of Shi'a Insurgency in Bahrain." Combatting Terrorism Center at West Point Policy Paper, January. https://ctc.usma.edu/evolution-shia-insurgency-bahrain.

Kuperman, Alan J. 2015. "Obama's Libya Debacle: How a Well-Meaning Intervention Ended in Failure." *Foreign Affairs,* March/April.

Lacher, Wolfgang, and Alaa al-Idrissi. 2018. "Capital of Militias: Tripoli's Armed Groups Capture the Libyan State." *Small Arms Survey Briefing Paper,* June 2018. http://www.smallarmssurvey.org/fileadmin/docs/T-Briefing-Papers/SAS-SANA-BP-Tripoli-armed-groups.pdf

Lacroix, Stephane. 2016. "Egypt's Pragmatic Salafis: The Politics of Hizb al-Nour." Washington, DC: Carnegie Endowment for International Peace, November 1. http://carnegieendowment.org/2016/11/01/egypt-s-pragmatic-salafis-politics-of-hizb-al-nour-pub-64902.

LaFranchi, Howard. 2012. "U.S. Lies Low on Egypt, Acting Behind the Scenes. Is That Approach Wise?" *Christian Science Monitor,* June 25.

Lake, Eli, and Josh Rogin. 2013. "Ambassador Anne Patterson, the Controversial Face of America's Egypt Policy." *Daily Beast,* July 10.

Landler, Mark. 2011. "Obama Tells Gaddafi to Quit and Authorizes Refugee Airlifts." *New York Times,* March 3.

———. 2019. "Egypt's President, Hoping to Be Allowed to Stay in Office Until 2034, Basks in Trump's Embrace." *New York Times,* April 9.

Lawson, Marian L., and Susan B. Epstein. 2019. *Democracy Promotion: An Objective of U.S. Foreign Assistance.* Congressional Research Service. January 4.

Lederman, Josh. 2018. "Trump Administration Approves Sale of $1.3 Billion in Artillery to Saudi Arabia." *PBS,* April 5. https://www.pbs.org/newshour/world/trump-administration-approves-sale-of-1-3-billion-in-artillery-to-saudi-arabia.

Lee, Matthew. 2011. "U.S. Recognizes Libyan Rebels as Libyan Government." *San Diego Union-Tribune,* July 15.

Levitsky, Steven, and Lucan Way. 2010. *Competitive Authoritarianism: Hybrid Regimes After the Cold War.* Cambridge: Cambridge University Press.

Linz, Juan J., and Alfred Stepan. 1996. *Problems of Democratic Transition and Consolidation: Southern Europe, South America, and Post-Communist Europe.* Baltimore: Johns Hopkins University Press.

Liptak, Kevin. 2017. "Trump Lands in Saudi Arabia as Controversies Swirl at Home." *CNN,* May 20.

Lipton, Eric, Brooke Williams, and Nicholas Confessore. 2014. "Foreign Powers Buy Influence at Think Tanks." *New York Times,* September 6.

Lizza, Ryan. 2011. "The Consequentialist: How the Arab Spring Remade Obama's Foreign Policy." *New Yorker,* May 2.

Lust-Okar, Ellen. 2009. "Reinforcing Informal Institutions Through Authoritarian Elections: Insights from Jordan." *Middle East Law and Governance* 1, no. 1: 3–37.

Lynch, Marc. 2012. *The Arab Uprising: The Unfinished Revolutions of the New Middle East.* New York: PublicAffairs.

———, ed. 2014. *The Arab Uprisings Explained: New Contentious Politics in the Middle East.* New York: Columbia University Press.

———. 2016. *The New Arab Wars: Uprisings and Anarchy in the Middle East.* New York: PublicAffairs.

———. 2017. "Obama and the Middle East, Rightsizing the U.S. Role." *Foreign Affairs,* September/October.

Mann, James. 2012. *The Obamians: The Struggle Inside the White House to Redefine American Power.* New York: Viking.

March, James G., and Herbert A. Simon. 1958. *Organizations.* New York: Wiley.

Marsden, Lee. 2005. *Lessons from Russia: Clinton and US Democracy Promotion.* Aldershot, NH: Ashgate.

Mason, Jeff. 2011. "U.S. Says Libya Has Spoken, Gaddafi Must Leave Now." Reuters, February 26.

Massoglia, Anna, and Geoff West. 2018. "Foreign Interests Have Spent Over $530 Million Influencing US Policy, Public Opinion Since 2017." *Open Secrets.* August 8. https://www.opensecrets.org/news/2018/08/foreign-interests-fara-lobby-watch-exclusive.

Matar, Hisham. 2016. *The Return: Fathers, Sons, and the Land in Between.* New York: Random House.

Mazzetti, Mark. 2013. *The Way of the Knife: The CIA, a Secret Army, and a War at the Ends of the Earth.* New York: Penguin Press.

McDaniel, Richard. 2013. "No 'Plan B': U.S. Strategic Access in the Middle East and the Question of Bahrain." Center for 21st Century Security and Intelligence, Brookings Institution Policy Paper, June. https://www.brookings.edu/wp-content/uploads/2016/06/24-us-strategic-access-middle-east-bahrain-mcdaniel.pdf.

McDermott, Mikaela A., and Brian Katulis. 2004. "Even the Word 'Democracy' Now Repels Mideast Reformers." *Christian Science Monitor,* May 20.

McEvers, Kelly. 2012. "The Crackdown." *Washington Monthly,* March/April.

McFaul, Michael. 2010. *Advancing Democracy Abroad: Why We Should and How We Can.* Hoover Studies in Politics, Economics, and Society. Lanham: Rowman & Littlefield.

———. 2018. *From Cold War to Hot Peace: An American Ambassador in Putin's Russia.* Boston: Houghton Mifflin Harcourt.

McGreal, Chris. 2011. "Egypt's Military Rejects Swift Transfer of Power and Suspends Constitution." *The Guardian,* February 13.

Mead, Walter Russell. 2002. *Special Providence: American Foreign Policy and How It Changed the World.* New York: Routledge.

Mearsheimer, John J., and Stephen M. Walt. 2007. *The Israel Lobby and U.S. Foreign Policy.* New York: Farrar, Straus and Giroux.

Miller, Andrew. 2018. "Trump Blinks, and Egypt's Sisi Wins." *Foreign Policy,* August 10.

Morgenthau, Hans J. 1948. *Politics Among Nations: The Struggle for Power and Peace.* First edition. New York: A. A. Knopf.

Morrell, Michael. 2016. *The Great War of Our Time: The CIA's Fight Against Terrorism—From al Qa'ida to ISIS.* New York: Twelve.

Muravchik, Joshua. 2009. "The Abandonment of Democracy." *Commentary,* June 19.

Murphy, Chris, and Ben Rhodes. 2019. "Democrats Should Stand for Democracy in Venezuela—And Democratic Values in America." *Washington Post,* January 29.

Nakamura, David. 2017. "Trump Welcomes Egypt's Sisi to White House in Reversal of U.S. Policy." *Washington Post,* April 3.

Nasr, Seyyed Vali Reza. 2014. *The Dispensable Nation: American Foreign Policy in Retreat.* New York: Anchor Books.

Nau, Henry R. 2010. "Obama's Foreign Policy." *Policy Review* 160: 27–47.

———. 2013. "Ronald Reagan." In *US Foreign Policy and Democracy Promotion: From Theodore Roosevelt to Barack Obama,* edited by Michael Cox, Timothy J. Lynch, and Nicolas Bouchet, 138–158. New York: Routledge.

Nauert, Heather. 2018a. Press Statement. Washington, DC, US Department of State, April 2. https://www.state.gov/r/pa/prs/ps/2018/04/280119.htm.

———. 2018b. "Readout of Secretary Pompeo's Meeting with Libyan Minister al-Sarraj." US Department of State. Washington, DC, December 4. https://www.state.gov/r/pa/prs/ps/2018/12/287880.htm.

Naylor, Sean D. and Nick Turse. 2019. "Libyan War Escalates Amid Lack of U.S. Strategy for Secret Missions in Africa." *Yahoo News,* April 10. https://www.yahoo

.com/news/libyan-war-escalates-amid-lack-of-us-strategy-for-secret-missions-in-africa-090000507.html.

Nelson, Louis. 2017. "Trump Praises Duterte for Doing an 'Unbelievable Job' Cracking Down on Drugs in the Philippines." *Politico,* May 24.

Nichols, John. 2011. "Biden Is on the Wrong Side of History." *The Nation,* January 31. https://www.npr.org/2011/01/31/133368321/the-nation-biden-is-on-the-wrong-side-of-history.

Nikitin, Mary Beth. 2012. "Proliferation Security Initiative." Congressional Research Service, June 15. https://fas.org/sgp/crs/nuke/RL34327.pdf.

Nye, Joseph S. 2004. *Soft Power: The Means to Success in World Politics.* First edition. New York: PublicAffairs.

Obama, Barack. 2004. *Dreams from My Father: A Story of Race and Inheritance.* New York: Crown.

———. 2006. *The Audacity of Hope: Thoughts on Reclaiming the American Dream.* New York: Crown.

———. 2009a. "A Just and Lasting Peace." Nobel Lecture. Oslo, December 20. http://nobelprize.org/nobel_prizes/peace/laureates/2009/obama-lecture_en.html.

———. 2009b. Speech at Cairo University. Cairo, June 4. https://obamawhitehouse.archives.gov/issues/foreign-policy/presidents-speech-cairo-a-new-beginning.

———. 2011a. "Remarks by the President in Address to the Nation on Libya." White House, March 28. https://obamawhitehouse.archives.gov/the-press-office/2011/03/28/remarks-president-address-nation-libya.

———. 2011b. "Remarks by the President on the Middle East and North Africa." White House Office of the Press Secretary, May 19. https://obamawhitehouse.archives.gov/the-press-office/2011/05/19/remarks-president-middle-east-and-north-africa.

———. 2011c. "Remarks by the President on the Situation in Egypt." White House, January 28. https://obamawhitehouse.archives.gov/the-press-office/2011/01/28/remarks-president-situation-egypt.

———. 2011d. "Remarks by the President on the Situation in Egypt." White House, February 1. https://obamawhitehouse.archives.gov/the-press-office/2011/02/01/remarks-president-situation-egypt.

———. 2011e. "Statement by the President on Bahrain." White House Office of the Press Secretary, February 27. https://obamawhitehouse.archives.gov/the-press-office/2011/02/27/statement-president-bahrain.

———. 2013. "Remarks by President Obama in Address to the United Nations General Assembly." New York, September 24. https://obamawhitehouse.archives.gov/the-press-office/2013/09/24/remarks-president-obama-address-united-nations-general-assembly.

———. 2015. "Remarks by President Obama to the United Nations General Assembly." New York, September 28. https://obamawhitehouse.archives.gov/the-press-office/2015/09/28/remarks-president-obama-united-nations-general-assembly.

Odinius, Daniel, and Philipp Kuntz. 2015. "The Limits of Authoritarian Solidarity: The Gulf Monarchies and Preserving Authoritarian Rule During the Arab Spring." *European Journal of Political Research* 54, no. 4: 639–654.

Osnos, Evan. 2014. "In the Land of the Possible." *New Yorker,* December.

Pack, Jason. 2015. "How to End Libya's War." *New York Times,* January 21.

Panetta, Leon. 2014. *Worthy Fights: A Memoir of Leadership in War and Peace.* New York: Penguin.

Pazzanese, Christina. 2018. "Samantha Power: The World in Her Rearview Mirror." *Harvard Gazette,* January 24. https://news.harvard.edu/gazette/story/2018/01/samantha-power-reflects-on-her-eight-years-helping-shape-u-s-foreign-policy.

Pearson, John. 2018. "US Quietly Increasing Air Strikes on ISIL in Libya." *The National,* March 10.

Pecquet, Julian. 2015. "Bahrain Bristles as U.S. Threatens to Move Fleet." *U.S. News & World Report,* May 19.
Penney, Joe, Eric Schmitt, Rukmini Callimachi, and Christoph Koettl. 2018. "C.I.A. Drone Mission, Curtailed by Obama, Is Expanded in Africa Under Trump." *New York Times,* September 9.
Perry, Tom, and Suleiman al-Khalidi. 2017. "Gulf Crisis Seen Widening Split in Syria Rebellion." Reuters, June 14.
Peterson, Scott. 2018. "In Iran's Surprise Uprising of the Poor, Dents to Revolution's Legitimacy." *Christian Science Monitor,* January 5.
Pew Research Center. 2007. "Global Unease with Major Powers." June 27. http://www.pewglobal.org/2007/06/27/global-unease-with-major-world-powers.
———. 2011. "Modest Support for Libya Airstrikes, No Clear Goal Seen." March 28. http://www.people-press.org/2011/03/28/modest-support-for-libya-airstrikes-no-clear-goal-seen.
Pincus, Walter. 2015. "Benghazi Was Familiar Ground for Amb. J. Christopher Stevens." *Washington Post,* October 19.
Pitter, Laura. 2012. "Delivered into Enemy Hands: U.S.-Led Abuse and Rendition of Opponents to Gaddafi's Libya." Human Rights Watch Report, September. https://www.hrw.org/report/2012/09/05/delivered-enemy-hands/us-led-abuse-and-rendition-opponents-gaddafis-libya.
POMED (Project of Middle East Democracy). 2018. "Candidates in Egypt's 2018 Presidential 'Election.'" January. https://pomed.org/fact-sheet-dropping-like-flies-sisis-purge-of-potential-candidates-in-egypts-2018-presidential-election.
Pompeo, Mike. 2019. "Mike Pompeo's Cairo Speech on Mideast Policy and Obama." *Haaretz,* January 11.
Power, Samantha. 2004. "Remember Rwanda, but Take Action in Sudan." *New York Times,* April 6.
Rapier, Robert. 2017. "Is the U.S. on Track for Energy Independence?" *Wall Street Journal,* November 15.
Reuters. 2011. "Factbox—International Recognition of Libya's Rebel Movement." June 22.
———. 2017. "Trump Says Ties with Bahrain Won't Be Strained Anymore." May 21.
———. 2018. "US 'Seriously Concerned' over Jailing of Bahraini Activist." February 21.
Rhodes, Ben. 2018. *The World As It Is: A Memoir of the Obama White House.* New York: Random House.
Rice, Condoleezza. 2000. "Campaign 2000: Promoting the National Interest." *Foreign Affairs,* January/February.
———. 2005. "Remarks at the American University in Cairo." US Department of State Archive, June 20. https://2001-2009.state.gov/secretary/rm/2005/48328.htm.
———. 2017. *Democracy: Stories from the Long Road to Freedom.* New York: Twelve.
Rogin, Josh. 2012a. "Obama Administration Seeks to Bolster Bahraini Crown Prince with Arms Sales." *Foreign Policy,* May 11.
———. 2012b. "State Department's New Middle East Fund Falls Victim to Capitol Hill Dysfunction." *Foreign Policy,* September 27.
———. 2017. "State Department Considers Scrubbing Democracy Promotion from Its Mission." *Washington Post,* August 2.
———. 2019. "Demands Grow to Release CIA Assessment of Khashoggi Murder." *Washington Post,* January 14.
Rosenau, James N. 1980. *The Scientific Study of Foreign Policy.* London: Frances Pinter.
Rothkopf, David J. 2006. *Running the World: The Inside Story of the National Security Council and the Architects of American Power.* New York: PublicAffairs.
Rucker, Philip, and Anne Gearan. 2019. "Trump Announced Nomination of Kelly Knight Craft to Be Ambassador to United Nations." *Washington Post,* February 22.

Ryan, Missy, and Sudarsan Raghavan. 2016. "U.S. Special Operations Troops Aiding Libyan Forces in Major Battle Against Islamic State." *Washington Post,* August 9.

Salloum, Shahira. 2011. "Bahrain's Al-Wefaq: Contemplating Compromise." *Al-Akhbar,* September 28.

Sanger, David E. 2012. *Confront and Conceal: Obama's Secret Wars and Surprising Use of American Power.* First edition. New York: Crown.

Sanger, David, and Eric Schmitt. 2017. "Rex Tillerson to Lift Human Rights Conditions on Arms Sale to Bahrain." *New York Times,* March 29.

Saunders, Elizabeth N. 2011. *Leaders at War: How Presidents Shape Military Interventions.* Ithaca: Cornell University Press.

Schein, Edgar H. 1984. "Coming to a New Awareness of Organizational Culture." *Sloan Management Review* 25, no. 2 (Winter): 3–16.

Schumpeter, Joseph A. 1942 (2010). *Capitalism, Socialism and Democracy.* New York: Routledge.

Shapovalova, Natalie, and Kateryna Zarembo. 2010. "Russia's Machiavellian Support for Democracy." *FRIDE Policy Brief,* no. 56 (October).

Sharp, Jeremy. 2018. "Jordan: Background and U.S. Relations." Congressional Research Service, October 17. https://fas.org/sgp/crs/mideast/RL33546.pdf.

Shehabi, Ala'a. 2014. "Why Is Bahrain Outsourcing Extremism?" *Foreign Policy,* October 29.

Shehata, Samer S., and Joshua Stacher. 2006. "The Brotherhood Goes to Parliament." *Middle East Report,* no. 240 (Fall): 32–39. https://samershehatadotcom.files.wordpress.com/2013/04/the-brotherhood-goes-to-parliament-middle-east-research-and-information-project.pdf.

Shelton, Judy. 2017. "Trump as a Democracy Promoter." *Wall Street Journal Asia,* June 9.

Simon, Herbert A. 1957. *Models of Man: Social and Rational; Mathematical Essays on Rational Human Behavior in Society Setting.* New York: Wiley.

———. 1983. *Reason in Human Affairs.* Stanford: Stanford University Press.

Slackman, Michael. 2007. "Rice Speaks Softly in Egypt, Avoiding Democracy Push." *New York Times,* January 16.

Slackman, Michael, and Nadim Audi. 2011. "Protests in Bahrain Become Test of Wills." *New York Times,* February 22.

Smeltz, Dana. 2012. "Foreign Policy in the New Millennium. Result of the 2012 Chicago Council Survey of American Public Opinion and the U.S. Foreign Policy." Chicago Council on Global Affairs, September 10. https://www.thechicagocouncil.org/publication/foreign-policy-new-millennium.

Smith, Tony. 2012. *America's Mission: The United States and the Worldwide Struggle for Democracy.* Princeton: Princeton University Press.

Snow, Donald M. 2016. *The Middle East, Oil, and the U.S. National Security Policy: Intractable Conflicts, Impossible Solutions.* Lanham, MD: Rowman & Littlefield.

Snyder, Richard C., ed. 1962. *Foreign Policy Decision-Making: An Approach to the Study of International Politics.* Glencoe, Illinois: Free Press.

Snyder, Sarah B. 2018. *From Selma to Moscow: How Human Rights Activists Transformed U.S. Foreign Policy.* New York: Columbia University Press.

Spence, Matthew. 2005. "Policy Coherence and Incoherence: The Domestic Politics of American Democracy Promotion." CDDRL Working Paper. https://cddrl.fsi.stanford.edu/publications/policy_coherence_and_incoherence_the_domestic_politics_of_american_democracy_promotion.

Starr, Barbara. 2017. "US Military Considers Ramping Up Libya Presence." *CNN,* July 10.

Sturm, Michael, and Nikolaus Siegfried. 2005. "Regional Monetary Integration in the Member States of the Gulf Cooperation Council." European Central Bank:

Occasional Paper Series, no. 31, June. http://www.ecb.europa.eu/pub/pdf/scpops/ecbocp31.pdf.

Sullivan, Kevin. 2016. "A Tough Call on Libya That Still Haunts." *Washington Post,* February 3.

Tapper, Jake. 2019. "Pentagon Official: 120-Day Syria Withdrawal Plan Aims to Please Trump 'and Not Get Everyone Killed.'" *CNN,* January 2.

Tau, Byron. 2012. "Muslim Brotherhood Delegation Meets with White House Officials." *Politico44 Blog,* April 4. https://www.politico.com/blogs/politico44/2012/04/muslim-brotherhood-delegation-meets-with-white-house-officials-119647.

Telhami, Shibley. 2011. "Arab Public Opinion: What Do They Want?" In *The Arab Awakening: America and the Transformation of the Middle East,* edited by Kenneth Pollack, Daniel L. Byman, Akram Al-Turk, Pavel Baev, Michael S. Doran, Khaled Elgindy, Stephen R. Grand, et al., 13–20. Washington, DC: Brookings Institution.

Thomas, Clayton. 2017. "Arms Sales in the Middle East: Trends and Analytical Perspectives for U.S. Policy." Congressional Research Service Report, October 11. https://fas.org/sgp/crs/mideast/R44984.pdf.

Thrush, Glenn, and Jennifer Steinhauer. 2017. "Stephen Miller Is a 'True Believer' Behind Core Trump Policies." *New York Times,* February 11.

Toaldo, Mattio, and Mary Fitzgerald. 2016. "A Quick Guide to Libya's Main Players." European Council on Foreign Relations, May 19. https://www.ecfr.eu/mena/mapping_libya_conflict.

Tran, Mark. 2011. "Bahrain Protests a Worry for the U.S. and Its Fifth Fleet." *The Guardian,* February 17.

Traub, James. 2008. *The Freedom Agenda: Why America Must Spread Democracy.* New York: Farrar, Straus and Giroux.

Tucker, Robert W., and David C. Hendrickson. 1990. "Thomas Jefferson and American Foreign Policy." *Foreign Affairs* 69 (Spring): 139.

Tyler, Patrick E. 2004. "Two Said to Tell of Libyan Plot Against Saudi." *New York Times,* June 10.

Ulrichsen, Cristian Coates. 2013. "Bahrain's Uprising: Regional Dimensions and International Consequences." *Stability: International Journal of Security & Development* 2(1): 14, pp. 1–12.

UNHCHR (United Nations High Commissioner for Human Rights). 2018. "Abuse Behind Bars: Arbitrary and Unlawful Detention in Libya." April. https://www.ohchr.org/Documents/Countries/LY/AbuseBehindBarsArbitraryUnlawful_EN.pdf.

United Nations. 2012. "UN Envoy Praises Libyan Election, Highlights Challenges Faced by New Government." *United Nations News,* July 9. https://news.un.org/en/story/2012/07/415102-un-envoy-praises-libyan-election-highlights-challenges-faced-new-government.

United Nations Development Programme. 2002. "The Arab Human Development Report: Creating Opportunities for Future Generations." United Nations Development Program.

US Department of Defense. 2018. "Remarks by Secretary Mattis at International Institute for Strategic Studies Manama Dialogue." October 27. https://dod.defense.gov/News/Transcripts/Transcript-View/Article/1674583/remarks-by-secretary-mattis-at-international-institute-for-strategic-studies-ma.

US Department of State. 2015. "Lifting Holds on Security Assistance to the Government of Bahrain." Press Statement by John Kirby. Washington, DC, June 29. https://2009-2017.state.gov/r/pa/prs/ps/2015/06/244478.htm.

———. 2017. "Bahrain." *Country Reports on Human Rights Practices for 2017.* https://www.state.gov/documents/organization/277481.pdf.

———. 2018. "U.S. Security Cooperation with Bahrain." Bureau of Political-Military Affairs, Fact Sheet. March 23. https://www.state.gov/t/pm/rls/fs/2018/279536.htm.

———. 2019a. "Secretary Pompeo's Meeting with Bahraini King Hamad Bin Isa Al Khalifa, Bahraini Crown Prince Salman Bin Hamad Al Khalifa, and Foreign Minister Khalid Bin Ahmed Al Khalifa." January 11. https://www.state.gov/r/pa/prs/ps/2019/01/288435.htm.

———. 2019b. "Secretary Pompeo's Meeting with Egyptian President Abdel Fattah Al-Sisi." January 10. https://www.state.gov/r/pa/prs/ps/2019/01/288405.htm.

US Embassy in Bahrain. 2018. "Secretary of Defense James N. Mattis' Meeting with Bahrain King Hamad bin Isa Al Khalifa." October 29. https://bh.usembassy.gov/secretary-of-defense-james-n-mattis-meeting-with-bahrain-king-hamad-bin-isa-al-khalifa.

Vanderhill, Rachel. 2013. *Promoting Authoritarianism Abroad.* Boulder: Lynne Rienner.

Vandewalle, Dirk. 2012. "After Qaddafi: The Surprising Success of the New Libya." *Foreign Affairs* 91, no. 6 (November/December).

Van Hüllen, Vera. 2015. *EU Democracy Promotion and the Arab Spring: International Cooperation and Authoritarianism.* New York: Palgrave Macmillan.

Wahlrab, Amentahru, and Michael J. McNeal, eds. 2018. *US Approaches to the Arab Uprisings: International Relations and Democracy Promotion.* London: I.B. Tauris.

Wald, Ellen R. 2018. "Saudi Arabia Has No Leverage." *New York Times,* October 18.

Walsh, Declan. 2018. "Tiny, Wealthy Qatar Goes Its Own Way, and Pays for It." *New York Times,* January 22.

Walt, Stephen M. 2014. "Is Barack Obama More of a Realist Than I Am?" *Foreign Policy,* August 19.

———. 2016. "Obama Was Not a Realist President." *Foreign Policy,* April 7.

Warrick, Joby. 2011. "U.S., Allies Seek to Maintain Arab Support for Military Intervention in Libya." *Washington Post,* March 21.

Watkins, Derek, and Declan Walsh. 2018. "Saudi Strikes, American Bombs, Yemeni Suffering." *New York Times,* December 27.

Wehrey, Frederic. 2012. "The March of Bahrain's Hardliners." Washington, DC: Carnegie Endowment for International Peace, May 31. http://carnegieendowment.org/2012/05/31/march-of-bahrain-s-hardliners-pub-48299.

———. 2013a. "The Forgotten Uprising in Eastern Saudi Arabia." Washington, DC: Carnegie Endowment for International Peace Paper, June 14. https://carnegieendowment.org/2013/06/14/forgotten-uprising-in-eastern-saudi-arabia-pub-52093.

———. 2013b. "The Precarious Ally: Bahrain's Impasse and U.S. Policy." Washington, DC: Carnegie Endowment for International Peace, Carnegie Papers, February. https://carnegieendowment.org/files/bahrain_impasse.pdf.

———. 2015. "Saudi Arabia's Anxious Autocrats." *Journal of Democracy* 26, no. 2: 71–85.

———. 2017. "Whoever Controls Benghazi Controls Libya." *The Atlantic,* July 1.

———. 2018. *The Burning Shores: Inside the Battle for the New Libya.* New York: Farrar, Straus and Giroux.

Weymouth, Lilly. 2013. "Rare Interview with Egyptian Gen. Abdel Fatah al-Sissi." *Washington Post,* August 3.

Whitehead, Laurence, ed. 2001. *The International Dimensions of Democratization: Europe and the Americas.* Oxford: Oxford University Press.

White House. 2002. "National Security Strategy of the United States of America." September. https://georgewbush-whitehouse.archives.gov/nsc/nss/2002.

———. 2011. "Statement by the Press Secretary on Recent Developments in Egypt." White House Office of the Press Secretary, November 25.

———. 2017. "National Security Strategy of the United States of America." December. https://www.whitehouse.gov/wp-content/uploads/2017/12/NSS-Final-12-18-2017-0905.pdf.

———. 2018a. "Readout of President Donald J. Trump's Call with President Abdel Fattah al-Sisi of Egypt." April 2.

———. 2018b. "Remarks by President Trump and President al-Sisi of the Arab Republic of Egypt Before Bilateral Meeting." September 24.

Wilson, James Q. 1991. *Bureaucracy: What Government Agencies Do and Why They Do It.* New York: Basic Books.

Winer, Jonathan. 2016. "Statement for the Record." US Senate Foreign Relations Committee, June 15. https://www.foreign.senate.gov/imo/media/doc/061516_Winer_Testimony.pdf.

Wittes, Tamara Cofman. 2008. *Freedom's Unsteady March: America's Role in Building Arab Democracy.* Washington, DC: Brookings Institution Press.

———. 2015. "Obama Administration to Sissi: Egypt-Bound Weapons Released with Caveat." Brookings Institution, April 6. https://www.brookings.edu/blog/markaz/2015/04/06/obama-administration-to-sissi-egypt-bound-weapons-released-with-caveat.

———. 2016. "The Slipperiest Slope of Them All." *The Atlantic,* March 12.

Worth, Robert Forsyth. 2016. *A Rage for Order: The Middle East in Turmoil, from Tahrir Square to ISIS.* First edition. New York: Farrar, Straus and Giroux.

Wroughton, Lesley, and Steve Scherer. 2015. "With Eye on Islamic State, Western Powers Push Libyans to Accord." Reuters, December 13.

Yergin, Daniel. 2013. "Congratulations, America. You're (Almost) Energy Independent: Now What?" *Politico Magazine,* November.

Yom, S. 2008. "The Dilemmas of American Democracy Promotion in the Arab World." *Yale Journal of International Affairs* 3 (Winter): 131–145.

Youssef, Nour, and Declan Walsh. 2017. "A Libyan Commander Says His Forces Have Taken Benghazi." *New York Times,* July 6.

Zakaria, Fareed. 2007. *The Future of Freedom: Illiberal Democracy at Home and Abroad.* New York: W. W. Norton.

———. 2012. "Zakaria: My Interview with President Obama." *CNN Global Public Square,* January 19.

Zayed, Dina. 2011. "Attack on Egyptian Women Protesters Spark Uproar." Reuters, December 21.

Index

Abdel-Jalil, Mustafa, 119
Abdullah (King), 161–162
Abrams, Elliott, 50
Abu Ghraib, 52
Activism, 198
Afghanistan, 66, 99, 129, 178
Africa, 95
Africa regional command (AFRICOM), 114, 120–121, 124–125, 202
Algeria, 57n7
Ali, Ben, 12, 34, 38
America First, 186–187
American model, 35, 38–39, 39tab
American University of Cairo, 48
Analogical reasoning, 21
Anti-Americanism, 64, 94–95, 145
Arab League, 97, 100
Arab Spring, 26; authoritarianism and, 11–12; Bahrain and, 138–141, 145–147; for democracy, 36; diplomacy in, 41–42; for DoD, 29–30; foreign policy after, 3–4, 138; for GCC, 27–28, 161–162, 175; for Gulf Arab States, 7; individual approach for, 65–66; Islam and, 11, 165–166; Israel and, 20; journalism for, 12; in media, 136; 9/11 and, 8; NTC after, 116; politics of, 6–7; psychology of, 99; for Qaddafi, 94; for regimes, 6; for State Department, 79, 137; for terrorism, 109n52; tribalism and, 65; for US, 2–3, 182–183. *See also* Egypt

Arab world, 2; anti-Americanism in, 64; Arab Human Development Report, 8, 47; authoritarianism in, 32n4; Bush, G. W., for, 55–56; corruption in, 52–53; democracy for, 48–49; diplomacy in, 26, 85–89; economic liberalization of, 38; foreign policy in, 42–51, 43tab–44tab; Israel and, 16; leverage with, 183–186; Muslim world and, 3; for Obama, 181–186; oil for, 14–15; politics in, 137–138; US and, 36
Arms sales: foreign policy for, 14, 184, 194; by US, 138, 142–145, 148, 151–153, 196
al-Asala Islamic Society, 170
Asia, 15. *See also specific countries*
al-Assad, Bashar, 16, 27–28, 182
Assistance, 39tab
The Audacity of Hope (Obama), 61
Austin, Lloyd, 105
Authoritarianism, 5; Arab Spring and, 11–12; in Arab world, 32n4; economics of, 166–171; in Egypt, 9–10, 181–182; for GCC, 175–177; in Jordan, 40–41, 108n11; in Libya, 29–30; military for, 78–79; of Mubarak, H., 48–49; national interest and, 35–36; politics of, 16–17, 37; protests against, 22–23, 87; scholarship on, 26–27; in US, 20–21, 192–195

232 Index

Autocracies, 7, 11, 15, 17, 19, 27; Arab Spring and, 138–141, 145–147; for DoD, 150–154; foreign policy and, 11, 150–154; individual approach in, 103–107, 110n76; institutions in, 127–132, 150–154; Islam in, 29, 130; Islamic State and, 147–148; Libya and, 170–171; in media, 158n55; military with, 46; Pearl Roundabout, 30, 132–135; politics of, 19; protests in, 132–135; regimes as, 42; Saudi Arabia and, 171–172; for Trump, 197–199; US and, 23, 111–112, 135–138, 141–145, 148–149, 185–186

Bachelet, Michelle, 198
Bahrain Independent Commission of Inquiry (BICI), 30, 137–138, 141–144, 148–150, 198
Bahraini Defense Forces (BDF), 128, 138
Bassiouni, Cherif, 137
BDF. *See* Bahraini Defense Forces
Beecroft, Robert, 90–91
Belgrave, Charles, 130
Ben Ali, Zine el-Abidine, 8
Benghazi. *See* Libya
Benghazi attacks, 99–100, 102, 116–118, 121–124, 126, 157n8
BICI. *See* Bahrain Independent Commission of Inquiry
Biden, Joe, 69, 102
bin Salman, Mohammed, 12, 189, 194
bin Zayed, Mohammed, 85
Blumenthal, Sidney, 157n4
Bolduc, Don, 124–125
Bolton, John, 190
Bosnia, 13
Bureaucrats, 23–25, 33n29, 59, 79, 111–112
Burns, William (Bill), 52, 60–61, 70, 106, 109n44, 137–138
Burr, Richard, 176
Bush, George H. W., 46, 62
Bush, George W., 3–4, 9, 128, 188, 210–211; for Arab world, 55–56; 9/11 for, 46–53; terrorism for, 53–55

Cambodia, 190, 193
Cameroon, 26
Canada, 15

Cardin, Ben, 194–195
Carlos, Juan (King), 144
Carpenter, J. Scott, 51
Carter, Jimmy, 45, 57n6, 73
Cato Institute, 17–18
Central Command (CENTCOM), 104–105, 153, 176
Central Intelligence Agency (CIA), 49, 107n9, 210–211; counterterrorism for, 70; DoD and, 117–118, 139–140, 156, 192–193; in Egypt, 81; FBI and, 117, 121; foreign policy and, 113; State Department and, 68
Challengers. *See* Gulf Arab States; Gulf Cooperation Council; Qatar; Saudi Arabia; United Arab Emirates
Chelabi, Ahmed, 183
Cheney, Dick, 47
Cheney, Elizabeth, 49–50
China, 15, 57n8, 62, 98–99, 197
Chollet, Derek, 177–178, 185
CIA. *See* Central Intelligence Agency
Civil society, 63
Clinton, Bill, 18, 46, 57n7, 95
Clinton, Chelsea, 108n11
Clinton, Hillary, 3, 8, 97, 104–105, 115, 132; Egypt for, 20, 66–72, 82, 154–155; Obama and, 108n11, 108n16; reputation of, 92, 100, 102–103, 201. *See also* Benghazi attacks
Cognitive scripts, 21–22
Cold War, 18, 45–47, 73; for Cuba, 10; for US, 5, 9, 26
Community, 24
Conditionality, 39*tab*
Congress, 185, 193–194, 199, 211–213; economics of, 75–76, 89–90, 119–120; in foreign policy, 3, 21, 45, 111–112, 143, 147, 157, 174
Corker, Bob, 194–195
Corruption, 52–53
Côte d'Ivoire, 7
Counterterrorism: for CIA, 70; as national interest, 10–11; after 9/11, 211; for Obama, 18; policy for, 90; for Trump, 201–202
Coup (2013), 65–66, 83–89, 175–178
Craft, Kelly Knight, 192
Credibility gap, 51–53
Cretz, Gene, 98, 113
Cuba, 10, 55, 187–188, 214n2, 214n8

Index

Daalder, Ivo, 97
DCA. *See* defense cooperation agreement
Defense, 13–14, 210. *See also* Department of Defense
defense cooperation agreement (DCA), 128
Democracy: Arab Spring for, 36; for Arab world, 48–49; diplomacy and, 209; in Egypt, 154–157; force and, 100–101; for Gulf Arab States, 165–166; Gulf War for, 18, 46; human rights and, 37–38, 60, 119, 197–198, 205, 212–213; individual approach and, 89–91; institutions and, 148–149; in Iraq, 52; in Libya, 114–116; in MENA, 63–64, 83–84, 178–179; as national interest, 103–104; NDI for, 80–81; NDP for, 72; NED for, 41; for NGOs, 40–41; for NSC, 113; protests for, 66–67; for SCAF, 79–80; for State Department, 193–195; for Trump, 196–203; violence and, 89
Democracy, Rights, and Labor (DRL), 23, 104–106, 131, 134, 195; in Bahrain, 138–143, 145–146; human rights for, 207
Democracy promotion. *See specific topics*
Dempsey, Martin, 87, 88
Department of Defense (DoD), 14, 103, 208–210; Arab Spring for, 29–30; Bahrain for, 150–154; CIA and, 117–118, 139–140, 156, 192–193; economics of, 103; in foreign policy, 127, 138–139, 142–145; intelligence for, 111–112; intervention for, 113; military for, 67–68; NEA and, 185–186; State Department and, 104, 147–148
Department of Homeland Security (DHS), 212–214
Diplomacy, 13, 39*tab*; in Arab Spring, 41–42; in Arab world, 26, 85–89; credibility gap for, 51–53; democracy and, 209; DRL in, 23; economics of, 195–198; foreign policy and, 191–192; Foreign Relations Committee for, 213; of individual approach, 78–81; for institutions, 138–141; with Libya, 69, 173–174; Marshall Plan, 75–76; with media, 175; with Mubarak, H., 68–69, 155; 9/11 and, 43–44, 44*tab*; NSC for, 21, 71; for Obama, 135–138, 177–178; psychology of, 19; with regimes, 150–154; stability and, 176–177; against terrorism, 121–122, 127; for UN, 174; for US, 57*n*14, 208
DoD. *See* Department of Defense
Donilon, Tom, 69, 78–79, 83, 101–103, 109*n*61
Dreams from My Father (Obama), 61
DRL. *See* Democracy, Rights, and Labor
Drones, 15–16
Duterte, Rodrigo, 188

Economics: of authoritarianism, 166–171; of Congress, 75–76, 89–90, 119–120; of defense, 13–14; of diplomacy, 195–198; of DoD, 103; economic liberalization, 38; Foreign Military Financing program, 207; foreign policy and, 128–129; ideology and, 25; IMF, 76–77; of institutions, 114–116, 142–145; of intervention, 120, 146; of Libya, 157*n*12; Middle East Response Fund, 108*n*19; of military, 149; of NGOs, 18; of NTC, 115; of regimes, 139; World Bank, 76–77
Egypt, 7, 13–14, 26, 38; authoritarianism in, 9–10, 181–182; CIA in, 81; for Clinton, H., 20, 66–72, 82, 154–155; Coup (2013), 65–66, 83–89, 175–178; democracy in, 154–157; Gulf Arab States and, 2; individual approach for, 68–70, 77–78, 83–89; institutions in, 154–157; Islam in, 164–165; Islamic State in, 156–157; Israel and, 45, 83, 88; Kerry in, 85–89, 92; leadership in, 33*n*16; Muslim world and, 56, 108*n*17; NDP, 72; NGOs and, 184, 204*n*34; for Obama, 92–93; Saudi Arabia and, 164–168; State Department and, 108*n*22; for Trump, 199–201; US and, 1, 18, 29–30, 46, 51, 85–89, 104. *See also* Morsi; Mubarak
ElBaradei, Mohamed, 86
Elitism, 28, 50
Ereli, Adam, 131, 137
EU. *See* European Union
Europe, 15, 32*n*10, 36, 97, 113. *See also specific countries*

European Union (EU), 36
External forces, 5–6

Fake news, 189–190
Federal Bureau of Investigation (FBI), 117, 121
Feltman, Jeffrey, 104, 134–135
Fishman, Ben, 114
Flynn, Michael, 84, 189–190, 202
Force, 39*tab*, 63, 81, 100–101
Foreign Military Financing program, 207
Foreign policy: anti-Americanism for, 94–95; after Arab Spring, 3–4, 138; in Arab world, 42–51, 43*tab*–44*tab*; for arms sales, 14, 184, 194; autocracies and, 11, 150–154; Bahrain and, 150–154; CIA and, 113; during Cold War, 18; Congress in, 3, 21, 45, 111–112, 143, 147, 157, 174; diplomacy and, 191–192; DoD in, 127, 138–139, 142–145; economics and, 128–129; of Europe, 32*n*10; *Foreign Affairs* (magazine), 46–47; Freedom Agenda, 3–4; Gulf Arab States in, 174–178; high policy, 40; history of, 31–32; human rights in, 5, 36, 51–53; individual approach as, 91–93; institutions in, 22–25; leadership and, 20–21; liberalism in, 35; libertarian politics, 17–18; Marshall Plan, 75–76; national interest and, 9–19; neutrality as, 7–8; before 9/11, 196–197; of Obama, 4, 10, 15–16, 66–68, 86–87, 150–154, 178–179, 187, 197–199, 201–202; process tracing, 31; of Qatar, 26; scholarship on, 5–6; for stability, 3; State Department and, 48–49, 68; for terrorism, 1; tools for, 38–39, 39*tab*; for Trump, 186–196
Foreign Relations Committee, 213
Free trade agreements (FTAs), 129
Freedom Agenda, 3–4, 52, 54, 65, 131, 187–188
FTAs. *See* Free trade agreements

Gabon, 26
Gates, Robert, 69, 71, 96–97, 101, 112, 134
General National Congress (GNC), 114, 119
General Protection Force Plan, 119–121

Gerson, Michael, 50
Ghonim, Wael, 108*n*18
Gibbs, Robert, 71, 161
global war on terrorism (GWOT), 53
GNA. *See* Government of National Accord
GNC. *See* General National Congress
Gorbachev, Mikhail, 47–48
Government of National Accord (GNA), 126, 203
Graham, Lindsey, 87, 194
Guantanamo Bay, 55
Gulf Arab States: Arab Spring for, 7; democracy for, 165–166; Egypt and, 2; in foreign policy, 174–178; military and, 171–174; monarchies in, 13, 16, 53; policy for, 166–171; politics of, 162–163; protests in, 164–165; Trump and, 195–196; US and, 178–179
Gulf Cooperation Council (GCC), 10–11, 129, 136; Arab Spring for, 27–28, 161–162, 175; authoritarianism for, 175–177; Islam for, 179*n*2; military of, 28; monarchies for, 165; Obama and, 169; Peninsula Shield Force, 172; politics of, 163; US and, 174
Gulf War, 18, 46
GWOT. *See* global war on terrorism

Haftar, Khalifa, 121–127, 170, 173–174, 202–203
Hagel, Chuck, 86, 88–89
Haiti, 7
Haley, Nikki, 192
Hamas, 50–51, 168
Hamzawy, Amr, 86
Hayden, Michael, 49
Herzegovina, 13
Hezbollah, 16, 51
High policy, 40
History, 7–8, 9, 28, 31–32, 60–61
Hughes, Karen, 51
Human rights, 1, 203; in Bahrain, 131–132; in China, 62; democracy and, 37–38, 60, 119, 197–198, 205, 212–213; for DRL, 207; in foreign policy, 5, 36, 51–53; Human Rights Watch, 106; ICC for, 95–96; for Kerry, 89–90; leadership in, 190–191; in Libya, 116–118; for Mubarak, H., 53;

NGOs and, 105, 133–134; after 9/11, 9; for Obama, 172, 204n8; stability and, 142–143; for State Department, 156; torture and, 148–149; Trump and, 194; for US, 73
Hun Sen, 190, 193
Hussein, Saddam, 9, 46, 52, 186

ICC. *See* International Criminal Court
Ideology, 25, 54, 65
IMF. *See* International Monetary Fund
Individual approach, 19–22; for Arab Spring, 65–66; in Bahrain, 103–107, 110n76; democracy and, 89–91; diplomacy of, 78–81; for Egypt, 68–70, 77–78, 83–89; as foreign policy, 91–93; institutions and, 67–68; in Libya, 93–103; with Morsi, 82–83, 108n26; for Mubarak, H., 66–67, 74–77; with NGOs, 81; for Obama, 59–65, 71–72; psychology of, 72–74; for Trump, 188–192
Indonesia, 62
Institutions, 22–25; in Bahrain, 127–132, 150–154; BICI and, 141–142; bureaucrats and, 111–112; democracy and, 148–149; diplomacy for, 138–141; economics of, 114–116, 142–145; in Egypt, 154–157; General Protection Force Plan, 119–121; Haftar for, 121–124; individual approach and, 67–68; IRI, 80–81; Islamic State and, 124–127; Libya for, 112–113; NDI, 80–81; PIL for, 118–119; protests for, 145–147; stability for, 132–135; terrorism for, 116–118, 147–148; for Trump, 192–195
Intelligence, 16, 67–68, 111–112, 206–207. *See also* Central Intelligence Agency
International Criminal Court (ICC), 95–96
International Monetary Fund (IMF), 76–77, 81, 214
International Republican Institute (IRI), 80–81
Intervention, 95–103, 112–113, 120, 146
Iran, 1, 16, 18, 129, 162, 175
Iraq, 9, 13, 16, 52, 186; Gulf War, 18, 46; Iraq war, 54, 210–211; ISIL, 90, 147–148, 157, 201–202; ISIS, 61; Islamic State and, 124–127, 147–148, 156–157; US and, 128, 183
IRI. *See* International Republican Institute
Islam, 17, 23, 129–130; Arab Spring and, 11, 165–166; in Bahrain, 29, 130; in Egypt, 164–165; fundamentalism in, 162–163; for GCC, 179n2; Islamophobia, 191; for Israel, 77–78; in Libya, 91, 109n54, 123, 165, 183–184; in MENA, 4, 20; for Morsi, 168; NGOs and, 131; politics of, 50, 79, 82, 97, 134–137, 142, 144–146, 174–175; protests and, 18; psychology of, 61; for Saleh, 53; terrorism and, 153–154, 173–174, 189; violence and, 124–127
al-Islam, Seif, 96, 109n54
Islamic State, 124–127, 147–148, 156–157
Islamic State in Iraq and Syria (ISIS), 61
Islamic State of Iraq and the Levant (ISIL), 90, 147–148, 157, 201–202
Israel, 10, 16, 20, 51, 168; Egypt and, 45, 83, 88; Islam for, 77–78

Japan, 15
Al Jazeera, 71, 136
JCPOA. *See* Joint Comprehensive Plan of Action
Jibril, Mahmoud, 119
Jihadist terror, 161
Johnson, Lyndon, 33n30
Joint Comprehensive Plan of Action (JCPOA), 16
Jones, Deborah, 120, 122
Jordan, 7, 13–14, 29, 40–42, 46, 108n11
Journalism, 12, 33n17, 68–69, 87, 136, 189–190
al-Jubeir, Adel, 176–177

Kennan, George, 13, 43
Kennedy, John F., 62
Kenya, 61–62, 121
Kerry, John, 20, 66, 107, 147–150, 157, 177; in Egypt, 85–89, 92; human rights for, 89–90; terrorism for, 125–126
al-Khalifa, Hamad bin Isa, 131, 134, 198
al-Khalifa, Salman bin Hamad, 130–131
Al-Khalifa, Shaikh Khalifa bin Salman, 132–133

al-Khalifa family, 17, 129–136, 138–142, 146–148, 171, 173, 182, 198
Khashoggi, Jamal, 12, 33n17, 193–194
al-Khawaja, Zaynab, 144
Kim Jong-un, 188–189
Krajeski, Tom, 130, 140–141, 145, 149–150
Kumar, Prem, 83
Kushner, Jared, 202
Kuwait, 13

Leadership, 20–21, 46, 186, 190–191, 205–206
Lebanon, 51
Leverage, 12–13, 28–29, 42, 73–74, 149, 183–186
Liberalism, 35, 38, 43–44, 50
Libertarian politics, 17–18
Libya, 2, 4, 13, 181–182; authoritarianism in, 29–30; Bahrain and, 170–171; Benghazi attacks, 99–100, 102, 116–118, 121–124, 126, 157n8; democracy in, 114–116; diplomacy with, 69, 173–174; economics of, 157n12; General Protection Force Plan, 119–121; Haftar for, 121–124; human rights in, 116–118; individual approach in, 93–103; for institutions, 112–113; Islam in, 91, 109n54, 123, 165, 183–184; Islamic State, 124–127; Libyan Political Agreement (2015), 90; PIL, 30; for Trump, 201–203; for UN, 125–126
Libyan National Army (LNA), 122–126, 170
Libyan Political Agreement (LPA), 126, 203
LNA. *See* Libyan National Army
LPA. *See* Libyan Political Agreement

Maduro, Nicolás, 187
Magarief, Mohamed, 119
Malinowski, Tom, 106–107, 110n76, 145–152, 194, 200
Malta, 124
Manama. *See* Bahrain
Marshall Plan, 75–76
Mattis, James, 84, 104–105, 176–177
McCain, John, 87, 115
McDaniel, Rich, 151
McDonough, Denis, 78
McFaul, Michael, 7, 69, 74, 77, 92

McMaster, H. R., 190
Media, 141, 158n55, 175; fake news on, 189–190; Al Jazeera, 71, 136; journalism, 12, 33n17, 68–69, 87, 136, 189–190; *Al-Wasat* (newspaper), 136
MENA. *See* Middle East and North Africa
MEPI. *See* Middle East Partnership Initiative
Methodology, 28–31
Mexico, 15
Middle East and North Africa (MENA), 3; democracy in, 63–64, 83–84, 178–179; for Europe, 97; history of, 7–8, 60–61; Islam in, 4, 20; journalism in, 68–69; national interest in, 65; for Obama, 123–124; policy in, 49; politics of, 13, 46; religion in, 77–78; security relationships in, 13–14; stability in, 27–28; for Trump, 195–196; for UN, 98; US and, 6, 178–179
Middle East Partnership Initiative (MEPI), 49, 108n19, 114, 131
Middle East Response Fund, 108n19
Military: for authoritarianism, 78–79; with Bahrain, 46; for DoD, 67–68; economics of, 149; force for, 63; Foreign Military Financing program, 207; of GCC, 28; Gulf Arab States and, 171–174; intervention and, 95–97; as leverage, 73–74; partnerships, 14–17; politics of, 18; terrorism and, 121; of US, 14–17, 100–101, 209–210
Miller, Stephen, 191
Monarchies, 12, 13, 16, 53, 73, 140, 165. *See also specific monarchies*
Moniz, Ernest, 15
Morgenthau, Hans, 43
Morocco, 4, 29
Morrell, Michael, 88, 109n52, 109n59
Morsi, Mohamed, 2, 85–89, 168, 171, 179n6; individual approach with, 82–83, 108n26; Muslim Brotherhood and, 66, 83–84, 161–162, 167
Mubarak, Hosni, 1, 4, 12, 33n16, 38; Abdullah (King) and, 161–162; authoritarianism of, 48–49; Clinton, B., and, 46; diplomacy with, 68–69,

155; for Donilon, 79; elitism for, 50; human rights for, 53; individual approach for, 66–67, 74–77; intelligence for, 67–68; Muslim Brotherhood for, 79–80, 177; for NGOs, 56; Obama and, 30, 69–70, 73–74, 77; psychology of, 72–73; Qaddafi and, 28–29
Mubarak, Suzanne, 108n11
Mullen, Mike, 98
Muravchik, Joshua, 188
Muslim Brotherhood, 8, 20, 25, 105, 168–169, 175; Morsi and, 66, 83–84, 161–162, 167; for Mubarak, H, 79–80, 177; for Rice, C., 79; terrorism and, 49–51, 90
Muslim world, 3, 56, 108n17. *See also* Islam

Nader, George, 196
Naga, Fayza Abou, 81
National Democratic Institute (NDI), 80–81
National Democratic Party (NDP), 72
National Endowment of Democracy (NED), 41
National interest, 9–18, 35–36, 65, 75, 103–104
National Salvation Front (NSF), 86
National security, 47
National Security Council (NSC), 21, 71, 205–208, 214n2; democracy for, 113; Obama and, 97–98, 155–156; Power at, 106
National Security Strategy (NSS), 186–187
National Transitional Council (NTC), 99–100, 115–116
National Unity Gathering, 170
Nation-building, 46–47
NATO. *See* North America Trade Organization
Naval Forces Central Command (NAVCENT), 103–105, 129, 137–140, 146, 149–150, 153
NDI. *See* National Democratic Institute
NDP. *See* National Democratic Party
Near Eastern Affairs (NEA), 106–107, 117, 133, 143–148, 153–155, 185–186, 200
NED. *See* National Endowment of Democracy

Neibuhr, Reinhold, 43
Neutrality, 7–8
NGOs. *See* Nongovernmental organizations
Nigeria, 37
9/11, 3, 8–9, 193, 209, 211–214; for Bush, G. W., 46–53; diplomacy and, 43–44, 44tab; foreign policy before, 196–197
Nixon, Richard, 14–15, 33n30
Nongovernmental organizations (NGOs), 8, 18, 81, 131, 140; democracy for, 40–41; Egypt and, 184, 204n34; human rights and, 105, 133–134; Mubarak, H., for, 56
Noor, Ayman, 48
North America Trade Organization (NATO), 97, 99, 192
North Korea, 188–189
NSC. *See* National Security Council
NSF. *See* National Salvation Front
NSS. *See* National Security Strategy
NTC. *See* National Transitional Council
Nuclear terrorism, 62

Obama, Barack, 1–2, 32n1, 107, 214n8; Arab world for, 181–186; Bahrain for, 133; Beecroft for, 90–91; Bush, G. W., and, 9; Clinton, H., and, 108n11, 108n16; counterterrorism for, 18; Cuba for, 214n2; diplomacy for, 135–138, 177–178; Donilon and, 109n61; Egypt for, 92–93; foreign policy of, 4, 10, 15–16, 66–68, 86–87, 150–154, 178–179, 187, 197–199, 201–202; GCC and, 169; human rights for, 172, 204n8; individual approach for, 59–65, 71–72; intervention for, 97–100, 112; Jordan and, 41–42; MENA for, 123–124; Mubarak, H., and, 30, 69–70, 73–74, 77; NSC and, 97–98, 155–156; Presidential Study Directive for, 8, 64; Qaddafi for, 114; reputation of, 99–103; SCAF for, 83; terrorism for, 55–56. *See also* Benghazi attacks; Egypt; Libya
Obey, David, 51
Office of Transitional Initiatives (OTI), 114
offshore balancing, 18

Oil, 14–15, 202–203
Oman, 4
Organization for Security and Cooperation in Europe (OSCE), 36
Organizational culture, 24
OSCE. *See* Organization for Security and Cooperation in Europe
al-Otaiba, Yousef, 85, 168–169, 176–177
OTI. *See* Office of Transitional Initiatives

Pakistan, 79
Palestine, 50–51
Panetta, Leon, 86
Patterson, Anne: career for, 78–81, 83–84, 86–87, 106–107, 147–148; reputation of, 91, 145, 167–168
Paul, Rand, 199
Pearl Roundabout, 30, 132–135
Pentagon. *See* Department of Defense
Philippines, 7, 45, 57n8
PIL. *See* Political Isolation Law
Policy, 47–49, 54, 61, 90, 166–171. *See also* Foreign policy
Political Isolation Law (PIL), 30, 118–119
Politics: of Arab Spring, 6–7; in Arab world, 137–138; of authoritarianism, 16–17, 37; of autocracies, 19; of bureaucrats, 23–24, 33n29, 59, 79; of Cold War, 45, 73; of consensus, 60; of GCC, 163; of Gulf Arab States, 162–163; of Islam, 50, 79, 82, 97, 134–137, 142, 144–146, 174–175; libertarian politics, 17–18; of MENA, 13, 46; of military, 18; 9/11 and, 209; of realist approach, 62; of religion, 90; of SCAF, 82; of security relationships, 17–18; of terrorism, 25–26; in US, 75–76
Pompeo, Mike, 1, 191, 199, 203, 204n34
Populism, 189
Posner, Michael, 104–106, 142, 144, 190
Powell, Colin, 8, 47, 62
Power, Samantha, 62, 89–90, 92–94, 95–103, 106, 116
Presidential Study Directive, 8, 64
Process tracing, 31
Protests, 18, 66–67, 73, 103–104, 198; against authoritarianism, 22–23, 87; in Bahrain, 132–135; in Gulf Arab States, 164–165; for institutions, 145–147; against regimes, 132–133; violence against, 141–142. *See also* Arab Spring
Psychology, 19, 24–25, 61, 72–74, 99
Public opinion, in US, 97
Puck, Wolfgang, 176
Putin, Vladimir, 186

Qaddafi, Muammar, 12, 27–28, 28–29, 94–103, 111, 114. *See also* Libya
al-Qaeda, 16, 84, 91
al-Qaradawi, Yusuf, 167
Qatar, 8, 13–14, 15, 26. *See also* Gulf Arab States

Rajab, Nabeel, 144, 198
Rational-choice theory, 33n26
Reagan, Ronald, 7, 32n4, 45–46, 62
Realist approach, 9, 17–18, 43–44, 47, 62; rational-choice theory compared to, 33n26; for US, 32n15
Regimes, 6, 42, 132–133, 139, 161; diplomacy with, 150–154; US and, 37, 105, 136, 199–201. *See also specific regimes*
Religion, 77–78, 90. *See also* Islam
Responsibility Doctrine, 98
Rhetoric, 39tab
Rhodes, Ben, 78, 82, 89, 97, 168–169; expertise of, 188; Obama and, 182
Ricciardone, Francis, 49
Rice, Condoleezza, 8, 46–52, 57n10, 69–70, 79
Rice, Susan, 95, 101–102, 115, 119–120
Roebuck, Bill, 149
Role theory, 33n27
Rubio, Marco, 149, 184
Rumsfeld, Donald, 47
al-Ruqai, Abdul-Hamed Nabil, 121
Rusk, Dean, 33n30
Russia, 98–99, 179n10, 186, 192, 197. *See also* Cold War; Soviet Union
Rwanda, 95, 101

Sahwat al-Faith movement, 170
Saleh, Ali Abdullah, 10–11, 27–28, 53, 178, 182
Salman, Ali, 145–147
al-Sarraj, Fayez, 203
Saudi Arabia, 1–2, 12, 17, 19, 82; anti-Americanism in, 145; Bahrain and,

171–172; Egypt and, 164–168; Morsi and, 179*n*6; regimes in, 161; Yemen and, 193–194, 199. *See also* Gulf Arab States
SCAF. *See* Supreme Council of the Armed Forces
Scholarship, 5–6, 26–27, 28–31
Scobey, Margaret, 78, 79, 85
Scowcroft, Brent, 62
Security relationships, 12–14, 17–18, 116–117
al-Senussi, Abdullah, 109*n*59, 157*n*2
Serbia, 7
Shafik, Ahmed, 82
Shale, 15
Shouting in the Dark (Al Jazeera), 136
al-Sisi, Abdel Fatah, 1–2, 16–18, 66, 189, 199–201; as General, 84–92; reputation of, 168–169, 171, 173–174, 179
Smith, Gayle, 97
Soft power, 38–39, 39*tab*
Somalia, 202
South Korea, 7, 11, 15, 45
Soviet Union, 47–48. *See also* Cold War
Spain, 144
Stability, 3, 11–12, 19, 27–28, 76–77; diplomacy and, 176–177; human rights and, 142–143; for institutions, 132–135
Stalin, Joseph, 11
State Department, 205–208; Arab Spring for, 79, 137; CIA and, 68; democracy for, 193–195; DoD and, 104, 147–148; DRL and, 138–140; Egypt and, 108*n*22; foreign policy and, 48–49, 68; human rights for, 156; Libya for, 114; 9/11 for, 193; protests and, 134
Stevens, J. Christopher, 99–100, 116–117, 183
Sudan, 93–94
Suleiman, Omar, 68, 107*n*9, 154
Supreme Council of the Armed Forces (SCAF), 75, 77–83
Syria, 13, 16, 165, 192. *See also* Islamic State in Iraq and Syria

Tahrir Square. *See* Arab Spring; Egypt
Tanzania, 121

Terrorism: Arab Spring for, 109*n*52; for Bush, G. W., 53–55; diplomacy against, 121–122, 127; foreign policy for, 1; GWOT, 53; Hamas as, 50–51, 168; Hezbollah, 16, 51; for institutions, 116–118, 147–148; Islam and, 153–154, 173–174, 189; jihadist terror, 161; for Kerry, 125–126; military and, 121; Muslim Brotherhood and, 49–51, 90; 9/11, 3; nuclear terrorism, 62; for Obama, 55–56; policy for, 61; politics of, 25–26; al-Qaeda, 16, 84, 91; for US, 11–12. *See also* Counterterrorism; Islamic State in Iraq and Syria
Tillerson, Rex, 190–191, 194–195, 204*n*34
Torture, 148–149
Transitology literature, 5, 33*n*30
Treasury Department, 214
Tribalism, 61, 65
Tripoli. *See* Libya
Trump, Donald J., 1, 16; democracy for, 196–203; foreign policy for, 186–196
Tunisia, 2, 8, 38, 124

UAE. *See* United Arab Emirates
UN. *See* United Nations
United Arab Emirates (UAE), 2, 82, 175–178, 179*n*10. *See also* Gulf Arab States
United Nations (UN), 21, 69–70, 98, 100, 192; diplomacy for, 174; Europe and, 113; Libya for, 125–126; Security Council, 27, 36
United States (US), 64; Arab Spring for, 2–3, 182–183; Arab world and, 36; arms sales by, 138, 142–145, 148, 151–153, 196; authoritarianism in, 20–21, 192–195; Bahrain and, 23, 111–112, 135–138, 141–145, 148–149, 185–186; China and, 15; Cold War for, 5, 9, 26; Coup (2013) for, 65–66; Cuba and, 187–188; diplomacy for, 57*n*14, 208; Egypt and, 1, 18, 29–30, 46, 51, 85–89, 104; Freedom Agenda, 3–4; GCC and, 174; Gulf Arab States and, 178–179; human rights for, 73; ideology in, 65; intelligence for, 16; intervention for, 100–103; Iraq and,

128, 183; Israel and, 10; journalism in, 87, 189–190; leadership of, 186; leverage for, 12–13, 28–29, 149, 183–186; MENA and, 6, 178–179; military of, 14–17, 100–101, 209–210; Morsi and, 161–162; national security of, 47; NGOs and, 8; politics in, 75–76; public opinion in, 97; Qatar and, 13–14; realist approach for, 32n15; regimes and, 37, 105, 136, 199–201; resources of, 37–38; Saudi Arabia and, 1–2, 17; security relationships for, 12–14, 116–117; soft power for, 38–39, 39*tab*; terrorism for, 11–12; Treasury Department, 214. *See also* Congress; Department of Defense; Foreign policy; *specific topics*

US Agency for International Development (USAID), 114, 213–214

Venezuela, 15, 187–188
Violence, 89, 124–127, 141–142, 148–149

Al-Wasat (newspaper), 136
Weinstein, Jeremy, 97
al-Wifaq, 131, 134–136, 144–146, 148
Wikileaks, 113
Williams, Stephanie, 137
Wilson, Woodrow, 35, 43
Winer, Jonathan, 123–126, 170, 201
Wisner, Frank, 70–72
Wittes, Tamara, 75–76
World Bank, 76–77, 81, 214
Wyden, Ron, 149

Yemen, 12, 46, 109n52, 182, 193–194, 199

Zeidan, Ali, 119–121
Zinatanis, 122–123

About the Book

Whether democracy promotion should play a role in US foreign policy continues to be a subject of considerable debate, perhaps nowhere more than with regard to the Arab World. But looking beyond the "whether," what explains why, where, and how the United States promotes democracy? What caused the shift from the Obama administration's support of the Arab Spring protests in 2011 to its retreat from democracy promotion only two years later? What explains the Trump administration's focus on relationships with autocrats?

In the context of these questions, Mieczysław Boduszyński explores the tensions between interests and ideals in US foreign policy and the possibilities and limits of US democracy promotion in a region where Washington has often supported autocracy over freedom.

Mieczysław P. Boduszyński is assistant professor of politics and international relations at Pomona College.

About the Book